THE ECONOMIC GEOGRAPHY OF FRANCE

The Economic Geography of France

JOHN TUPPEN

CROOM HELM
London & Canberra
BARNES & NOBLE BOOKS
Totowa, New Jersey

© 1983 J. Tuppen
Croom Helm Ltd, Provident House, Burrell Row,
Beckenham, Kent BR3 1AT

British Library Cataloguing in Publication Data

Tuppen, John N.
    The economic geography of France.
    1. France—Economic conditions—1945-
    I. Title
    330.944   HC275
    ISBN 0−7099−2412−7

First published in the USA 1983 by
Barnes & Noble Books
81 Adams Drive
Totowa, New Jersey, 07512

Library of Congress Cataloging in Publication Data

Tuppen, John N.
    The economic geography of France.

    1. France—Economic conditions—1945-
I. Title.
HC276.2.T85   1983   330.944'0838   83−6036
ISBN 0−389−20399−8

Printed and bound in Great Britain

CONTENTS

LIST OF TABLES

LIST OF FIGURES

PREFACE

Over the last thirty years successive changes have
led to the substantial remodelling of the French
economy. Following an initial and extended phase of
unprecedented expansion and modernisation, latterly
growth rates have moderated substantially,
accompanied by new priorities in the direction of
the economy. Emphasis is now being given to
restructuring, involving the improvement of efficiency and the need to channel investment into those
activities capable of inducing expansion and in
which French competitiveness is likely to be
greatest. Such changes are not unique to France,
but have become features of most other advanced
capitalist societies, indicating the extent to which
the international economic environment has been
greatly modified over the last decade. Just as
growth trends have altered, so too has the political
context in which the French economy has been
managed. In the recent past the most pronounced
change has been the alternative philosophy of development offered by the Socialists. These are some
of the themes which provide the background to the
present appraisal of the French economy.
     The text is based upon an assessment of each of
the three main sectors of activity, aiming to
portray the principal features of and contrasts in
their respective patterns of development during the
post-war period. Within the individual sectors,
discussion is centred upon an examination of the
dominant structural and locational characteristics,
emphasising the manner in which these have altered,
particularly over the more recent past. To reinforce this approach, selected branches of activity
are studied in greater detail, while to highlight
key themes or topical issues a number of specific
case studies are also incorporated.

In writing this account I have been extremely grateful for the assistance given by numerous people in response to my enquiries. Amongst colleagues in French universities, I would like to thank in particular Pierre Barrère, Jacques Bethemont, Jacques Bonnet, Marc Bonneville, Micheline Cassou-Mounat, Jean-Paul Diry, Pierre Estienne, André Fel, François Gay, Christian Jamot, Yannick Lageat, Serge Lerat, Jean-Paul Martin, Christian Mignon, Paul Mingret, René Neboit, Henri Nonn, Albert Odouard, René Pijassou, Janine Renucci and Pierre Vitte. Many other individuals in public and private organisations have provided information and advice; my thanks are extended especially to Guillaume Astier, Maria Ferrari, Josette Gourlier, Bernard Higel, Liliane Kasparian, Jocelyne Lerouge, Jacqueline Letellier, Jean-Louis Masson, Marie Masson, Catherine Poirieux, Christophe Tampon-Lajariette and Jean-Paul Verdier. I greatly appreciate the kindness and excellent hospitality shown on so many occasions by my friends Germain and Marguerite, Monique and José, Françoise and Vincent, Françoise and Jean-Yves and the Fuch's family.

Equally, I am indebted to those who have worked so hard to enable me to complete the manuscript. Marie Partington and Moira Armitt have proved indefatigable typists, while Christine Warr and Gustav Dobrzynski have skilfully designed and drawn the accompanying figures. My thanks are also extended to the staff of the University's Library for their assistance in obtaining numerous items of reference. I would also like to thank Ian Thompson for his continuing interest in my work and particularly my parents for their support and considerable help. To my family I owe a special debt of gratitude, not least to Emma and Helen for doing their best to divert 'daddy's' attention from his work! Above all, however, it is to my very patient wife Valerie that I would like to say 'thank you', especially for typing the camera-ready copy.

Chapter One

A BACKCLOTH TO CHANGE

The French economy is no longer expanding at the
high rate which became such a distinctive feature of
growth throughout the greater part of the post-war
period. Nonetheless, the substantial value and
volume of the country's output, the underlying
strength and competitiveness of many of its industries and the large scale of foreign trading all
testify to the position of France as a leading world
economic power. Yet, in the immediate aftermath of
the second world war, with the economy badly disrupted and burdened by a long heritage of stagnation
and limited structural modifications, the likelihood
of this achievement seemed remote. However, over
the following two decades France experienced a
period of exceptional and unprecedented economic
expansion, notable for the profound transformation
of the country's agricultural and industrial activities. It was not until the mid-1970s that various
economic forces of largely external origin combined
to moderate the pace and volume of growth, leading
to new priorities in economic policy, with a marked
emphasis upon increasing the efficiency rather than
the capacity of the productive system. Like most
western economies, France has been adversely
affected by the recession, notably through the rise
in unemployment and inflation, although the amplitude of these problems has been less than in a
number of other industrialised countries. However,
whereas the French record of economic growth in the
period from the early 1950s to the mid-1970s was
unequalled in Western Europe, the more recent
performance of the country's economy has been less
impressive.

POST-WAR ECONOMIC CHANGE

From the early 1950s the need to re-establish and
restructure many productive activities and to adapt
agricultural, industrial and commercial enterprises
to a changing and more competitive trading environment contributed to a rise in output and a transformed economy. The strength of growth is illustrated by the increase in gross domestic product which,
between 1949 and 1969, averaged 5 per cent per annum.
As the economy expanded, substantial rises also
occurred in incomes, living standards and levels of
household consumption, although not all social
groups or all regions of the country benefited
equally (1). As output increased trading activity
grew equally rapidly as France moved away from a
policy of protection towards increased integration
with other industrialised nations, notably its
European partners in the Common Market; during the
1960s intra-community exchange progressed rapidly.
These changes relied upon a much higher level of
investment, both in plant and infrastructure. In
the former case, not only did this respond to the
need to increase capacity, but also to improve
productivity, involving much higher levels of mechanisation and automation as capital was progressively
substituted for labour. However, despite this trend,
the size of the French labour-force continued to
increase (not least in the industrial sector),
emphasising the strength of economic growth. Fundamental to the development of the economy, however,
was the necessity to improve the country's outdated
and neglected infrastructure. This requirement gave
rise to an impressive programme of investment,
notably in the fields of energy supply and communications. Since then, priorities within these fields
have shifted and the pace of change slackened, but
impressive advances continue, demonstrated by the
inauguration of the new rail link and high speed
train between Paris and Lyon in 1981 (2).
    The transformation and expansion of the economy
represented only part of a much wider process of
revival and change in post-war France, exemplified
by the reversal of previous demographic trends as
the country's population began to grow rapidly.
This increase was also accompanied by a pronounced
redistribution and urbanisation of the population,
processes linked to other mutations within society;
as material standards of well-being improved, so too
did the range and quality of educational opportunity
and welfare provision.

Backcloth to Change

By the early 1970s there were many overt signs of a 'new' France, dominated by an urban and industrial society, and characterised by the rapid growth of tertiary activities within the economy. The key theme of change had been modernisation, but certain weaknesses remained. There were still large sectors of agriculture and industry which were outdated and often moribund, with many areas of the country untouched by change, except for the continuing and often increasing loss of their populations. At the same time, a gradual increase in unemployment and inflation, coupled with an unstable foreign trading balance suggested a still fragile base to the country's economic resurgence. Nonetheless, the expectation was that a high rate of growth would be maintained throughout the following decade.

This assessment did not take account, however, of the quadrupling of oil prices in 1973. The recession triggered by this action radically altered the outlook not only for the French economy but also for the economies of other leading industrial nations. While the rise in the cost of crude oil was significant in itself as a major cause of ensuing problems, it was not the only factor. One principal effect was to aggravate considerably an already worsening economic situation related largely to influences beyond the direct control of the French government such as the growing disorganisation of international money markets (3). For France there were numerous repercussions, including the increase in the cost of oil-derived products and various other raw materials, a slowing in investment, a worsening of the balance of payments' deficit and a rise in the rate of inflation (Table 1.1). Together this produced a marked deterioration of the country's economic performance, a tendency emphasised by the much lower and variable character of the growth of gross domestic product since 1974 (Table 1.1). Moreover, the extent of the change in economic conditions compared with the preceding decade is illustrated by reference to the mean annual growth rate of gross domestic product and retail prices for the years 1960-73 and 1974-9; in the former case it fell from 5.7 per cent to 3.0 per cent, while in the latter accelerated from 4.6 per cent to 10.7 per cent (4).

By 1978 some success had been achieved in overcoming these difficulties, particularly in limiting inflation and improving the foreign trading balance, but this had only been achieved at the cost of a substantial rise in unemployment. Almost

Table 1.1:   Indicators of the Changed Economic
Situation

	Rise in GDP (%)	Rise in retail prices (%)	Unemployed (yearly average) ('000)	Balance of payments (billion francs)
1974	3.0	13.7	615	-29.8
1975	0.0	11.3	902	- 1.0
1976	4.9	9.8	993	-27.3
1977	3.1	9.0	1,073	-15.2
1978	3.5	8.6	1,182	+14.8
1979	3.4	10.3	1,355	+ 5.3
1980	1.1	13.6	1,452	-33.1
1981	0.3	14.0	1,696	-40.6

Source: INSEE, Rapport sur les Comptes de la Nation,
various years.

immediately, however, economic problems were intensified by the further doubling in the price of crude
oil over the period 1979-80.

Since its election in 1981, a major strand of
the socialist government's strategy has been to
attempt to reduce the seemingly intractable problem
of unemployment, allied to greater state intervention in the economy and policies designed to stimulate demand. By mid-1982, however, despite a relative stabilisation of the number of people out of
work, other problems remained or had intensified,
including an upward trend in inflation and an
increased budget deficit, provoking a number of
deflationary measures. Investment has again fallen,
linked to the combined influence of depressed
demand, a reduction in world trade, the high cost of
borrowing and the low profit levels of many companies. Similarly, over the latter part of 1980 and
1981 manufacturing output dropped noticeably and
unemployment rose sharply, while in 1981 GDP
increased by only 0.3 per cent, although by the
standards of certain European partners this represented a relatively creditable performance.

Many of the above problems have been compounded
by basic changes in the pattern of work manufacturing. The dominant position previously held by a
limited number of the advanced industrial nations
has been progressively eroded as the technology
which they formerly monopolised has been

disseminated to an increasing range of developing
countries; this trend is particularly marked where
the techniques of production are relatively straightforward and the skills required by the labour-force
comparatively modest. For the manufacture of many
items such as textiles and footwear, electrical
goods, toys, and basic metal and chemical products,
therefore, French firms are being strongly challenged by third-world producers. Thus, from a position
where raw materials for industry and energy production were widely and cheaply available and manufacturing technology limited to a restricted number of
countries, the former have become in shorter supply
and more expensive and the latter has been diffused
ever more rapidly. At the same time, with the
freeing of world trade, France has had to counter
increasing and often intense competition from other
leading industrial producers, notably Japan. In
view of the importance of industrial expansion to
the post-war economic resurgence of France, these
changes have been particularly problematic, reinforcing the need to improve productivity and competitiveness, and to specialise in activities dependent
upon advanced technology. Given that France is not
the only country to have embarked on such a strategy,
however, intense competition is also a feature of
many of these latter fields of production.

STRUCTURAL AND SPATIAL CHANGES IN THE FRENCH ECONOMY

The Structure and Size of the Labour-Force
Although the marked expansion in the overall size of
the French economy has been a dominant feature of
post-war change, there have also been equally pronounced internal modifications of the country's
economic structure, related particularly to the
altered contribution made by each of the main
sectors of activity to employment and output (5).
Reference to the changing pattern of employment
illustrates these transformations (Table 1.2). In
contrast to the heavy and continuing decline of the
agricultural work-force, the evolution of employment
in the secondary sector has varied; an accelerating
rate of growth throughout the greater part of the
1960s and early 1970s has been replaced by a decline
in both the absolute size and relative strength of
jobs in industrial activities since the mid-1970s.
Conversely, the dominance of the tertiary sector has
been reinforced so that by 1981 it accounted for

Table 1.2: The Sectoral Distribution of the Labour-Force

Sector	1954	1962	1968	1975	1981
			(%)		
Primary	28	20	15	10	9
Secondary	36	38	40	39	33
Tertiary	36	42	45	51	58
	100	100	100	100	100

Source: Calculated from INSEE, _Recensements_ and _Rapport sur les Comptes de la Nation de l'Année 1981_ (1982).

58 per cent of total employment (6), although by the early 1980s its rate of growth had fallen substantially, reflecting the sluggish performance of the economy as a whole. Reviewing the pattern of employment change in terms of broad sectors often conceals, however, conflicting internal trends; thus, within industry, for example, those firms concerned with the manufacture of capital goods have experienced a very contrasting evolutionary tendency compared with producers of consumption goods. The above changes have also had a related effect upon the size and relative significance of different occupational groups, with two trends predominating: the decline of the farmer and farm worker, counterbalanced by a strong upward surge in the number of white-collar employees.

Throughout the early post-war period, modifications in the sectoral distribution of the workforce occurred against the background of a relatively stable total active population. It was not until the 1960s that the latter began to experience a substantial increase. In part this reflected the arrival on the labour market of the first of the much larger generations born after the war when birth rates rose significantly: it also resulted from the growing number of immigrants attracted to France (7), responding to the expansion of the economy and increased demands for labour. At this time, however, the rate at which the work-force grew was well below that at which the economy was expanding, indicating the importance of improvements to productivity. Certain other influences moderated the rise in the active population; as education opportunities were enlarged, proportionally fewer young people under 25 sought employment, while the tendency towards earlier retirement has also with- drawn further workers from the labour market (8). Since 1974 restrictions placed on the arrival of foreign immigrants have had a further depressive effect (9). Conversely, from the latter 1960s an increasing number of women have joined the labour market, linked partially to changing attitudes to- wards female employment and to the expansion of full and part-time jobs in the service sector. The greater part of the subsequent net increase in total employment has resulted from this movement (10).

Spatial Patterns of Employment Change
Over the early post-war years sharp contrasts existed in the employment structures of different regions. Whereas areas such as Nord-Pas-de-Calais and Lorraine exhibited a pronounced bias towards industry, an almost equally strong dependency upon agriculture characterised regions such as Limousin, Bretagne and Basse-Normandie (Figure 1.1). Since then the widespread decline of agricultural employ- ment, particularly heavy in those areas most depen- dent upon farming, a similar although more recent reduction of industrial jobs in the older manu- facturing regions, and a more uniform increase in the importance of the tertiary sector have helped attenuate these contrasts. However, although regional employment profiles now portray a greater degree of homogeneity, differences persist. Many western regions still rely comparatively heavily upon agriculture and have a weak proportion of industrial jobs; conversely, the northern and north- eastern areas of France remain characterised by a large industrial sector, just as Ile-de-France and Provence-Alpes-Côte d'Azur are made distinctive by the strength of tertiary employment. Other signifi- cant changes have also occurred, not least the expansion of industrial employment in many areas of the Paris Basin and western France (despite in certain cases the persistence of a relatively large agricultural labour-force). This trend, although now less apparent, has been linked to decentrali- sation and particularly to a limited series of industries, including vehicles, electrical engi- neering and electronics and mechanical engineering (11). More generally, the size of the labour-force

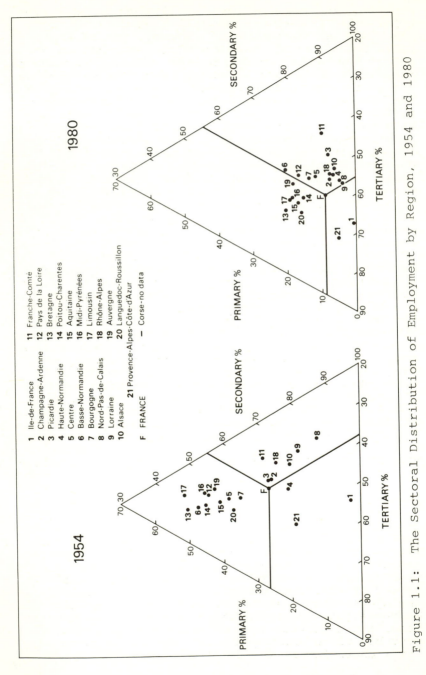

Figure 1.1: The Sectoral Distribution of Employment by Region, 1954 and 1980

8

has evolved unequally over the country, even during a period of strong economic expansion. Thus, over the 1960s and early 1970s, although much of the Paris Basin and south-eastern France exhibited a pattern of an increasing rate of growth, throughout many central and south-western areas the picture was one of accentuating decline.

In many instances changes in an area's economic performance have given rise to or been associated with both inter and intra-regional movements of population. Throughout much of the 1950s and 1960s regions such as Ile-de-France, Rhône-Alpes and Provence-Alpes-Côte d'Azur acted as major reception areas for migrants (reflecting the dynamism of their economies or their appeal for living) while the areas of western, central and south-western France experienced a heavy outflow of population as new employment opportunities failed to compensate for the decline of activities in rural areas. By the 1970s, however, a modified pattern had emerged. The Paris region had become a net exporter of population and many parts of its hinterland and western France were experiencing a reversal of previous demographic trends dominated by out-migration, both tendencies linked to the induced and spontaneous forces of decentralisation (12). At the intra-regional scale, although the drift of rural population towards urban centres is still perceptible, patterns of movement have become more complex, notably as central and inner urban areas have witnessed a growing outflow of residents to peripheral or exurban locations. The development of commuting satellites, symptomatic of this trend, is most evident around the capital.

TWO KEY ECONOMIC PROBLEMS

Unemployment
With the number of people out of work by mid-1982 oscillating around 2 millions, unemployment has become a prominent and undesirable feature of the French economy. France is not alone amongst western industrialised countries in experiencing such a problem (Table 1.3) but, following an extended period of strong economic growth and virtually full-employment, the inability of the economy to generate adequate jobs has been difficult to accept; nonethe-less, the amplitude and speed with which unemploy-ment has risen emphasises that certain weaknesses still characterise the country's productive system.

Table 1.3:   Unemployment in the EEC, 1982

	Registered unemployed as proportion of labour-force* (%)
France	8.8
Belgium	13.0
Ireland	12.0
United Kingdom	11.7
Italy	10.3
Denmark	10.2
Netherlands	9.4
Western Germany	7.3
Greece	2.0
Luxembourg	1.3
EEC	9.7

*average for first three months

Source: Eurostat.

　　　Although unemployment began to rise progressively from the mid-1960s, there were still less than
250,000 people unemployed in 1970 and around
420,000 out of work in the early part of 1974; by
the latter part of the following year, however, the
total had more than doubled (Figure 1.2). Since
then the upward trend has continued, with a particularly strong surge over the year between the latter
part of 1980 and 1981 when the number of unemployed
increased by nearly 500,000. With the rise in
unemployment there has also been a corresponding
decrease in the number of vacancies, exacerbating
the problem. As in 1974/5 these trends corresponded
with the depressive effect upon economic activity
related to the substantial rise in oil prices.
　　　By the early part of 1982 nearly 9 per cent of
the active population was registered as unemployed,
although considerable variations exist between
different regions (Figure 1.2). Unemployment rates
tend to be higher in many of the country's southern
and western peripheral areas, although this is also
a feature of parts of central and northern France.
Conversely, rates are substantially lower throughout
the greater extent of the Paris region and selected
parts of eastern France. These regional contrasts
reflect the interplay of various factors, which may

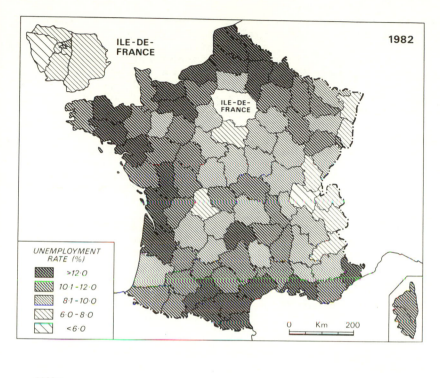

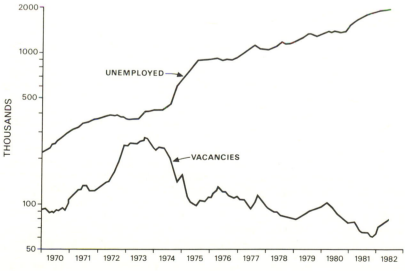

Figure 1.2:   The Pattern of Unemployment

be illustrated by reference to areas where this
condition is particularly problematic. In many
traditionally rural regions, relatively high levels
of unemployment have long been characteristic,
symptomatic of the extent to which the agricultural
sector in particular has shed labour (13). In
certain instances (Bretagne, Pays de la Loire) this
effect has been lessened by industrial expansion,
but this trend has also slackened with the recession;
moreover, despite the general characteristic of
underindustrialisation, selected localities have
been adversely affected by the decline of staple
industries (for example, shipbuilding in the region
of Nantes-St. Nazaire). In industrialised regions
of northern France the high rate and recent rise of
unemployment reflect the problems encountered by the
many branches of manufacturing, particularly heavy
metallurgy and related industries. Mediterranean
regions also feature high unemployment rates, their
varied cause demonstrating the complexity of the
problem. Despite signs of a buoyant economy
(through tourism, for example), traditional activities in many rural areas continue to decline or
require fewer workers. Jobs offered by many formerly large employers such as the construction
industry have fallen sharply with the completion of
major development projects, while despite the
tourist boom, many related employment opportunities
are insecure and of short duration. In addition,
the area has been a major focus for immigrants from
North Africa, many of whom have few skills or qualifications and are ill-adapted to the demands of the
labour market.

Few categories of workers have been unaffected
by the rise in unemployment, and although rates are
highest amongst the unskilled, since the latter
1970s the number of skilled workers and qualified
employees seeking employment has increased noticeably (14). There are still, however, important
structural and regional contrasts (15); for example,
in an area of declining heavy industry such as Nord-
Pas-de-Calais high male unemployment has become
endemic. Over recent years two dominant trends have
caused growing concern - the substantial rise in
youth unemployment and in the number of women out of
work; of the total unemployed, around 55 per cent
are women and over two-fifths under 25. In each
case the problem is greatest amongst the least
qualified. For young people the difficulty of
obtaining a job is aggravated by the large number of
school leavers and graduates joining the labour

market, currently totalling between 700-800,000 each
year (16). More than a sixth of the active population under 24 is now without a job (17). For those
who eventually find work there is often considerable
delay, now a general feature of unemployment; as the
number out of work has risen, so has the average
length of time over which people are unemployed.

Reduced demand has exerted a major influence on
the increase in unemployment. Enforced redundancies,
largely motivated by this cause, fluctuated between
200,000 and 330,000 each year between 1975 and 1980,
affecting various industries including textiles,
metals, building and public works and, more
recently, vehicles (18). Other factors are relevant,
many linked to the continuing need for rationalisation to improve competitiveness; numerous jobs have
disappeared through technological change and
improved working practices. In addition, there are
problems of structural unemployment, with workers'
skills or qualifications failing to match job
opportunities. The country's demographic structure
has also played a role. Since the early 1970s the
much larger age groups born after the war have
started to enter the labour market. With the
labour-force expanding rapidly until 1974, this
increase could be absorbed relatively easily, but
with a virtually stable total working population
since that date, this has become more difficult
(Figure 1.3). In addition, over the latter 1970s
fewer people retired due to the comparatively small
number who were of retirement age, related to the
depletion of these age bands during the first world
war (19). Together, these influences led to a net
increase in the active population, through demographic factors alone, of around 200,000 persons
each year between 1975 and 1980. Both trends are
now lessening; on the contrary, funding the pensions
of a growing retirement population is likely to
place, in the longer term, an added strain on the
economy.

The gravity of the unemployment problem has
produced a series of measures designed to increase
jobs. During the first year of their mandate, the
Socialists' general economic strategy was linked to
stimulating output and demand (and, therefore, jobs),
although by mid-1982 with the rate of inflation
averaging more than 14 per cent, this strategy was
moderated. But the government had also pledged
itself to the creation of employment in the public
sector, aiming at the ambitious target of over
200,000 new jobs in the period 1982-3. A number of

13

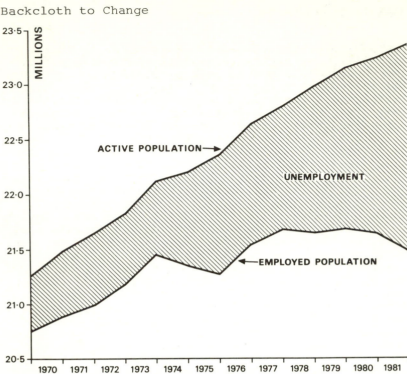

Figure 1.3: Changes in the Size of the Active Population and Employed Population

more specific initiatives and innovative policies have been introduced, based on the Socialists' philosophy of a greater sharing of available employ-ment. One example is the idea, launched in 1981, of solidarity contracts (<u>contrats de solidarité</u>) by which a firm, agreeing to reduce the working hours of its employees or encourage early retirement in return for the creation of new jobs, becomes eligible for various payments from the government (20). So far the scheme's impact appears modest. More generalised, socially inspired policies such as the reduction of the working-week also aim to generate new employment (21).

Greatest attention has been given to the problem of youth unemployment, continuing and en-larging upon measures introduced by the Barre government. In 1977 the first of a series of three <u>Pactes Nationaux Pour l'Emploi</u> was launched, designed principally to encourage the employment of young workers for a limited period (six months) by reducing employers' social security contributions. The benefits of the policy have been arguable, with

the new jobs created being achieved at a relatively
high cost, although in the latter half of 1980 over
300,000 people were covered by this scheme. Between
1981-2 a wider strategy (Plan Avenir Jeunes) based
on the above system was adopted; now the government's aim is to negotiate aids through employment
contracts concluded with firms prepared to take on
young workers (22). Particular emphasis is also
being given to providing professional training and
work experience to school-leavers, aged 16-18, who
lack qualifications and are especially disadvantaged
in the labour market (23). Naturally, these and
other policies to reduce employment are highly
justified on social grounds (and appear to be having
some impact) but this has to be balanced against
their cost to a now slow moving and indebted economy.

Energy Supply
Over the last decade a radical transformation of the
energy market has occurred within France, precipi-
tated by the rise in oil prices in 1973. Not only
has energy become far more expensive (as the price
of other fuels has followed that of oil), but weaknesses in the country's system of supply have also
been highlighted (24). France is relatively poorly
endowed with fossil fuels; it possesses very little
oil and its reserves of coal and natural gas are
becoming increasingly depleted. At the same time
the ability to develop further the generation of
hydroelectric power has become restricted, reflecting the extent to which the country's undoubted
potential in this field has already been harnessed.
Above all, the events of 1973 gave prominence to the
extent to which France relied upon external sources
for the supply of raw materials for its energy
requirements and the resulting vulnerability of the
economy to fluctuations in price and availability.
    Together these difficulties led to the develop-
ment of a revised energy policy, based around a
number of interrelated strategies. The main objective became a reduction in the dependency upon oil,
a diversification of supply and economy in the use
of power; to meet the first two aims, priority was
accorded to the large-scale expansion of the nuclear
industry. Since then, significant changes have
occurred. Table 1.4 indicates the altered pattern
of primary energy consumption, illustrating the
recent relative decline in the role of oil and the
increasingly more important position of nuclear
power. Both trends are also reflected in the

Table 1.4:   The Consumption of Primary Energy

	Proportion of total consumption (%)		
	1960	1973	1981
Coal	53.4	17.2	17.1
Oil	30.8	66.0	48.3
Natural gas	3.4	8.4	13.2
Hydroelectric	10.2	5.6	7.8
Nuclear	-	1.7	11.8
Other	2.2	1.1	1.8
	100.0	100.0	100.0

Source: Comité Professionnel du Pétrole, Statistiques Petrolières et Enérgetiques.

reduction of the country's reliance upon external sources of supply, which fell from 79 per cent in 1973 to 67 per cent in 1981 (25). Oil consumption has been lowered, declining over the same period from 117 to 91 million tonnes, while between 1974 and 1980 it is estimated that the savings in energy amounted to 24 million tonnes of oil equivalent (26). Nevertheless, despite such efforts the cost of energy to the economy rose from 1.8 per cent of GDP in 1973 to 5.2 per cent in 1980. Other forms of energy supply using solar or geothermal sources currently make little contribution to consumption, but to encourage research into these areas and to promote further economies, the government established the Agence Française pour l'Energie in 1982 (27). With the development of new forms of energy generation, changes have also occurred in the distribution of production units (28). The nuclear programme, for example, has resulted in the creation of a number of important generating centres in western France, an area previously largely devoid of production sites. However, unlike the period of the 1960s and early 1970s, when the consumption of energy was expanding rapidly (by an average of 5.4 per cent per annum between 1958 and 1973), the above changes have taken place against a background of relative stability, reflecting lower rates of economic growth, but also the more efficient use of energy; between 1973 and 1980 consumption rose by an annual average of 1.1 per cent (29).

Energy Industries (30). Although coal production
has stabilised over recent years (21.5 million
tonnes in 1981), the industry's main characteristic
since the latter 1950s has been the inexorable
decline of production and manpower (Figure 1.4).
The highly localised nature of activity and, thus,
of reductions in employment, has posed considerable
problems of restructuring for many communities,
particularly in the northern coal-mining districts.
Various plans (31) have been proposed to remodel the
industry and improve efficiency, and over recent
years greater priority has been given to coal as an
energy source, leading to the postponement of the
cessation of mining in the Nord-Pas-de-Calais field.
Nonetheless, French output remains high-cost and
heavily subsidised and the now modest but comparatively stable position of coal as a source of
primary energy has been achieved through increasing
lower-cost imports (29.8 million tonnes in 1981).
New reception facilities have been created at ports
such as Le Havre and Fos to cater for this traffic,
a number of previously oil-fired power stations have
been converted to use coal, and new plants based on
coal are being developed (32). However, the costs
of conversion are considerable, and given the
unpredictable nature of the energy market, there is
a reluctance by potential users and handlers to
engage in the necessary investment (33).
        Changing patterns of energy consumption have
produced two major difficulties for the oil industry. Reduced demand has created a substantial
excess of refining capacity. In 1981 capacity stood
at 158 million tonnes, yet only 97 million tonnes of
crude were refined. Given the underlying trend
towards the contraction of the industry, companies
have sought to rationalise operations by closing
production units including complete refineries (34).
This has occurred already at Vern-sur-Seiche (near
Rennes), for example, and plans exist to shut plants
at Dunkerque, Valenciennes and Hauconcourt
(Lorraine) (35). Although the scale is less than in
the coal industry, the fall in employment induced by
a decline in refining activity has had severe repercussions on local employment markets; the reduction
of Shell's operations at Berre (12,000 inhabitants)
resulted in the loss of around 650 jobs in 1981, in
an area where 60 per cent of jobs are dependent
upon the oil and related chemical industries (36).

17

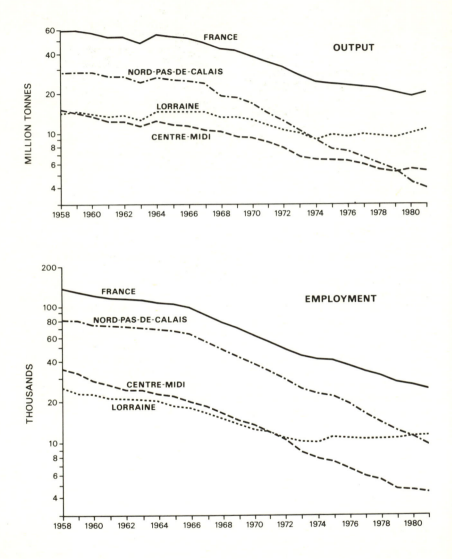

Figure 1.4:   Production and Employment in Coalmining

The other significant problem is adapting the range
of production to changing demand, largely due to the
decline in requirements for heavier fractions.
Thus, despite the recession, oil companies have been
obliged to invest in new plant. One other problematic feature of the industry is the continued heavy
reliance upon a limited area of supply - the Middle
East (and particularly Saudi Arabia). In 1981 65
per cent of the supply of crude oil originated from
this area; but, the benefits of diversification have
to be balanced against preferential trading and
price agreements.

The importance of natural gas as a source of
primary energy has increased significantly since the
early 1960s, now accounting for nearly 13 per cent
of consumption. Furthermore, despite the low overall upward trend in the use of energy, gas consumption rose by an average of 3.6 per cent each year
between 1973 and 1980 (37), reflecting its attractions as a fuel. However, certain doubts over cost
and security of supply surround its future use.
Indigenous supplies now provide only a quarter of
French requirements, with their role likely to
decline further. Thus, France has to rely to an
ever greater extent upon imports. The Netherlands
is currently the principal external supplier but its
resources too are being progressively exhausted.
Long term contracts have been negotiated with two
other present suppliers, Algeria and the USSR, but
at a relatively high cost as attempts have been
made, notably by the former country, to align gas
prices with those of oil. Supply from the latter
source also raises certain moral and political
issues and depends upon the completion of the trans-
Siberian pipeline (38).

Despite the construction of new conventional
thermal power stations and the continued inauguration of hydroelectric plants (along the course of
the Rhône, for example), the outstanding feature of
change in the production of electricity over the
last decade has been the development of nuclear
power; over 40 per cent of electricity now originates from this source (39). The nuclear programme
has attracted considerable criticism on environmental and security grounds and due to its 'imposed'
nature, involving little consultation with interested parties at a local level. However, its development represents a major strand in the policy of
diversifying the forms of energy provision and
reducing dependency upon external sources of supply.
Particular emphasis was accorded to this strategy

under the presidency of Giscard d'Estaing, a
priority which has been largely maintained under the
Socialists, despite initial expressions to the
contrary. A limited number of proposed developments
will not be pursued (notably Plogoff on the Breton
coast) and the pace of expansion has been slowed
(40), but this reflects the fall in demand as much
as a fundamental revision of energy policy. The
economic arguments in terms of the cost of production and the ability to reduce expensive imports of
oil, weigh heavily in favour of the nuclear option.
Moreover, pursuit of this strategy has given birth
to a series of strongly linked industrial activities
(manufacture of the nuclear plant, the enrichment of
uranium and the reprocessing of waste material)
providing employment as well as expertise which,
commercially, is of great value. Construction of
power stations has also generated many jobs, often
in regions with high unemployment, further compli-
cating the debate over the desirability of this form
of energy (41). However, despite the undoubted
emphasis still placed upon the nuclear programme,
the socialist government's energy policy differs
from its predecessor's in giving greatest priority
to economising the use of energy.

Government Intervention in the Economy
French economic progress over the last three decades
is remarkable due to the scale and pace of change.
It is also distinctive due to the extensive character of government involvement in the process. For,
despite an increasing liberalisation of the economy,
initiated as France became integrated into the
Common Market and considerably reinforced through
Barre's economic philosophy in the latter 1970s,
strong state leadership has been maintained in
planning, financing and implementing measures to
stimulate growth. Government intervention is apparent in each sector of the economy. There is a long
tradition of assistance to French farmers, reflective both of the nature of their activity and its
inherent risks, and the strength of their lobby, in
spite of diminishing numbers. The state's influence
in industrial activity is even greater, indicative
of the importance of this sector to national economic growth and to achieving balance in regional
employment opportunities. For similar reasons
interest has increased in the tertiary sector,
involving, for example, the decentralisation of
government offices and research establishments and

promotion of the expansion of tourism. Intervention
has been directed by a highly centralised administrative system, frequently reinforcing the
dirigiste and 'imposed' nature of decisions and
strategy. Major development programmes ranging from
nuclear energy to the new towns have been characterised by the lack of consultation with local
officials, let alone the inhabitants! Yet, it might
be argued that it is for this reason that such substantial transformation has been accomplished.
      Government involvement in the economy is
readily apparent through the series of National
Plans which have guided French development since
1947 (42). The orientation and form of individual
Plans have varied. Since the mid-1960s greater
emphasis was accorded first to promoting industrial
growth and restructuring (Vth and particularly the
VIth Plans), and subsequently to combating the disruption of the economy by the recession and changing
patterns of world trading and manufacturing. This
was largely to the neglect of social policies. At
the same time growth targets became more difficult
to achieve, reflected in the revision of the VIIth
Plan mid-way through its course and the lack of
precision attached to the broad objectives outlined
for the now defunct VIIIth Plan, originally prepared
for the period 1981-5 (43). These problems highlight one of the limitations and inherent contra-
dictions of the French planning system, that through
its indicative rather than compulsory nature,
implementation and the fulfilment of its objectives
are invariably compromised. Nonetheless, until the
economic disorders engendered by the oil crisis of
1973 and the resulting difficulties of accurate
forecasting, there is little doubt that the Plans
offered valuable guidelines and a positive contribution to the country's economic expansion.
      Following a relative decline in the 'Plan's'
role, since 1981 the socialist administration has
sought to re-establish its influence. A ninth Plan
is in preparation for launching in 1984 but until
that time an Interim Plan (Plan Intérimaire)
covering the years 1982-3 has been published. It is
primarily a statement of the main objectives of
government policy for this period. Priority in the
economic field is given to the creation of employment, allied to a series of social policies to
improve working conditions and assist the lower paid,
all dependent upon achieving a high rate of growth
of national output. Extension of state control in
the economy is central to these proposals, a goal

achieved in early 1982 by approval of a major
programme of nationalisations.
    There is a much longer tradition, however, of
state ownership, dating principally from a series of
nationalisations immediately following the second
world war (44), which gave the government control,
in particular, of industries related to transport
and energy, and of a limited number of key financial
institutions. There has been a reluctance to intervene in the running of these companies: far greater
influence has been exercised by government funding
and lending policies, frequently operated through
the state's own credit organisations. By the same
means, pressure has been exerted in the private
sector, with selective but often generous aid
accorded to industrial and research activities.
Under Giscard d'Estaing, for example, investment in
high technology industries became a major priority
(45). In many cases financial commitments have been
linked to the joint negotiation of development
programmes between the government and representa-
tives of different industries, a feature characteristic of branches such as textiles, steel, shipbuilding, machine tools and computers.
    Nonetheless, the nationalisations carried
through by the Socialists represent a vast extension
of direct public control. Nine large industrial
groups now lie within the state's orbit, providing
a major stake in the production of basic metals,
chemicals, glass and electrical and electronics
goods, including data processing equipment. With
the industries already under its authority such as
Renault and SNIAS (aerospace), this places a series
of key activities in the state sector; overall,
around 30 per cent of turnover and 24 per cent of
employment in industry is now controlled by the
government (46). At the same time, 36 banks and the
two major financial groups of Paribas and Suez have
been nationalised giving the state almost exclusive
control of the distribution of credit. A programme
of this scale corresponds in part with the ideo-
logical and political commitments of the Socialists;
it is also linked to their credibility, in offering
an alternative economic strategy to that of the
government under Giscard. Mitterand's contention is
that a coherent and efficient economic strategy is
dependent upon the lead given in investment and
restructuring by a strong state sector. Nonetheless,
the nationalisations were stoutly contested, not
least due to the high cost of compensation and fears
of a lessening of competitiveness amongst the firms

affected.

Since the mid-1950s and the government's first
tentative steps towards a regional policy, state
intervention in the economy has also been given a
marked spatial dimension. Subsequent action has
been guided and implemented largely by the work of
the DATAR (Délégation à l'Aménagement du Territoire
et à l'Action Régionale). Progressively, policies
have become more comprehensive, covering a wider
area, a greater range of activities and more diverse
forms of involvement (47). With the exception of
the central part of the Paris Basin, some form of
financial incentive for the location of industrial
or tertiary businesses is available throughout the
remainder of the country. Within the broad framework of its area-based policies, the government has
also launched other initiatives. These include
regional investment banks, special development companies to undertake specific projects of agricultural improvement, tourist expansion and the build-
up of research complexes, as well as major construction projects, exemplified by Fos. Broad planning
strategies for regions encountering particular
difficulties, yet often with resources which are
under-exploited, have also been launched, notably in
the Massif Central and south-west France.

One of the fundamental objectives of regional
policy has been to reduce the weight of the capital
within the French economy. Some success might be
claimed in this respect, particularly as a result of
the amount of investment and the number of jobs
diverted away from Paris. However, the effectiveness of such action has often been questioned due to
the contrasting lack of decentralisation of
decision-making power, a feature of both public and
private business activities and of government administration. There are signs now of a gradual
change, emphasised by the major socialist reforms
adopted in March 1982 involving the devolution of
far greater responsibility and accountability in
local government to the départements and régions.
The authority of the Préfet (now termed Commissaire
de la République) is much restricted, executive
power has been transferred to the president of the
departmental general council, accompanied by an
enhanced policy-making role for this body, and
regional councils are to be directly elected (48).
In addition, the region's financial resources are
also augmented. Such measures have been long ac-
claimed; while ensuring that decisions affecting a
local area are more democratic, inevitably they risk

inducing antagonism where the priorities of
departmental or regional assemblies conflict with
those of central government, especially where there
is a difference of political complexion. These
reforms undoubtedly represent a significant advance
over legislation introduced in 1972 but the extent
to which, in the context of economic development,
they will reduce the power of central government and
contribute to more dynamic regional economies is
open to question.

NOTES

1. Mary, S. and Turpin, E., 'Panorama
Economique des Régions Françaises', Les Collections
de l'INSEE, R42-3 (1981), 20.
2. Tuppen, J.N., 'Le train à grande vitesse:
its development and implications', Geography, 67
(1982), 343-4.
3. For a fuller discussion see Chevalier,
J-M., L'Echiquier Industriel (Hachette, Paris,
1981), 211-29.
4. 8ème Plan de Développement Economique et
Social 1981-1985 (La Documentation Française, Paris,
1980), 53.
5. More detail of these changes is given in
Cessieux, R., 'L'emploi' in Pagé, J-P. (ed.),
Profil Economique de la France (La Documentation
Française, Paris, 1981), 71-2.
6. Similar trends are reflected in changes in
the contribution to gross domestic product made by
different sectors of the economy; for example,
whereas the primary sector generated nearly 11 per
cent of GDP in 1959, by 1981 this had fallen to
around 5 per cent.
7. In the early 1960s there was also an
important influx of repatriates from North Africa.
8. Fixed at the age of 60 by the socialist
government in 1982.
9. Ogden, P.E., 'French population trends in
the 1970s', Geography, 66 (1981), 312-15.
10. Marchand, O. and Revoil, J-P., 'Emploi et
chômage: bilan fin 1980', Economie et Statistique,
No.130 (1981), 40.
11. Mary and Turpin, Panorama Economique,
15-16.
12. Recent demographic trends are discussed in
Tuppen, J.N., France (Dawson, Folkestone, 1980),
4-9.
13. Mary and Turpin, Panorama Economique, 16.

14.   Marchand and Revoil, 'Emploi et chômage', 35; Le Monde, 29 Sept. 1981.

15.   Mormiche, P., 'Chômage et qualification dans les régions', Economie et Statistique, No.119 (1980), 23-34; Parodi, M., L'Economie et la Société Française depuis 1945 (Armand Colin, Paris, 1981), 28-9.

16.   Marchand and Revoil, 'Emploi et chômage', 39.

17.   Bilan Economique et Social 1981 (Le Monde, Paris, 1982), 17.

18.   Marchand and Revoil, 'Emploi et chômage', 34-6.

19.   8ème Plan de Développement, 51-2.

20.   Le Monde, 18 Oct. 1981. Independently of these 'contracts' the government has encouraged early retirement, particularly in industries badly affected by the recession such as steel.

21.   Fixed at 39 hours in 1982 with the aim of a further reduction to 35 hours by 1985.

22.   Le Monde, 30 July 1982.

23.   Le Monde, 26 March 1982.

24.   For a wider view of energy problems see Cremieux, M., 'L'énergie', in Pagé, Profil Economique de la France, 133-58.

25.   La France en Mai 1981: Les Activités Productives (La Documentation Française, Paris, 1982), 29.

26.   La France en Mai 1981, 34.

27.   Although new, this organisation results from the fusion of a number of bodies previously concerned with individual aspects of this question - e.g. Commissariat à l'Energie Solaire.

28.   Such aspects are discussed in more detail in Tuppen, France, 20-7.

29.   La France en Mai 1981, 11.

30.   Detailed reviews are given in Pinchemel, P., La France (Armand Colin, Paris, 1982), vol.2, 79-101; Baleste, M., L'Economie Française (Masson, Paris, 1981), 130-61; Dézert, B., La Crise Mondiale de l'Energie (SEDES, Paris, 1981), 161-72.

31.   Lepidi, J., 'Le charbon en France', Notes et Etudes Documentaires, Nos.4441-2 (1976).

32.   Dézert, La Crise Mondiale de l'Energie, 172.

33.   'Le retour au charbon en France et des implantations industrielles', Problèmes Economiques, No.1699 (1980), 10-14.

34.   Many refineries have reduced capacity or are working below capacity. The Shell refinery at Petit-Couronne, for example, has a theoretical

annual refining capacity of 18.8 million tonnes, yet
in 1981 produced only just over 5.2 million tonnes.
Similar problems of underuse also affect related
infrastructure such as pipelines.

35. Le Monde, 17 April 1982.
36. Le Monde, 22 and 23 Nov. 1981.
37. Le Monde, 26 Jan. 1982.
38. Natural gas is already received from
Russia, amounting to 15 per cent of total consumption. The contract signed in January 1982 relates
to supplies to be received from 1984. Building of
the Trans-Siberian pipeline offers an important
spin-off for French industry.
39. This also accounts for the rise in the
overall use of electricity which now accounts for
around 28 per cent of final energy consumption.
40. For 1982-3 the programme outlined by the
Barre government has been cut by about a third.
Some more detail of recent developments is contained
in Boyle, M.J. and Robinson, M.E., 'A further note
on French nuclear energy', Geography, 67 (1982),
148-9.
41. An example of the regional impact is given
in George, P., 'Tricastin 1980', Annales de
Géographie, 89 (1980), 401-23.
42. These are well documented in Pinchemel,
La France, vol.1, 223-33; Parodi, L'Economie et la
Société Française, 35-45. House, J., France: An
Applied Geography (Methuen, London, 1975), 304-17
provides an earlier summary.
43. This was prepared under Giscard d'Estaing
but never voted by Parliament. Not unnaturally, the
Socialists chose to prepare their own strategy.
44. For more details see Chenot, B., Les
Entreprises Nationalisées (Presses Universitaires de
France, Paris, 1972), and Brémond, J., Les
Nationalisations (Hatier, Paris, 1981).
45. Giscard d'Estaing, V., L'Etat de la France
(Fayard, Paris, 1981), 73.
46. Bilan Economique et Social, 28. Some
further details of nationalisation in the industrial
sector are given in Scarth, A., 'New nationalisations
in France', Geography, 67 (1982), 155-6.
47. Numerous more detailed accounts of
regional policy exist. Two recent examples are
Pinchemel, La France, vol.1, 233-44 and Perrin, N.,
'L'aménagement du territoire et le développement
régional' in Pagé, Profil Economique de la France,
393-433.
48. For a much more detailed discussion of the
background of proposals see Nivollet, A. (ed.),

Backcloth to Change

'La décentralisation', _Les Cahiers Français_, No.204
(1982) and Ardagh, J., _France in the 1980s_ (Penguin,
Harmondsworth, 1982), 187-205.

Chapter Two

FRANCE AS AN AGRICULTURAL NATION

During the nineteenth century France was dominated
by a rural society in which agriculture played a
pre-eminent role. Yet, for the most part production
methods were inefficient, relying heavily upon an
archaic system of cultivation and undertaken primarily upon a subsistence basis. Even by the early
1950s over 28 per cent of the French work-force was
still employed in agriculture, while more than 44
per cent of the total population lived outside urban
areas: much of France retained the image of a rural
and largely agriculturally based society which had
altered little since the early part of the preceding
century. Now, however, agriculture employs less
than a tenth of the active population and the
countryside houses barely more than a quarter of the
population. Both have undergone a profound
mutation.
        Over the last thirty years spectacular progress
has been achieved in the modernisation of French
agriculture. Production has risen substantially,
productivity has increased significantly and France
has become one of the world's major exporters of
agricultural products. Nevertheless, since the mid-
1970s a combination of factors have disrupted the
advances of previous years and demonstrated the need
for the continued, if more selective, transformation
of the agricultural sector. Since the initial sharp
rise in energy prices in 1973, the costs of farmers'
inputs have in general risen more sharply than the
retail prices for their products. The instability
of European currencies and the introduction of monetary compensatory amounts have acted against agricultural producers in countries with relatively weak
currencies such as France. More generally, the
difficulty of regulating supply and demand and the
shortcomings of the Common Agricultural Policy have

been shown by the growing volume of surplus
production and the disorganisation of certain
markets, notably those for products typically produced in Mediterranean regions. The strains provoked amongst French farmers by these problems have
been illustrated by a series of protests in many
areas of the country, and an indicator of farmers'
difficulties is given by the agreement of the
government to grant special subsidies in 1980 and
1981 to maintain the purchasing power of their
incomes.

THE ROLE OF AGRICULTURE

Despite the diminished role of agriculture as a
source of employment and generator of national
income, now accounting for just over 5 per cent of
GDP, and irrespective of current problems, France is
still a major farming nation. Within the EEC it
holds a dominant position, notably in relation to
the value and volume of output. Over 32 million
hectares of land are in agricultural use, amounting
to nearly 59 per cent of the country's total surface
and representing more than a third of the productive
area of the Common Market. Forest and woodland
represent a further major category of rural land
use, covering 15 million hectares (27 per cent of
the total area), which amounts to more than half of
the afforested area within the EEC.
    France is the Community's major agricultural
producer, accounting for around half the output of
wine and oil seed, nearly two-fifths of all cereals,
a third of sugar beet and approximately a quarter of
the production of beef, milk and poultry. Over the
1970s the country's dominant position was reinforced,
aided by the development and extension of the EEC;
by the end of the decade more than 28 per cent of
the total value of output originated from France.
Exports of agricultural and food products now represent nearly a fifth of the total value of exported
goods, giving some indication of the significance of
the country's pétrole vert to the economy (1). The
majority of trading is with other Common Market
countries, although over recent years there has been
a trend towards the diversification of outlets for
French produce, particularly for major commodities
such as cereals (2).
    As an agricultural nation, France is
undoubtedly favoured by the vast extent of its productive area, although qualitative features of this

land surface play an equally influential role (3).
The country has the substantial advantage, particularly for arable farming, of an extensive area of
relatively flat, fertile land, benefiting from few
extremes of climate. Not only are soils and climatic conditions widely conducive to farming, but
their diversity is also considerable, giving France
an aptitude for a broad range of production.

Regional Patterns of Production
Despite widespread modernisation, the infinite
variety of natural conditions contributes to the
still extremely heterogeneous nature of French
farming. This is seen in the multiplicity of output, the contrasting forms of production technique,
differences in the size and ownership of holdings
and in varying rates of change. Small and often
fragmented farms in areas such as Brittany and
Alsace continue to support varied forms of polyculture; many such holdings are marginal in character, although where worked intensively may be highly
remunerative. Conversely, in parts of the Paris
Basin, areas such as the Beauce house some of the
largest, most efficient and profitable farms within
the country, their production orientated almost
exclusively towards cereals. Human factors also
play a significant role in explaining such contrasts, not least the willingness and ability of
farmers to accept innovation and adopt new techniques. Rather than attempt a comprehensive study of
the complex mosaic of farming patterns the following
review seeks to provide an overview of major
regional contrasts in agricultural activity (4).
    At a national level 54 per cent of agricultural
land is used for arable farming (Table 2.1) yet its
distribution is uneven (Figure 2.1). The greatest
concentration lies in a broad arc stretching from
northern France through to Brittany and is associated particularly with the rich limon soils of the
Paris Basin. Conversely, permanent grassland, which
covers 40 per cent of farmland, predominates in
mountainous regions such as the Massif Central,
Alps, Jura and Vosges, as well as in certain western
areas, notably Basse-Normandie. The pattern of land
use in this latter region provides an interesting
contrast with that of Brittany. Despite similarities of soil and climate, there is far greater
emphasis upon arable farming in Brittany, reflecting
much higher population densities which over a long
period have provided an incentive for the adoption

France as an Agricultural Nation

Table 2.1:   Agricultural Land Use

	Extent (million hectares)	Total (%)
a. Distribution of Agricultural Land (1980)		
Arable	17.3	54.4
Permanent grassland	12.9	40.6
Other (e.g. vines, orchards)	1.6	5.0
	31.8	100.0
b. Distribution of Arable Land (1980)		
Cereals	9.9	57.2
Forage crops	5.0	28.9
Root crops	1.1	6.4
Other	1.3	7.5
	17.3	100.0

Source: Eurostat.

of more intensive forms of production (5). More specialised land uses (6 per cent of the total agricultural area), associated particularly with the growth of vines, fruits and vegetables, are found throughout the country, although in most instances on a very restricted scale. Viticulture only occupies a significant proportion of the land in the southern regions of Languedoc-Roussillon and Provence-Alpes-Côte d'Azur and to a lesser degree in the western areas of Poitou-Charentes and Aquitaine. It is also principally in the Midi that fruit and vegetable production occupies a proportion of the land markedly above the national mean.

Land use patterns, however, are not necessarily an accurate guide to the relative value of output. Although more than half of the agricultural area is in arable use, animal production generates a greater amount of revenue. In 1980 54 per cent of the total value of output was contributed by this sector (Table 2.2), a bias which indicates the extent to which a considerable volume of the output of cereals is used for animal feedstuffs and that over 30 per

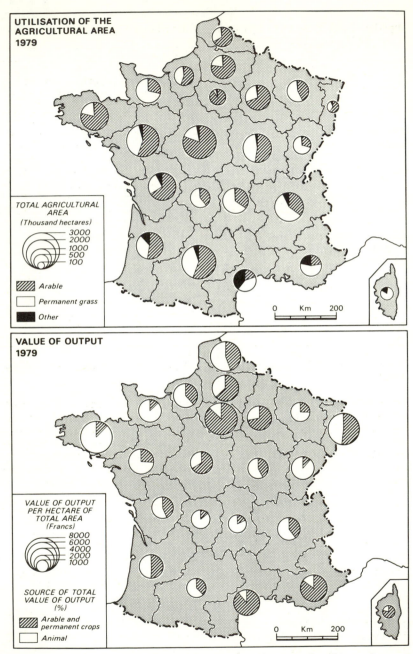

Figure 2.1:   Regional Contrasts in Agricultural Activity

Table 2.2: Distribution of Agricultural Production
(by value), 1980

	Total output (%)	
Production from arable land and crops under permanent cultivation	46.2	
of which cereals		17.2
fruit and vegetables		10.8
vines		10.2
industrial crops		5.3
Animal production	53.8	
of which milk		17.9
beef and veal		17.0
pork		7.0
poultry		4.9
Total	100.0	

Source: INSEE, Les Comptes de l'Agriculture en 1980,
1981.

cent of arable land is used to produce forage crops.
On a regional basis this latter feature is illustrated in Nord-Pas-de-Calais and particularly Brittany,
where despite the predominance of arable land-use, a
greater proportion of revenue derives from animal
production (Figure 2.1); at the same time the above
average value of output indicates the relatively
intensive use of land in these regions, a feature
also applying particularly to Alsace. Conversely,
in many of central areas of the Paris Basin, the
origin of the greater part of agricultural income
from cereals confirms the dependence upon arable
farming; although a relatively extensive form of
production, the large size of holdings combined with
high grain prices results in some of the richest
farms in France (6). In a similar way, for many
areas with a high proportion of land under permanent
grass, the majority of the total value of output
derives from animal production, amounting to over 80
per cent in Auvergne, Limousin and Franche-Comté.
Specialised crops rarely cover an extensive area of
agricultural land, yet the revenue they generate is

often considerable: in Ile-de-France, Nord-Pas-de-Calais, Languedoc-Roussillon and Provence-Alpes-Côte d'Azur vegetables account for over 10 per cent of the value of production, while in Champagne-Ardenne and Alsace vines represent around 20 per cent of the total. It is farmers in the Midi who depend most upon specialised cultivation. Fruits, vegetables and wine provide 60 per cent of total revenue in Provence-Alpes-Côte d'Azur, and more than 80 per cent in Languedoc-Roussillon where the vine remains unchallenged as the major source of income; despite occupying little more than a third of the agricultural area, it alone provides the basis for 60 per cent of the value of output in this latter region. Under such systems of cultivation the use of land is often extremely intensive, reflected in the high incomes generated per unit area. However, due to the extremely small size of holdings in certain major production areas such as the lower Rhône valley (7), farm incomes are often comparatively modest; both features contrast strongly with cereal farming in the Paris Basin.

MAJOR AGRICULTURAL ACTIVITIES

The range of output is extremely wide, but rather than examine all agricultural enterprises in detail, emphasis here is focused upon a restricted number of key areas of production. Reference is also made to forestry and fishing. Although they share relatively few characteristics of other spheres of the agricultural economy, each makes a significant contribution to the production of the primary sector.

Cereals
France is a major producer of cereals. Their cultivation occupies 57 per cent of the country's arable land and they account for over 17 per cent of the total value of agricultural output. There are few regions of the country in which cereals are not grown, although the bulk of production originates from a relatively restricted number of regions. Wheat is the major cereal, covering over 4.3 million hectares: annual production has now risen to around 21.5 million tonnes. It is cultivated predominantly throughout much of the Paris Basin and to a lesser degree in parts of western France (Figure 2.2). In the former instance not only are natural conditions frequently ideally suited to this form of activity,

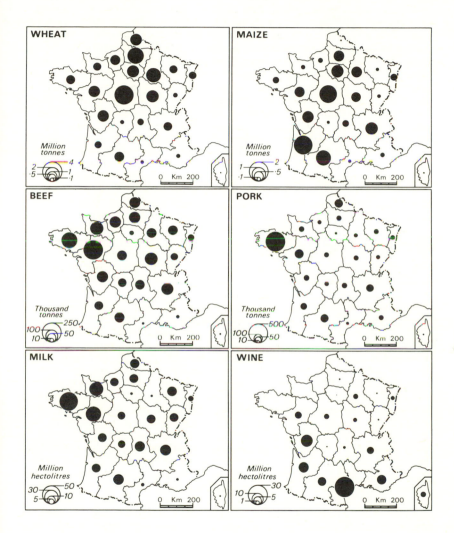

Figure 2.2: The Production of Selected Agricultural
Commodities, 1980

but the areas are also well placed geographically to serve a range of potential markets and over a long period have ranked amongst the most advanced areas of production within France. The growing of barley shows a similar distribution, with total output now exceeding 11 million tonnes; much of this is utilised as a basis for animal feeds and accounts for the considerable expansion of production. Maize grain has now become the third most importance cereal, with an annual output of around 9.5 million tonnes. Originally cultivated mainly in south-western France, it is now grown extensively in the Paris Basin, particularly to the south and east of the capital (Figure 2.2). Other cereals such as oats, rye and rice are characterised by a much lower level of output and a general decline in their pro-duction and extent.

The most prosperous region of cereal production is unquestionably the central area of the Paris Basin. By French standards farms are often extremely large, in certain instances covering up to 700-800 hectares; yet, such a holding would be run by less than 10 workers, indicating the extent of mechanisation and motorisation, and the capital intensive nature of farming. Wheat and maize are often grown in rotation, although this may be widened to include barley, sugar beet, rape and lucerne - essentially any enterprise which lends itself to the same degree of mechanisation as the cultivation of cereals (8). Yields are well in excess of the national mean, rising in a good year to up to 8 tonnes per hectare for maize and over 6 tonnes for wheat.

Grain production is characterised, nonetheless, by certain problematic features. Much of the profi-tability of cereal growing derives from the high prices guaranteed through the CAP; but, outside of the major areas of cultivation, these have enabled many marginal producers to remain viable, reducing their incentive to become more efficient or to switch to other forms of production. The high level of cereal production has enabled France to become a major exporter, particularly of wheat and barley, but to an essentially European market which is becoming increasingly saturated. New outlets are necessary if production is to continue to increase, although so far exports have been facilitated by rebates paid by the EEC. In the long term, however, this is an unsatisfactory basis upon which to main-tain production.

France as an Agricultural Nation

Livestock

Animal production is widespread within France and
nearly 20 million hectares of farming land are related directly (permanent grassland) or indirectly
(artificial pasture and fodder crops) to livestock
rearing (9). This sector is, however, extremely
heterogeneous both in relation to the type and quantity of livestock kept and to the conditions under
which they are reared. Production generally is less
intensive than in certain other Common Market
countries, particularly the Netherlands and Denmark,
for despite the wide extent and undoubted significance of livestock, there are relatively few areas
of intensive and specialised animal production.
Frequently, livestock rearing still represents but
one activity amongst several others on the small,
mixed farm. Nevertheless, considerable progress has
been achieved in improving standards over the last
two decades, partly as a result of the stimulus to
production and increased competition which have
accompanied the development of the EEC (10). But,
as this has occurred, the number of cattle farmers
has declined, especially in dairying, although the
average size of herd has risen.
    With the principal exception of the Midi, beef
and dairy cattle are commonly found throughout
France, although with a marked concentration in the
lowland areas of western France, stretching from the
region of Nord-Pas-de-Calais to that of Pays de la
Loire (Figure 2.2). A secondary band where cattle
rearing is dominant stretches from north-eastern
France to the country's south-western regions,
focusing predominantly upon the upland areas of the
Ardennes, Vosges, Jura and Massif Central. Even in
these areas, however, the average size of herd is
often modest, the density of cattle per hectare is
low and the input of labour comparatively high.
    Dairying is a major farming occupation, accoun-
ting for nearly a sixth of the total value of agricultural output (approximately the same proportion
as cereals) and now amounting to the production of
over 33 million tonnes of milk per year. It is a
particular feature of western France, the central
and eastern parts of the Massif Central and selected
areas of eastern France, notably around Lyon (11).
Even amongst these regions, however, farming
conditions vary considerably. Although some of the
French dairy herds are now amongst the largest and
most productive in the EEC, there are still many
small, often marginal farms with fewer than 10

animals, particularly in upland areas. Here natural
pastures on poor soils provide inadequate nourishment, a deficiency frequently exacerbated by the
poor running of the farm, related to a lack of
willingness or inability (due to financial constraint, for example) to modify the system of production. Inevitably, yields of milk are low, often
well under half those obtainable in more advanced
and specialised areas in parts of western and
northern France. Yet, many farmers, despite such
conditions, view dairying as the only means by which
to extract, at best, a meagre living from their
holding.
    Apart from the supply of fresh milk, much of
the output is processed to form an extensive array
of dairy produce ranging from yogurt to powdered
milk. Again, there is some evidence of regional
variations in the nature of this production.
Whereas in Basse-Normandie the bias is towards
butter and condensed milk, in Auvergne cheese is of
far greater significance; in the département of
Cantal over half of the production of milk is used
for this purpose.
    The rearing and fattening of beef cattle is a
highly varied and often speculative operation. It
is frequently linked to the regions of dairying,
particularly for the raising of calves for slaughter
at a very early age. Increasingly, these are reared
intensively indoors on a variety of feeds, an
activity also accompanied by the more questionable
use of hormones and other stimulants (12). Traditionally, however, true stockbreeding is the
speciality of a more limited number of areas such as
eastern Brittany and the western and northern flanks
of the Massif Central (13).
    Beef and dairy cattle represent only part of a
much wider range of animal production. Sheep are
reared for both meat and milk, although their number
is now considerably diminished compared with their
former significance. Flocks are now concentrated in
the southern half of the country in areas such as
the north-west fringe of the Massif-Central, the
Basque country, the Causses and the southern Alps.
With the output of meat not yet matching demand,
scope exists for an extension of the activity. Pig
rearing and poultry farming offer two examples of
the rapid progression of highly organised factory
farming. In the former case industrialised techniques now dominate and the activity has become
highly localised in Brittany and to a lesser degree
Nord-Pas-de-Calais (Figure 2.2). Such concentration

reflects, in part, proximity to food supplies such
as the by-products of milk production, but it also
results from the presence of local initiative and
pressures for a more remunerative form of agricultural activity.

Considerable scope exists within France for the
more intensive and efficient rearing of livestock.
However, standardisation and mechanisation tend to
be less easy to achieve in this area than in cereal
production, particularly due to the large number and
wide range of producers. Moreover, modernisation
requires heavy investment. Other problematic issues
are apparent relating to the orientation of production. Dairy products are generally in surplus due
partly to high prices, while, conversely, France
imports both pork and lamb. Stimulation of home
output is limited in the former case by the increasing cost of imported concentrated foodstuffs and
strong competition from other EEC producers, and in
the latter by low Community prices. To ensure a
more rational pattern of production, eradication of
such imbalances is essential but this is part of the
much wider question of the reform of the CAP.

Specialised Production
French agriculture is also characterised by the
significant contribution made to the total value of
output by a limited range of more specialised and
intensively cultivated enterprises, generally occupying only restricted areas of land. This is illustrated by the production of wine, fruit and vegetables which together account for approximately 21
per cent of the value of output, yet only 4 per cent
of the cultivated area.

Viticulture. France possesses one of the world's
most important series of vineyards, expressed not
only in terms of their extent and volume of output,
but also in relation to the quality and value of the
production. This is despite a gradual but progressive reduction in the area planted with vines, which
now totals a little over 1.1 million hectares. The
volume of output varies considerably between years,
reflecting the vine's susceptibility to variations
in climatic influences, but between 1977 and 1980 it
averaged 66 million hectolitres each year. Vin
ordinaire represents the greatest part of production,
accounting for over 60 per cent of the total; the
remainder is constituted by quality wines (AOC and

VDQS) and wine produced for the manufacture of cognac. Considerable quantities of wine are imported and exported - around 8 million hectolitres in each case in 1980. However, while the former is represented largely by imports of low grade Italian wines, the latter is orientated towards products of higher quality, with the result that the value of exports exceeds that of imports by a ratio of approximately 4:1.

With the exception of the north-western third of the country, vines are found throughout France, yet relatively few areas stand out due to the high volume of production (Figure 2.2). Amongst the major areas of viticulture there are also sharp contrasts in the pattern and quality of production (14). There is little in common between the virtual monoculture of the vine over an extensive area for the production of predominantly low grade wines, as throughout much of the Languedoc plain and in parts of Provence and Corsica, and the far more limited areas of high quality output; these are dispersed chiefly amongst the wine growing districts of Bordeaux, Burgundy, Champagne, Charentes and the Rhône valley (Figure 2.3).

Despite many outward signs of prosperity, the activity is not without its problems. Overproduction of vin ordinaire has long been a difficulty faced by the wine growers of Languedoc, aggravated in the past by imports of cheaper Algerian wines and more recently by the similar inflow of Italian produce (15). Now, there is also a declining market. Measures to encourage alternative activities or an improvement in the quality and a reduction in output have met with only limited success; nor has an entirely successful formula been reached within the framework of the CAP to assist in the regularisation of the market. Less well publicised, however, are the problems encountered by vine growers in other regions. Along the Rhône valley, for example, between Vienne and Valence, the area under vines is decreasing. Producers are handicapped by the excessively small and fragmented size of holdings and the difficulties of working the steep slopes which severely limit an increased use of motorised equipment. Even in areas of more favourable relief higher returns from alternative land uses, particularly housing, or even other crops such as fruit, act as further incentives to abandon production (16). Nevertheless, these constraints are more apparent for the producers of lower grade wines; the much higher prices commanded by the limited areas of

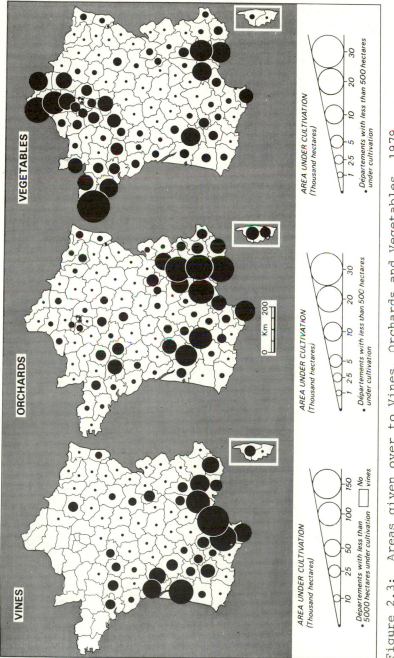

Figure 2.3: Areas given over to Vines, Orchards and Vegetables, 1979

high quality output have assured the permanence of
these vineyards. The production of wine is a speculative business and it is not unusual for the area
under vines to fluctuate; this has long been dis-
played in the Bordeaux region (17). Moreover, in
contrast to the decline of the vine in certain
areas, in other districts there is a reverse tendency. In Alsace, a region renowned for the general
excellence of its wine, vineyards have been extended
over the last ten years and output has risen,
reflecting careful planning and management, and a
considerable effort to increase exports.

Fruit and Vegetables. Production of these products
is a traditional feature of farming patterns on the
outskirts of urban areas; from an early date
favourable climatic conditions also encouraged such
specialisation in a limited number of other regions,
illustrated by the growing of vegetables along the
northern coastal fringe of Brittany. However, it
was not until the early part of the present century
that these activities became more widespread, responding to improvements in communications and transportation technology and a rapid increase in demand,
the latter also partly linked to changing dietary
patterns. Cultivation is now characterised by a
wide variety of products (Table 2.3) and techniques.
Vegetables are just as much a feature of the fields
of relatively large farms in the Paris Basin or
northern France as they are of extremely small,
intensively worked holdings of the lower Rhône
valley (18). It is in the Midi where specialisation
in the production of vegetables and especially fruit
is most marked, notably in Roussillon, parts of the
Languedoc plain, western Provence and the Rhône
valley (Figure 2.3). The volume of output here is
also considerable; for example, south-eastern France
(19) accounts for around 40 per cent of the
country's total production of apples and pears and
over 80 per cent of peaches. Other important areas
for the cultivation of fruit and vegetables include
the lower Loire valley and the départements of Lot-
et-Garonne and Tarn-et-Garonne, and for vegetables,
the départements of Nord, Pas-de-Calais and Somme,
and western Brittany (Figure 2.3).
    There are two main problems associated with
these activities. Firstly, the rising costs of inputs, especially heating costs, for the increasing
volume of output grown under at least partially
artificial conditions (for example, under glass or

Table 2.3:   Production of Selected Major Fruits and
Vegetables, 1978-81

	Mean annual production ('000 tonnes)
Apples	1,701
Tomatoes	813
Carrots	499
Cauliflowers	466
Pears	430
Peaches	400
Lettuces	289
Leeks	243
French and runner beans	207
Melons	197
Grapes	188
Plums	152

Source: Eurostat, Crop Production 1982.

plastic). Secondly, fruit growers in particular are
faced with a market which is increasingly over-
supplied. French output receives strong competition
from other Mediterranean producers (such as Italy
and Spain) where production costs are frequently
lower and the season longer. Even within France
there is often great rivalry between different
growing regions. Languedoc and Corsica, through the
extension of their fruit production, now compete
with established areas such as the Comtat Venaissin
(lower Rhône). Competition, however, has acted as a
spur to improvement, encouraging increased standardisation and mechanisation in an activity which
traditionally is labour intensive. Conversely, it
has also contributed to a reduction in the area
under orchards, further encouraged by EEC grants, to
help reduce the problem of overproduction.

Forestry
French forests and woodland represent a vast but
generally under-exploited resource, covering more
than a quarter of the country's total area. Despite
losses due to hazards such as fire or resulting from
urban encroachment, the extent of the forest cover is
gradually increasing with around 35,000 hectares
planted each year. The afforested area is, however,

far from homogeneous, both in terms of distribution
and dominant species. Much of the north-western and
western parts of the country have a relatively
sparse covering, although the region of 'les Landes'
in south-western France is a major exception, being
one of the country's most densely forested areas
(Figure 2.4). Apart from this, the most extensively
wooded areas are associated with the country's mountainous massifs. In these areas, as in the Landes,
are found the major coniferous forests, although
overall nearly two-thirds of the country's forest
cover is of deciduous species.

     This resource fulfils various economic, social
and ecological functions, although within the same
area all are not necessarily compatible. It also
generates a considerable number of employment opportunities. Around 80,000 people are employed
directly in the maintenance of the forests and in
associated sawmills, while an estimated further
500,000 jobs result from industries dependent upon
the use of wood as a raw material; these range from

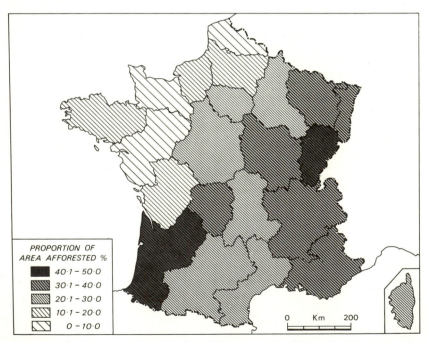

Figure 2.4: Regional Variations in Forest Cover,
1980.

the manufacture of furniture to paper and packaging.
Yet, despite the richness and potential of France's
forest resources, the country is a net importer of
wood products, particularly of soft-wood for the
paper industry. To help redress this imbalance the
state has responded by improved management and increased planting, but the anticipated improvements,
inevitably, are long term. Furthermore, the State
Forestry Service is only responsible for approximately a quarter of the country's resources. The
rest is under private control, often split amongst
numerous relatively small owners. Here change has
proved difficult to implement and co-ordinate.
    The problems of management are well illustrated
by the forests bordering the Mediterranean, where
they cover more than 4 million hectares. Now
largely abandoned for their economic use (contrasting with the rigorous management of the forests of
les Landes), they still represent an important
resource for recreation and play a vital role in
controlling soil erosion; yet almost each year they
are ravaged by fire, with over 320,000 hectares
destroyed between 1970 and 1979 (20). Various forms
of control have been tried, but part of the problem
relates to neglect of the forest, enabling the
growth of garrigue scrub vegetation which in turn
facilitates the spread of fire. Once destroyed,
however, replacement is often difficult due to the
resulting soil erosion.

Fishing

Many areas of France's extensive coastline have had
a long association with fishing, although increasingly the activity is becoming concentrated in a
limited number of centres. Fishing is of greatest
importance along the Atlantic and Channel coasts,
focused in the former instance upon the ports of
southern Brittany (particularly Lorient and
Concarneau) and in the latter upon Boulogne, the
country's principal fishing port.
    Despite the wide distribution of fishing ports,
various weaknesses characterise the structure and
operation of the industry, restricting its efficiency. Part of the activity's difficulties results
from the excessive number of small, undercapitalised operators which exist both for inshore
and deep-sea fishing. In addition, quay-side facilities are frequently out-dated and the handling of
the catch inefficient and thus expensive. These
problems have been exacerbated by other developments.

French fishermen have faced growing competition from
cheaper imports (the EEC having taken little action
to limit such imports), which has resulted in a
reduced demand for their products and had a depressant effect upon prices. At the same time costs
have risen, most noticeably in relation to fuel.
Many of the small independent fishermen have been
forced to cease their activities, while even the
larger operators have rationalised their undertakings; the industry's labour-force which stood at
over 42,000 in the mid-1960s is now less than 25,000
(21). Protests by the fishing community at such
events culminated in the violent action in the
summer of 1980; since then the government has agreed
to provide additional financial assistance, aimed
above all at modernisation and increased efficiency.
With these objectives a five-year plan was launched
jointly by the government and the industry in 1982.
    A further and more serious problem also affects
the industry's viability. Overfishing in the past
has depleted fish stocks, leading now to lower
catches. The feature is by no means unique to
France and over an extended period has formed the
basis of discussions between the Common Market partners aimed at the protection and improved management
of fish resources. However, despite the setting up
of a 200 mile limit for territorial waters around
the member states, the Community has still failed to
reach agreement on the fishing limits of members
within this zone; such action is essential to safe-
guard the fishing industry, not only of France, but
of all the Common Market members, yet as delays
continue, countries have begun to take unilateral
action.

FRENCH AGRICULTURE - DIRECTIONS FOR THE 1980S

Scope for increased efficiency undoubtedly exists
and further modernisation appears essential if
France is to remain a competitive producer in the
European and world market. This need is increased
by the relatively slow expansion of the demand for
food products yet the continued growth in competition to supply this market. Numerous strategies
have been outlined to further improve the performance of the agricultural sector, many of which
represent the continuation of existing but uncomple-
ted policies; for example, increasing the rate at
which land is consolidated and encouraging the more
widespread application of techniques such as

irrigation.   Certain action, however, appears
critical.   Too few farms are managed effectively and
run as a commercial operation, thus reducing their
efficiency.   Equally, the educational standards of
farmers, their access to and utilisation of the
findings of modern research, and the speed and
efficiency with which new techniques are diffused
all appear limited.   Finally, ample scope remains to
improve the marketing of produce by making far more
extensive use of specialised operators capable of
dealing in large quantities of a standardised
product, thus allowing a much greater level of scale
economies to be realised.   In turn, the food processing sector remains underdeveloped in France, yet
offers considerable potential not only to enhance
greatly the value of 'raw materials' produced by
agriculture, but also to stimulate output.

   Achievement of these objectives in an economic
climate of reduced growth and lower public expenditure poses many problems, apart from the difficulties of deciding upon the most effective means by
which to attain the above goals.   It also means a
choice of priorities.   Producing a more efficient
and competitive agricultural system implies encouraging the more dynamic and successful farmer, yet
France is faced with a still substantial number of
marginal and sub-marginal producers which the
government has pledged to subsidise.   The basic
incompatibility of the two policies is an inevitable cause of conflict and compromise.

NOTES

   1.   Reference to agriculture in this way was
first made by Valéry Giscard d'Estaing in 1978 when
emphasising the country's rich potential as an agricultural nation and the need to further exploit this.
   2.   The EEC (9 members) accounts for approximately 65 per cent of exports and 47 per cent of
imports.
   3.   Klatzmann, J., L'Agriculture Française
(Seuil, Paris, 1978), 101-3.
   4.   More detailed accounts are given in
Thompson, I.B., Modern France (Butterworths, London,
1970) and Klatzmann, J., Géographie Agricole de la
France (Presses Universitaires de France, Paris,
1979), 32-42.
   5.   Klatzmann, L'Agriculture Française, 31.
   6.   For more details of the spatial variation
of incomes see Klatzmann, L'Agriculture Française,

39-43.

7. In the region of Provence-Alpes-Côte d'Azur as a whole over 60 per cent of holdings are below 5 hectares in size.

8. Estienne, P., La France (Masson, Paris, 1979), vol.1, 63-6.

9. A detailed account of livestock farming is given in Spindler, F., 'L'élevage en France', Notes et Etudes Documentaires, Nos.4341-2 (1976).

10. Estienne, La France, vol.1, 66.

11. Estienne, La France, vol.1, 68.

12. Le Monde, 19 Sept. 1980.

13. Estienne, La France, vol.1, 68-9.

14. For a detailed discussion see Froment, R. and Lerat, S., La France (Bréal, Montreuil, 1977), vol.2, 24-8, and Baleste, M., L'Economie Française (Masson, Paris, 1981), 75-9.

15. Stevenson, I., 'Sour grapes for rich harvests', Geographical Magazine, 48 (1976), 262-4.

16. See, for example, Gadille, R., 'L'héritage d'une viticulture antique, vignes et vins de Côte-Rôtie et Condrieu', Revue de Géographie de Lyon, 53 (1978), 7-22 and Roux, C., 'Heures et malheurs des coteaux rhodaniens dans la région valentinoise', Revue de Géographie de Lyon, 53 (1978), 23-35.

17. For a detailed history of the changing fortunes of one district in this area see Pijassou, R., Un Grand Vignoble de Qualité: le Medoc (Tallandier, Paris, 1980). A summary is published in L'Information Géographique, 44 (1980), 209-13.

18. More general details of such production are given in Lerat and Froment, La France, 47-56. For a fuller study of the small but intensely culti-vated holdings in one area of the lower Rhône see Daudé, G., 'L'agriculture de Châteaurenard: tradi-tion, difficultés et perspectives', Revue Géographique de Lyon, 47 (1972), 167-219.

19. The regions of Provence-Alpes-Côte d'Azur, Languedoc-Roussillon and Rhône-Alpes.

20. Le Monde, 4 Jan. 1980.

21. It is estimated, however, that the industry generates a further 100,000 dependent jobs in ancillary and processing activities.

Chapter Three

THE CHANGING FACE OF FRENCH AGRICULTURE

THE BACKGROUND TO CHANGE

The Position in 1945
By 1945 French agricultural activity and rural
society had evolved comparatively little since the
end of the preceding century (1). Agriculture was
still dominated by an excessive number of small,
self-sufficient family farms. Production was
centred upon a variable but basic system of polyculture combined with livestock, characterised by
its inefficiency. Mechanisation was limited and
those machines which did exist were frequently old.
The use of fertilisers was not yet common practice
and little attention was accorded to either the
selection and care of animals or to the development
of improved strains of crops. Under such conditions
output frequently varied greatly in quality and
quantity, not only between years and regions, but
also between farms. Few areas were intensively
farmed, and generally yields per hectare and productivity per worker were low. Agriculture was thus
based upon high cost production and, due to the
extravagent use of manpower, labour requirements
remained high. In addition, the country was self-
sufficient in few agricultural commodities, with the
need to import placing unwanted pressure on the
balance of payments. Farmers' attitudes were still
dominated by the need to supply the family: the
production of a surplus for commercial sale was a
valuable addition but an essentially secondary consideration. There was, therefore, little thought
given to adapting supply to demand and orientating
production towards consumer preferences (2). Nor
were there yet any signs of the now increasingly
common association, and even integration, between

agricultural producers and food manufacturers.

Thus, in the period immediately following the second world war agriculture was in a critical state. Overmanned and unproductive and having suffered the ravages of the war, it was incapable of responding to a growth in demand which became essential as the French nation entered into a belated but intense phase of urbanisation and industrialisation.

Change was crucial in three areas. Firstly, farmers had to be educated and encouraged to utilise new technology; above all, farming had to become more highly mechanised, enabling substantial gains in productivity but also implying severe reductions in manpower. Secondly, to facilitate this movement, farm structures had to be reformed to enlarge the general size of holdings and reduce the degree to which they were subdivided. Thirdly, inefficient systems of distribution and marketing required rationalisation, not least to improve the return to the farmer. Such changes presupposed a radical upheaval of traditional agricultural society, with the implication that they would not be achieved without a difficult period of transition. Furthermore, for transformation of this scale to be accomplished, the outlook and attitudes of both government and farmers required substantial modification; the government needed to stimulate progress and offer the incentives for greater efficiency rather than continue to support an outdated system of production, while for the farmer it was essential that he should view farming as a commercial operation based upon the specialisation and maximisation of output. For effective and durable modernisation to occur it was equally necessary that both these parties should accept a commitment to investment on an unprecedented scale.

Progress Since 1945

In the early post-war years, innovation and reform tended to take second place to the urgent need to re-establish production, hit by the loss of manpower, the disruption of markets and the frequently extensive damage to the land and buildings of farms. Considerable emphasis was given to the achievement of this goal in the 1st National Plan (1946-53), aided by the programme of Marshall Aid. Modernisation, however, was by no means ignored and, indeed, the encouragement of a substantial increase in mechanisation and motorisation (with the beneficial

side-effect of releasing labour for industry where
there was an acute shortage) became a major priority
in the attainment of higher output and greater
productivity. By the early 1950s, with production
now rising, the government sought to widen and
strengthen the basis of its policy towards agriculture. Attempts were to be made to relate more
effectively supply to demand, particularly as a
means of preventing low prices depressing farmers'
incomes. Similarly, strong emphasis was to be given
to encouraging a rise in the volume of exports, not
least because the output of various products began
to exceed the demands of the home market (3); moreover, in view of the country's undoubted potential
for further increasing production, this appeared an
obvious policy to pursue in order to reduce imports
and ease pressure on the balance of payments. More
generally, recognition was given to the need to
improve the living environment of farmers through
the provision of water and electricity supply,
better housing and new roads.

During the 1950s some progress was made towards
the attainment of these objectives but agriculture
remained beset by problems, many of them serious and
fundamental in character. Despite a substantial
rise in output, a slimming of the labour-force and
some increase in productivity, agricultural improvement was restricted by the extent to which the
sector was tied to an inequitable system of price
support. In theory such a policy should have stimulated output and protected incomes, but in practice,
through inadequacies in its implementation, it
favoured a limited range of products, notably
cereals, and the larger producers who were already
often relatively efficient. Little progress was
made towards improving the standards of the still
numerous class of small and frequently marginal
farmers.

Throughout the 1950s discontent was manifest
amongst the farming population, expressed in a
series of demonstrations and protests, many of them
violent in character (4). There was a growing and
forceful expression of opinion for more radical
change, led by an increasingly organised and articu-
late group of young farmers. The movement grew
partly out of the activities of the <u>Jeunesse
Agricole Chrétienne</u>, an organisation with originally
religious aims but, due to its spread amongst young
people in rural areas, it became a means of co-
ordinating their views and voicing their disenchantment (5). In turn, it helped give birth in the

latter 1950s to the Centre National des Jeunes
Agriculteurs (CNJA) which became the junior body of
the main farmers' union, the Fédération Nationale
des Syndicats des Exploitants Agricoles (FNSEA) (6).
The CNJA advocated strongly the need for basic
structural reform, rather than manipulation of the
market through the price mechanism, as the only
effective means by which to render agriculture more
efficient and to raise farmers' incomes. To achieve
this it was prepared to accept a reduction in the
farming labour-force. By the end of the decade constant pressure and increased protests led to a
series of government measures to restructure the
agricultural sector.

The reforms of 1960 and 1962 (Loi d'Orientation
Agricole and Loi Complémentaire d'Orientation
Agricole) sought to raise farmers' and farm workers'
earnings to a level comparable with similar socio-
economic groups in other areas of employment and to
ensure that production was based upon holdings of a
viable size and structure to enable the efficient
utilisation of manpower and machinery (7): the basic
unit was seen as a holding employing at least two
full-time workers throughout the year - in essence
the family farm. Achievement of these objectives
implied a significant reduction in manpower and
marginal production units, and an agricultural
system organised upon a much stronger commercial
basis.

This legislation, which is notable for the
changes it introduced relating not only to the economic basis upon which agriculture was to be organised, but also to the social welfare of the farmer
and farm worker, has remained the basis for agricultural reform ever since. It also has a wider significance, marking an important threshold in progress
towards the post-war modernisation of French agriculture and a modification of attitudes towards such
transformation. The institution of the Vth Republic
led to a fresh outlook towards economic change in
France, guided by a new team of ministers and a new
generation of technocrats ready to consider the
views and aspirations of the progressive elements of
the farming community forcefully presented by one of
their most ardent leaders, Michel Debatisse. A
further vital stimulus for change arose from the
establishment of the Common Market and the creation
of a Common Agricultural Policy, despite its protec-
tionist character. Once the policy had been firmly
established by the mid-1960s, relatively high and
guaranteed prices became of great significance in

assuring a healthy income for at least a part of the
French farming community. Thus, during the 1960s a
series of increasingly influential internal and
external policies underpinned the advance and profound transformation of agriculture.

From the early 1970s, however, a new set of
problems emerged. Farmers were adversely affected
by the slowing in growth induced by the energy
crisis, while the weaknesses as well as the
strengths of the CAP were becoming increasingly
apparent. The result was to disrupt the steady rise
in output and improved performance of agriculture in
the export market, and to induce a lower rate of
income growth, tending to widen the differential
between the farming population and other groups of
workers. Structural problems remained and other
trends provoked concern, particularly the increasing
level of indebtedness and the progressive ageing of
farmers. Together these factors have produced a new
wave of legislation in the early 1980s seeking to
achieve better control over the land market and
speed up the enlargement of holdings, as well as
encouraging younger people to enter farming.

FARM STRUCTURES AND RELATED PROBLEMS

As in many other European countries, modernisation
of agriculture in the post-war period has been
greatly hampered by an increasingly irrational
pattern of land distribution. In the 1950s France
was characterised by a large number of agricultural
holdings, an excessive proportion of which were of
very small size; many were also subdivided to an
exaggerated degree into numerous, often minute, non-
contiguous parcels. Frequently these conditions co-
existed. In 1955 there were over 2,300,000 holdings,
of which 35 per cent were less than 5 hectares in
size. It was also estimated that up to 18 million
hectares of farmland were susceptible to consolidation. Small, sub-divided holdings were the consequence of various factors, including the legacy of
medieval openfield agricultural systems, a response
to population pressure, the consequences of inheritance laws, or the reflection of terrain conditions.
But whatever the cause, their impact was to render
farming inefficient and uneconomic and, above all,
to retard or make impractical the introduction of
extensive mechanisation. These conditions varied
throughout the country, being less apparent in parts
of the Paris Basin yet particularly problematic in

selected areas such as Alsace. Here a long
tradition of openfield farming combined with high
rural population densities had produced a pattern of
very small and intensely divided holdings, although
these features were more apparent in the latter part
of the nineteenth century when rural population
densities were at their highest (8).

The problems produced by the above features had
long been recognised and over an extended period had
resulted in a substantial reduction in holdings (9),
an increase in the average size of farm, and progress towards consolidation. In general, however,
the pace of change was relatively slow with the exception of the widespread disappearance of very
small holdings; conversely, there was little
increase in the number or proportional significance
of larger farms above, for example, 20 hectares in
size. Thus, as greater emphasis was placed upon
structural reform, it became essential to accelerate
these tendencies, largely through the various forms
of state intervention embodied in the legislation of
the early 1960s.

Significant changes have occurred since this
period, notably in the creation of substantially
larger farming units. The total number of holdings
has continued to decline, (with little sign of a
marked easing of this trend), falling to around 1.2
millions by the end of the 1970s (Table 3.1). Whereas
in 1955 approximately 56 per cent of all holdings
were less than 10 hectares in size and only 8 per
cent were above 35 hectares, by 1979 these proportions had changed to 42 per cent and 20 per cent
respectively. Thus, the overall change is accounted
for essentially by a spectacular decline in holdings
below 20 hectares in size and a marked rise in those
above 35 hectares. Small holdings are still numeri-
cally the most dominant with farms below 20 hectares
representing over 60 per cent of the total number of
holdings. However, the growing significance of
larger production units is indicated by the fact
that approximately 43 per cent of all agricultural
land is concentrated in farms exceeding 50 hectares,
which also account for more than a third of the
total value of output (10).

These broad national trends conceal a number of
divergent regional patterns, although the continued
decline in holdings is a virtually universal feature
of all rural France; where the proportion of small
holdings is particularly high there is frequently a
correspondingly elevated rate of decrease in
holdings, as for example in Alsace. Regional

Table 3.1:   Distribution of Agricultural Holdings by Size

Size in Hectares	1955		1970		1979	
	No. ('000)	%	No. ('000)	%	No. ('000)	%
< 5.0	807	35	493	31	357	29
5 - 9.9	482	21	251	16	167	13
10 - 19.9	540	23	355	22	243	20
20 - 34.9	298	13	263	16	232	18
35 - 49.9	83	4	107	7	116	9
50 - 99.9	76	3	93	6	114	9
> 99.9	21	1	27	2	35	2
Total	2,307	100	1,589	100	1,264	100

Source: Ministère de l'Agriculture, Recensement Général de l'Agriculture 1979-80, 1981.

variations in the size of farms are complex, with marked differences occurring even within a single department.   Nonetheless, there is a notable contrast between a broad central zone of the Paris Basin where holdings are significantly above the mean size, and the Mediterranean fringe and parts of north-eastern France where the average size is significantly below the mean (11) (Figure 3.1). Comparison of the départements of Bas-Rhin (Alsace) and Aube (Champagne-Ardenne) illustrates this disparity and the dissimilar ways in which the two areas have evolved (Table 3.2). The former is characterised by a predominance of small, intensively worked holdings, traditionally based around a system of polyculture in association with livestock but now showing an increasing specialisation in cereals: the latter is dominated by the cultivation of cereals and a greater proportion of much larger farms - over 43 per cent of the agricultural area is accounted for by farms exceeding 100 hectares.

Market forces have acted as a natural stimulus to the decline in the number of holdings and to the general enlargement of those remaining. These trends have been encouraged by increased mechanisation, motorisation and associated economies of scale, as well as the departure of owners, thus releasing land. The government, however, has sought to

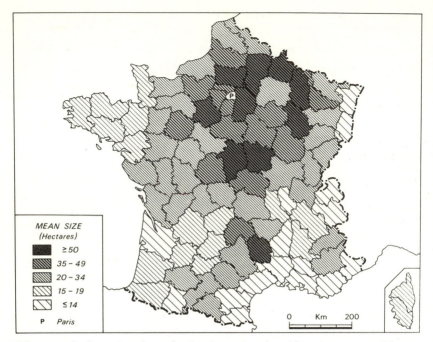

Figure 3.1: Regional Contrasts in the Average Size of Farm Holdings, 1979.

structure and facilitate these processes. Two mechanisms have been particularly significant. By the laws of 1960 and 1962 it established the first of a series of Sociétés d'Aménagement Foncier et d'Etablissement Rural (SAFER). These are semi-public, non-profit making bodies which now operate throughout most regions of France with the principal aim of trying to regulate the land market. They intervene to purchase land which becomes available, subsequently redistributing it to enable the enlargement of farms. To assist in this action a SAFER may pre-empt other potential purchasers and may constitute and offer for sale entirely new holdings from the land it has purchased. Through such activity it was also hoped that a moderating influence would be exerted on the rise in land values, although the SAFER are involved in only a limited proportion of all land transactions (12). Thirty-one SAFER now operate within France.
To accelerate the release of land, it was deemed logical to encourage elderly farmers to accept early retirement, which ought also to offer

The Changing Face of French Agriculture

Table 3.2: Comparison of the Size and Number of
Holdings in the Départements of Aube and Bas-Rhin

a. Distribution of Holdings

Size of holding (hectares)	1955		1970		1979	
	No.	%	No.	%	No.	%
Bas-Rhin						
< 5.0	20,934	54	9,456	45	7,444	45
5 - 9.9	12,283	31	4,100	20	2,467	15
10 - 19.9	5,394	14	4,844	23	2,912	18
20 - 49.9	478	1	2,383	11	3,055	19
> 49.9	35	-	165	1	444	3
	39,124	100	20,948	100	16,322	100
Aube						
< 5.0	2,050	20	1,834	24	2,097	27
5 - 9.9	1,049	10	503	7	495	7
10 - 19.9	1,460	14	560	7	448	6
20 - 49.9	3,844	36	2,057	26	1,535	20
> 49.9	2,104	20	2,825	36	3,031	40
(of which						
> 99.9	425	4	796	10	1,031	14)
	10,507	100	7,779	100	7,606	100

b. Mean Size of Holding (hectares)

	1955	1970	1979
Bas-Rhin	5.2	9.4	11.9
Aube	36.6	46.1	48.8

Source: Ministère de l'Agriculture, Recensement
Général de l'Agriculture 1979-80 (1981).

the advantage of allowing young farmers to assume
responsibility at an earlier age. Thus, in 1962 the
government set up a special fund, the Fonds d'Action
Sociale pour l'Amélioration des Structures Agricoles
(FASASA) (13), to finance the payment of early or

supplementary pensions - the <u>Indemnité Viagère de Départ</u> (IVD) (14). Collaboration between farmers enabling them to work their holding jointly and therefore, in principle, realise certain economies of scale, is a further means by which some of the inefficiencies of the small farm may be overcome. Various forms of such co-operation exist, and this has been achieved notably through the creation of a <u>Groupement Agricole d'Exploitation en Commun</u> (GAEC), a system established by government legislation passed in 1962. A slightly different formula was proposed by the <u>Groupement Foncier Agricole</u> (GFA), aimed at the joint ownership of a holding (to facilitate, for example, the retention of a farm within a single family) rather than in the case of the GAEC, some form of co-operative scheme of working (15).

State intervention has also taken place to help tackle the major handicap of the fragmentation of holdings, seeking to sponsor consolidation schemes. The disadvantages of excessive fragmentation are many, but above all it limits or renders more costly the use of machines and frequently tends to act as a brake against change and innovation. Recognition of these problems has produced a long history of compensatory measures; examples include private agreements amongst a limited number of individuals to exchange plots, buying out of the other inheritors by a single heir to avoid subdivision, or the leasing of adjacent land to enlarge the plot (and the holding as a whole) to make its operation more efficient. Nonetheless, their effectiveness and application have always been limited, and in recognition of the need for more direct and far-reaching action the government instituted as early as 1918 a semi-official policy of consolidation (<u>remembrement</u>). Its role was greatly increased by legislation passed in 1941 which has remained the basis for subsequent action. In general, remembrement involves not only a regrouping of holdings but also associated improvements such as the remodelling of the local road system.

THE EFFECTIVENESS OF RESTRUCTURING MEASURES

These measures all aimed to improve the efficiency of French farming through a rationalisation of productive units. Moreover, with the accelerated decline of rural population they also became a reflection of the extent to which holdings within an

area were no longer adapted to its demographic
characteristics. Their achievements and effectiveness, however, have been variable.

Since their creation, the SAFER have acquired
over 1.1 million hectares of land. The greater part
has been used to enlarge existing holdings and a
further substantial amount to constitute new proper-
ties. Considerable regional variations exist in the
role played by the SAFER, but generally their action
has been greatest in areas of traditionally small
and often marginal farms in central and southern
parts of the country (Figure 3.2). In these areas
they have undoubtedly played a valuable role in the
redistribution of land. However, despite substantial activity, overall the purchases of the SAFER
account for less than 20 per cent of land which has
become available on the market. In part this
reflects certain limitations placed on their possibilities of intervention by the government (16) and,
despite some financial advantages, their relatively
limited resources. A further handicap arises from
the obligation of the SAFER to resell land within 5

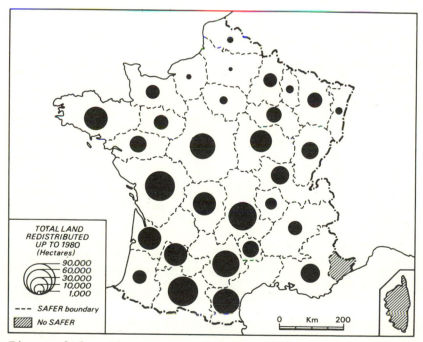

Figure 3.2:   The Action of the SAFER

years of its acquisition, frequently limiting the
possibilities of a substantial regrouping of land,
and their requirement to sell rather than lease
land. Certain criticism has also been expressed at
the preference in certain regions for the SAFER to
redistribute land in favour of a series of small
farms, with only marginal benefit to any one unit,
rather than constitute much larger, more viable
holdings. Their impact, therefore, is debatable,
although in view of some of the above limitations
the government revised the legislation relating to
the SAFER in 1980, notably increasing their capital
and thus their possibilities for action. In a wider
sense the SAFER have had little impact on the regularisation of the market for land or on the stabilisation of prices, largely due to the relatively
minor role they play in land transactions. The
demand for rural land, however, is strong, the
greater part of it still originating from farmers.
An enlarged land area is not only an important
factor in increasing output; it is also a form of
security and a means of achieving an increased
social standing (17). Invariably, however, such
possibilities exist only for the already larger and
more affluent landowner, particularly where supply
is restricted.

Certain reservations also apply to the effectiveness of the IVD, although by 1980 over 560,000
farmers had benefited from these grants (offering
for redistribution more than 10 million hectares of
land) suggesting the measure has had a substantial
influence (18). Nonetheless, the number of benefi-
ciaries has declined very substantially from a peak
of over 80,000 in 1969 to 14,000 in 1979 with a
corresponding decrease in the amount of land libera-
ted. Partly this resulted from a natural fall in
the numbers potentially available to benefit from
this measure but it also reflected the considerable
decline in the attractiveness of the grant as its
value has been eroded by inflation, although its
level was raised in the latter 1970s. The notion of
land being released for redistribution or the
creation of new holdings is also partially misleading, for in many cases the payment of the IVD has
simply hastened the process of transfer of the
holding from father to son. Overall, although
certain economic benefits have resulted from this
policy, it has had more effect as a social measure
facilitating premature retirement (19).

Although there are now more than 11,000 GAEC
the success of the measure also appears questionable;

this is despite government grants to encourage their
formation and running and the availability of loans
at preferential interest rates through the Crédit
Agricole (20). The majority of GAEC have been
formed within families (for example, between father
and son) and thus the measure has generally failed
to promote wider co-operation. While the theory of
their establishment is sound, in practice it has
sometimes proved difficult to rationalise successfully two or more small farms. Nonetheless, where
the system does function effectively it has brought
obvious benefits and where father and son or
brothers have joined together has provided one means
of encouraging young people to remain in agriculture.
For the latter group, further incentives are available. In 1973 the government launched a scheme to
assist young farmers to become established through
the payment of a special grant (<u>Dotation
d'Installation des Jeunes Agriculteurs</u> - DJA) and
the provision of very low interest loans. Initially,
it was aimed specifically at favouring the retention
of the young in mountainous regions, but given the
desirability of the policy's general objective, its
scope was enlarged in 1978 to cover the whole
country. Nevertheless, the size of grant remains
higher in upland regions and areas of difficult
farming. After a relatively slow start (with only
22,000 grants allocated between 1973 and 1980) the
measure has increased in popularity. In 1981 the
value of the grant was raised substantially and
under the Socialists the provision of assistance to
young farmers has become a major strand of agricultural policy. This was further demonstrated in 1982
by the extension of the role of the SAFER to give
preferential aid to this group to enlarge their
holdings. Such priority reflects the still large
number of farmers nearing retirement.

Since 1945, official programmes of consolidation have affected over 10.5 million hectares of
agricultural land, although progress has been relatively slow, notably throughout the period until the
early 1960s. Currently remembrement is completed
annually over an area of approximately 300-400,000
hectares. Progress has been greatest in those areas
of advanced farming where natural conditions have
facilitated the process, as throughout the Paris
Basin and northern France (Figure 3.3). Equally,
substantial advances have been achieved in similarly
progressive regions with a strong tradition of sub-
division such as Brittany and Alsace. Conversely,
consolidation has progressed only slowly in many

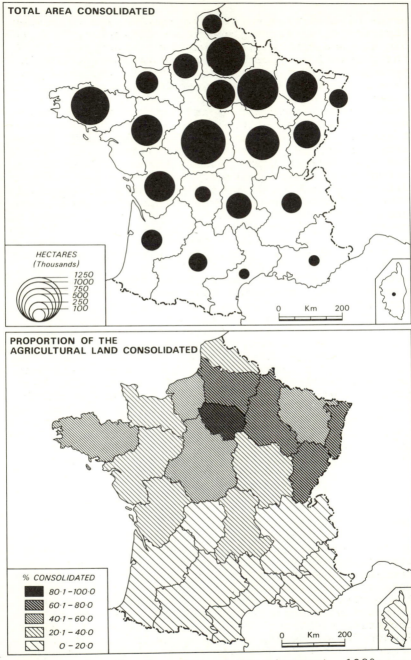

Figure 3.3:   The Progress of Remembrement, 1980

areas of central and southern France, its extension
thwarted by a mixture of influences ranging from the
old age and general conservatism of many farmers, to
the difficulties posed for the exchange of plots by
enterprises such as the vine where micro-variations
in soil, climate and aspect are frequently highly
significant (21). More generally, there are various
factors which have slowed or limited the effectiveness of remembrement operations. Although generous
financial assistance is offered by the state, consolidation depends upon the agreement of two-thirds of
the landowners within a given commune. This has
often been difficult to obtain, particularly due to
differences over the eventual pattern of redistribution. Remembrement represents only a partial
grouping of a holding and in itself does not of
course augment its size. Moreover, it has been
argued that the operation might be more effective if
it was combined with a greater range of ancillary
projects. Although new roads, drainage schemes,
water and electicity supply have often accompanied
remembrement, little has been done to effect a more
rational distribution of settlement.

There appears to be little disagreement over
the desirability of all the above measures as an
important part of the modernisation of French
farming. More questionable is their impact (22),
but at the very least they have greatly accelerated
otherwise much slower natural tendencies. Structural reform is a vital component of change and the
legacy of an excessive number of minute holdings has
long been an anachronism of French farming. However,
merely taking into account the extent of a farm is a
poor indicator of its economic importance. For a
realistic appraisal of a holding's potential profitability, size ought to be viewed in relation to the
nature of the activity.

IMPROVEMENTS IN TECHNIQUES

While French agriculture has been progressively
transformed by fundamental structural changes during
the last three decades, over the same period it has
been revolutionised by improvements in technique and
the organisation of productive activities. When
compared with agricultural activity in European
countries such as the Netherlands and Great Britain,
French farming in the immediate post-war period
demonstrated many features of backwardness and
inefficiency. Subsequently, progress has been such

that French agriculture is now highly competitive
within the EEC. Various factors have contributed to
such a vastly improved performance, ranging from a
great increase in mechanisation to a far more scientific approach to farming. In turn, these changes
represent a response to a series of pressures; these
have included the need to increase output to satisfy
both home and export markets, the reduction of the
agricultural labour-force to enable greater efficiency and encourage a sectoral shift of manpower,
and the desire to raise farmers' financial returns
and reduce the physical burden of their work.

A major role in the increase of output and productivity has been attributed to the large-scale and
widespread advances in mechanisation and motorisation (23). Initial progress in this area was slow,
despite the priority given by the 1st National Plan,
with draught animals still providing the major
source of energy in the early 1950s (24). Progress
started to become rapid from the middle of the
decade, symbolised by the very substantial rise in
the number of tractors utilised (Table 3.3) and
facilitated by the belated development of France's
own agricultural machine industry. The tractor has
now become an integral part of farm operations
throughout the country, although inevitably the
emphasis tends to be stronger in areas of cereal-
based rather than animal-based activity. By 1979,
on 76 per cent of all holdings a tractor was owned
or jointly owned. As this has happened, the rate of
increase in the number of tractors has slowed;
instead, since the early 1970s, there has been a
substantial rise in the use of more powerful units
capable of a wider range of tasks. High levels of
mechanisation are not only features of cereal
farming, but are equally apparent in relation to a

Table 3.3: The Number of Tractors in Operation

	Total tractors
1955	337,000
1963	950,000
1970	1,200,000
1975	1,346,000
1980	1,485,000

Source: Ministère de l'Agriculture.

wide range of other activities, with a noticeable increase in their use in the production of fruit, vines and vegetables. Generally, the problem of under-equipment has now been overcome; the current emphasis is upon the introduction of a more sophisticated range of machines and, given the substantial increases in productivity, the extension of the range of activities capable of mechanisation. For the smaller farmer, unable or unwilling to purchase equipment himself, the formation of co-operatives for its joint acquisition has been encouraged by the government. There are now over 8,200 Co-opératives d'Utilisation de Matériel Agricole (CUMA) established for this purpose which benefit from government grants to assist in purchases. The nature and organisation of farming activities have been altered radically by these changes, but their introduction has not been without problems, not least due to the large investment which the acquisition of new machinery entails.

These trends have been accompanied by an equally significant biological revolution. Production and yields of major cereals have increased significantly through the introduction of hybrid and improved varieties, while arable farming generally has also been associated with the use of an ever growing quantity and range of chemical products to enhance output and eradicate or reduce the likelihood of disease or unwanted growth. Evidence of the importance of these tendencies is given by the dramatic rise in the application of fertilisers (Table 3.4), and in the level of yields (Table 3.5).

Table 3.4: Consumption of Fertilisers

Agricultural year	Total consumption ('000 tonnes)
1954/5	1,470
1959/60	2,064
1964/5	3,088
1969/70	4,220
1974/5	4,679
1979/80	5,652

Source: INSEE, Annuaire Statistique de la France (various volumes), and Assemblée Permanente des Chambres d'Agriculture.

Table 3.5:   The Increase in Yields of Selected
Cereals

	Yield (tonnes per hectare)		
	1950	1970	1981
Wheat	1.8	3.4	4.8
Barley	1.6	2.7	4.2
Maize	1.2	5.1	5.6

Source: Eurostat.

Similar attempts have been undertaken to raise the
efficiency of animal production especially through
concentration upon a smaller range of more specialised breeds, allied to the improvement of related
buildings and fixed installations (25). Control of
livestock to help prevent infection is now far more
widespread, as is the use of techniques such as
artificial insemination. Generally, there has been
a growing standardisation of production methods and
the quality of output. To this end the nourishment
of animals has altered greatly. Animal feeds now
include a variety of cereals, sugar beet pulp,
powdered and skimmed milk and high protein manufactured foodstuffs. Consumption of the latter has
increased markedly, rising from 600,000 tonnes in
1960 to over 13 million tonnes by 1978 (26); it has
also led to greater production of oil seed and much
higher imports of soya. The use of high protein
feeds was originally linked to poultry and pig
farming, notably in Brittany; now it has become a
growing feature in the feeding of cattle and the
spread of totally stall-fed rearing. One index of
progress is provided by the increase in the mean
annual milk yield of cows, which in 1960 was little
more than 2,000 kilogrammes per head, yet by 1980
had reached nearly 3,600 (27).
    All the above features have tended to raise the
extent to which agricultural activity occurs within
an artificial or controlled environment. Fertilisers have increasingly removed the need for a rotation of production, the latter determined far more
by the relative demand for and, therefore, financial
return of different enterprises. Similarly, with
the advent of industrialised production techniques,

natural conditions now need place few limitations
upon the rearing of livestock. A further example of
an extension of control over the environment is
offered by the spread of irrigation, although only
3 per cent of agricultural land in France is
actually irrigated. Nonetheless, the practice is
increasing, affecting 800,000 hectares in 1979 compared with 539,000 in 1970. Although the concentration of irrigated areas is greatest in southern
France (not unnaturally in view of the summer
drought conditions), the last decade has been noticeable for the spread of the technique to areas such
as western France and the Paris Basin. Here it is
linked, for example, to the expansion of maize cultivation where the yield is frequently greatly
increased through irrigation. Techniques have also
evolved, seeking to increase efficiency and econo-
mise water. One example is the use of perforated
pipes embedded in the soil to feed water directly to
plant roots (28), a system which is applied in parts
of the areas of fruit and vegetable production in
the lower Rhône valley and Languedoc.

COMMERCIALISATION AND MARKETING

Just as it was apparent in the early post-war years
that a radical modification of production methods
was essential to increase the output and competitiveness of French agriculture, it was equally evident that the sector's efficiency also depended upon
the modernisation of distribution channels and
marketing practices. The markets for relatively few
products were controlled, making it difficult to
regulate supply and demand, not only in terms of the
volume of output but also in relation to its quality;
there was often little attempt to standardise the
product. This latter feature was to gain far
greater importance as production activities have
become more closely linked to and reliant upon agricultural processing industries, reflecting the shift
away from polyculture and a high degree of auto-
consumption to a much more highly commercialised
agriculture. Moreover, the nature of demand has
changed, implying the need for not only the pattern
of production to alter correspondingly, but also the
related marketing processes. Traditionally, the
distribution of many products was characterised
either by its complexity, involving a series of
intermediate agents, or by the individualistic attitude of the producer. Costs rose accordingly and,

therefore, a rationalisation of this activity represented, as with technical progress, an important means by which to help raise the revenue of farmers.

Marketing practices still vary greatly in their form and efficiency between different agricultural products, but there are a number of general trends which characterise their evolution since the 1950s. Three tendencies have been particularly strong. First, as part of its general policy of improving the control and organisation of markets, the government has attempted to strengthen the marketing structure for products such as cereals, sugar and milk over which there was already a strong element of control; in part this was also encouraged by the creation of the CAP and its price support policies. Second, particular emphasis has been placed upon trying to rationalise the commercialisation of products where previously there had been little official organisation, notably for items such as fruit, vegetables and eggs. With this objective, proposals were introduced in 1982 to extend the principle of marketing boards to cover such products, and to achieve a much closer relationship between supply and demand. Third, there has been an increasing tendency for farmers to produce under contract for processing firms or distribution chains, or to become more closely tied to the industries which supply their inputs. In a wider sense marketing has also been rendered more efficient by ancillary changes, as for example the increasing use of road transport as a more flexible means of movement, despite the continued existence of special express train services between areas such as southern France and Paris.

Marketing boards were first established with the principal aim of regulating production through a policy of price support. The first of these, now the Office National Interprofessionnel des Céréales (ONIC), for cereals, was originally established in 1936 (29), to be followed in 1953 by others relating to milk, sugar, meat and wine (30). In 1961 these were complemented by the creation of a special organisation (Fonds d'Orientation et de Régularisation des Marchés - FORMA), with the original function of intervening via the marketing boards to purchase and stock excess production. Its role is now wider, concerned with the preparation and execution of government policy in the general field of market regulation. Moreover, once the CAP had been fully established, much of the activity of FORMA and that of the marketing boards was dictated and financed by the Community's policy. The boards themselves have also widened their spheres of action. For example, the Office National Interprofessionnel des Vins de Table (ONIVIT) is concerned as much with improving the marketing of these wines and promoting an improvement in their quality, as with regulating production (31). Certain of the markets controlled by these organisations function highly efficiently, notably for cereals, for which the collection and stockage is strictly organised through a series of powerful co-operatives acting on behalf of the ONIC. In contrast, the marketing board for livestock and meat (Office National Interprofessionnel du Bétail et de la Viande - ONIBEV), in trying to improve the supply of meat, is faced with the complexities produced by a varied and traditional set of commercialisation procedures.

For those markets lacking official organisation the situation has frequently been far less satisfactory, notably in the sale of fresh fruit and vegetables, where traditionally the amounts offered by producers have been small and variable in quality; furthermore, due to the absence of adequate knowledge of the markot, and a lack of unity amongst them, farmers were able to exert little pressure upon the variety of middlemen or wholesalers to whom they sold their produce. To overcome these and other inadequacies, two main policies have been followed. In the early 1950s the government sanctioned the creation of a series of Marchés d'Intérêt National (MIN), although many were not completed until the latter part of the decade or early 1960s. Their aim was to facilitate contact between producers and purchasers and to increase the efficiency with which products were distributed. Eighteen of these centres now exist (32), biased generally towards either the dispatch of fruits and vegetables (for example, Châteaurenard, Cavaillon and Agen in the southern part of France) or to the supply of large urban markets such as Lyon, Toulouse and principally Paris (Rungis) (Table 3.6). However, with the growth of much larger purchasing groups dealing directly with producers the need for these centres, particularly in the former instance, has been diminished, although they still offer an important service to the smaller grower and dealer.

The other main strand of policy has been to encourage greater unity of action amongst producers through the formation of a variety of co-operative organisations. Such bodies have long existed and

Table 3.6:   Regional Wholesale Market Centres
(Marchés d'Intérêt National)

Market	Tonnage handled 1980 (tonnes)
Agen	109,062
Angers	43,280
Avignon	148,905
Bordeaux	141,236
Cavaillon	434,362
Châteaurenard	260,953
Grenoble	110,350
Lille	253,249
Lyon	219,232
Marseille	166,078
Montauban	97,356
Nantes	259,515
Nice	153,178
Nîmes	53,805
Rouen	113,364
Rungis	1,484,779
Strasbourg	107,622
Toulouse	210,513

Source: Fédération Française des Marchés d'Intérêt National.

played an important role in the marketing of products such as cereals, wines and milk (33), but in its 'orientation' laws of 1962 the government sought to extend the concept to a far wider range of products as part of its policy to organise production more effectively and regularise markets. Equally, if better organised, producers ought to possess a stronger negotiating position vis à vis purchasers. Thus, to facilitate such action the government encouraged, through a series of financial aids, the creation of Groupements de Producteurs Reconnus - GPR (34); over 1200 have since been created. In certain cases they have been formed through existing co-operatives or Sociétés d'Intérêt Collectif Agricole (SICA) (35), although these latter organisations still function independently. The achievements of these various co-operative organisations appear mixed. In many areas they have grown rapidly and undoubtedly brought benefits to their adherents (36), but there are criticisms. Bad

management, partly reflecting too many divided
interests, has limited their impact, while all too
frequently there is still an important part of the
market which remains outside of this organised
sector. Individualism, the traditional desire for
independence and the hope that a better price might
be obtained where the market is not controlled all
contribute to this situation. For example, in the
département of Lot-et-Garonne, a major producer of
fruits and vegetables, co-operatives still control
less than 40 per cent of the market (37). Furthermore, these bodies represent an extremely heterogeneous group of organisations, ranging from those
which are small and locally based, to larger, more
influential units covering a much wider territory.
Rationalisation is essential to enable the co-
operatives to function more efficiently and effectively, above all as selling organisations. Certain
co-operatives have also sought to extend their
influence by enlarging their activities and controlling a greater part of the productive process: as
such they have become involved in the purchase and
supply of many of the farmer's inputs and not only
the disposal of his produce, but also its transformation.

Even amongst the activities of traditional
dealers in agricultural produce, change and rationalisation has taken place, with a growing role being
played by a number of large forwarding agencies for
which farmers often now grow under contract. This
forms part of an increasing tendency for sales to
take place directly between producers and large
consumers. Such action takes various forms, ranging
from direct purchases by large hyper and super-
market chains and by the largest wholesalers, to the
supply of canning industries. Similar links are
also evident in the rearing of poultry, pigs and
calves, in all cases increasing agriculture's link
with other sectors of the economy, principally with
the food processing and the animal feedstuffs
industries. The trend is marked in Brittany through
the role played by companies such as Dusquesne-
Purina, leaving little scope for the initiative of
the individual farmer, and is similarly apparent in
the regions of Bresse and Dombes (Rhône-Alpes) for
poultry farming (38). Inevitably, under such
systems the element of control is extremely high,
for the industrial customer seeks the regular supply
of a uniform product. There ought, however, to be
various benefits which accrue to the producer. Not
only has he an assured market for his output

(although as a consequence he may be paid slightly less), he also will undoubtedly be obliged to employ modern techniques and be given expert advice; furthermore, the parent firm is often a valuable source of credit to finance necessary improvements, with all these factors increasing the farmer's security (39). There are dangers and some sacrifices which the farmer much accept. Not all contracts offer strong security, the uncertainty of the weather is ever present, and the farmer is no longer a free agent, for many, the most significant drawback. Nonetheless, it would appear that if French agriculture is to maintain progress towards higher efficiency, such trends need to continue, as must the tendency towards a greater degree of collective action.

AREA-BASED POLICIES

The majority of measures outlined already relate to national policies covering the whole country, although due to factors such as the varying intensity of the problem they are designed to tackle, their impact frequently varies from one region to another. Other initiatives, however, again largely sponsored by the state, have been taken to focus or encourage improvement within specific areal limits where farmers are faced with unavoidable and difficult problems or where, despite constraints, there is adequate potential for development provided sufficient investment is undertaken. In many instances projects of this type form part of wider programmes of economic improvement.

One strategy adopted by the government, although partly financed through the Guidance section of the CAP, is the provision of additional financial assistance to farmers living and working in particularly unfavourable areas, the latter reflected in conditions such as a harsh climate, intense depopulation, or poor soils (40). Such zones have been classified in various parts of the country (Figure 3.4), but their major concentration, not unnaturally, is in mountainous regions, with the greater part of the Vosges, Jura, Massif Central, Pyrenees and Corsica included within this definition. In recognition of the special problems of farming in such areas and of the desirability of lessening the associated heavy outward movement of population, the government offers an additional series of aids for these zones, notably the payment of an Indemnité

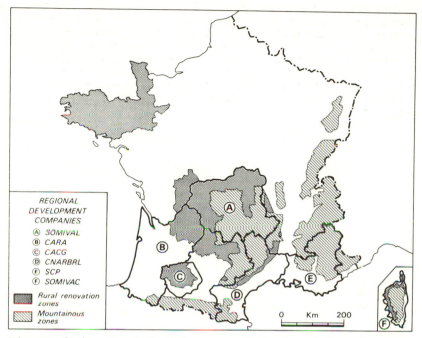

Figure 3.4: Assisted Zones and Regional Development Companies in Rural Areas

Spéciale de Montagne (ISM), in effect a grant based on the number of head of cattle. Other special measures include the payment of subsidies to facilitate the purchase of machinery, while, as indicated previously, under schemes such as the grants available to young farmers (DJA), the amount payable is much higher in mountainous areas. These various measures offer some compensation for farming and living in a difficult environment, but in view of the many factors which discourage such an existence, it is questionable whether their impact is more than marginal.

More specific assistance to a limited number of areas has been provided by the activities of regional development companies (Sociétés d'Aménagement Régional - SAR), first established by the government in the latter 1950s and early 1960s. Seven companies were originally formed, of which six are still functioning (Figure 3.4): all are concentrated in the central and southern parts of France (41). Each of these organisations varies in its precise form and objectives, the latter also frequently having been modified in the light of new experience or changing conditions. In general, however, they possess the status of 'mixed economy companies' (42), and were created not only with the aim of improving agriculture but also as part of a wider policy of regional development to help promote economic expansion in the regions in question. Their launching coincided with a period of increasing awareness and action by the government over the problem of regional imbalance within France. Moreover, in the early 1960s much of southern France faced the problem of absorbing repatriates from Algeria, many of whom wished to preserve an interest in farming; by transforming or extending agricultural activity, these companies were able to exert a valuable influence in this process. To enable fuller discussion of such general aims, as well as of the specific tasks set for individual organisations, a more detailed account of a number of these bodies will follow.

First established in 1955, the Compagnie Nationale d'Aménagement de la Région du Bas-Rhône et du Languedoc (CNARBRL) has become one of the best-known and most successful of the regional development companies. Its primary objective was to help revitalise the rural economy of Languedoc-Roussillon, a region which at that time was characterised by a low intensity of economic activity, little industry, a general tendency towards the outward migration of population, and an excessive dependency upon viticulture (43). To achieve this, it was proposed to irrigate an extensive area of the Languedoc plain, split between two sectors of intervention, transforming the previous structure and pattern of agriculture to a new system based upon the production of fruit and vegetables. Progress has been less than anticipated, although in the eastern sector approximately half of the 130,000 hectares proposed for irrigation is now equipped. This has been accompanied by a substantial transformation of farming, shown in the growth of fruit and vegetable production for the département of Gard, the area principally affected by such changes; as an example, the volume of peaches produced increased from little more than 2,000 tonnes in the late 1950s to over 57,000 tonnes in the latter 1970s. Apart from providing the necessary facilities to permit irrigation, the CNARBRL has been active in promoting and encouraging the use of irrigated farming techniques, the creation of new farms and restructuring the layout of holdings. Moreover, if farmers were to be

persuaded to reorientate their production, it was
also essential to provide the necessary distribution
and marketing facilities; this has been attempted
through promoting the growth of producers' marketing
organisations or co-operatives, and the attraction
of a modern canning and processing industry. There
are, thus, many positive aspects to the developments
which have taken place, not least the technical
success of the irrigation works.

Against these, however, must be balanced
various less satisfactory features. Progress has
been much slower than anticipated and farmers have
been reluctant to modify their pattern of production.
Many factors contribute to this, but in part it reflects the relatively high cost of water and the
ambiguous record of transformation; in the latter
1960s, for example, those farmers who had planted
apple trees in place of the vine were badly affected
by over production of this fruit. The same situation has arisen with peaches. Partly as a consequence of these problems, the policy of the CNARBRL
has altered, notably in the use of the water it
controls which is now supplied to meet the needs of
various towns (e.g. Montpellier) and to irrigate the
vine, a use which was inconceivable when the company
was first set up. This latter policy aims not only
at increasing the sale of water, but also at improving the quality of the wines produced; unfortunately, little progress has been achieved in this
field by the use of irrigation alone, which has done
more to increase yields, exacerbating a long-
standing problem of over-production (44).

The action of the CNARBRL has not, therefore,
matched expectation in all the areas of its operation. A similar assessment might apply to the
Société de Mise en Valeur de la Corse (SOMIVAC),
created in 1957 to assist in the revitalisation of
Corsican agriculture, not an easy task in view of
its generally degraded state and the widespread depopulation of the countryside (45). Greatest emphasis was placed on the clearance and drainage of the
eastern plain, to be followed by the creation of new
farms specialising in the production under irrigation of fruits, vegetables, fodder crops or flowers.
Again, considerable technical assistance and advice
was to be made available to farmers by SOMIVAC.
Throughout the island SOMIVAC has now equipped over
25,000 hectares for irrigation, of which over half
is actually irrigated, but this has not been without
difficulty and controversy. In the early years
there were problems in attracting new farmers to the

eastern plain, reflecting local scepticism of the
project; this was resolved by the arrival of
Algerian repatriates willing to experiment with new
techniques, although their subsequent success only
served to further inflame local feeling. More
serious has been the reluctance of producers to move
away from cultivation of traditional crops such as
the vine, to the production of citrus fruits and
vegetables. Thus, much of the irrigated eastern
plain is given over to viticulture, producing essentially wine of a relatively low quality for an
already saturated French and European market. Nonetheless, SOMIVAC has enabled the radical transformation of the agricultural landscape of a significant area of Corsica.

The role of the Société du Canal de Provence et
d'Aménagement de la Région Provençale (SCP) is somewhat different. Founded in 1957, its primary
purpose then was to ensure an adequate supply of
water to meet the needs of agriculture in the
départements of Bouches-du-Rhône and Var, and to
help meet the requirements of the city of Marseille.
Almost inevitably, however, in view of the severe
shortage of water which characterised this area in
the post-war period, the project was to assume a
wider significance. Most of the water is taken from
the Verdon to be distributed southwards towards Aix,
Marseille and Toulon by a series of canals, over
half of which have been constructed underground.
The bulk of the infrastructure is now completed but
once again the scheme's original expectations have
not been entirely fulfilled. Despite a long history
of attempts to introduce irrigated farming to this
region, the use made of the new facilities by
farmers has been less than anticipated. In part
they have been slow to experiment with and adopt new
techniques; in addition, there has been a reluctance
to invest in the essentially speculative production
of fruit and vegetables, despite their suitability
for irrigation. In contrast, greater quantities of
water than were originally anticipated are now con-
sumed by urban and industrial users in the regions
of the Etang de Berre, Aix, Marseille and Toulon,
although even here the reduction in the scale of the
Fos scheme has slowed the expected growth of demand.
Nonetheless, it is these latter sales which account
for over two-thirds of the revenue of SCP and have
assured its viability (46).

Although the three companies discussed above
have encountered problems, others have been far less
successful. The Compagnie d'Aménagement des Landes

de Gascogne, established in 1958, aimed to diversify
the rural economy through the creation of a series
of large arable farms located on clearings within
the forest (47). Although maize is now grown under
irrigation with some success, there were many
failures in the early years, resulting in the original company being reformed in 1972 (to become the
Compagnie d'Aménagement Régional d'Aquitaine - CARA)
and given a wider, but modest brief. The activities
of the Compagnie d'Aménagement des Coteaux de
Gascogne (CACG) have also been limited in scope (48,
49).

There is considerable variation in the scale of
operations of these various development companies,
but all have sought as part of their operations to
transform and improve agricultural activity, frequently through programmes of irrigation. Equally,
they all share certain problems. Progress has been
slower than anticipated, farmers have frequently
been reluctant to accept change, notably in their
pattern of output and, partly as a result of these
factors, the companies have modified the orientation
of their development programmes. In certain cases
agricultural improvement represents only part of a
wider sphere of intervention. Also, in parts of the
areas affected by these schemes, other agencies have
introduced improvements (notably irrigation) as one
of their wider range of activities, illustrated by
the action of the Compagnie Nationale du Rhône and
Electricité de France. While this may be generally
beneficial, this does raise the issue of the desirability of the duplication of administrative,
research and technical teams, not only between
various state bodies, but also between the regional
development companies themselves. Nonetheless, in
partial recognition of this anomaly, but also testifying to their undoubted expertise in hydraulic
engineering and agricultural improvement, these
latter bodies have combined to form a joint company
(Groupement d'Etudes et de Réalisations des Sociétés
d'Aménagement Régional) to promote their activities
abroad, principally in the developing countries.

KEY FACTORS UNDERLYING THE TRANSFORMATION OF
AGRICULTURE

Having considered some of the principal ways in
which agricultural activity has been transformed
over the post-war period, a limited series of key
influences which have been an integral part of and

an important motivating force behind such change are
now discussed. Emphasis is focused upon four
themes.

The Growth of Indebtedness

Prior to the 1950s, borrowing on a large scale by
farmers was a relatively rare occurrence, with the
principal exception of the large farms of the Paris
Basin where, over a long period, farmers have invested heavily in new technical innovations. Purchases
of equipment or land were frequently financed
through savings within the family, particularly by
the smaller landholder. However, the subsequent
revolution in the techniques and organisation of
farming not only transformed this practice but was
only made possible by heavy reliance upon external
funding. As agriculture has become more capital
intensive and machinery has been increasingly substituted for labour, there has been a spectacular
increase in borrowing by farmers. Loans have become
essential to purchase new equipment, to finance the
re-organisation of holdings or their improvement
(through drainage or irrigation), to enable the
construction of new buildings (often essential in
the increasingly widespread adoption of factory
farming) and not least to permit the acquisition of
additional land. Many owners of small or medium-
sized farms have been reluctant to extend their
holding through the lease of extra land, preferring
to purchase, a reflection not only of a strong
traditional attachment to the land, but also of the
general soundness of the investment given the rise
in land values. The need for borrowing has grown
partly due to the increased scale and sophistication
of the equipment which is required, and also as a
result of the rapidity of change and, to remain competitive, the need for constant adaptation (50).
    The main agent in the distribution of credit to
the farming community has long been the Crédit
Agricole. Not only is it the traditional farmers'
bank, but it also operates as an important official
outlet for the payment of various government-backed
subsidies. Not unnaturally younger farmers have
demonstrated a greater readiness to borrow, while
the level of indebtedness is generally greater for
the larger holdings. Loans may be essential for
modernisation, but this does not lessen their burden,
particularly for the smaller operator. Interest
charges are now often a significant part of the
farmer's outlay. Yet, there is some relief. Many

loans are subsidised by the government as one of
its policies for encouraging modernisation, and thus
attract very low rates of interest. In addition,
relatively rapid inflation has reduced the effective
value of repayments. It is often the small-scale,
marginal farmer who suffers most, unable to give
sufficient guarantees to secure such loans.

Education and Research

Access to an adequate source of finance may be
important in effecting change, but educating the
farmer in the use of new techniques and increasing
his awareness of current research and its results
are equally fundamental. Traditionally, the level
of educational attainment amongst farmers has been
low, with relatively few progressing beyond the
secondary sector; even fewer have possessed any academic qualifications directly related to farming.
For improvement to be successful and for it to occur
rapidly, it became essential to raise these standards. Moreover, as farm management has become far
more complex, the necessary degree of competence has
risen accordingly. An early effort to improve the
availability and standard of farming education,
particularly at a secondary level, was made in the
context of the legislation of 1960 (51). Attempts
have also been undertaken to increase the possibilities for training at a higher level, but generally
the degree of educational qualification amongst
farmers remains extremely modest, particularly for
those living in the more remote and marginal areas.
Since the mid-1960s, however, there has been a significant increase in the number of farmers partici-
pating in specialised courses designed to improve
their knowledge or competence (52).

A strong emphasis upon research is an equally
important factor in achieving progress. Government
sponsored research has expanded considerably, principally through the work of the Institut National
de la Recherche Agronomique (INRA), first created in
1946. Its achievements are numerous and diverse,
although there is some criticism that its work has
been more theoretical than applied and that results
of research have been slow to disseminate (53).
Extensive and valuable research is also undertaken in
the private sector, illustrated by the improvements
in the varieties of maize achieved by the company
Limagrain which specialises in the production of
seed maize. Unfortunately, the diffusion of new
ideas appears to remain in many instances relatively

slow and haphazard, despite the increased and often important role played by co-operatives, the agricultural processing industry and professional organisations to explain new techniques and processes, and encourage their adoption. Nevertheless, the situation has improved with, for example, a range of expert advice from technicians available to farmers from such sources as the Chambres d'Agriculture professional bodies existing within each département. Groups such as the Centres d'Etudes Techniques Agricoles (CETA), a discussion forum for local farmers, and the CNJA also promote the exchange of ideas and offer advice. Obstacles remain, however, not least the conservative and individualistic character of certain farmers and the reluctance of many of the more elderly to accept new practices.

State and EEC Policies

Throughout the post-war period the French government has taken an active and influential role in promoting the modernisation and reorganisation of agriculture. It has done this through legislation and a wide array of systems of aid, frequently guided by the general economic and social strategies embodied in the country's National Plans. Not all its action, however, has been linked with change and increased efficiency: the state has also acted in an important supportive capacity which for social reasons has often involved maintaining otherwise inefficient forms of production. The extent of government intervention in both spheres is indicated by the amount of financial assistance accorded to the farming community, which in 1981 exceeded 5 billion francs. Priorities have changed: no longer is the overriding need to improve productivity. Emphasis is now being given to resolving the activity's intrinsic demographic problems by encouraging young people to farm, to a further remodelling of still unsatisfactory marketing procedures and to the development of food processing industries.

Whatever the aims and strengths of the French government's own policy towards agriculture, however, the evolution and regulation of this sector of the economy have become increasingly dependent upon the Common Agricultural Policy of the EEC. As a major original advocate of the policy, it is of little surprise that France should have benefited from the system. The introduction of guaranteed prices for many commodities at levels above those previously practiced in France, and the very considerable enlargement of the potential market for these products, acted as major stimuli for the expansion of production, and supported a significant increase in farmers' incomes. This at least was representative of trends from the mid-1960s until the early 1970s. Since then the advantageous position of French agriculture has been less apparent, although the Common Market still absorbs two-thirds of French agricultural exports. France, like other member countries, has been adversely affected by the effects of the recession and by the dramatic increases in raw material costs, but also particularly by currency fluctuations. During the 1970s this latter feature posed a major difficulty for the CAP as its common pricing policy was based upon the maintenance of fixed exchange rates. To overcome the inequalities in intra-community trading caused by changes in the value of different currencies, the EEC introduced a series of Monetary Compensatory Amounts (54). These acted in effect as a subsidy on agricultural exports for countries where the value of the currency moved upwards and as a tax on exports where movement was in the reverse direction. While in theory an equitable if complex system, in practice France, with a relatively weak currency, was disadvantaged: not only by an effective tax on its exports, but also by the higher production costs caused by more expensive imports (e.g. fertilisers, animal feedstuffs) resulting from a devalued currency. With some renewed order brought to the money markets by the introduction of the European Monetary System in 1979, attempts are being made to phase out these adjustments.

French agriculture has been adversely affected in other ways. While the country is largely unrivalled as a producer of cereals and its grain farmers have profited greatly from the CAP, it encounters strong competition from other European and external producers for the provision of fresh fruits, vegetables and wines. Moreover, Community policy has generally been less effective in regulating supply and demand for these commodities and in maintaining prices. As a major producer of these items, French farmers have suffered accordingly, although the impact has been localised, affecting above all those operating in the southern areas of the country (55). Overall, French farming still benefits considerably from the CAP, but the advantages are selective, less pronounced than in the early years of the market's existence, and further threatened by the enlargement of the EEC. Hence, the considerable interest and concern by the French over proposals to modify the Community's agricultural policy.

The CAP also seeks to encourage structural improvements, despite the majority of its budget being spent on price support policies. Ever since the publication of the Mansholt Plan in 1968 measures such as a reduction in the number of uneconomic small-holdings have been advocated, but in view of the slender resources available little effective action has resulted. More recently, the EEC has sought to intervene by aiding existing national policies which have this objective; subsidising the early retirement pensions (IVD) paid to farmers is one example. Various other initiatives have been launched to encourage farmers, particularly in upland and Mediterranean regions, to improve the efficiency and viability of their holdings as a means of raising incomes. Since the early 1970s aid has been available to farmers willing to undertake long-term investment and prepare a development programme detailing their proposals. Although intended to assist the small-scale farmer, there is little evidence that this has happened in France, reflecting the low level of financial assistance and the lack of interest amongst such farmers in this type or measure.

Farmers - A United Front?
The traditional independence of the French farmer has been progressively eroded, partly through the successful operation and spread of many joint forms of action, such as co-operatives, and partly through the realisation by farmers of their greater bargaining strength when represented as a united body. Just as the government has played a vital role in initiating change, farmers' organisations have exercised an increasingly significant influence in persuading governments of the necessity for intervention and of its most appropriate form. In the pre-war period the views of farmers were essentially those expressed by a minority representing the more affluent, large-scale farmer (56). Since then, not only have farmers' associations grown in strength and number, they have also tended to become more democratic.

Amongst the various professional organisations which now represent farmers, two are of prime importance in defending their interest. The <u>Fédération Nationale des Syndicats d'Exploitations Agricoles</u> is

the principal farmers' union, with a membership of
over 600,000. It is complemented and in part
rivalled by the Centre National des Jeunes
Agriculteurs which acts in a similar capacity for
members of the profession below the age of 35 (57).
Inevitably its membership is more restricted, totalling approximately 90,000 but its impact has been
substantial, notably as the driving force behind the
major reforms of the early 1960s. Younger farmers
have become more highly unionised and an effective
pressure group, aided by a series of able and arti-
culate spokesmen, not least in the influential years
of the late 1950s and early 1960s when led by
Michel Dabatisse who subsequently became president
of the FNSEA and later Secretary of State for Food
and Agricultural Industries in the government of
Raymond Barre.

The front presented by farmers is not, however,
entirely united, a feature to be expected in view of
their extremely heterogeneous character. Other
unions exist to defend their interests, such as the
Mouvement de Défense des Exploitants Familiaux
(MODEF), founded in 1959. It is a generally more
militant, communist inspired organisation, designed
principally to protect and represent the smaller
farmer. For farm labourers, their representation
is generally through the established major trade
unions such as the CFDT, although due to their
dispersed location, organisation of such labour is
rendered more difficult than in the industrial
sector.

Through a variety of methods, ranging from consultation to disruptive and at times violent demonstrations, farmers' organisations have been successful in defending and improving the status of their
profession, despite the declining significance of
their numbers. Not only have they been influential
in the rejuvenation of French agriculture, but they
have also played a vital role in gaining special
privileges for the farming community, not least
through the special tax levied to counteract the
effects of the drought in 1976 and the additional
financial aid granted to farmers, due to a relative
fall in their incomes, in 1980 and 1981. Moreover,
their role has been much wider, encouraging the
diffusion and use of new techniques. Despite such
benefits, as with the general transformation of
French agriculture, it still appears that the
interests of the more dynamic and efficient farmers
have been defended most strongly, providing little
benefit for the smaller, more marginal and often

older operator.

NOTES

1. For a review of French agriculture in the eighteenth and nineteenth centuries see for example, Clout, H.D., Agriculture in France on the Eve of the Railway Age (Croom Helm, London, 1980); Clout, H.D., 'Agricultural change in the eighteenth and nineteenth centuries', in Clout, H.D. (ed.), Themes in the Historical Geography of France (Academic Press, London, 1977), 407-46; Gervais, M. et al., Une France sans Paysans (Seuil, Paris, 1965).

2. Sorlin, P., La Société Française, 1914-68 (Arthaud, Paris, 1971), 95-6.

3. Gervais, M. et al., Histoire de la France Rurale - Tome 4: La Fin de la France Paysanne - 1914 à nos Jours (Seuil, Paris, 1976), 113.

4. Ardagh, J., France in the 1980s (Penguin, Harmonsworth, 1982), 208.

5. Ardagh, France in the 1980s, 208-9.

6. Chombert de Lauwe, J., L'Aventure Agricole de la France de 1945 à nos Jours (Presses Universitaires de France, Paris, 1979), 143-61.

7. Chombert de Lauwe, L'Aventure Agricole, 230.

8. Juillard, E., Atlas et Géographie de l'Alsace et de la Lorraine (Flammarion, Paris, 1977), 36-8 and 89.

9. By comparison with the figures for 1955, in 1929 there were nearly 4 million holdings of which approximately a quarter were less than 1 hectare in extent.

10. Chombert de Lauwe, L'Aventure Agricole, 58. It is interesting to note that more recently the number of very small holdings (less than 1 hectare) has remained stable reflecting a variety of trends such as the increase in part-time and hobby farming as well as industrialised farming techniques.

11. A more detailed discussion of this and related factors is given in Pinchemel, P., La France (Armand Colin, Paris, 1981), vol.2, 18-37.

12. For more details of SAFER see Chombert de Lauwe, L'Aventure Agricole, 242-6 and Klatzmann, J., L'Agriculture Française (Seuil, Paris, 1978), 167-73.

13. This is now controlled by the Centre National pour l'Aménagement des Structures des Exploitations Agricoles (CNASEA) which also intervenes in the education of young farmers and in the payment of grants to help farmers retrain for other

professions.

14. Fuller details are given in Chombert de Lauwe, L'Aventure Agricole, 235-8 and 314, and Klatzmann, L'Agriculture Française, 173-7.

15. Chombert de Lauwe, L'Aventure Agricole, 254-5.

16. Chombert de Lauwe, L'Aventure Agricole, 243.

17. Chombert de Lauwe, L'Aventure Agricole, 31.

18. Most of the land released in this way has been used directly for the creation or enlargement of holdings; a small proportion has been bought by the SAFER.

19. Klatzmann, L'Agriculture Française, 175.

20. Chombert de Lauwe, L'Aventure Agricole, 248-50.

21. For more details see Percheron, S., 'Le remembrement: bilan et facteurs justificatifs', Revue de Droit Rural, No.75 (1979), 91-3 and Froment, R. and Lerat, S., La France (Bréal, Montreuil, 1977), vol.2, 95-6.

22. Gervais, et al., Histoire de la France Rurale, 612.

23. Chombert de Lauwe, L'Aventure Agricole, 18.

24. Gervais, et al., Histoire de la France Rurale, 145.

25. Le Roy, P., L'Avenir de l'Agriculture Française (Presses Universitaires de France, Paris, 1975), 67-70; Pinchemel, La France, 69-70. An interesting account of change in dairy farming is given in Boichard, J., 'Le lait et les problèmes de l'élevage laitier en France', Revue Géographique de Lyon, 47 (1972), 99-135.

26. Direy, J-P., L'industrie française de l'alimentation du bétail', Annales de Géographie, 8 (1979), 671.

27. This is still well below the average figure for countries such as Denmark and the Netherlands.

28. The technique is explained in Atkinson, K., 'Trickle irrigation - a new technology in irrigated agriculture', Geography, 64 (1979), 219-21.

29. When originally formed it was concerned solely with wheat.

30. Baleste, M., L'Economie Française (Masson, Paris, 1981), 96-100.

31. Chombert de Lauwe, L'Aventure Agricole, 124-5.

32. For a general discussion of these centres and a more detailed review of one MIN, see Djelal, M., 'Le marché d'intérêt national de Toulouse',

Revue de Géographie des Pyrénées et du Sud-Ouest, 50 (1979), 84.

33. Sceau, R., 'La coopération agricole dans la région Rhône-Alpes', Revue de Géographie de Lyon, 47 (1972), 259-96.

34. Le Roy, L'Avenir de l'Agriculture Française, 54-6.

35. The SICA is a form of co-operative which has the advantage of being able to sell the production of farmers other than that of its members.

36. Detailed case studies are provided in Charrié, J-P., 'La commercialisation des fruits et légumes en Lot-et-Garonne', Revue Géographique des Pyrénées et du Sud-Ouest, 50 (1979), 59-80 and Bozon, R., 'Une coopérative fruitière exemplaire: Vivacoop (Ardèche)', Norois, 95ter (1977), 21-35.

37. Charrié, 'La commercialisation des fruits et légumes', 69.

38. Direy, 'L'industrie française d'alimentation', 682-93. Sceau, 'La coopération agricole', 284-6.

39. Chombert de Lauwe, L'Aventure Agricole, 50-1.

40. For more general details see Madiot, Y., L'Aménagement du Territoire (Masson, Paris, 1979), 165-75.

41. The seventh, the Société d'Aménagement des Friches et Taillis de l'Est (created in 1958) has been disbanded.

42. The originality of such companies lies in their combination of both public and private interests either in the administration/management of the company or in the constitution of its capital. Although this type of company may benefit from advantages such as low interest loans it is expected to operate on commercial lines without, for example, any government subsidy.

43. These problems are discussed more fully in Thompson, I.B., Modern France (Butterworths, London, 1970), 424-6.

44. A more detailed account of the CNARBRL and an evaluation of its policies are given in Ferras, R. et al., Atlas et Géographie du Languedoc et du Roussillon (Flammarion, Paris, 1979), 155-78.

45. This is discussed in Livet, R., Atlas et Géographie de Provence, Côte d'Azur et Corse (Flammarion, Paris, 1978), 238-9.

46. A fuller account is provided in Tarlet, J., 'Un grand aménagement régional à objectif hydraulique: la société du canal de Provence et d'aménagement de la région provençale, Méditerranée,

39 (1980), 37-64.

47. Papy, L., 'Les Landes de Gascogne; la maîtrise de l'eau dans la 'lande humide'', _Norois_, 95ter (1977), 199-210.

48. Estienne, P., _La France_ (Masson, Paris, 1978), vol.4, 162.

49. SOMIVAL is not discussed here. Its aims are more varied and it forms the basis of a more detailed discussion in the following chapter.

50. A specific case study related to these features is given in Maury, R., 'L'endettement de l'agriculture française: l'exemple du département d'Indre-et-Loire', _Norois_, 25 (1978), 511-32.

51. Pinchemel, _La France_, 67.

52. Chombert de Lauwe, _L'Aventure Agricole_, 263.

53. Chombert de Lauwe, _L'Aventure Agricole_, 264-8.

54. For more details see Guth, J-J., _Comprendre l'Europe_ (Etudes Vivantes, Paris, 1980), 47-54; Chombert de Lauwe, _L'Aventure Agricole_, 306-8.

55. Discamps-Dheur, A-M., 'Les conséquences régionales de la politique agricole commune', _Revue Economique du Sud-Ouest_, No.4 (1980), 57-69.

56. A detailed appraisal appears in Gervais et al., _Histoire de la France Rurale_, 396-449.

57. Constitutionally the CNJA is part of the FNSEA.

Chapter Four

AGRICULTURE TRANSFORMED - THE IMPACT AND
CONSEQUENCES OF CHANGE

The radical transformation of French agriculture
over the last thirty years has resulted in impressive modifications in the spatial pattern and techniques of production, and in a vast increase in
output. Change has brought undoubted benefits,
although these have not accrued equally to all
levels of the farming community or to all regions of
the country: in terms of incomes and living standards, farmers and farm workers remain an extremely
heterogeneous sector of French society. Progress
has also involved certain costs. For the individual
farmer it has often meant a heavy reliance upon
borrowed capital, while the community as a whole has
had to bear the burden of the substantial financial
aid accorded to support the farming population and
to make improvement possible. Innovations have been
slow to spread to certain traditionally backward
areas, including parts of the Massif Central and
other mountainous regions of the country, although
in some more dynamic areas, notably Brittany, the
inability of pre-existing farming systems to provide
an adequate return has acted as a stimulus to change.
The very success of efforts to raise output has led
to its own problems, particularly the overproduction
of certain commodities, while the high gains in productivity have often been paid for by a massive
reduction in labour requirements.
    However, the modernisation and restructuring of
agriculture represent but part of the wider transformation of rural France, a process which at one
extreme is characterised by the inexorable decline
of population and economic activities, typical of
more remote, upland areas, and at the other by the
intense pressures for urbanisation, a common feature
on the fringes of many towns and cities. Just as
the state has intervened to promote change in

farming activities, it has also acted in an attempt to resolve the problems and conflicts inherent in rural society generally. It is this theme of the nature and consequences of change in agriculture and in other rural occupations which is considered more fully in the present chapter.

THE TRANSFORMATION OF AGRICULTURE: THE IMPACT UPON PRODUCTION AND EMPLOYMENT

Changing Patterns of Production
Under the pressure of the above processes widespread and unprecedented changes have occurred in the agricultural landscapes of France. Action to improve farm structures has eradicated from many areas former patterns of small enclosed fields, while variations in the demand for and profitability of different products have considerably altered the spatial distribution and production levels of enterprises.
    Change in the volume of output is particularly evident in relation to grain production, although the overall pattern of increase conceals divergent trends (Table 4.1). Similar modifications have occurred in the areal extent of cultivation. Both tendencies are illustrated by the marked expansion in the growth of maize which first developed in the 1950s. High yielding varieties of the grain, adapted to the climatic conditions of a more northerly location, have enabled the spread of maize

Table 4.1: The Increase in Production of Cereals

	Mean annual output (million tonnes)		
	1962-4	1969-71	1979-81
All cereals	25.4	33.8	45.6
Wheat	12.7	14.2	22.0
Barley	6.7	8.8	11.0
Grain maize	2.6	7.4	9.5
Oats	2.6	2.8	2.3
Rye and maslin	0.4	0.3	0.4

Source: Eurostat.

throughout many areas of the Paris Basin and eastern France (Figure 4.1), encouraged by the strong demand throughout the EEC for the cereal as a food base or for animal feedstuffs. Not only have yields and output risen, but the area under maize has been extended from less than 400,000 hectares in the early 1950s to currently over 2 million hectares. (In contrast, the overall area under wheat has changed little over the same period, although yields and output have risen substantially). More efficient cultivation, however, is only part of the far greater modernisation and reorganisation of cereal production which also includes the introduction of new systems of stockage and distribution (1).

Major changes have also occurred in the growth of forage crops. With animal feeding techniques revolutionised, and the declining significance of natural pastures and other forms of traditional feed such as beetroot, new trends have emerged. Artificial grasses are now grown more commonly, but above all there has been a spectacular increase in the cultivation of forage maize and its use for silage, particularly in western France in the regions of Bretagne and Pays de la Loire. The total area given over to such maize throughout France rose from 279,000 hectares in 1970 to 1.1 million hectares in 1979.

The growth of fruits and vegetables is an equally dynamic, although far more competitive and speculative activity. Competition has been intensified by imports from areas benefiting from lower production costs and often an earlier or longer season. However, this pressure allied to an underlying growth in demand for such produce has acted as a spur to changing patterns of cultivation. In traditional areas of fresh vegetable cultivation such as the small market gardens of the lower Rhône valley one of the most spectacular changes has been the introduction of large 'plastic' greenhouses within which the conditions of growth can be strictly regulated. Improved yields and advancing the date at which the produce is ready for marketing more than offset the additional cost of the equipment, and its efficacity is demonstrated by the extension of cultivation under this system (2). In France the total area utilised in this manner increased from 1,060 hectares in 1970 to 3,498 in 1979, while in the département of Bouches-du-Rhône the respective figures for the two dates were 116 and 926 hectares. So competitive is the market, yet the advantages of capturing the early season when

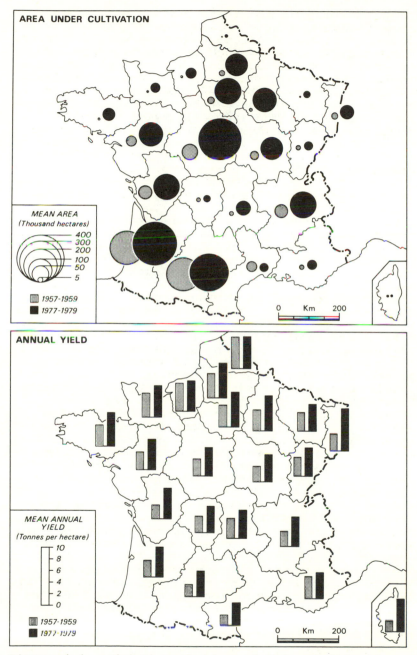

Figure 4.1:   The Distribution of Maize Cultivation

prices are highest so great, that various other
innovations have taken place; for example, the
import of unripened melons from Africa to be ripened
under plastic in areas such as Cavaillon prior to
sale (3). Where irrigation has been employed, techniques have required modification, sometimes also
entailing a reorientation of production, illustrated
by the changes which have taken place in the
Languedoc plain. The availability of water for
irrigation has not, however, always led to its utilisation; despite the vast extension of the area in
which irrigation has become possible in the Rhône
valley below Lyon, there has frequently been a
reluctance to adopt new farming techniques and incur
additional investment costs, particularly for the
supply of an uncertain market (4).

Such changes are not confined to areas of
arable farming and permanent crops but are also evident, in many diverse forms, in regions of animal
rearing. The increasingly widespread occurrence of
the intensive raising of pigs, poultry and calves
represents a prime illustration, not only of
changing techniques but often of a delocalisation of
production away from traditional areas of rearing.
Similarly, dairying groups in Brittany, seeking new
outlets for their produce, now manufacture an
increasing amount of emmenthal cheese, reducing considerably the market share of customary production
centres in eastern France. Even in more remote
mountainous areas, traditional pastoral economies
have become modified. In the Cantal the summer
grazing of dairy cattle on mountain pastures,
centred upon the buron of each individual family
where cheese was manufactured, long remained an
essential element of the local economy. However,
the inherent inefficiencies of such a system, particularly in terms of labour requirements and the duplication of activities, has led to its virtual
demise; yet, the mountain pastures remain an important area for summer grazing. Now their prime
function is to support young heifers still unsuited
for milk production or young calves prior to their
sale for fattening and slaughter. The operation is
frequently organised by large co-operatives, although managed by a very small work-force. Electri-
fied fences (le berger électrique) and barbed wire
are now the essential agents in controlling herds.

The forces behind these changes are symptomatic
of two wider tendencies underlying the post-war evolution of agricultural activity - a growing uniformity in the units and techniques of production and

an increasing specialisation in output.
Consolidation of holdings and the eradication of the
smallest farms, promotion of the family farm, and
the widespread development of mechanisation and
motorisation for all forms of cultivation, whether
it be for the production of cereals or fruit, are
all representative of the first trend. The second
is typified by the disappearance of polyculture,
replaced by concentration upon a single or limited
range of enterprises. This tendency has also been
accompanied by a growing intensification and often
simplification of production systems, all these
processes dictated by the need for the agricultural
sector to become more competitive and by its increasingly capitalistic character (5).

At the same time, the relative independence of
agriculture in relation to other sectors of the
economy has been replaced by its increasingly strong
association with industry and commerce. Farming
relies upon an ever growing range of inputs from
industry, while the productive process has become
but one stage in the much wider agricultural processing industry. Such integration has enabled agriculture to develop as an important influence in the
generation of employment in other branches of activity. The farming sector is now a major user of an
extensive range of chemical products, notably fertilisers (6), of specialised animal foodstuffs, of
numerous varieties of seeds and of many diverse
forms of machinery. For many industrial groups it
represents, therefore, a highly significant market.
Companies such as Renault, John Deere, and Massey-
Ferguson are heavily involved in the production of
machinery, the market for fertilisers is dominated
by a limited number of large national firms such as
APC and COFAZ, while the more general supply of
chemical products is a feature of the activities of
many of the large multinational groups such as
Bayer, Ciba-Geigy and Rhône-Poulenc (7). On the
downstream side, agricultural products have become
raw materials which subsequently undergo various
forms and stages of transformation, frequently
involving not only sophisticated systems of collection and storage, but also a highly organised distribution chain for the finished product. Measured
by turnover, food processing and drink industries
now represent one of France's major industrial activities, with many of the above operations dominated
by a limited number of large national or multinational companies such as BSN-Gervais-Danone. Co-
operatives have also become involved increasingly in

the processing of produce (in addition to such basic
functions as distribution), reflecting the higher
value-added of this activity and its potentially
greater profitability. Despite these trends, there
are still numerous small-scale, relatively inefficient food industries, giving considerable scope for
rationalisation and an increase in productivity.

A Pronounced Decline in the Agricultural Population
Since 1955 there has been a net loss of over 3.4
million workers from the primary sector, so that by
1981 there were little more than 1.8 million workers
employed in agriculture representing only 8.6 per
cent of the total active population (Table 4.2) (8).

Table 4.2: Active Population Working in Agriculture

	Total (millions)	Proportion of total active population (%)
1954	5.2	27.4
1962	3.9	20.0
1968	3.1	15.3
1975	2.1	10.1
1981	1.8	8.6

Source: INSEE, Recensements and Rapport sur les
Comptes de la Nation de l'Année 1981 (1982).

Throughout the 1950s and early 1960s the decline in
agricultural workers averaged over 3 per cent per
annum, accelerating to a yearly mean of 4.6 per cent
during the intercensal period 1968-75. Since then
the rate has shown a noticeable tendency to slacken,
falling to an annual average of 2.1 per cent between
1975 and 1981. This does not necessarily indicate a
major change in underlying trends. In part it reflects the short-term effect of the smaller generations born during the 1914-18 war reaching the age
of retirement; it also indicates an increased reluctance to leave farming as the recession has reduced
the availability of alternative employment. While
agriculture has thus shed labour in a continuous and
pronounced manner over the post-war period (9), it
has been only part of a wider process of decline and
outward movement of population from rural areas.

The two conditions, however, although undeniably linked, are not necessarily synonymous. For example, over the period 1962-75 the number of people working in farming in Alsace fell by an average of around 7 per cent per annum, yet the total rural population remained stable. In part, this is explained by the importance of part-time farming, a dispersed pattern of industry and a dense network of urban centres enabling easy commuting from existing villages to alternative employment. Conversely, there are many areas where the decline of rural population and the reduction of employment in agriculture exhibit a close relationship, notably in the Massif Central. In Auvergne the rural population fell from 502,000 persons in 1962 to 425,000 in 1975, while the number of people employed in agriculture declined from 176,000 to 90,400, the total having now fallen to less than 70,000.

The reduction in the agricultural population over the last thirty years has been generalised throughout rural France, being just as much a feature of the Paris Basin as it has of areas such as Brittany or the Massif Central (Figure 4.2). Inevitably, however, the consequences of population loss have varied spatially, with numerous small communities within many of the mountainous regions of France now experiencing a series of social and economic problems provoked by severe depopulation. Nonetheless, despite considerable regional variation in rates of population decline and a corresponding narrowing of the gap between those regions with a high and low proportion of employment in agriculture, the spatial distribution of agricultural families in France is still characterised by the persistence of broad regional contrasts which have altered little over the post-war period. Thus, it is possible to discern a basic division between the western, central and southern regions of France where it is still common to find over 20 per cent of the population living in farming households, and the majority of northern and eastern areas where the proportion is often well below 10 per cent (Figure 4.3).

The shedding of labour has been a necessary and fundamental component of the modernisation of French agriculture (10). Increased mechanisation and improved efficiency have been a major cause, although their influence needs to be viewed in the wider context of the aggregate level of demand. Increases in productivity have been far greater than the rise in demand, leading to an inevitable decline in labour requirements. But other factors have

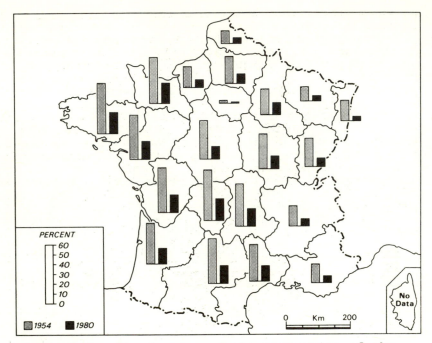

Figure 4.2: The Decline of the Proportion of the Labour-Force working in Agriculture

contributed to the reduction in manpower. The exceptional expansion of the French economy led to a strong demand for labour, particularly in industry, where the financial rewards were likely to far exceed those to be gained from agriculture. Moreover, the failure of modernisation to occur, or its general slowness, and the associated persistence of low incomes and poor living standards have represented further incentives to abandon agriculture. The factors influencing this decision are, not unnaturally, numerous and complex, although economic motives appear to be of primary importance (11).

Closer examination of the pattern of employment change in agriculture suggests, however, that the greater part of the loss of population is due to the retirement or death of farmers and farm workers. A more modest proportion is accounted for by those who have changed employment, while both the above trends are compensated to only a limited extent by new entrants into the activity, principally the sons of parents who are already farmers (12). The government's policy of offering farmers an enhanced

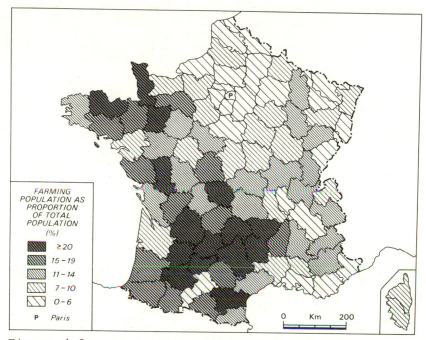

FARMING POPULATION AS PROPORTION OF TOTAL POPULATION (%)

- ≥20
- 15 – 19
- 11 – 14
- 7 – 10
- 0 – 6

P   Paris

0   Km   200

Figure 4.3:   Regional Variations in the Farming Population, 1980

pension through early retirement (IVD) has contributed to their departure, but the heavy decline is also attributable to the age-structure of the farming population which is strongly distorted in favour of the higher age-ranges. At the same time, better pay and an improved standard of living, less arduous working conditions, and access to a wider range of opportunities are amongst the many factors which have persuaded workers to exchange agricultural work for other forms of employment. Moreover, they have often been strongly solicited by alternative employers (13). Many of the above factors have also discouraged young people from entering farming. There is some suggestion, however, that in more profitable farming districts there is a growing willingness on their part to farm, as incomes have improved and alternative employment openings become scarcer, although this desire is often frustrated by the high cost of land; hence, the government's system of financial aid (DJA) (14).

The reduction in manpower has not been shared uniformly by all categories of worker within the

agricultural sector. Proportionally, losses have
been greatest amongst family labour and hired farm
labourers (15), whereas in absolute terms the
decrease has been most evident amongst farmers and
female members of their families. There are now
relatively few full-time permanent farm labourers.
During the 1970s their number fell by a yearly
average of 5 per cent, resulting in a total of less
than 140,000 by the end of the decade (16). Overall,
full and part-time workers, whether employed on a
temporary or permanent basis, now account for only
15 per cent of the work performed on the farm, the
remainder undertaken by the farmer and his family
(17). Even here change has been considerable. The
recent decline of the part played by women in the
family labour-force has been particularly marked,
testifying to the unattractive and arduous nature of
the work, as well as illustrating the impact of
mechanisation upon the demand for labour.

Rather than cease farming altogether, for many
farmers there is the possibility of combining this
activity with some other form of employment.
Various influences have encouraged this tendency.
Where the income from the farm is low, this offers
an obvious means by which it might be supplemented;
frequently, such second incomes become of greater
significance than those generated by the farm.
Similarly, where a holding is small, providing insufficient full-time employment, a condition which
has increased substantially through greater mechanisation, the incentive to take on an additional job
is strong. Increased specialisation of production
has also facilitated this possibility, particularly
as the work on the farm has become more highly pro-
grammed enabling the farmer to gauge accurately his
available time. Inevitably, the possibilities for a
'second employment' vary throughout the country,
depending upon factors such as the size of holding,
the nature of the enterprise and the degree of availability of alternative jobs. While the justification for this practice is sound, precise measurement
of its incidence is potentially more difficult.

In 1979 21 per cent of the heads of farming
families declared that they had a double employment, most commonly combining their responsibility
on the farm with a manual job in industry (18).
Thus, in the case of the individual it is relatively
easy to determine the extent of this phenomenon.
However, if the farm is viewed as a family unit in
which certain members work in an occupation external
to agriculture, then the concept becomes less easy

to define, particularly as it has become
increasingly common for the wife or remaining children to work at least partially in this manner.
Viewed in the narrower sense of the head of the
family, there is a wide regional variation in this
practice, with it being most developed in parts of
eastern and southern France, reflecting the variable
influence of the factors mentioned above. In Alsace,
for example, 40 per cent of farmers have a second
job, a trend particularly strong amongst those
owning the smallest holdings. Taken in the wider
sense, this feature affects 57 per cent of all the
region's holdings and over 40 per cent of the agricultural land area. Its occurrence has been aided
not only by the diversity of industrial employment
within Alsace, frequently dispersed throughout the
rural area, but also by the rapid industrial expansion of neighbouring German and Swiss areas and the
growth of trans-frontier commuting. Whatever the
attraction in terms of higher incomes or greater
security, there are also handicaps, not only for the
farmer himself who undertakes two jobs, but also his
employer. In both cases fatigue is an obvious problem. Nonetheless, combining employment in agriculture with another job is certainly not a recent
phenomenon, although its incidence has tended to
increase since the early 1960s (19), emphasising the
extent of underemployment in agriculture.

The decline of the agricultural labour-force
has been an essential and inevitable component of
the process of modernisation, but it has also been
accompanied by the less desirable and related trends
of an ageing farming population and the rejection by
many young people of a career in agriculture. There
is a marked under-representation of the younger
generations amongst farmers, despite a modest
natural attenuation of this tendency due to the
effects of higher birth rates in the early post-war
period (20). By 1979, 58 per cent of the heads of
farming families were over 50 years old (compared
with 54 per cent in 1970) and 16 per cent were 65 or
older (Table 4.3) (21). Moreover, the present age-
structure also implies, at least in the medium term,
a continuing strong outflow of population from
agriculture as more farmers reach the age of retirement. Regional variations of this characteristic
exist, with the ageing of the population most pronounced in the more remote or marginal areas of
farming where there has also been a strong tradition
of emigration, features which are particularly
marked in many central and southern areas.

Table 4.3:   Distribution of Farming Population by
Age

Age band	France 1970 (%)	France 1979 (%)	Marne 1971 (%)	Marne 1980 (%)	Corrèze 1970 (%)	Corrèze 1979 (%)
0 - 34	8	˙1	13	18	6	8
35 - 49	38	31	41	31	39	29
50 - 64	37	42	32	36	37	46
65	17	16	14	15	18	18

Source: Ministère de l'Agriculture, Recensement
Général de l'Agriculture 1979-80 (1981).

Comparison of the départements of Marne (Champagne-
Ardenne) and Corrèze (Limousin) illustrates such
variability, the former dominated by an advanced
system of farming centred on cereals and viticulture,
the latter distinguished by the mediocrity of its
upland agriculture based on polyculture and livestock; here over 63 per cent of farmers are over 50
(Table 4.3). One disquieting feature of an ageing
population is the implications which it has for the
outlook and attitudes of a large proportion of
farmers. Not unnaturally, with increasing age the
incentive for further investment or modernisation
diminishes, especially in the absence of a son or
daughter prepared to take over the farm. In areas
of less prosperous farming, where there is a high
rate of farm ownership, a trait which is again more
pronounced in the southern half of the country, this
acts as a significant restriction on progress.

Farmers' Incomes
After three decades of profound transformation and
modernisation of the agricultural system, it is to
be expected that the incomes of farmers and farm
workers should also have been modified. Moreover,
in recognition of the generally accepted low level
of these incomes, their improvement became a fundamental aim of the CAP and of the French government's
legislation of the early 1960s. Measurement of income and particularly comparison with other branches
of employment poses certain difficulties, for a
farmer's income often serves not only as a

remuneration for his labour but also for a diverse range of other obligations such as repayment of debts and investment in new equipment or land. In general, however, it appears that the mean value of farmers' incomes increased by at least the same rate as that of other socio-economic groups for much of the period from the early 1960s until the mid-1970s, giving the average farmer a salary equivalent to that of a junior white collar worker or small shop-keeper (22). Similarly, the average sum of the farm labourer has improved to give approximate parity with other manual and relatively unskilled occupations (23); inevitably, though, the wage is modest, exceeding the minimum wage (SMIC) by only a limited amount. Some confirmation of an improvement in agricultural incomes is offered by the now generally high rates of ownership amongst the farming population of consumer durables such as cars, refrigerators, freezers and television sets.

These, however, are all average conditions, concealing very wide deviations from the mean (24). Farmers' incomes vary greatly according to the size and efficiency of their holding and the nature of their activities, giving rise to equally marked regional contrasts in income. The revenue from agriculture for the small-holder engaged in poly-culture in upland areas such as the interior of the Massif Central or Alps or in parts of the south-west or Lorraine is often extremely low, leading to con-ditions of severe poverty. Conversely, the incomes generated by the large cereal farms of the Beauce or Picardie are very substantial, giving rise to a highly prosperous farming community; yet, the same profitability is not apparent amongst the much smaller arable farms of the Pays de la Loire or Midi-Pyrénées. The level of farmers' earnings is also adversely affected by unfavourable climatic variations, disease and, particularly for those products for which the market is inadequately guaranteed such as fresh fruit, wines and vegetables, sharp falls in demand and thus in prices. As opposed to workers in other sectors of the economy, therefore, there is also often a far greater degree of uncertainty over the level of remuneration. Con-versely, particularly for the small-scale farmer, a useful supplement to his income and an increase in security is afforded by undertaking a second job. There may also be the benefit to the farmer of the consumption of part of his production.

Since the mid-1970s the upward trend in incomes has been arrested. The increased outlay of farmers, occasioned by rises in oil prices and their repercussions on other costs generally, has not been compensated by a corresponding rise in the price of agricultural products. To these general trends were added the adverse effects of exceptional events such as the drought of 1976. By the beginning of the present decade, with continually rising production costs reflecting factors such as the high level of imported inputs and the relative weakness of the French franc, the maintenance of farmers' incomes came to rely increasingly heavily upon government subsidy. Even so, for many small farmers incomes have declined in real terms, contributing to a renewed wave of discontent, forcible expressed in demonstrations in the latter part of 1981 and early months of 1982.

While there is some disagreement over the level and adequacy of farmers' incomes, their quality of life appears in many cases to be inferior to that of other social groups (25). Conditions which reflect this include the generally much longer hours of working, poor housing, the inferior standard of education and lack of holidays. Farmers are thus still faced with many inequalities of opportunity, but again their impact is selective, affecting primarily the less efficient smallholder, rendering his task more arduous and increasingly less attractive.

Change and the Persistence of Regional Contrasts
The post-war modernisation of French agriculture has led to many fundamental changes in farming practices but it has not eradicated regional contrasts in the scale and efficiency of agricultural activity. Within France there are many examples of farms where highly sophisticated techniques of production are employed, yet at the same time extreme conditions of poverty persist in certain rural areas. However, to sub-divide agriculture into a modern advanced sector opposed to a backward traditional system would be an unrepresentative simplification of reality - the spectrum is much wider and a more appropriate frame is offered by the adoption of a basic three-fold classification, although even this inadequately covers all forms of farming unit (26). A vital role in French agriculture is now played by the large capital intensive farm, frequently managed rather than owned, where the application of the most advanced techniques is commonplace and where the income generated by the holding is high. Often, in such areas the density of agricultural population is low.

A second broad group is represented by a series of smaller farming units where the amount of investment and size of holding are less, but where agricultural activity now displays a strong inherent dynamism. These are frequently family-owned farms, often in regions of still relatively dense rural population, where modernisation has progressed rapidly but has produced its own problems, particularly the level to which many farmers have had to finance improvement through borrowing. It is within this category of farms that change tends to be most apparent. Finally, there is the small farm in the process of decline where incomes are low, the incentive for modernisation is absent and thus techniques have evolved but slowly and spasmodically. Such holdings are invariably linked to regions displaying an increasingly ageing farming population and a strong net outflow of inhabitants, and their persistence frequently relies upon special government subsidy.

It is less easy to generalise about the spatial distribution of these different groups, although certain broad trends are apparent. The large capitalist farm dominates in the central areas of the Paris Basin, extending notably into northern France; it is also a feature of parts of the vineyards of Languedoc. A far wider distribution characterises the second group of smaller but dynamic farming units, but they are a notable feature of the southern and western fringes of the Paris Basin, Alsace and western areas of France such as Brittany. France's upland regions represent the primary location for the small uneconomic holding, frequently destined to disappear through lack of a successor; but this ought not to imply that farming in mountainous regions is everywhere unprofitable or on a small scale. The Massif Central, Jura and Alps all house many large and prosperous dairy farms: hence the difficulty of regional characterisation.

CHANGE IN THE WIDER RURAL ENVIRONMENT

An Inexorable Decline of Population?
Emigation has long been a feature of many areas of the French countryside, although it was not until the middle of the nineteenth century that it became widespread and pronounced (27). Since then, a virtually continuous outward movement has led not only to fragile and imbalanced demographic structures, but also to a disappearance of employment and a

disintegration of society within many rural communities. The belated industrialisation of the French economy began to generate an unprecedented demand for labour in urban areas, while the impoverishment of many rural communities, coupled with the slow advance of mechanisation in agriculture, provided further incentives for out-migration. At the same time, continuing improvements in communication, above all through the extension of the railway network, facilitated the process. Flows became complex, but the unequal spread and pace of industrialisation throughout the country produced certain distinctive patterns of migration. These were dominated by movement to the capital, as its rapid economic growth drained an ever wider hinterland of its surplus labour, leading to extensive migration from regions such as Brittany, Limousin and Auvergne. The reduction of the agricultural labour-force has played a vital but not exclusive role in this process. As rural-based industries and services contracted or closed, and the demand locally for craftsmen declined, with no alternative employment outlets, workers and their families also left. Furthermore, the limited economic and social opportunities offered by a rural community have long acted as a strong incentive for young people to leave, often before they enter the labour market.

Since the second world war, the decline in rural population has been substantial, although over the last decade there are indications of a slowing and reversal of this trend. Between 1954 and 1975 rural communes experienced a net loss of nearly 3.5 million inhabitants (Table 4.4), while the proportion of the country's population living in these areas diminished from 41 to 27 per cent. Where

Table 4.4: Population Living in Rural Areas

	Total (millions)	Proportion of total population (%)
1954	17.7	41
1962	17.0	36
1968	14.2	28
1975	14.3	27

Source: INSEE, Recensements.

population has continued to decrease, the average
age of those people remaining has tended to increase,
as has the imbalance between the sexes, with a
higher proportion of male than female residents, a
trend which has led to an elevated incidence of
celibacy. Many remote, upland regions have continued to lose population since the early or mid-
nineteenth century, accentuating these tendencies;
as a result, such areas now frequently display the
further problem of a net loss of population through
natural change. Spatial patterns of movement have
also become more complex; emphasis upon Paris has
long since declined, partly through the reduction in
the rate of the capital's economic expansion and
through other influences such as the far greater
range of large regional employment centres now
accessible to the potential migrant.

   Not all rural zones feature the above characteristics; in many areas the recent tendency has
been for population to expand rather than decrease
(28). This is illustrated at a broad regional scale
by Figure 4.4, which indicates substantial increases

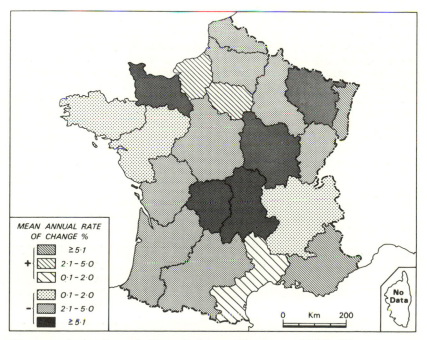

Figure 4.4: Rural Population Change, 1968-75

of rural population along parts of the Mediterranean
fringe and in Alsace, and to a lesser degree in the
inner parts of the Paris Basin and in Haute-
Normandie; (it also portrays certain regions where
the intensity of outward movement is still extremely
high as in Limousin and Auvergne). However, broad
regional sub-division of this scale fails to demonstrate adequately the much more dispersed character
of rural areas experiencing a net increase in population. Generally, they are located near or adjacent to the larger urban centres, particularly
dynamic but smaller rural towns, or in areas of
major tourist activity (29). Invariably, their
growth relates to an influx of population, while in
general their demographic and employment structures
exhibit marked contrasts with those of areas experiencing depopulation. This may not always occur,
notably where retirement-migration is the main cause
of population increase; in this instance it may even
aggravate existing problems. Thus, population change
in rural areas is a complex process, with considerable variation in tendencies often occurring over
only a limited area.

AID AND POLICIES FOR RURAL AREAS

Although the pressures for the movement of population away from the more remote and disadvantaged
rural areas are frequently strong, various initiatives have been taken in an attempt to at least
restrict, if not reverse, the trend. Many of the
measures implemented have been advocated by the
government as, over the last twenty-five years, a
specific development strategy towards rural areas
has slowly but unsystematically evolved. The need
for action to limit the decline of population and
employment in rural areas is suggested by a number
of factors, the majority of which relate to the
desire to provide people wherever they live with an
equality of living standards and, wherever possible,
of opportunity. There are frequently considerable
differences in living conditions between urban and
rural dwellers, a reflection of the generally lower
average incomes of the latter group (30). Housing
conditions are often poor and still lack such essential items as the telephone; equally, accessibility
is often difficult and public transport non-existent.
Moreover, as a community declines, many of its vital
services also disappear - village shops, the post
office, doctors' surgeries and schools (31). In the

absence of corrective measures the process of
decline becomes irreversible, as a reduction in
population induces further closures which in turn
encourage more of the population to leave. For
those remaining, often nearing or at retirement age,
the outlook is bleak, while local councils are often
powerless to act to improve conditions as the loss
of population and business leads to an inevitable
fall in their income. Moreover, if young people are
to be persuaded to become farmers or exercise their
profession in rural areas, an improvement in living
conditions is vital. In a wider context, growing
concern has been expressed, principally by a variety
of environmental and ecological groups, over the
need to preserve the country's rural heritage,
represented as much by its work-force, activities
and settlements as by its natural aesthetic quali-
ties. The rural dweller thus has a significant role
to play in safeguarding a valuable resource.
     Many rural communes, however, face other prob-
lems requiring alternative development strategies.
On the fringes of urban areas where the pressures
for housing or industrial expansion are strong, the
main priority is often how to control and limit more
effectively this process; inevitably, many conflicts
of interest arise, not least between those wishing
to preserve the former village community and new
inhabitants demanding change and additional
amenities. Similar difficulties may arise where
tourism has expanded rapidly. This has led to the
need for more effective planning policies and controls over the nature and form of development in
sensitive rural areas (32). A planned approach to
investment and change is likely to be beneficial to
any commune, however, and some encouragement for the
more widespread adoption of this practice in other
rural zones has been given by the government.

The Creation of Employment

Where there is a need to counteract depopulation,
enlargement of the employment market through the
creation of a greater number and wider range of jobs
is essential, although the means by which to achieve
this is frequently less certain. The modernisation
of agriculture has generally produced, at least in
the short term, the reverse effect of reducing
labour requirements and thus population. However,
where activities remain viable, this ought in the
longer term to help stabilise the population.
Furthermore, the 'artificial' support of agriculture

in regions naturally ill-disposed to such activity,
through for example the payment of grants on livestock in mountainous zones, helps slow the rate of
decline. New jobs may result in other ways.
Increases in output and the sophistication of production techniques may generate employment in ancillary occupations such as food processing or in firms
servicing machinery or providing technical advice,
although these activities need not of course be
rural-based. For certain areas the extension of
afforestation and related industries offers a
further means by which to provide additional jobs,
although with few exceptions little success appears
to have been realised in revitalising an activity
which nationally is declining (33).

The secondary and tertiary sectors would appear
to offer a greater range of opportunities. Rural-
based industries have a long history in France and
remained of considerable significance until the
inter-war period when their decline was hastened by
the increasing growth and concentration of industry
in urban centres. Nonetheless, around 15 per cent
of all wage-earners in French industry are still
employed in firms located in rural areas, although
the extent to which this occurs varies between
regions; generally, it is more pronounced in areas
of traditional industrial activity such as Nord-Pas-
de-Calais, Alsace, Franche-Comté and Rhône-Alpes
(34). The range of industries is extremely mixed,
including textiles, shoes, wood products, metal
working, plastics and electronics; the building
industry is also strongly represented. In all cases,
however, firms are generally of very modest size.
There is, therefore, already a long established and
diversified rural industrial base, which despite an
overall tendency to contract in size, is characterised in many regions by its dynamism, lending
credibility to a policy to promoting industry in
rural areas.

However, whether it be an attempt to solicit
new industrial activities or prolong the life of
existing industries, there are many problems which
may limit the effectiveness of such action. In the
latter case, these frequently include diseconomies
induced by the poor location of factories or their
outdated and run-down condition, combined with an
insecure financial base and management which has
failed to adapt to changing and more competitive
marketing conditions (35). New activities may not
be faced with such difficulties but the industrialist still has to assess the disadvantages likely to

result from a relatively isolated location, while the apparent advantage of an ample reserve of labour through the decline of other traditional activities is often illusory. Even a relatively well-paid factory job is insufficient to arrest the departure of many young people, thus limiting the potential supply of a work-force; frequently, the available labour is also unskilled. In addition, the practice of agricultural workers seeking to supplement their incomes through an industrial job may pose problems such as absenteeism (at harvest time, for example) which are disruptive and costly for the industrialist.

Nonetheless, considerable efforts have been undertaken by a variety of bodies ranging from government to local councils in attempts to promote industrial growth in rural areas. Use has been made of numerous forms of aid including a series of financial incentives, the creation of industrial estates and the construction of advance factories. Overall assessment of the efficacity of these policies is difficult, but there are many examples of success, illustrated by development in the regions of Choletais and Jura. Here expansion has been due, at least partly, to a willingness to adopt and exploit new technology and to capitalise upon the traditional skills of local craftsmen (36). For industrial policies to function effectively, it is essential to co-ordinate their implementation with other strategies such as the improvement or provision of housing, schools and recreational facilties. There are also many failures, and the wisdom of trying to persuade industrialists to locate in isolated areas lacking a sizeable urban centre, as in many upland areas of France, seems highly questionable.

Within the tertiary sector, the opportunities for creating additional employment in rural areas appear most favourable in relation to tourism. Not only is it an activity which is expanding rapidly with increased affluence, mobility and leisure time, but it is also represented in many diverse forms, offering a range of possibilities for employment. Moreover, the growth of tourism frequently has a beneficial impact upon other activities. The construction or improvement of second homes, which has enabled many local building firms to flourish, is but one illustration of this process. Again, as with industry, there are many regional examples where tourism has played an important role in the stabilisation or even growth of rural population.

The northern Alps is one such area where many
communities have prospered from the exceptional
growth in the popularity of skiing and often from
the expansion of summer tourism as well. In this
area it is the tertiary sector as much as industry
which offers the agricultural worker the opportunity
of a second job; in winter, the 'dead season' for
agriculture, winter sports provide a series of
openings ranging from ski-instructor to waiter.
However, resulting employment is frequently of short
duration and not necessarily well-paid. Moreover,
not all regions possess the necessary appeal to
function as tourist centres. For many rural areas
there is also a problem of attitude and the need to
educate the population in the arts and finesse of
attracting and retaining a tourist clientele. To
exploit the tourist market may also require substantial investment in the construction or improvement
of accommodation, which despite the availability of
low-interest loans for this purpose, is often a
dissuasive factor. The absence of services and
shops, frequently consequent upon depopulation also
discourages the tourist: the Parisian holidaymaker
who travels daily a considerable distance in eager
search of his Le Monde, only to find that the one
copy the local shop takes has already been sold, may
well be reluctant to return to the area a second
time! Obstacles to the expansion of tourism may
arise from other sources, not least from individuals
and organisations opposed to such development on
environmental grounds (37).

The 'Actors' Involved
Attracting new employers to rural areas, which in
many instances appear to offer few natural attractions, or persuading those already present to maintain or even expand their operations, has proved a
difficult task. The government has intervened
directly in various ways, but bodies such as
Chambers of Commerce, departmental and regional
councils, employers' associations and various forms
of special development company have equally been
involved. Success has also often depended upon the
initiative and persuasiveness of local officials,
notably the mayor, and in certain cases a degree of
political patronage (38).
     Many of these factors have been influential in
attempts to revitalise much of the Massif Central,
where problems of population and employment loss
remain critical. However, a major guiding force has

been the <u>Société pour la Mise en Valeur de la Région Auvergne-Limousin</u> (SOMIVAL) (39). It first became operational in 1964, created as one of several regional development companies proposed by the government in the latter 1950s. As with these similar organisations, the initial objectives of SOMIVAL were directed primarily at the revitalisation of agriculture and forestry, although subsequently the role of the company has been considerably widened to include the promotion of tourism, the regulation of water supplies and the development of industrial and craft activities in rural areas. Equally, since 1976 its territorial competence has been enlarged to encompass those areas of Rhône-Alpes, Languedoc-Roussillon and Midi-Pyrénées lying within the Massif Central; this coincided with the launching by the government of a major development programme for this region in which SOMIVAL was to act as a principal co-ordinating agent. The latter role has always been the company's primary task, seeking to interest farmers, industrialists or developers in particular projects, and at the same time preparing the necessary related studies and organising the financial backing for their realisation, largely through obtaining government grants and subsidies.

Since its inauguration SOMIVAL has played a major contribution to the modernisation of many farm holdings, particularly through encouraging improvements in the quality of livestock, the introduction of new techniques (for example the recent use of irrigation), and co-operation between farmers. In the tourist sector it has been involved in the development of a diverse range of facilities, including the construction of over 50 holiday villages and a similar number of camping sites, as well as more modest undertakings such as swimming pools and tennis courts. Its more recent attempts to promote industrial and handicraft activities have resulted in the creation of over 500 jobs. Yet, when viewed in relation to the overall problems of the Massif Central these achievements, although commendable, have had but a relatively marginal impact. Greater effectiveness undoubtedly requires far more substantial investment. More efficiency might also result from wider consultation and co-operation between those agencies responsible for promoting development; despite the role of SOMIVAL as a co-ordinating body, this is more effective at a local level rather than between government departments concerned with financing projects.

Government Policy

Throughout much of the early post-war period the
government accorded relatively low priority to
policies designed to encourage development in rural
areas. However, the increasing depopulation and
progressive abandonment of many of these regions,
allied to the widespread disappearance of industrial
and commercial activities and services, has led to
the gradual evolution of a more comprehensive, if
not entirely coherent and generous policy or rural
improvement. For example, one of the priority programmes of the VIIth Plan was directed specifically
at the improvement of job prospects and living conditions in rural districts (40). Largely through
various systems of financial aid, the government has
sought to support traditional activities (notably
agriculture), to diversify the rural employment base
through the expansion of manufacturing and tourism,
and to maintain and improve the number and range of
shops and private and public services. Other action
to achieve these objectives has included the
improvement of infrastructure, notably to ameliorate
access by road and up-grade the telephone service.
By improving living conditions, the aim is to reduce
or wherever possible reverse the continuing trend
towards depopulation.

Action and legislation in favour of rural
improvement have grown spasmodically leading to both
complexity and overlap, although a number of distinct policies may be discerned, the majority guided
by the action of the DATAR. A first sphere of
intervention relates to the development of a number
of area based initiatives designed to aid the worst
affected regions. The major upland areas of central,
eastern and southern France, together with a number
of their peripheral zones and Brittany have been
designated for priority intervention (Zones de
Rénovation Rurale et de Montagne), a strategy which
has evolved progressively since the early 1960s (see
Figure 3.4). Due to the seriousness of the problems
in these regions the government has appointed four
special commissioners to help co-ordinate and stimulate intervention (41). The idea of selective
regional assistance was embodied in the creation of
the regional development companies (SAR). More
recently, the government has sponsored the preparation and implementation of various differing forms
of general development plan to cover each of the
major upland regions of the country, although in
most cases their scope is limited essentially to
offering planning guidelines rather than a

commitment to investment: a major exception is the
Massif Central (42). In 1975 a more diffuse areal
policy was launched offering financial assistance to
small groups of communes, suffering from problems
such as depopulation, which were prepared to submit
a detailed programme of remedial action; this might
include the construction of advance factories,
improvements to roads or the creation of social and
medical centres. If acceptable, a contract was concluded with the government (<u>contrat de pays</u>) outlining the proposed action and levels of state
financial assistance (43).

The provision of various forms of grant to
assist in the growth of new economic activity represents a second element of government strategy.
Regional development grants have long figured as
the most widespread form of assistance available in
France. For industrial projects the areas in which
the maximum rate is payable include parts of
Brittany, the Massif Central and Corsica. Here the
prerequisites in terms of size of investment and the
number of new jobs created are also lower. However,
these grants tend to have more relevance for the
generation of employment in urban centres within
broadly rural regions rather than in remote countryside areas. Other forms of grant, such as the <u>prime
d'installation artisanale</u> (44), have been available
to small businesses setting up in rural zones. More
flexibility in the type of project funded and its
location is likely to result from the socialist
government's recent revision of investment incentives. Regional Councils are now empowered to offer
grants for the expansion of various business activities, largely dependent upon the Council's own order
of priorities. Loans, at low interest rates (underwritten by the government) are also available, distributed essentially by the Crédit Agricole (45).

A third major component of official policy has
been the provision of a series of funds designed to
enable selective intervention in rural areas to help
finance diverse projects ranging from new industrial
zones to additional services. In order to simplify
the administration of such aid, to try to avoid
unnecessary duplication and to co-ordinate investment in manufacturing, services and infrastructure
with that destined for agriculture (for example,
grants to assist young farmers), the government
established a new central fund in 1979 – <u>Fonds
Interministériel de Développement et d'Aménagement
Rural</u> (FIDAR). It is managed by an interministerial
committee and has become the main mechanism for the

provision of this form of financial assistance, with the government agreeing to invest over 360 million francs in 1981. Although spread over a wide area of the country, the majority of the aid is destined for the regions of most intense rural depopulation, where a number of new initatives are also being encouraged. For various essential public services, it is proposed to extend the idea of local post offices acting as a focal point for their provision; as for employment, increased emphasis is to be given to providing a greater range of part-time activities which farmers might undertake to supplement their incomes - for example, developing part of their house as a gîte or shop (46).

The results of such policies appear contradictory. A considerable increase in investment in rural areas has occurred over the last decade, particularly in the less favoured regions, but in many of the same zones there has been little modification of pre-existing demographic trends. Partly, this is a reflection of the belated introduction of many forms of assistance; it is only in recent years that a distinctive strategy towards rural areas has begun to emerge. Moreover, where new jobs have been created they have often been located in the already more dynamic smaller rural centres, shunning less attractive localities which have therefore continued to decline. It is also arguable that despite an increase in assistance, the total volume of investment in rural areas is still too low, with inevitable consequences; equally, the money that is dispensed is spread too widely. However, whatever the level of aid and the manner of its distribution, for it to be effective it needs to be backed by a coherent and continuing policy. In the past this has been lacking.

THE CHANGING COUNTRYSIDE

The now apparent upward trend in the number of rural dwellers might indicate a lessening of the problem of depopulation and imply some success for the policies designed to protect existing jobs or provide new employment. However, this overall picture conceals many divergent trends, the continuing strong outflow of people from much of rural France contrasting with the rapid demographic growth of a comparatively restricted number of areas located principally on the outskirts of major urban settlements. The balance of employment is less favourable;

there is still an overall net loss of jobs in rural
areas, with the creation of new employment in manufacturing and services failing to counteract the
continued contraction of the agricultural labour-
force (47).

Change in the size of population is but one
aspect of the profound upheaval of rural society.
Once dominant, the farming community now plays an
increasingly minor role, although the occupational
characteristics of the population are often relatively complex (48). Many of the activities encouraged through government or local initiatives,
rather than providing totally new, full-time employment, have offered the farmer the opportunity of
supplementing a low income from agriculture by an
additional seasonal or part-time job. This renders
the division between the agricultural and non-
agricultural population less distinct.

An even greater diversity of socio-economic
structure now typifies rural communes on the fringe
of urban centres. Here farm workers represent a
small minority of a much more diverse employment
structure. Often few of the people work in their
local settlement, the majority commuting to an adjacent agglomeration which increasingly determines
their lifestyle. Here the rural world is far from
being isolated, inward-looking and self-sustaining.
Furthermore, these features no longer apply to many
rural communes, even in relatively remote areas; as
the telephone, television, improved road access,
many diverse forms of contact with outside people
and the widening of family horizons by children
seeking employment in different areas and non-
agricultural activities have all contributed to the
breakdown of the traditional barriers of isolation.

Change continues within rural France. In many
areas depopulation and the decline of the agricultural work-force will undoubtedly persist, yet
tourism, industrial expansion (particularly of small
craft industries) and retirement migration have
helped revive many communities. But, whereas the
transformation of society was revolutionary in
character for much of the period from the end of the
war until the early 1970s, subsequently the pace of
change has moderated.

NOTES

1. Lerat, S., 'Collecte et commercialisation des céréales en France', L'Information Géographique, 42 (1978), 15-27.
2. The comparative cheapness and greater flexibility and manoeuverability of plastic covered enclosures has led to a considerable decline of the traditional 'glasshouse'.
3. Cavaillon has long been renowned for the growth of its own melons.
4. These and many other aspects of agricultural activity in this region are discussed in Bethemont, J., Le Thème de l'Eau dans la Vallée du Rhône (Université de St. Etienne, St. Etienne, 1972). A useful summary is given in Carrière, P., 'Le thème de l'eau dans la vallée du Rhône', Bulletin de la Société Languedocienne de Géographie, 7 (1973), 295-8.
5. Verrière, J., 'Le progrès agricole est-il devenu un mythe dangereux?' Norois, 95ter (1977), 47-9; Calmès, R. et al., L'Espace Rural Français (Masson, Paris, 1978), 136-40.
6. France is the major producer and consumer of fertilisers in the EEC.
7. Bombal, J. and Chalmin, P., L'Agro-Alimentaire (Presses Universitaires de France, Paris, 1980), 28-9.
8. A similar decrease characterises the total number and proportional significance of farmers and their families within the total population: by 1980 their number had fallen to 4.3 millions, representing 8 per cent of the population.
9. The reduction in the agricultural labour-force in France is not a feature confined to the post-war years. It has existed since the middle of the nineteenth century, although even in the early part of this century the rate of decline was relatively modest, averaging approximately 1 per cent per annum. See Moliner, J. 'L'évolution de la population agricole du XVIII siècle à nos jours', Economie et Statistique, No.91 (1977), 79-84.
10. Pitié, J., L'Exode Rural (Presses Universitaires de France, Paris, 1979), 77.
11. Clout, H.D., 'Rural-urban migration in Western Europe', in Salt, J. and Clout, H.D. (eds.), Migration in Post-War Europe (Oxford University Press, London, 1976), 40-3.
12. Chombert de Lauwe, J., L'Aventure Agricole de la France (Presses Universitaires de France, Paris, 1979), 22, and Royer, J-F., 'L'exode agricole:

des départs sans relève', Economie et Statistique, No.79 (1976), 59-63.

13. A typical example is Michelin. As its activities at Clermont-Ferrand expanded rapidly in the 1960s and early 1970s, given the inadequate local supply of labour, special bus services were provided over an extensive area to collect rural-based workers. Michelin also offered its workers various other social and material benefits.

14. Ardagh, J., France in the 1980s (Penguin, Harmonsworth, 1982), 217-18.

15. See Girard, J-P. et al., 'Les agriculteurs - Tome 1', Collections de l'INSEE E 46-7 (1977), 272, and Vial, B., L'agriculture' in Pagé, J-P. (ed.), Profil Economique de la France (La Documentation Française, Paris, 1981), 176; Gombert, M., 'De moins en moins d'agriculteurs', Economie et Statistique, No.100 (1978), 26-34.

16. Commissariat Général du Plan, Agriculture, Industries Agricoles et Alimentaires (La Documentation Française, Paris, 1980), 173-7.

17. Recensement Général de l'Agriculture, 1979-80. It should be noted that only 9 per cent of all farm holdings now have at least one employed worker in addition to the farmer and his family.

18. This gives an indication of the problem of underemployment in agriculture, also reflected in the sector's weak contribution to GDP (5.1 per cent) compared with its proportion of manpower (8.6 per cent).

19. The question is discussed in Girard, et al., 'Les agriculteurs', 89-112, and Livet, R., 'A propos des agriculteurs à temps partiel', Norois, 95ter (1977), 129-38.

20. Gombert, 'De moins en moins d'agriculteurs', 26.

21. The head of the family, however, need not necessarily run the farm.

22. Chombert de Lauwe, L'Aventure Agricole, 60.

23. For more detail see Cazenave, G., and Monteil, J., Les Revenus des Agriculteurs (Presses Universitaires de France, Paris, 1980), 7-9, and Giraud, et al., 'Les agriculteurs', 123-4.

24. See, for example, Gombert, M., 'Les revenus fiscaux des agriculteurs en 1975', Economie et Statistique, No.124 (1980), 29-38.

25. A fuller discussion appears in Girard et al., 'Les agriculteurs', 195-238, and Jeannot, C., 'Conditions et problèmes de l'agriculture française', Profils Economiques, No.2 (1980), 16-17.

26. See Gervais, M. et al., Une France sans

Paysans (Seuil, Paris, 1965), 75-61, and Calmès, R.
et al., L'Espace Rural Français (Masson, Paris,
1978), 153-6.
    27. See Pitié, L'Exode Rural, 79-89 and Calmès
et al., L'Espace Rural Français, 41-52.
    28. Limouzin, P., 'Les facteurs de dynamisme
des communes rurales françaises', Annales de
Géographie, 89 (1980), 549-87; Fruit, J-P., 'L'évolution récente de la population active rurale en France
(1968-75)', L'Information Géographique, 42 (1978),
159-66. Preliminary results of the 1982 census con-
firm there is now a net increase in rural population.
    29. Limouzin, 'Les facteurs de dynamisme',
549-87.
    30. De Farcy, H., L'Espace Rural (Presses
Universitaires de France, Paris, 1975), 31-6.
    31. In the département of Ain (Rhône-Alpes),
for example, by no means one of the least prosperous
or isolated areas of rural population, over 200
schools have closed in the last 15 years.
    32. Various forms of control over development
are discussed in Pagès, M., La Maîtrise de la
Croissance Urbaine (Presses Universitaires de
France, Paris, 1980), 35-64.
    33. Béteille, R., 'L'industrie en milieu rural
en France', L'Information Géographique, 42 (1978),
32.
    34. Béteille, 'L'industrie en milieu rural',
28.
    35. Béteille, 'L'industrie en milieu rural',
34-5.
    36. Limouzin, 'Les facteurs de dynamisme',
570-3.
    37. This issue is referred to again in the
chapter on tourism.
    38. Pinchemel, P., La France (Armand Colin,
Paris, 1981), vol.2, 286.
    39. There has been a net loss of over 200,000
jobs since the early 1960s.
    40. VIIe Plan de Développement Economique et
Sociale (Union Générale d'Editions, Paris, 1977),
283-8.
    41. The commissioners cover the Massif
Central, Alps-Jura-Vosges, Pyrenees and the western
area centred on Brittany.
    42. In 1975 the government launched a special
development plan for the Massif Central with the
general aims of improving living conditions and
living standards; encouraging agriculture was but
one of a number of policies advocated, amongst which
other priorities included the improvement of

communications and stimulating industrial and tourist development. In 1978 a similar programme was announced for south-western France.

43. A similar initiative was launched in 1970 with the passing of legislation enabling the creation of rural development plans (<u>Plan d'Aménagement Rural</u>), although in this case without the guarantee of government financial backing. See Pinchemel, <u>La France</u>, 289-90; Melleray, G., 'Bilan provisoire d'une expérience d'aménagement rural: le plan d'aménagement rural (PAR)', <u>Revue de Droit Rural</u>, No.74 (1979), 51-8.

44. Madiot, Y., <u>L'Aménagement du Territoire</u> (Masson, Paris, 1979), 159-61.

45. Madiot, <u>L'Aménagement du Territoire</u>, 161-2.

46. <u>Le Monde</u>, 9 and 10 Jan. 1981.

47. Limouzin, 'Les facteurs de dynamisme', 579.

48. See, for example, Fruit, 'L'évolution récente de la population active', 159-66 and Kayser, B., 'Le changement social dans les campagnes françaises', <u>Economie Rurale</u>, No.135 (1979), 5-6.

Chapter Five

THE POST-WAR GROWTH AND PRESENT STRUCTURE OF INDUSTRY

The post-war transformation of the industrial sector has been just as remarkable as the progress achieved in agriculture. It is not unrealistic to suggest that over the last three decades French industrial activity has been revolutionised, reflected in the radical changes which have been a feature of the increase in volume and range of manufacturing output and the distribution of production units. Although by the early 1950s industry represented the main sector of employment (accounting for approximately 37 per cent of the active population), plant was often outdated and there were large areas of the country within which modern manufacturing activity was totally absent. Since then France has become a leading world industrial power ranking behind the USA, Western Germany and Japan. French productive capacity has risen very substantially, the country is now a major exporter of manufactured goods and has gained an international reputation in a variety of industrial fields, including aerospace, armaments, telecommunications, nuclear engineering and the production of vehicles.

From the late 1950s until the early 1970s French industrial production rose at a continuously high level, this growth underpinning the country's economic revival and sustaining a remarkable rise in living standards. Since then progress has continued, its rate even accelerating in certain fields such as microelectronics, but the preceding period of largely uninterrupted and unimpeded expansion has been replaced by a phase of modest growth and readjustment. The upward trend in the level of output has been moderated, investment has stagnated and the marked upsurge in unemployment is largely attributable to the reduced labour demands of the secondary sector. Structural change, so much a feature of

past growth, has become even more essential to
enable French industry to enhance its competitiveness.

Nevertheless, the direct role of industry
within the economy remains substantial. In 1981,
the secondary sector (including building and public
works) employed approximately 7.2 million workers,
representing 33 per cent of the country's labour-
force, and accounted for around 38 per cent of gross
domestic product. Moreover, industrial goods represent over three-quarters of the value of French
exports (including services), while nearly 30 per
cent of industrial output is exported.

THE BACKGROUND TO CHANGE

Change within the industrial sector has been directed not just at increasing the volume and diversifying the range of output, but also at raising
efficiency. It has resulted in a significant reorganisation of manufacturing activity, including a
substantial reduction in the number of small industrial firms and the growth of a series of large
multinational groups which have come to control an
increasing proportion of output. The character and
extent of such transformation have been influenced
by broad changes in the manufacturing environment.
Productive activities have been greatly modified by a major technological revolution involving
the introduction of new machines, improved manufacturing processes and the use of new materials (1).
Just as innovations themselves have prompted change,
the birth of new industries such as nuclear energy
has demanded different products and manufacturing
techniques. At the same time, computerised systems
of control and the use of robots to perform many
tasks previously performed manually have become more
widespread. Such changes have implications for manpower requirements and, in the current state of a
depressed labour market, a conflict of interest has
tended to arise where technological progress has
improved productivity without a corresponding
increase in demand for the product.
The market areas exploited by manufacturers
have altered radically, a change dominated by the
growth in international trading. However, just as
French industrialists have been strongly encouraged
to increase their foreign sales, the same strategy
has been adopted by other countries. Thus, many
companies within France have been challenged for

their share of the domestic market. Moreover, such
competition has originated not only from the
advanced manufacturing nations such as Japan but
also from a new and forceful set of producers
amongst the developing nations, including Brazil,
Mexico and various south-east Asian countries.

In responding to increased competition, French
manufacturers have been hampered by a number of
problems beyond their direct control, not least
those provoked by the country's relatively poor en-
dowment in raw materials for industry and for the
production of energy (2). Over the last decade conditions of supply have altered radically, as the
cost of imported products has risen dramatically.
France is particularly disadvantaged by the extent
of its imports of energy materials (3); the cost of
oil imports alone rose from 14.1 billion francs in
1973 to 128.8 billion francs in 1981. One strategy
to reduce the unfavourable impact of the facture
pétrolière (and of the cost of other imports) on the
balance of payments, has been the encouragement of
industrial exports. However, despite a reduction in
oil consumption and a rise in the export of manufactured goods, the benefits of these trends have
failed to compensate for the steadily increased cost
of energy imports (Table 5.1). Moreover, although
French industrial exports have shown an overall

Table 5.1: Trade Balance of Industrial and Energy
Products

	Balance (billion francs)	
	Energy	Industrial goods
1973	-17.9	9.3
1974	-51.5	11.0
1975	-45.7	37.6
1976	-60.9	23.5
1977	-64.6	43.0
1978	-62.1	49.3
1979	-83.8	46.6
1980	-132.9	34.2
1981	-161.0	54.5

Source: INSEE, Rapport sur les Comptes de la Nation
de l'Année 1981 (1982).

tendency to increase substantially in value and volume since the early 1970s, it has only been in the areas of capital goods for industry and vehicles that France has shown a significant trading surplus.

As many of these changes have occurred, the pattern of demand has altered. Following its high level during the 1960s and early 1970s, demand generally throughout the world had declined by the beginning of the present decade as the recession intensified following the second choc pétrolier. Thus, more recently manufacturers have often been faced not only with rising costs, but less demand for their goods in an increasingly competitive market.

Features of the Labour-Force

These changes in marketing conditions, levels of demand and the techniques of production have all affected the labour requirements of firms, tending over recent years to considerably depress employment within industry. This has also been related, however, to a longer term underlying shift of the work-force away from secondary to tertiary activities. As a result there is now a well-established trend of a decline in the absolute and proportional signifi-cance of industrial employment within the total labour-force (Table 5.2). In a wider context, however, industry remains influential in the genera-tion of employment within the economy, spawning a growing number of jobs in tertiary occupations ranging from researchers and technicians to finan-cial and marketing consultants. Frequently, this multiplier effect has operated to the benefit of non-industrial businesses, but it has also led to an

Table 5.2: The Size of the Industrial Labour-Force

	Total (millions)	Proportion of labour-force (%)
1974	8.1	38
1977	7.7	36
1981	7.2	33

Source: INSEE, Rapport sur les Comptes de la Nation de l'Année 1981 (1982).

expansion of tertiary employment within manufacturing firms; nearly a fifth of the total employment in industry is accounted for by 'tertiary' jobs.

Despite its decline, the secondary sector is still a major source of employment. The majority of jobs it provides, however, are for male workers. Although over recent years the growth of employment within the economy has been strongly linked to an increase in the number of women in the labour-force, this tendency has been most apparent in the tertiary sector (4). Where it has occurred in industry, it has generally been linked to tertiary occupations within firms. Overall, approximately 30 per cent of employment in manufacturing industry is represented by women and it is only amongst the group of textile, clothing and footwear industries that women dominate the work-force (5).

Immigrant workers, largely originating from the lesser developed countries of the Mediterranean region, still represent a sizeable and significant sub-section of the labour market, despite a reduction in their number since the mid-1970s. In 1980 there were approximately 1.5 million foreigners officially registered as working in France (Table 5.3), the majority employed in industry. Most are poorly skilled, with over 70 per cent engaged as manual workers, predominantly in industries such as heavy metallurgy, chemicals, car production and,

Table 5.3: The Number and Origin of Immigrant Workers in France, 1980

Nationality	Total	%
Portuguese	430,611	28.9
Algerian	322,736	21.7
Spanish	157,723	10.6
Italian	146,406	9.8
Moroccan	116,120	7.8
Tunisian	65,320	4.4
Yugoslavian	32,232	2.2
Others	216,344	14.6
	1,487,492	100.0

Source: INSEE, Enquête sur l'Emploi d'Octobre 1980 (1981).

above all, building and civil engineering (6). In
the 1960s and early 1970s they represented a vital
means of overcoming the shortfall of labour, while
increasingly they have undertaken jobs shunned by
Frenchmen due to the occupation's dirty, repetitive
or dangerous character.

Traditionally, certain weaknesses have been
ascribed to the French industrial work-force (7).
By international comparison the standard of technical training in the past has been mediocre. The
need for industry to become more efficient and competitive has helped change attitudes and promote
improvement, especially as production techniques
have evolved more rapidly, demanding retraining and
new skills. Criticism has also been levelled at the
inferior quality of certain aspects of French
management, not least a lack of professionalism and
aggressiveness compared with German and Japanese
rivals (8). In part this originates from the heritage of a large number of small, family-owned
businesses. Again, under the pressure of competition, companies are being forced to change or be
threatened with closure.

The Government: an Important Agent of Change and
Support
Amongst the many influences which have affected the
development of industry, the role of the government
has been crucial. The motives for involvement are
numerous, frequently inspired not only by economic
imperatives but also by social and political considerations. Various examples illustrate these
diverse factors. Reasons of strategic importance
partly explain the government's involvement in
industries such as aerospace and nuclear energy,
while the desire to promote and, often in the
initial stages, protect key growth sectors reflects
its interest in the computer and telecommunications
industries. Branches of declining activity also
attract government attention, not uncommonly with
the aim of reducing the impact of high unemployment
in specific localities; thus, in recent years the
state has intervened significantly to support
industries such as textiles, shipbuilding and above
all, steel. Broader ambitions lie behind the
Socialists' extension of state control, linked to
the desire for more effective management of the
economy and the achievement of various social goals
such as a marked overall reduction in unemployment.
General guidelines to orientate and facilitate

long-term investment in industry have been provided
over an extended period through the country's
National Plans (9), but there are many diverse and
more specific ways by which the government intervenes in the economy. These range from its legisla-
tive role to its position as a major client of both
public and private enterprises. One key area of
intervention is in the provision of financial assistance, in the form of grants, loans and tax concessions. These are offered through a variety of
mechanisms including regional policy, subsidies to
assist with research costs or encourage exports, and
aid to foster growth in key sectors of production
such as aerospace and electronics or to alleviate
the worst effects of concentration in others.
Greatest assistance has been given to these latter
sectors (10), but in economic terms it is arguable
that priority ought to have been accorded to the
former group due to their potential for growth. The
government also supports various major research
organisations, particularly in areas of advanced
technology. These include the Commissariat à
l'Energie Atomique (CEA), Centre Nationale d'Etudes
Spatiales (CNES) and the Agence de l'Informatique
(ADI). Generally, however, the level of research
spending in France is below that of its main industrial rivals, potentially adversely affecting the
country's competitiveness.

     To assist in its funding operations, the govern-
ment has created a series of specialised organisations (11). Two examples are represented by the
Fonds de Développement Economique et Social (FDES),
set up in 1955, and the more recent Comité
Interministériel d'Aménagement des Structures
Industrielles (CIASI), established in 1974. The main
aim of the former body is to help finance major
restructuring programmes, while in the latter case it
is to manage and co-ordinate the government's investment strategy, essentially for those companies in
difficulty. Nonetheless, there is now an extensive
and even confusing array of organisations offering
both finance and advice, suggesting the need for
rationalisation and a more coherent policy of intervention (12). However, whether to assist ailing
industry or enhance the growth prospects of more
flourishing activities, one common thread to government strategy has been the joint negotiation of
development programmes with particular industries or
even individual firms. Such agreements first became
significant in the mid-1960s with the preparation of
plans for the steel and computer industries. Since

then their scope has been greatly extended, more recently under the Socialists with the preparation since 1981 of restructuring plans for a series of industries including steel, textiles, chemicals, shipbuilding, paper and machine tools.

Thus, government finance has been vital in maintaining or improving the health of French industry, but there is now some disquiet at the extent to which the state exerts control over financial resources, particularly for borrowing (13). Various government controlled bodies ranging from the large Caisse Centrale de Crédit Hôtelier, Commercial et Industriel to the smaller regionally-based Sociétés de Développement Régional have long provided the greater part of loans to industrialists, but with the nationalisation of most of the banking sector in 1982, the state now exercises a virtual monopoly over such financing.

Even greater direct control over manufacturing activity has resulted from the nationalisation of a series of the country's major manufacturing groups: these include Sacilor and Usinor (steel), Compagnie Générale d'Electricité (industrial electrical goods), Saint-Gobain (glass, metals, computers), Pechiney-Ugine-Kuhlmann (metals, especially aluminium, and chemicals), Thomson-Brandt (electrical goods and electronics) and Rhône-Poulenc (chemicals, textiles). The government has also acquired 51 per cent of the shares (as opposed to 100 per cent in the above cases) of the two companies of Dassault-Breguet (aircraft) and Matra (military equipment, electronics) (14). This gives the state extensive control of key sections of industry (particularly when existing nationalised companies are added to this list). For much of the post-war period only around 6 per cent of the industrial work-force lay within the public sector, but the proportion has now risen to nearly a quarter. This extension of the state's influence has not been without controversy and, evaluated in purely economic terms, the necessity for these takeovers has been stoutly contested, not least due to the past records of success of most of these groups (15).

THE POST-WAR DEVELOPMENT OF INDUSTRY

The Position in 1945
In the period immediately following the second world war the prospect of sustained industrial growth

appeared remote (16). Apart from the general
disruption within the country resulting from the war,
there were many underlying weaknesses in the
country's economic and social structures likely to
impede expansion. The economy had exhibited little
dynamism throughout much of the earlier part of the
century, a situation mirrored in the country's poor
demographic performance: in 1946 the total population (40.1 millions) was less than in 1901. In
addition, much of the infrastructure essential to
foster growth, related principally to the supply of
energy and communications, had suffered from a long
period of under-investment.

Compounded with these general problems were the
more specific inadequacies of the industrial sector.
Despite change and progress, industry was still
based to an excessive degree upon increasingly outdated technology, too many small, undercapitalised
and often inefficient firms, an under-representation
of activities capable of generating increased output
and employment, and management unwilling to accept
change and unused to competition. Thus, an excessive proportion of manufacturing activity was still
tied to inefficiently sized productive units, unable
to realise scale-economies and frequently vulnerable
to cyclic variations in the economy (17). Moreover,
industry was spread unevenly thoughout the country,
with many areas of western, southern and central
France lacking either a strong or diversified industrial base, or both. Yet, in spite of these deficiencies, France evolved into a powerful industrial
nation. In assessing subsequent change, discussion
is focused upon three contrasting phases of economic
growth (18).

Industrial Growth Between 1945 and the Late 1950s
Over this period industrial policy was related to
two fundamental objectives; first, the need to re-
establish industrial output (which even in 1949 was
still no larger than in 1929) (19) as part of the
more general post-war reconstruction programme, and
second, the longer-term necessity to provide France
with a modern and competitive manufacturing sector.
With industrial output increasing by a rate of over
5 per cent per annum throughout the greater part of
this period, it is not unrealistic to suggest that
both aims were largely met. Their attainment was
facilitated by various factors. An important initial
impetus to modernisation resulted from the American
programme of Marshall Aid, together with the priority

accorded by government planning to the raising of industrial production. The First National Plan (1947-53) concentrated upon the re-equipment and extension of the country's basic industries, while in the Second Plan (1954-57) emphasis shifted to support for transforming industries. Increased output was also stimulated by the growth of the home market, consequent upon the country's demographic revival and a rise in purchasing power; moreover, throughout the greater part of the 1950s this remained a protected market, thus helping to nurture the newly expanding industrial sector. Industry's efficiency was similarly improved, with a substantial rise in productivity reflecting increased automation and technological improvements, as well as a general shortage of labour, encouraging greater investment in productive capital. Other broader initiatives benefited industry, notably the improvement of infrastructure, although the modernisation of the telephone system and of the road network (through motorway construction) were exceptions to this policy, despite their significance to the process of industrial development (20).

Many of these tendencies were to be reinforced during the following decade, but in certain areas little progress was achieved during the 1950s. For example, industry remained dominated by a host of small and medium-sized firms and, despite a growing number of mergers, lacked the presence of an influential sector of large national or internationally based groups.

From Common Market to Oil Crisis: Unimpeded Expansion

When the French government elected to join the EEC in 1957 doubts were expressed over the ability of the country's still seemingly fragile industrial sector to withstand the increased competition from other member states which this decision implied. On the contrary, over the next fifteen years the French economy expanded at an exceptional pace, reflecting in part the modernisation of agriculture and the beginning of the rapid growth of tertiary activities, but above all the substantial and sustained rise in industrial output, perpetuating and accentuating the trend established during the 1950s. Between 1960 and 1973 both French GDP and industrial production grew annually by an average of approximately 6 per cent, with yearly rates varying little from this mean; this high and regular pattern of expansion was

unrivalled elsewhere in the Common Market, not even
in Western Germany.

During this period the transformation of French
industry became even more radical, linked to the
rapid expansion of new growth sectors such as oil
refining and petrochemicals, the continuous development and application of new techniques, the widespread construction of new factories and the considerable enlargement of product ranges. These
changes were accompanied and assisted by the high
level of investment in industry (representing
annually between 16 and 19 per cent of the total
value of output between 1960 and 1974) and its
strong annual rate of increase (21). Increased
mechanisation and automation and a growing substitu-
tion of capital for labour produced a substantial
rise in productivity, averaging over 5 per cent per
annum during the same period (22). Employment in
industry also jumped significantly with the net
yearly increase in workers averaging 62,000 between
1963 and 1969 and 93,000 between 1969 and 1973 (23),
these latter years being regarded generally as the
peak period of post-war economic and industrial
growth. The strength of the demand for labour was
reflected in an upsurge in immigration and by the
importance attached to the availability of labour in
the location strategies of many expanding companies.

Growth also embodied a modification of the
structure of industrial output and activity, exemplified by the belated development of a series of
large French owned multinational groups, strongly
encouraged by the government. Other changes included a shift in the orientation of production, away
from traditional consumption goods to intermediate
and particularly equipment goods. Similarly, an increasing proportion of output was exported as
foreign trading expanded, notably with other
countries of the Common Market to the detriment of
the former French colonial empire (24). Within
France, this period of expansion coincided with
significant shifts in the location of industrial
activity, strongly conditioned at this time by the
government's preoccupation with decentralisation.

Many of the influences promoting the growth and
transformation of industry during this period were
already apparent in the 1950s. Thus, an increasingly
buoyant home market, linked to higher incomes and
living standards, a growing population and nearly
full employment all continued to represent a major
spur to increased output. Government planning also
accorded a high priority to industrial development,

particularly to the restructuring of industry and to
the expansion of key growth sectors such as electronics and aeronautical industries. These objectives
were central to the Vth Plan (1966-70) and were supported by extensive state funding. The government
also encouraged the private sector of industry to
invest heavily, partly through increasing the availability of low interest loans; while this undoubtedly prompted change, equally it had the
potentially problematic consequence of greatly
increasing industry's indebtedness. Other factors
prompted expansion. Rather than stifle increased
output, the creation of the EEC and the progressive
freeing of trading with other European countries
characterised by large and expanding markets acted as
an important stimulus to growth. Throughout the
world, protective barriers generally were reduced,
with both these latter trends linked to an increased
contribution being made to industrial investment by
foreign firms as a growing number expanded their
manufacturing operations in France.

By the early 1970s remarkable progress had been
achieved in the development of a strong and competitive industrial sector in France, although deficiencies in its structure persisted, suggesting that the
process of transformation was incomplete. Despite
the increased dominance of large industrial groups,
by international standards French industry remained
weakly concentrated. Similarly, specialisation in
growth industries and especially those involving the
application of advanced technology, although
increasing, was still relatively modest, indicating
that possibly too much emphasis had been accorded to
the quantitative rather than qualitative aspects of
expansion. There also existed a large and varied
group of small, marginal firms largely untouched by
change, with many doomed ultimately to disappear,
posing at the regional level the problem of the
need to regenerate employment.

The Oil Crisis and the Changed Pattern of Economic
Growth
In the early 1970s the prospects for the continued
expansion of industry at a high rate appeared good
(25). However, the huge rise in oil prices in 1973
and the recession triggered by this action radically
altered the outlook not only for the French economy,
but also for the economies of other leading industrial nations, all heavily dependant upon oil.
Problems were only intensified by the further

substantial rises in the cost of oil between 1979 and 1980 (26). Thus, over much of the last decade industry has been faced with the difficult task of adapting to an unstable economic environment and major increases in the costs of energy and many raw materials. It has also been forced to change in resonse to other factors, not least a major revolution in manufacturing techniques, led by developments in microelectronics (27). World trading patterns have also been modified, with two related processes proving particularly significant: the continued freeing of world trade and the increased integration of certain developing countries into the world economy, not just as suppliers of raw materials and semi-finished goods but now as industrial producers of growing importance benefiting particularly from lower labour costs. In both instances the effect has been to increase competition from other world manufacturers, to the detriment of certain branches of French industry. Importers now take a growing share of the market for domestic appliances, textile and leather goods and, belatedly, cars. Moreover, much of this competition is from other advanced industrial nations. Despite the growing role of third-world producers, these countries account for less than 5 per cent of the imports of manufactured goods (28), although in selected areas, notably textiles, the impact has been much greater, depressing substantially the level of home production.

Against this background, industrial activity has altered significantly. Output has increased less rapidly and more inconsistently (Table 5.4), suffering noticeably in the wake of the two major rises in oil prices. Similarly, the rate of investment growth has declined and gains in productivity are now lower. Both trends are partly related to the fall in demand and an excess of productive capacity, this latter feature also testifying to the high level of previous investment in equipment. Above all, however, employment in the secondary sector is now falling substantially; whereas between 1969 and 1975 there was a net annual increase in industrial jobs of nearly 95,000, between 1975 and 1981 there was a net yearly decrease of over 104,000 (29). Furthermore, the scale of loss has recently increased dramatically, as short-term expedients such as temporary lay-offs and short-time working have become inadequate to deal with the fall in demand (Table 5.5). The extent of industry's difficulties has also been evident from the increase in

Growth and Structure of Industry

Table 5.4:   Variation in Volume of Industrial Output[*]

	Rate of change (%)
1960 - 70 (annual average)	+ 6.4
1970 - 73 (annual average)	+ 6.8
1974	+ 3.2
1975	- 6.6
1976	+ 8.4
1977	+ 1.6
1978	+ 2.0
1979	+ 3.5
1980	+ 0.1

* excludes branches of energy, agricultural and food industries, and building and public works.

Source: INSEE, Les Comptes de l'Industrie 1980 (1981) and Commissariat Général du Plan, Industrie (1980).

Table 5.5:   The Decline of Employment in Industry

	Net loss of jobs
1976/7	-37,000
1977/8	-127,000
1978/9	-123,000
1979/80	-74,000
1980/1	-219,000

Source: Calculated from INSEE, Rapport sur les Comptes de la Nation de l'Année 1981 (1982).

the number of firms going out of business or experiencing major financial problems, tendencies which are not confined to small businesses: they have also been a feature of large companies such as Agache-Willot (textiles), Terrin (ship-repair) and Usinor and Sacilor (steel).

Although France remains a powerful manufacturing nation these problems indicate the persistence of structural weaknesses in the industrial sector and the continuing process of mutation. The recession and changing world patterns of production have affected industry unequally. While output and employment have fallen substantially in certain industries, notably heavy metals and textiles, other branches such as industrial electronics and food and drinks have been affected less severely. The differential performance of various branches of industry and the varying impact of technological progress are also indicative of the progressive re-orientation and specialisation of French manufacturing. The aim is to increase investment in the production of goods with a high-value added which require the use of advanced technology and a skilled labour-force. Less progress has been achieved than amongst competitors such as Japan, but the current challenge to French industry is to complete successfully this conversion (30).

CONCENTRATION AND THE GROWTH OF LARGE INDUSTRIAL GROUPS

Over the last twenty years a key element in the profound transformation of the French economy and its progressive integration with other national economies has been the growth in the concentration of the ownership and organisation of manufacturing (31). As in other western nations, industry within France has become dominated increasingly by the activities of large, generally multinational industrial groups. Yet traditionally French industry has been associated with a host of small companies, complemented by only a limited series of larger enterprises. Small firms still predominate in terms of their number, but their significance as employers and producers is extremely modest (32).

The Development of Concentration

The linkage and association of industrial firms through takeovers, mergers or various other forms of amalgamation have long been features of the expansion and reorganisation of industry within France (33). Already by the end of the nineteenth century such action was occurring in the textile and iron and steel industries. Such trends continued into the present century, covering a wide range and greater number of industries. Nonetheless, despite the progressive formation and growth of a number of large companies such as Saint Gobain and Kuhlmann (chemicals), Renault and Citroën (automobiles) and Pont-à-Mousson, de Wendel and Schneider (steel), there was relatively little concentration of

industrial capital at this time (34). On the
contrary, the phase of more rapid industrial growth
initiated in the 1890s led to the creation of
numerous small firms, accentuating the dispersion of
employment and investment, and generally counteracting the tendency towards a more restricted
grouping of companies.

Thus, despite continued mergers, by the out-
break of the second world war there were still
relatively few large industrial companies within
France; moreover, their incidence and influence were
restricted to limited areas of production, particularly those which were capital intensive in character such as steel and chemicals. Over the post-war
period the scale and extent of concentration have
greatly increased. Three trends are recognisable.
There has been a steady decline in the number of
industrial firms, (partly through merger and partly
as the result of closure), companies have generally
increased in size and, above all, the control of
French industry has been vested, at an accelerating
rate, in the hands of an ever smaller number of
large and influential industrial corporations. Thus,
central to these processes has been the formation
not only of larger manufacturing companies but also
of extremely powerful and complex industrial groups,
where generally the main link between constituent
firms is financial (35). The development of such
groups is not confined just to industrial concerns
but is equally a feature of companies engaged in
financial or commercial affairs. All these activities may become combined within a single group, but
where this does not occur there are often strong
links between different groups where interests are
complementary, as in the fields of banking and manufacturing. However, groups differ widely in their
form and, given the intricate nature of the linkages
between companies, it is often difficult to define
accurately their exact spheres of operation (36).
What is clear, however, is that the weight of large
companies and groups within the economy has
increased very substantially since the latter 1950s
(37).

Stages in the Post-War Growth of Concentration
Despite the general trend towards increased concentration, the nature and intensity of the process
have varied over the post-war period, enabling a
number of evolutionary phases to be distinguished.
It was not until the latter 1950s that the tendency

towards the creation of larger companies intensified.
Prior to that period, although many small and often
marginally efficient firms disappeared, this was not
accompanied by a significant strengthening of the
role of large enterprises. In part this resulted
from the absence of a sufficiently strong stimulus
for concentration, reflecting the still protected
character of the French market.

With the creation and expansion of the Common
Market, the trading environment was modified radically. It became apparent that if French companies
were to remain competitive within the home market
and to challenge effectively in other European
trading areas, their size and efficiency needed to
be augmented. Thus, the movement towards concentration accelerated, effected in part 'externally'
through a growing number of mergers and amalgamations of firms, but also 'internally' through
companies financing an increase in their size and
productive capacity by an issue of additional shares
or by borrowing the necessary capital. By the mid-
1960s this tendency had further intensified, responding to a variety of influences. Greater size and
the associated potential to realise various economies of scale became essential to enable firms to
penetrate or increase their dominance within markets.
To remain competitive, however, particularly in
fields of advanced technology, requires extensive
and continuing investment in research and development, and the means to undertake this is again
related to the size and financial capacity of the
firm; production has to be on a large-scale to generate the necessary income to finance such activity
(38). Marketing of the product is equally important
and depends upon an efficient and comprehensive
distributive network; once more it is generally only
the larger companies which have the resources to
establish such systems. In all these processes,
access to loan capital is often vital and again size
tends to be a controlling factor, with major groups
usually able to exert the greatest influence in
financial markets; moreover, as the reliance upon
such funding has risen, so have the links between
industrial firms and financial institutions, frequently within the framework of the same group.
Large industrial corporations also wield considerable
power and the more significant a group's role within
the economy, the greater tends to be its ability to
place pressure upon the government or influence its
policy, a position of some importance in relation to
investment or location strategy. Thus, increased

size implies numerous potential benefits, its
attainment often becoming a self-reinforcing process.
    All these factors helped promote an intense
movement of concentration during the period from the
mid-1960s until the early 1970s. Further and substantial encouragement was given by the government,
notably under the late President Pompidou.
L'impératif industriel was one of the main strands
of his economic policy, involving strong support for
industry, especially in the creation of a number of
large groups capable of rivalling those of competing
industrialised nations. In certain instances the
government acted directly forming, for example, the
Entreprise de Recherche et d'Activité Pétrolier -
ERAP (oil refining and exploration) in 1966 (now
Elf-Aquitaine) and the Société Nationale Industrielle
Aerospatiale (SNIAS) in 1970; equally, it promoted
plans and provided financial assistance to further
restructuring in various industries such as steel,
shipbuilding, electronics and data-processing. It
was also during this period that large private
groups such as Wendel-Sidélor (steel), Thomson-
Brandt (electrical engineering and electronics), BSN
(glass) (39) and Ugine Kuhlmann (chemicals) were
constituted. Such changes represented the beginning
of a marked reorganisation of various key sectors of
industry, a process largely dominated by the merger
of companies rather than through the internal expansion of firms. Just as these types of changes were
affecting the company structure of French industry,
modifications were also occurring in the number and
size of the individual plants owned by firms. For
example, in certain instances the amalgamation of
companies provoked a rationalisation and specialisation of productive units, associated with the elimi-
nation of the least efficient or of those where
activities were duplicated, and with the search for
greater economies of scale.
    Over the last decade many of these trends have
continued, associated in particular with the further
development and strengthening of a series of large
French-based multinational corporations. The
presence of such groups became essential if French
companies were to penetrate successfully world
markets, as restrictions on trading have progressively diminished and new market areas have grown
amongst the more industrialised developing countries,
notably those which are oil producers. Similarly,
to remain competitive French companies needed to
adjust their manufacturing strategies to take
account, for example, of an increased international

division of labour and the much lower production
costs in many of the world's emerging industrial
nations.

Just as French companies have modified their
business strategies in this way, foreign-based
groups have similarly increased their investment in
France. American firms (such as IBM and Bendix)
have invested most heavily, although the role of
European companies (particularly West German) is now
of increased significance, indicated by the total of
new jobs foreign firms created between 1971 and 1980
(Table 5.6). Not unnaturally, penetration has been
generally greatest in branches of industry which, at
least in the past, have been characterised by a
strong demand for their products: these include,
data processing, electronics, oil, parachemicals and
pharmaceuticals. Overall, although the number of
such companies is relatively modest, they account
for over 17 per cent of industrial employment and
nearly a quarter of the sales of manufactured goods
in France (40).

Whereas the earlier development of large groups
was often associated with the absorption by one
company of a series of smaller firms, subsequently
there has been a trend towards the merging of
already sizeable and diversified parent companies.
Thus, in the early 1970s very large groups such as
Pechiney-Ugine-Kuhlmann and Saint Gobain-Pont-à-
Mousson (41) were formed, while more recently
Peugeot has greatly enlarged its operations through

Table 5.6: Foreign Industrial Investment in France

Country of origin	Total jobs 1971-80	%
USA	34,964	40
Western Germany	26,177	30
United Kingdom	8,203	9
Switzerland	5,533	6
Benelux	4,296	5
Scandinavia	1,668	2
Spain	1,880	2
Other	4,815	6
Total	87,536	100

Source: DATAR

the acquisition of Citroën in 1976 and Talbot (ex Chrysler - Europe) in 1978. Certain recent changes in investment strategy are also evident, partly induced by the more difficult trading conditions created by the recession as well as the changing spatial pattern of world manufacturing. During the very intense phase of concentration of the late 1960s and early 1970s the principal objective was to increase the size of the company and its financial resources, sometimes almost irrespective of the nature of the activities of the firms absorbed in the process. Inevitably, a number of diversely structure conglomerates resulted. More recently the emphasis has shifted, leading to a series of internal and external adjustments (42). In the search for greater efficiency and profitability, there has been a trend towards increased selectivity in the nature of companies' activities; this has also frequently been linked to a policy of disinvestment in sectors which are unprofitable or in which the group is weakly represented. Conversely new investment has been directed towards areas of existing strength or growth. Thus, for example, in 1980 Rhône-Poulenc sold its interests in the manufacture of basic chemicals to Elf-Aquitaine. For Rhône-Poulenc this represented a move away from a highly competitive, low profit-generating area of the market in which it was a relatively small producer, enabling the company to specialise further in fields in which it was already a major manufacturer and where there was a high-value added, such as fine chemicals and pharmaceuticals; for Elf-Aquitaine it represented an opportunity to dominate to an even greater extent a sector in which it was already a leading producer.

Reorientation may be geographic as well as sectoral, and a further trend, reinforced in recent years, is the increase by French firms of investment outside France. This policy is frequently guided by the desire to penetrate large existing markets, illustrated by Renault's links with American Motors and Mack Trucks in the USA. Alternatively, it may be prompted by lower production costs abroad (seen in Thomson-Brandt's investment in Singapore) and by the attraction of rapidly growing markets, both factors influencing Lafarge (cement) and Rhône-Poulenc to invest in Brazil and Peugeot to undertake production in Nigeria. Thus, the activities of major French groups have become organised increasingly on an international basis, although generally to a lesser degree than competitors in other advanced industrialised nations (43).

THE EXTENT OF CONCENTRATION

Following the second world war, one of the main structural deficiencies of French industry was its weak level of concentration; France lagged noticeably in this area by comparison with countries such as Britain and the USA. Now, however, following a belated but intense movement of restructuring, the general dominance of industrial activity by larger companies has become pronounced (Table 5.7). Although less than one per cent of the 31,000 firms employing more than ten workers has a work-force exceeding 2,000, these companies account for 40 per cent of employment, 53 per cent of turnover and nearly 65 per cent of investment in industry. Conversely, for the far greater number of firms employing less than 100 workers (80 per cent of the total), the respective figures are 18, 13 and 9 per cent.

Amidst this general tendency, one of the most significant features has been the emergence of a restricted number of major industrial and financial groups which, in contrast to the position in the 1960s and early 1970s, now rival those of France's main competitors (44). These groups play an important direct role within the economy, related to the number of people they employ, the income they generate, their investment policies and the level of their exports. Table 5.8 indicates that France's fifteen largest companies (measured by turnover) have over 1.5 million employees and in many cases

Table 5.7: Structure of French Companies Employing more than Ten Workers

Size (No. of workers)	Number of companies (%)	Labour-force (%)	Turnover (%)	Investment (%)
10 - 99	80.0	18.0	13.3	8.6
100 - 499	16.0	22.8	17.7	12.8
500 - 1999	3.2	18.9	15.9	13.9
2000+	0.8	40.3	53.1	64.7
	100.0	100.0	100.0	100.0

Source: Commissariat Général du Plan, Industrie (1980).

Table 5.8:   Major Industrial Groups in France, 1980

Group	Principal activities	Turnover (billion francs)	Employ- ment ('000)	Turnover from overseas sales (%)
Compagnie Française des Pétroles	Oil	101.0	44	56
Renault	Vehicles	80.1	232	47
Elf-Aquitaine	Oil	76.6	37	23
Peugeot SA	Vehicles	71.1	245	50
Compagnie Générale d' Electricité	Electrical engineering; Electronics	45.7	180	30
Saint-Gobain	Glass; Mechanical engineering	43.5	163	60
Shell Française	Oil	42.0	8	2
Pechiney-Ugine- Kuhlmann	Metals; Chemicals	38.0	90	53
Thomson-Brandt	Electrical engineering; Electronics	36.5	128	46
Esso-France	Oil	35.9	5	-
Michelin	Tyres	32.6	115	59
Schneider	Metallurgy	31.6	117	46
Rhône-Poulenc	Chemicals	30.2	95	59
Générale Occidentale	Food	29.1	60	80
Usinor	Steel	21.5	34	29

Source: L'Expansion, No.180 (1981).

generate over half of their sales outside the
country through exports or foreign-based production,
emphasising their multinational character. They
also exert a much wider indirect influence through
the numerous, diverse firms which are dependent upon
their decisions.

Despite the general trend towards increased
concentration, the extent to which this feature
affects different sectors of industry varies significantly. Generally, it is developed most fully
amongst activities which are capital intensive in
character and in which control traditionally has
been vested in a limited number of producers. Thus,
the dominance of relatively few large companies is
characteristic of the energy, iron and steel and
motor vehicle industries. The degree of concentration is also relatively high in the manufacture of
consumer durables, partly reflecting the competitive
nature of the market but also its considerable size
and growth. More generally, particularly since the
onset of the recession, large industrial and financial groups have tended to concentrate investment
and reinforce their positions in high technology
industries in which the potential for growth is
considerable (45). Conversely, many older consumer
industries related to products such as foods and
textiles are still characterised by a generally dispersed pattern of ownership and control.

LIMITS TO CONCENTRATION

The formation of a series of large, multinational
groups has played an essential role in restoring and
enhancing the competitiveness of the country's
industrial base. However, size in itself does not
ensure a group's profitability and problems as well
as benefits have been associated with the growth of
very large companies. One of the major difficulties,
particularly where a group has expanded rapidly, has
been to rationalise effectively its operations;
often the diverse nature of the various activities
brought under common ownership has rendered this
task extremely complex (46). Furthermore, this problem has been exacerbated (especially in the
depressed economic climate of recent years), in
cases where a company that has been taken over is
already suffering from structural deficiencies or
financial weaknesses (47). Other complications have
arisen in establishing effective organisational and
administrative structure, not only due to the large

size and intricate nature of groups but also to the inheritance of ill-conceived or cumbersome systems of management.

Objections have also been raised over the desirability of certain aspects of the growing con- centration of industrial activity. Where it has resulted in an increasingly oligopolistic organisa- tion of an industry and the reduction of competi- tion, it is not necessarily beneficial to all interested parties. Certainly, where this leads to price fixing and market sharing it is not generally to the advantage of the consumer. Similarly, the large size of these groups bestows a particular significance upon their investment and locational strategies, yet these may not necessarily coincide with government or regional priorities; however, given the power of multinationals and their ability to switch investment between various countries it is often a difficult and delicate task to influence their decisions.

Large Companies: a Reappraisal?

A shift has also occurred in attitudes to large groups. While not denying the importance of their role within the economy, renewed recognition has been given to the contribution made by a host of medium sized firms (50-500 workers); together they account for over 30 per cent of employment in industry. Such firms are representative of all activities, but traditionally their presence has been most marked in industries such as clothing, leather goods, metal working and machine tools (48); frequently, they act as important suppliers or sub- contractors for larger companies. Although an extremely heterogeneous group of businesses which includes many firms of only marginal efficiency, the more dynamic companies display a number of merits. Often they possess the advantage of greater flexibi- lity enabling them to respond rapidly to changing product demands. Equally, they have proved an important source of innovation and experimentation, particularly in areas of advanced technology.

More generally, there is also an important regional dimension to support for this sector; given the predominance of such firms in many small urban and rural communities they often represent a vital means by which to help stabilise employment and population, in this case sometimes responding more to social than economic imperatives. Official policy has responded to the renewed interest in such companies and reflects an enhanced appreciation of the contribution made by the country's petites et moyennes entreprises (PME). More financial aid has been offered, notably through the increased availability of low-interest loans (49); equally, for many small centres the notion of supporting indigeneous firms and stimulating local initiative seems a more appropriate means by which to encourage the growth of employment than through decentralisation.

NOTES

1. This issue is discussed more fully in Gachelin, C., 'Crises et défis de l'industrie française', La Documentation Photographique, No.6056, (1981).
2. See Tuppen,J.N., France (Dawson, Folkestone, 1980), 15-20. An example of the country's paucity is given by the following production figures (million tonnes) for 1980:- coal 20.7; oil 1.4; iron ore 29.0; bauxite 1.9; potash 2.0; sulphur 1.8.
3. Only Japan, of the advanced industrial nations, imports a greater proportion of its requirements in primary energy.
4. Huet, M., 'Emploi et activité entre 1968 et 1975', Economie et Statistique, No.94 (1977), 59-76.
5. This excludes employment in building and public works which is dominated by male workers.
6. More details are given in Gachelin, 'Crises et défis'.
7. Stoffaës, C., 'Les talents industriels des Français', in Reynaud, J.D. and Grafmeyer, Y. (eds.), 'Français qui êtes-vous?', Notes et Etudes Documentaires, Nos. 4627-28 (1981), 157-74.
8. La France en Mai 1981: Les Activités Productives (La Documentation Française, Paris, 1982), 230.
9. Tuppen, France, 83-5.
10. La France en Mai 1981, 243-5.
11. See Tuppen, France, 94-5.
12. La France en Mai 1981, 243-8.
13. Ardagh, J., France in the 1980s (Penguin, Harmondsworth, 1982), 119.
14. The government has also taken a majority holding in three subsidiaries of foreign companies - ITT (electronics), CII - Honeywell-Bull (computers) and Roussel-Uclaf (pharmaceuticals).
15. Ardagh, France in the 1980s, 117-9.

16. For details of the earlier development of French industry see, for example, Clout, H.D., 'Industrial development in the eighteenth and nineteenth centuries' in Clout, H.D. (ed.), Themes in the Historical Geography of France (Academic Press, London, 1977), 447-82; Carré, J.J. et al., Abrégé de la Croissance Française (Seuil, Paris, 1973); Tuppen, France, 37-40.

17. Thompson, I.B., Modern France (Butterworths, London, 1970), 159.

18. Stoffaës, C., La Grande Menace Industrielle (Pluriel, Paris, 1980), 246.

19. Carré, Croissance Française, 31.

20. Stoffaës, Grande Menace, 201-2.

21. Roux-Vaillard, P., 'L'industrie', in Pagé, J.P. Profil Economique de la France (La Documentation Française, Paris, 1981), 190.

22. Roux-Vaillard, 'L'industrie', 193.

23. Dubois, P., 'La rupture en 1974', Economie et Statistique, No.124 (1980), 7.

24. Guibert, B. et al., 'La mutation industrielle de la France', Collections de l'INSEE, E31-32 (1975), vol.2, 41-8.

25. 'Les performances de l'économie française depuis 1955: une étude du Hudson Institute', Problèmes Economiques, No.1482 (1976), 3-6.

26. Hannoun, M., 'L'industrie française face au second choc pétrolier', Economie et Statistique, No.135 (1981), 59-63.

27. Stoffaës, Grande Menace, 34.

28. 'Redéploiement ou protectionnisme?', Les Cahiers Français, No.192 (1979).

29. See Marchand, O. and Revoil, J-P., 'Emploi et chômage: bilan fin 1980', Economie et Statistique, No.130 (1981), 23-44.

30. Stoffaës, C., 'L'industrie française prise en tenailles', in 'Redéploiement ou protectionnisme?' 6-8.

31. Gilly, J.P. and Morin, F., 'Les groupes industriels en France', Notes et Etudes Documentaires, Nos.4605-6 (1981), 5.

32. Brocard, R., 'Les entreprises françaises', Collections de l'INSEE, E64 (1979), 16.

33. For more details see Morvan, R., La Concentration de l'Industrie en France (Armand Colin, Paris, 1972), 252-3; Chevalier, J-M., L'Echiquier Industriel (Hachette, Paris, 1981), 140-1; Allard, P. et al., Dictionnaire des Groupes Industriels et Financiers en France (Seuil, Paris, 1978), 16-17.

34. Bellon, B., Le Pouvoir Financier et

l'Industrie en France (Seuil, Paris, 1980), 121-42.
        35. For a discussion of the notion of the term
group see Bellon, Le Pouvoir Financier, 25-57, and
Gilly and Morin, 'Les groupes industriels en France',
9-24.
        36. Morvan, La Concentration de l'Industrie en
France, 96.
        37. Gilly and Morin, 'Les groupes industriels
en France', 25-9.
        38. Stoffaës, Grande Menace, 266.
        39. BSN then became part of BSN-Gervais-Danone
(foods and drinks) and has now sold all its
interests in glass.
        40. DATAR Newsletter, No.26, 1981/2.
        41. The parent company is now Saint-Gobain.
        42. A more general view of companies' strate-
gies of diversification is given in Camus, B. and
Rousset, M., 'La polyvalence des entreprises',
Economie et Statistique, No.125 (1980), 3-14.
        43. Le Monde, 29 May 1980.
        44. Gilly and Morin, 'Les groupes industriels
en France', 39-52; Stoffaës, Grande Menace, 266.
        45. Gilly and Morin, 'Les groupes industriels
en France', 84.
        46. Stoffaës, 'Les talents industriels des
français', 169.
        47. A prime example is the takeover of
Chrysler's operations in Europe by Peugeot in 1978.
        48. Chevalier, L'Echiquier Industriel, 32.
        49. Le Monde, 24 Sept. and 9 Oct. 1981.

Chapter Six

THE LOCATION OF INDUSTRY: PATTERNS AND TRENDS

REGIONAL CONTRASTS IN THE EVOLUTION OF INDUSTRIAL
EMPLOYMENT SINCE 1954

By the mid-1950s little change had occurred in the
spatial distribution of industry since the early
part of the century (1). Industrial employment was
spread unequally throughout the country, concentrated above all in Paris and more generally in a
broad arc centred upon northern and eastern France,
extending from Haute-Normandie to Rhône-Alpes (2).
Within these areas the proportion of the active
population working in industry was noticeably higher
than in the rest of the country, particularly in
Nord-Pas-de-Calais and Lorraine where it accounted
for well over half the labour-force. However,
despite this zone's industrialised character, within
it there was still a marked lack of homogeneity in
the intensity and nature of industrial activity.
The four regions of Ile-de-France, Rhône-Alpes,
Nord-Pas-de-Calais and Lorraine alone housed more
than 51 per cent of the country's total employment
in industry, but even here areas of large-scale
manufacturing based upon modern plants were limited
in number and areal extent. Industrial activities
ranged from a bias towards energy, intermediate
goods (such as steel and chemicals) and textiles in
Nord-Pas-de-Calais, Lorraine and to a lesser degree
Rhône-Alpes, to a far greater emphasis upon the production of capital goods (for example, cars,
machines and electrical appliances) in Ile-de-France.
     In contrast, much of the remainder of the
country, particularly in western, central and
Mediterranean regions, was comparatively underindustrialised. There were exceptions, with the development of industry in urban centres such as Clermont-
Ferrand, Bordeaux and Nantes, and around the

Etang de Berre. However, much of the manufacturing
activity which existed outside of these areas was
orientated towards the production of consumer goods
in the textile, leather and wood industries. These
activities were relatively labour intensive, relied
little upon modern technology, featured a low rate
of growth and were generally dispersed amongst a
large number of small factories. Thus, not only was
industry frequently developed only to a limited
extent but also characterised by various structural
weaknesses.

Since the early 1950s the regional pattern of
industrial employment has been modified substantially, linked for an extended period to the regular
and sustained growth of manufacturing activity; this
provided greatest benefit for certain of those areas
previously lacking industry (3). Conversely, many
traditional regions of industrial activity, notably
within Ile-de-France and Nord-Pas-de-Calais,
experienced a decline of industrial employment.
More recently, with the worsening of the country's
economic problems, the upward trend in employment in
areas of previous growth has been reversed, leading
now to a general decrease in industrial jobs; in
regions which were already experiencing such a loss
the tendency has been accentuated.

The Growth and Redistribution of Industrial Employment

Although employment in industry increased throughout
most of the country until the mid-1970s, growth was
exceptionally strong in the two broad areas of the
Paris Basin and western France (Table 6.1). Already
by the end of the 1950s there was an established
trend towards a net increase of industrial jobs in
parts of the former zone, notably in the regions of
Centre and Picardie. Throughout the 1960s this
trend was accentuated, particularly in areas to the
south and west of the capital, and became equally
apparent in western France in the regions of
Bretagne, Pays de la Loire and Poitou-Charentes,
benefiting numerous towns such as Rennes, Lannion,
Cholet and Poitiers; whereas the rate of growth of
industrial employment nationally averaged 1.1 per
cent per annum between 1962 and 1968, within this
broad belt annual rates well in excess of 3 per cent
were recorded (4). Although the pace of expansion
tended to moderate between 1968 and 1975, it was
again in the above areas that rates were generally
highest.

The Location of Industry

Table 6.1: Employment Change in Industry

	Mean annual rate of increase			
	1954-62	1962-68	1968-75	1975-81
		(%)		
Paris Region				
Ile-de-France	+1.5	-0.1	-0.4	-2.2
Paris Basin				
Champagne-Ardenne	+1.0	+1.5	+0.9	-1.9
Picardie	+2.0	+2.1	+1.6	-1.7
Haute-Normandie	+1.4	+2.2	+1.8	-1.5
Centre	+2.0	+4.1	+2.4	-0.4
Basse-Normandie	+0.8	+3.7	+2.9	-0.2
Bourgogne	+1.5	+2.3	+1.5	-1.1
Northern France				
Nord-Pas-de-Calais	-0.4	-0.6	-0.2	-2.5
North-eastern France				
Lorraine	+0.3	-0.5	+0.3	-2.5
Alsace	+0.3	+0.4	+1.7	-0.4
Franche-Comté	+1.5	+1.8	+1.8	-1.4
Western France				
Pays de la Loire	+1.2	+3.4	+2.4	0.0
Bretagne	+0.5	+3.8	+2.0	-0.2
Poitou-Charentes	+1.4	+3.4	+2.0	-0.2
South-western France				
Aquitaine	+1.2	+1.9	+0.6	-0.8
Midi-Pyrénées	+1.2	+1.6	+0.7	-1.0
Limousin	+0.8	+1.8	+1.1	-0.4
Central-eastern France				
Rhône-Alpes	+1.7	+0.7	+0.9	-1.8
Auvergne	+1.0	+2.0	+1.0	-0.6
South-eastern France				
Languedoc-Roussillon	+1.6	+2.4	+0.1	-0.2
Provence-Alpes-Côte				
d'Azur (and Corse)	+2.4	+1.8	+1.2	-1.3
France	+1.5	+1.1	+0.8	-1.4

Source: Calculated from INSEE, _Recensements_ and _Emploi Salarié_.

Further evidence of the exceptional strength of this growth is given by spatial variations in the volume of increase of new employment. Thus, of the net gain of over 1 million jobs in manufacturing within France between 1954 and 1975, 40 per cent was located in the Paris Basin; similarly, over 30 per cent of the net rise in such employment between 1962 and 1975 (650,000 jobs) was accounted for by growth in the three western regions cited above (5). Nonetheless, despite the vigour of industrial expansion, in certain areas this failed to compensate for employment losses in other activities, notably agriculture. This was the case in Brittany and Poitou-Charentes and more generally throughout central and south-western regions of France. Nor was growth equally spread, even in the regions of strong increase (Figure 6.1); for example, some of the highest growth rates were in the areas on the southern and western periphery of the capital and in a ring of towns such as Dreux, Chartres and Orléans surrounding this zone (6). The extent to which the general expansion of industry has modified the employment structure is shown in Figure 6.2. It also demonstrates the still weak development of the secondary sector, even by 1975, in many parts of western, central and southern France, despite an

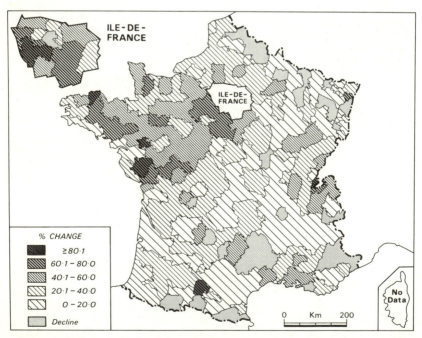

Figure 6.1: Regional Contrasts in the Growth of the Industrial Labour-Force, 1962-75

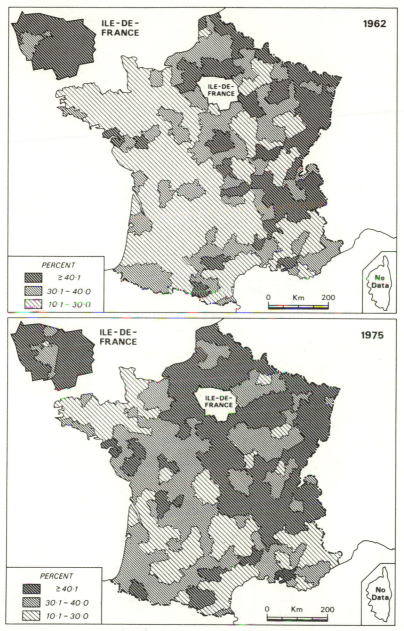

Figure 6.2: Regional Variations in the Proportion of the Active Population Working in the Secondary Sector

extended period of intense industrialisation.

The Recession and the Decline in Industrial Employment

Since the mid-1970s, the previous widespread
tendency for employment in industry to expand
rapidly has been radically reversed (Table 6.1).
However, prior to this period there were already
certain regions in which industrial jobs were
declining (Figure 6.1). For example, many of the
older centres of industry in Nord-Pas-de-Calais and
Lorraine were losing employment by the 1960s, while
since then this tendency has become progressively
stronger in certain parts of Ile-de-France, notably
the inner areas of the capital. With the onset of
the recession many of these traditional manufacturing areas have become characterised by a high
rate of decrease of employment, averaging more than
2 per cent per annum between 1975 and 1981 in the
three regions of Ile-de-France, Nord-Pas-de-Calais
and Lorraine: a similarly pronounced downward trend
is also evident in Rhône-Alpes. In each case there
has been a substantial fall in the number of workers
in industry (Table 6.2). At the same time, in the

Table 6.2: The Decline of Industrial Employment in
Selected Regions, 1975-81

Region	Net loss of wage-earners ('000)
Ile-de-France	218
Nord-Pas-de-Calais	94
Rhône-Alpes	89
Lorraine	59

Source: Calculated from INSEE, Emploi Salarié.

formerly dynamic regions of the Paris Basin and
western France industry has ceased to be a net
generator of employment. Moreover, it is within the
broad area of the capital's hinterland (particularly
in Haute-Normandie, Picardie and Champagne-Ardenne)
that the reversal of previous tendencies has been
most evident.

The Location of Industry

Employment Change and Differential Industrial Performance

Just as the nature of change in the level of
industrial employment has varied between regions of
the country, it has also differed between branches
of industry; equally, the same industry has not
always evolved in the same manner in all parts of
the country (7). Furthermore, the strong growth or
decline of industrial employment has often been
limited to a restricted range of activities.
Various examples illustrate these general themes.
During the latter 1950s and 1960s much of the apparent vitality of the secondary sector in southern
France was related to the rapid rise of employment
in the building and civil engineering industry,
reflecting the launching of a series of major
regional development projects and the strength of
urbanisation throughout much of this area; the majority of manufacturing industries expanded only
modestly. More recently, over the period 1968-75,
three groups of industries stood out as being most
significant in the generation of new jobs; of the
net increase in manufacturing employment, 80 per
cent related to the growth of the automobile, electrical engineering and electronics, and mechanical
engineering industries (8). It was the expansion of
these activities that represented a major component
in the very rapid growth of industry in many areas
of the Paris Basin and western France.
    Part of the more general process of industria-
lisation of these regions has been related to the
decentralisation of jobs or diversion of new employment away from the Paris region, although in the
case of the manufacture of cars and electronics and
electrical goods this did not lead, until recently,
to a net reduction of the labour-force of these
industries in the capital. Nonetheless, the government's policy towards industry contributed to the
overall decline of industrial employment which first
became apparent in Paris in the 1960s. Other forces
have contributed to this trend, related to the diseconomies of continued operation in a large urban
centre. Conversely, the decrease of jobs in Nord-
Pas-de-Calais, which dates from an earlier period,
was linked to the pronounced contraction of manpower
requirements in the coal, iron and steel and textile
industries, basic pillars of the region's industrial
economy; however, had it not been for the government's policy of decentralisation, it is likely that
the overall reduction of employment would have been
far more severe.

In many regions the reversal of trends since
the mid-1970s corresponds with a marked loss of
dynamism amongst these activities which had
previously created jobs at a high rate, such as the
vehicle, electrical and electronics and mechanical
engineering industries. At a national level these
branches now all exhibit a net loss of jobs, largely
reflecting the fall in demand for their products.
Inevitably, therefore, this has adversely affected
the more recently industrialised regions heavily
dependent upon such activities, notably in the
regions of the Paris Basin and western France such
as Centre, Basse-Normandie and Pays de la Loire
(Table 6.3). In addition, the ability of these

Table 6.3: Employment Change in Selected 'Growth'
Industries

Region	Vehicles		Electrical engineering and electronics		Mechanical engineering	
	1975	1981	1975	1981	1975	1981
			('000)*			
Haute-Normandie	26.5	28.4	30.4	25.7	20.2	17.8
Basse-Normandie	18.6	16.3	19.4	18.9	7.3	7.3
Centre	17.2	17.9	31.4	30.2	29.7	27.2
Bretagne	13.9	16.0	16.9	18.3	8.8	8.6
Pays de la Loire	21.5	21.2	30.6	31.7	25.2	22.0

*number of employees

Source: INSEE, Emploi Salarié.

industries to generate new jobs in the above areas
through decentralisation is now greatly diminished.
The repercussions of such decline have also been
felt in regions where these activities have been
located over a much longer period, such as the urban
centres of Lyon and Lille. Moreover, it is arguable
that in these areas the forces promoting decline are
likely to be greater: in regions of more recent
expansion, production and employment may have a
better chance of being maintained due to the newness
of plant and its greater efficiency and adaptability
(9).

The Location of Industry

An Assessment of Change
It is possible to relate varying regional trends in
the evolution of industrial employment to the contrasting mix of industries within different regions.
Thus, areas in which employment has been biased
towards activities with a declining demand for
labour such as textiles, inevitably, have tended to
perform less satisfactorily than those in which the
emphasis was upon industries such as electrical
engineering and electronics which have expanded
rapidly, significantly increasing their manpower
requirements. However, the industrial performance
of regions has also been strongly influenced by the
spatial redistribution of activities, a process
which in certain cases has produced a reverse tendency to the one outlined above (10). In the Paris
region, for example, jobs in industry have fallen
markedly over the last twenty years, despite the
existence in the 1950s of an employment structure
dominated by industries which at a national level
have shown a strong underlying tendency towards
growth over the greater part of the post-war period.
Much of this decline is related to the government's
relocation policies. Similarly, expansion well in
excess of that indicated by the industrial mix
twenty years ago in regions to the south-west of
Paris and in western France, is also largely
explained by the influx of decentralised activities.
Again, in northern France and Lorraine it is only
the arrival of such industries which has prevented
the much more severe decline of employment implied
by the region's traditional pattern of industrial
activity. Finally, in terms of general trends, the
growth of employment in certain regions has been
enhanced by the particular strong indigenous expansion of selected industries; food and drink industries, for example, have been especially dynamic in
much of western France, benefiting from the richness
of the area's agriculture (11).

Inevitably, broad areal generalisations need to
be viewed with some caution for they may conceal
various sub-regional contrasts in the pattern by
which employment has evolved. The region of Rhône-
Alpes, for example, now appears to have lost part of
its former vitality as an industrial centre (independently of the effects of the recession) (12);
this reflects the above average decline of many of
its staple industries (coal, heavy metallurgy,
textiles, and more recently heavy goods vehicles)
notably in the areas of St. Etienne and Lyon, a
tendency allied to the progressive

deindustrialisation of these two urban centres. Conversely, there are a number of smaller towns within the region, located in attractive natural environments and benefiting from good accessibility, such as Annecy, which have experienced a vigorous expansion of light industry.

Although industrial structures and growth rates still exhibit considerable variability at both regional and sub-regional scales, a further underlying consequence of change has been the reduction of contrasts between regions in terms of their range of industrial activities and the relative weight of employment in industry (Figure 6.3). The latter trend has derived largely from the declining role of the secondary sector in the country's older industrial regions, while both tendencies have been encouraged by the wider areal spread of industry throughout the country. In recent years, however, the combination of the adverse effects of the recession upon industrial employment and the dominance of the tertiary sector in the creation of new jobs has

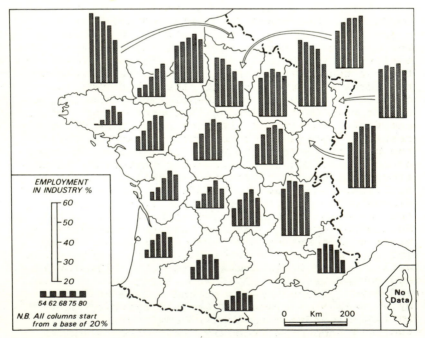

Figure 6.3: Changes in the Proportion of the Labour-force Working in Industry, 1954-80

resulted in a general reduction in the proportional
significance of industry within regional employment
structures (Figure 6.3).

Unquestionably major changes have occurred in
the distribution of industry throughout France.
Numerous industrial operations have spread to
'western' France, not least to parts of Brittany or
to cities such as Bordeaux and Toulouse where there
has been a pronounced expansion of advanced technology industries in the fields of electronics and, in
the two latter cases, aerospace. Nevertheless,
industrial activity is still spread unevenly
throughout the country and many of the more remote
areas of central and southern France still lack a
modern industrial base. The arc of nine regions in
northern and eastern France which housed two-thirds
of manufacturing employment in 1954, still accounted
for 60 per cent of the total in 1981. Similarly,
broad regional contrasts in the nature of industrial
activity persist, now represented increasingly by
differences in the nature of the manufacturing
process.

GOVERNMENT POLICY AND INDUSTRIAL LOCATION

The contrasting regional patterns of industrial
employment growth and the ensuing revised distribution of industry within France are the outcome of
the interplay of a series of locational forces,
certain of which have altered in their significance
over time. This reshaping of the areal pattern of
manufacturing activity has not been, however, the
result of entirely spontaneous processes. Just as
the government has sought to promote the development
of the industrial sector within the economy, according preferential treatment to various branches of
activity, it has also given an important regional
dimension to its strategy, aimed at the selective
spatial allocation of new employment in industry.
Such a policy has formed part of the government's
wider commitment to reduce regional inequalities in
job opportunities, incomes and living standards, as
well as to counteract high rates of employment loss
and unemployment in localities experiencing specific
and severe economic difficulties. The varied means
by which the government currently intervenes to
influence locational decisions have evolved from
the relatively modest initiatives first taken in
the 1950s; although there have been substantial
changes in the scale and orientation of policies,

restrictions on expansion in and around the capital,
coupled with financial inducements to develop in
disadvantaged, provincial areas of the country have
remained central to the government's strategy.
     The promotion of industrial expansion has
played a key role in regional planning. In part
this is a reflection of the sector's relatively
strong growth rate for much of the post-war period,
allied to its valuable local multiplier effect,
particularly through the creation of additional
employment opportunities, essentially in service
activities. Equally, the underindustrialised
character of extensive areas of the country,
patently evident in the 1950s, called for remedial
action, just as the more recent heavy job losses
from a variety of staple activities in the older
industrial regions, has prompted increased action to
remodel and diversify the pattern of activity.
Similarly, many predominantly rural areas still
exhibit a strong outflow of population which, if it
is to be eased, requires the generation of new jobs.
However, the deteriorating economic climate since
the mid-1970s, combined with the now general
decline in industrial jobs at a national level, has
greatly reduced the opportunities for manipulating
the distribution of industrial employment (13).

Constraints on Expansion and Aids to Industrial
Development
Despite the demonstration of a growing awareness of
regional inequalities within France, in the early
post-war years, the government's more immediate concern was re-establishing the country's manufacturing
base; it was not until the mid-1950s that the first
tentative steps towards an official regional planning strategy were taken, involving measures to
assist in the redistribution of industrial activity.
From 1955 the creation or extension of industrial
premises in Paris above an initial threshold of 500
square metres became dependent upon (and thus
limited by) the need to obtain government approval
through the granting of an agrément; conversely, a
limited number of heavy industrial zones in which
unemployment was high (such as St. Etienne, Alès and
Montceau-les-Mines where coal mining was already
showing signs of decline) became eligible for grants
to assist in the attraction of new firms. Since
then these provisions have been revised and extended.
In 1960, further control over expansion in the Paris
region resulted from the introduction of a

development tax (<u>redevance</u>), levied on new or
additional floorspace at a varying rate according to
the location of the project. However, from 1972 the
agrément was required only for developments above
1,500 square metres and since 1980 a more liberal
attitude has been adopted towards its granting (14),
reflecting in part the extent to which industry has
disappeared from the capital. The system of grants
and the areas to which they apply have been modified
on various occasions, most recently in 1982 (15).

Two main subventions are now payable, a
Regional Development Grant (<u>La Prime d'Aménagement
du Territoire</u>) and a Small Business Grant (<u>La Prime
Régionale à l'Emploi</u>). The former is a revised and
simplified form of the previous development grant
and also replaces the Special Industrial Adaptation
Fund (<u>Fonds Spécial d'Adaptation Industrielle</u>) (16)
introduced between 1978 and 1981. Sanction of the
grant depends upon agreement to a minimum size of
investment and the creation of a minimum number of
jobs over a period of three years: its value and the
total amount payable vary according to the nature of
the development area in which the project lies.
Areas now qualifying for maximum assistance are
situated predominantly in central and southern
France (including Corsica) as well as in parts of
western Brittany and in a discontinuous belt along
the country's northern and north-eastern fringes
(Figure 6.4). One major change is that within areas
qualifying for assistance large urban centres (above
100,000 inhabitants) have been excluded and will
only be granted aid in exceptional cases. The
rationale behind this decision is that, in general,
within development regions it is the larger cities
such as Bordeaux and Toulouse which have been most
successful in attracting industry; this has been to
the detriment of many smaller centres where the
disappearance of employment in traditional manufacturing activities has often had a much more severe
impact upon the job market. Hence, the desire now
to accord them greater priority.

In accordance with the Socialist's philosophy
of decentralisation, grants will be authorised by
the Regional Council (although funded by central
government) unless the project is particularly large,
in which case the decision will rest with the
Minister for Planning and Regional Development. The
Small Business Grant is a more flexible form of aid,
financed and accorded by the Regional Councils.
Certain general guidelines dictating its use are to
be laid down by the government, but each region is

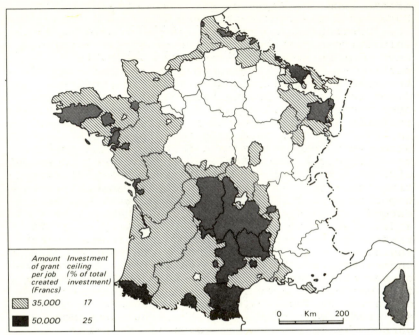

Figure 6.4: Government Grants and Assisted Areas for Industrial Operations, 1982

able to establish its own priorities for providing assistance. The subsidy cannot, however, be used to supplement the regional development grant.

Various additional incentives are available to industrialists, notably in the form of tax relief, which apply throughout the greater part of the country (excluding the central part of the Paris Basin). The principal measure is the total or partial exemption from the local business tax (taxe professionnelle) for a maximum of five years (17). Compared with the initial measures of regional aid, there is now a more comprehensive system of grants, covering a much wider area of the country; similarly, in the determination of an award greater significance is now attached to the level of employment to be generated rather than the size of the investment, and grants have become far more generous. Moreover, the ability of the government to finance industrial projects in development areas has been enhanced by funds deriving from a variety of sources funded by the Common Market, including conversion grants from the European Coal and Steel Community, development

grants from the Regional Fund and loans from the
European Investment Bank (18).
     There are also a number of other more varied
initiatives which have been launched. Governments
have shown a growing willingness to negotiate,
particularly with larger companies such as Renault,
the size and location of investment programmes.
Given the now far greater degree of state control
over such enterprises, and the socialist government's
reaffirming of its commitment to this approach, it
is likely to take on a more significant role; it
also gives the government a means by which to link
more closely its sectoral and regional strategies of
aid. The agrément, despite its seemingly restrictive character, has also been used as a basis for
negotiation. Companies agreeing to relocate or
extend at least part of their productive capacity in
a development zone have received more sympathetic
treatment of applications to expand within the Paris
region (19). Major companies have also shown a lead
themselves in attempting to facilitate the creation
of new firms and factories to take on their redun-
dant employees in areas in which they have reduced
operations. Such schemes were pioneered by the coal
and steel industries in the 1960s but have now been
pursued by various large groups such as Elf-
Aquitaine and Rhône-Poulenc, the latter having established a subsidiary firm, Sopran, to undertake such
activity (20). Commercial motives (for example, the
sale of equipment and factory space, or the attraction of a component supplier) partly explain such
action, as does the desire to protect or enhance the
corporate image of the firm; but it also reflects a
growing appreciation of the severe social and economic consequences upon communities which result from
the closure of major factories, as well as apppre-
hension over stricter legislation on redundancies
which might follow if no action were taken.

Other Measures to Encourage Industrial Development.
Restrictive controls and financial incentives form
only one aspect of government measures to influence
industrial location decisions (21). Various policies have sought to improve the industrial environment of regions, notably through the amelioration of
communication networks (22). Thus, the development
of motorways such as the A4 to eastern France and
more recently the A10 to south-western parts of the
country has been used as an instrument of regional
policy to help stimulate economic expansion in these

areas (23); the similar priority that was given to
upgrading the telephone system in such regions was
aimed at least in part at the same goal. Improved
accessibility, however, does not necessarily in
itself stimulate a wider dispersion of economic
activity; on the contrary it may encourage its
further polarisation.

Other strategies include the provision and
equipment of industrial estates, although their size
and quality are highly variable; they range from
small zones financed by local authorities or
Chambers of Commerce to extensive industrial sites,
underwritten by the government, created in areas
such as the ports of Dunkerque, St. Nazaire, Le
Havre and Fos (24). It is not only the amount and
differing forms of assistance to industry which are
instrumental in remodelling location patterns, but
also the effectiveness with which development programmes are planned, managed and co-ordinated.
Since 1963 this task has been largely entrusted to
DATAR (25).

The Consequences of Government Intervention
Assessment of the impact and effectiveness of
measures taken to influence the spatial distribution
of industrial activity is rendered difficult due to
the many varied forms of intervention by the government, the conflicting nature of certain of its
policies and a number of revisions to the objectives
of regional strategy since the mid-1950s (26).
Nonetheless, certain aims appear to have been accomplished successfully. Estimates suggest that since
the introduction of restrictions to dissuade industrialists from investing in the region of the
capital, decentralisation has resulted in the
creation of nearly 500,000 jobs in provincial France,
many of them by major companies such as Renault,
Citroën, Thomson and SNIAS (27). The extent to
which such moves have been directly attributable to
government policy is less easy to determine, particularly as the bulk of decentralisations occurred
during the 1960s, a period when industrial companies
generally were expanding rapidly and the lack of
adequate space for development at original locations
in Paris gave firms little option but to invest
elsewhere. Since the late 1960s, decentralisation
has eased greatly as the supply of industry susceptible to transfer has shrunk, a depressed economic
climate has curtailed investment and government
priorities have shifted, not least in response to

the heavy loss of manufacturing jobs from the
capital. Other, and at times, conflicting policies
have acted against decentralisation, illustrated by
the emphasis given to relocation within Ile-de-
France, favouring for example the region's new
towns. Certainly, however, decentralisation has
contributed greatly to a reduction of the degree to
which employment in a number of activities was formerly concentrated in the capital; in the early
1950s over 60 per cent of the labour-force of the
car industry was located in the Paris region but by
1981 this proportion had fallen to less than 30 per
cent. Overall, just over 20 per cent of the
country's industrial workers are now employed in
Ile-de-France compared with nearly 24 per cent in
1954. As industry has declined, however, remaining
activities have become more specialised, orientated
towards the manufacture of relatively sophisticated
products with a high value-added.
    While the shift of manufacturing activities
away from Paris may have helped decongest the
capital, the extent to which it has responded to the
government's objective of industrialising less
developed industrial regions is questionable. Thus,
in terms of actual transfers from the Paris region,
for example, around 45 per cent of related employment has been created within close proximity to the
capital, principally in the regions of Haute-
Normandie, Picardie, Champagne-Ardenne, Bourgogne
and Centre (28). Furthermore, in areas in which the
industrial base is declining, even when new industries are attracted, there is often an additional
shortcoming. Delay in the realisation of development projects is inevitable, leading to short-term
hardship or encouraging workers to attempt to seek
employment in other regions.
    Regional development grants and other financial
incentives have undoubtedly exerted an influence
upon the locations to which decentralised activities
have moved. Such inducements exist, however, to
attract any industrialist, irrespective of links
with decentralisation. There are again grounds for
suggesting that the government's aid programme has
been relatively successful. For example, between
1972 and 1980 over 6,500 projects were funded,
designed to create more than 360,000 jobs; moreover,
new employment has been concentrated in the priority
areas of western and south-western France and the
regions of Nord-Pas-de-Calais and Lorraine (Figure
6.5), although the strong emphasis placed upon
investment in these two latter zones dates only from

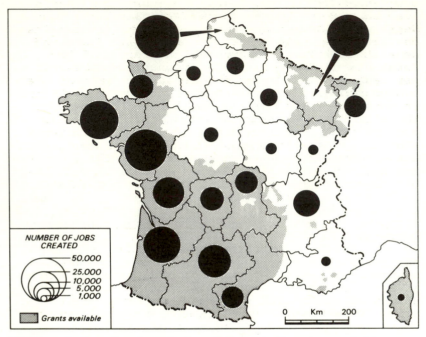

Figure 6.5: Regional Development Grants and the Creation of New Industrial Jobs, 1972-80

the latter 1960s. Regional totals are somewhat misleading, however, due to the varying areal extent of regions and the assisted areas within them, and the size of their work-forces. For example, despite the relatively modest total of jobs created in both Limousin and Auvergne, it might be argued that the impact has been much greater in the former due to the smaller size and weaker proportional signifi- cance of the secondary sector within this area (29). Few jobs have been created in southern regions of the country , perpetuating their underindustrialised character. In part this relates to the absence in certain areas of development grants, but it also suggests that while the government's aid programme has exerted some influence upon industrialists' choice of location, other factors have also played a role.

During its relatively short existence the more generous and flexible Special Industrial Adaptation Fund appears to have been particularly successful in orientating investment to areas affected by the acute decline of jobs in heavy industry. Over 123

projects have benefited from the fund, and should
lead to the creation of more than 20,300 new jobs.
Nearly 35 per cent are being generated in Nord-Pas-
de-Calais, notably by Peugeot at Valenciennes and
Renault at Douai. A further 33 per cent of the
total has been agreed in Lorraine, with around 11
per cent to result from development in each of the
two regions of Marseille-Toulon and the lower Loire;
in both cases aid has been accorded principally to
the electronics and microelectronics industries. In
view of its apparent success, it is perhaps surprising that the system should have been discontinued,
but more generous grants are now available under the
new and more uniform scheme of regional aid, in many
of the areas previously benefiting from the FSAI.

Regional Policy and Industrial Development: an
Overview
By the 1960s, in marked contrast to the early post-
war years, Paris ceased to expand as an industrial
centre. Instead growth became much more pronounced
in areas of provincial France, a trend which continued until the middle of the last decade (Table 6.4).
Since then the decline of industrial employment has
become generalised, although outside Paris the
average rate is considerably lower. Government
strategy has strongly influenced these trends;
arguably, without a regional policy, employment losses
in many provincial areas of northern and western
France would be much higher. However, other factors
have intervened, illustrated in the past by some of
the highest growth rates lying within regions adjacent to the capital in which no incentives for

Table 6.4: The Evolution of Industrial Employment:
Ile-de-France Compared with Provincial France

| | Mean annual rate of change | | | |
| | 1954-62 | 1962-68 | 1968-75 | 1975-81 |
		(%)		
Ile-de-France	1.5	-0.1	-0.4	-2.2
Provincial France	1.0	1.5	1.2	-1.2

Source: Calculated from INSEE, Recensements and
Emploi Salarié.

development have been available (30). Moreover,
certain general doubts have been expressed over the
efficiency and utility of the government's industrial location strategy. It has been suggested that
in relation to the scale of the problems the amount
of money allocated to regional policy has been
inadequate; certainly France has spent less than
other European countries, notably Britain (31),
but it has also been argued that such investment has
been more productive, reflected in a much lower unit
cost per job created (32). There is also evidence
that the initial employment and investment targets
set by firms have been generally met or exceeded, a
possible reflection of the government's policy of
reclaiming part of the grant if expectations are not
fulfilled (33). Furthermore, since the latter 1970s
spending on regional aid has risen substantially
(34).

More generally, the whole idea of selective
regional aids to industry has been questioned, related to the notion that their effectiveness is
limited (35). Not only are the potential benefits
restricted in value but also in time, with the
result that industrialists tend to give greater consideration to locational factors affecting the
longer term viability of the firm such as accessibility or the quality of the local industrial environment. Consequently, it has been argued that it
might be more advantageous to invest in improving
these features through, for example, the amelioration of the communication infrastructure, rather
than to pay development grants (36). Moreover, in a
period of recession and reduced investment it has
become more difficult to persuade industrialists to
locate in areas which are inherently unattractive
for manufacturing activity. The desirability of
such a strategy anyway, given the highly competitive
nature of the market for industrial products in
European and world markets, is also debatable (37).

FACTORS INFLUENCING INDUSTRIAL LOCATION

A General Review
Whatever the precise role of government incentives,
they still represent only one of a number of factors
likely to influence the industrialist's location
decision. Given the extent of expansion away from
Paris throughout much of the 1960s and early 1970s,
either through the transfer of manufacturing

activities or the need to expand capacity, a number
of studies have sought to determine the major
factors which have guided the selection of locations
(38). These suggest that decisions were strongly
conditioned by the availability of a work-force, the
essential feature being an adequate quantity of
labour rather than its level of skill or qualification. Secondary considerations related frequently
to the maintenance of close contact with the
company's head office (inferring the need to remain
relatively close to Paris) and to the quality of the
local industrial environment, particularly the cost
and availability of factory space located on an
equipped industrial estate. Conversely, much less
influence appears to have been exerted by factors
such as government grants or the presence of potential local sub-contractors.

Part of the explanation for the importance
attached to a reservoir of labour relates to the
major role played in the spatial diffusion of industry by activities such as the manufacture of cars,
machinery and electrical appliances; all were industries which had heavy manpower requirements at a
time when there was a general shortage or strong
competition for labour in many traditional manufacturing centres (39). It is also linked to manufacturing techniques. Thus, the greater the extent to
which the production process is standardised and
repetitive, and reliant upon well-proven technology
and a relatively unskilled work-force, the greater
tends to be the degree of locational freedom:
assembly operations in the car and domestic appliances industries illustrate these characteristics.

Therefore, many of the predominantly rural
areas of the Paris Basin and western France, with
the release of a large surplus of labour from agriculture, were potentially very attractive for the
location of these types of industries, despite the
general absence of technical skills (40). Furthermore, in certain areas there were originally the
additional attractions of paying lower wage rates
than in the Paris region, and of a work-force with
little tradition of union membership or militancy.
One constraint, however, was often the desire to
seek a location close to the capital. Nonetheless,
the interaction of these factors is seen in the
strong growth of industrial employment in the
departments adjacent to the capital throughout much
of the 1960s and early 1970s, a trend which adds
support to the contention that government aids have
acted in a comparatively minor way to influence the

selection of locations. Maintaining easy
accessibility with the Paris region was not always
related only to facilitating exchanges between
mother and branch plants; it might also be desirable
to enable continued contact with sub-contractors and
suppliers, relatively few of which appear to have
decentralised their activities in response to a
similar move by the companies they serve (41); a
centralised location permits these firms to continue
working for a range of customers, a possibility
frequently not easily available with movement away
from the capital. The persistence of such links
helps explain the generally weak integration of many
decentralised firms into the local industrial
environment, although this may also relate to the
production strategy adopted by the firm.

Such generalisation inevitably masks many contrasting situations. The relocation of the steel
industry in favour of the coastal sites of Dunkerque
and Fos, for example, was strongly determined by
accessibility to raw materials, while even in the
search for labour in areas such as the Paris Basin,
manufacturers of relatively sophisticated industrial
products such as machine tools have given greater
consideration to the qualitative rather than quantitative aspects of the available labour-force (42).
Thus, depending on the nature of the industrial
process a reordering of locational priorities may
occur. However, locational decisions rarely rely
solely upon economic justification. Political considerations are often significant, particularly in
the explanation of otherwise unusual choices, such
as the decision by Ford to invest on the outskirts
of Bordeaux and the development of the electronics
industry at Lannion in Brittany. Moreover, where
the government controls a company it is obviously in
a position to influence its locational policy as is
suggested by Renault's commitment to investment in
the regions of Nord-Pas-de-Calais and Lorraine.

Industrial Location and the Firm
The size, pattern of organisation and the business
strategy of a firm may all influence the policy it
pursues relative to the location of its constituent
plants. While companies' locational decisions
generally have an underlying economic logic, often
this needs to be viewed in the context of a firm's
spatial field of operations rather than within a
regional or national operating framework. This may
be particularly important for those large industrial

groups where a significant porportion of linkages
are internalised.

Generalisation concerning the distribution of
firms' factories and the areal expansion policies
which they have pursued is difficult, partly due to
a lack of relevant empirical studies. Certain
trends, however, are discernible. For example, the
wider the range of a company's manufacturing activities, the greater is the tendency for its plants to
be dispersed over an extensive area, particularly if
there is a strong emphasis towards the production of
a variety of finished goods rather than intermediate
products (43). This tendency has frequently been
reinforced where concentration has resulted in the
formation of large conglomerates such as Saint
Gobain. Spatial development strategies may be
influenced by the manner in which the firm has
evolved. Companies which have grown largely internally (i.e. through the creation of additional
branch plants) have often sought to widen their
spatial field of operations. Conversely, for those
firms which have expanded through merger, the resulting need to rationalise production facilities and
close factories may lead to greater spatial concentration (44). As companies have grown in size and
the volume of their production has increased, there
has also been a tendency for the manufacturing
activities of individual plants to become far more
highly specialised, frequently leading to concentration upon a single product or limited range of items,
with the higher distribution costs which may result
more than offset by the increased scale-economies
realised by each factory. This process has
generally been accompanied by a reduction in the
required labour skills, facilitating the recruitment
of workers and leading, in relation to location,
towards a bias in favour of those areas of plentiful
supply (45).

The simplification of manufacturing processes
and the search for a labour-force that is readily
available and cheap to employ have encouraged an
increasing number of firms to invest outside France
in low cost areas such as south-east Asia, contributing to the more generally emerging processes of the
delocation of industrial activity and the deindustrialisation of the country. Other factors, however,
such as market penetration influence firms to base
part of their production in other countries and,
just as this has led to French firms locating abroad,
it has also encouraged many foreign multinational
companies to invest in France. Their location

policies appear to have been guided in part by the
desire to minimise risks, with a bias apparent in
favour of large urban centres such as Paris or Lyon,
or in border regions giving greatest proximity to
the parent company (46). Thus, a high proportion of
German investment is located in Alsace and Lorraine,
although in the past the presence of a relatively
abundant and cheap labour-force (by German standards) has often enhanced the attraction of such a
location.

Since the onset of the recession many companies'
location strategies have been guided not by the need
for expanion, but by the necessity to reduce output
and rationalise production facilities. Where the
closure of plants has resulted, frequently this has
been at the expense of older and less efficient
units, many of which inevitably are located in
traditional industrial centres. In the steel industry, for example, Usinor has reduced its operations
in areas in which the industry was originally
focused in northern France, such as Denain and
Valenciennes, to the benefit of the coastal works at
Dunkerque; similarly, Sacilor has closed plants in
Lorraine and reorientated more of its activities
towards Fos. Despite the overall decline of industrial employment and an economic climate unconducive
to large-scale investment, many activities are still
expanding, leading to the construction of new
factories. In such circumstances, however, there is
some evidence of greater selectivity in the choice
of location, with an avoidance of those areas, such
as small rural centres, where the risks are potentially greater (47).

While there has been a general tendency
throughout much of the post-war period towards the
wider distribution of many manufacturing activities,
a similar trend has not been evident in relation to
the decision-making, research and strategic functions of firms. On the contrary, these activities
have remained highly concentrated, polarised upon a
limited number of urban centres, above all Paris
(48). Moreover, as industry grew rapidly and
factories became more dispersed, the centralisation
of control was reinforced. Thus, somewhat paradoxically, decentralisation and the general movement
towards industrial location in provincial centres
has led to the increased dependency of these areas
upon Paris, emphasising the extent to which major
firms have sought to separate, spatially, decision-
making and manufacturing functions. In many cases
the enlargement of companies through mergers and

takeovers has contributed significantly to the
concentration of head offices and related functions
in the Paris region.
    Highly trained and qualified employees and
highly skilled workers remain strongly concentrated
in Paris and, to a lesser degree, other major
cities. As a result two trends are apparent in the
employment profiles of industries based in the
capital: the relatively small proportion of production workers and amongst this group, the predominance of skilled labour (49). Conversely, the
creation of new employment in provincial areas has
been linked largely to semi or unskilled jobs,
frequently depressing the general level of qualification of a region's labour-force (50). Both
features are illustrated by regional contrasts in
the pattern of employment in the electrical and
electronic industries. In the Paris region the proportion of semi-skilled workers represents only
around 13 per cent of the total labour-force, whereas in areas of the Paris Basin and western France
such as Basse-Normandie, Bourgogne and Pays de la
Loire (where expansion in the 1960s and early 1970s
was exceptionally rapid) it is approximately 50 per
cent. Thus, decentralisation and the government's
industrial policies have contributed towards a more
equitable spatial distribution of industrial jobs
within France, but this has been accompanied by the
maintenance and even reinforcement of marked
regional inequalities in the character of
employment.

NOTES

    1. For a discussion of earlier changes in the
distribution of industry see Pinchemel, P., La
France (Armand Colin, Paris, 1981), vol.2, 112-14.
    2. Tuppen, J.N., France (Dawson, Folkestone,
1980), 52-4. The regions included in this zone are
Haute-Normandie, Picardie, Nord-Pas-de-Calais,
Champagne-Ardenne, Lorraine, Alsace, Franche-Comté,
Rhône-Alpes and Ile-de-France.
    3. Mary, S. and Turpin, E., 'Panorama
économique des régions françaises', Collections de
l'INSEE, R42-3 (1981), 101.
    4. It should be remembered that strong growth
was a feature of other parts of the country,
although not over such a continuous area. Towns
such as Melun and Meaux on the eastern outskirts of
Paris, Reims, Châlons-sur-Marne and Dijon in the

eastern Paris Basin and Bourg-en-Bresse, Annecy,
Avignon and Montpellier in the central eastern and
southern parts of the country were all characterised
by a high rate of increase of employment in industry.
    5. Mary and Turpin, 'Panorama économique',
101-4. For a more detailed discussion of the evolution of employment in industry in the various French
regions see also Battiau, M., 'Quelques remarques
sur l'évolution de la répartition géographique des
emplois industriels en France entre 1954 et 1975',
L'Information Géographique, 42 (1978), 170-88.
    6. In addition, a significant proportion of
the new jobs created were often related to the
development of a relatively limited number of large
plants in a restricted number of locations.
    7. For example, the slowing in the growth
rate and then decline of employment in the car
industry in Ile-de-France during the 1960s and 1970s
contrasts with its expansion in regions such as
Nord-Pas-de-Calais, Lorraine and Haute-Normandie.
    8. Mary and Turpin, 'Panorama économique',
105.
    9. Turpin, E., 'Disparités régionales,
croissance et crise', Economie et Statistique,
No.133 (1981), 96.
    10. See Turpin, 'Disparités régionales', 93-6
and Mary and Turpin, 'Panorama économique", 127-9.
    11. Battiau, 'Evolution des emplois
industriels en France', 181.
    12. See Mary and Turpin, 'Panorama économique',
127-9 and Carrère, P. et al., 'Evolution de la
situation économique des régions françaises de 1972
à 1977', Economie et Statistique, No.100 (1978), 39-
50.
    13. For more details of regional strategy see,
for example, Monod, J. and de Castelbajac, Ph.,
L'Aménagement du Territoire (Presses Universitaires
de France, Paris, 1978), 21-9; Durand, P., Industrie
et Régions (La Documentation Française, Paris, 1974),
13-29; Beaujeu-Garnier, J., 'Toward a new equilibrium in France', Annals of the Association of
American Geographers, 64 (1974), 113-18; Tuppen,
France, 85-9.
    14. Perrin, N., 'L'aménagement du territoire
et le développement régional', in Pagé, J., Profil
Economique de la France (La Documentation Française,
Paris, 1981), 420.
    15. For details of earlier changes and the
previous system of grants see Durand, Industrie et
Régions, 61-5; Hull, C., 'Regional incentives in
France', in Yuill, D. et al., (eds.), Regional

Policy in the European Community (Croom Helm, London, 1980), 57-77.

16. Details are given in Yuill, D. and Allen, K. (eds.), European Regional Incentives (Centre for the Study of Public Policy, University of Strathclyde, 1981), 184-92.

17. See Hull, 'Regional incentives in France', 71-7, and Yuill and Allen, European Regional Incentives, 173-83.

18. Madiot, Y., L'Aménagement du Territoire (Masson, Paris, 1979), 29-42.

19. Ferniot, B., La Décentralisation Industrielle (IAURIF, Paris, 1976), 15-16.

20. DATAR Newsletter, No.23 (1980), 10-12.

21. For more detail see Tuppen, France, 95-7, or Merlin, P., 'Aménagement du territoire et localisation des activités en France', Tijdschrift voor Economische en Sociale Geografie, 65 (1974), 372-3.

22. The government has established, for example, special programmes to improve roads in Brittany and the Massif Central.

23. Tuppen, J.N. 'Road of the toll', The Geographical Magazine, 49 (1977), 483-6.

24. For a more detailed discussion see Tuppen, France, 95-6; for more details of the planning of Fos, see Tuppen, J.N., 'Fos - Europort of the south?', Geography, 60 (1975), 213-17.

25. Its role is discussed more fully in Durand, Industrie et Régions, 43-4 and Chardonnet, J., L'Economie Française (Dalloz, Paris, 1976), vol.3, 309-15.

26. Madiot, L'Aménagement du Territoire, 227; Tuppen, France, 106.

27. Although decentralisation is usually associated with movement from Paris or the expansion in provincial areas of firms based in the capital, it is also a feature of industrial growth generated from other centres within France. The scale is limited but examples include the spread of Renault's commercial vehicles group (RVI) away from Lyon to smaller, surrounding centres and the dissemination of Michelin factories from Clermont-Ferrand to localities such as Bourges, Orléans and Cholet.

28. 'Un bilan de la décentralisation industrielle', Problèmes Economiques, No.1747 (1981), 6-7. See also Aydalot, P., L'aménagement du territoire: une tentative de bilan', L'Espace Géographique, 7 (1978), 246; Ferniot, La Décentralisation Industrielle, 19; Chardonnet, L'Economie Française, 376-7; Merlin, 'Aménagement du

territoire', 375-6; Durand, Industrie et Régions, 106-8.
   9. It should also be noted that only limited areas of Nord-Pas-de-Calais and Lorraine qualify for aid, unlike western regions. Major urban centres such as Lille, Dunkerque, Metz and Nancy have always been excluded from areas qualifying for grants.
   30. Tuppen, France, 103-5.
   31. Monod and Castelbajac, L'Aménagement du Territoire, 117-18. Chardonnet, L'Economie Française, 385-8.
   32. Perrin, 'L'aménagement du territoire', 428.
   33. Hull, 'Regional incentives in France', 80.
   34. La France en Mai 1981: Les Activités Productives (La Documentation Française, Paris, 1982), 245.
   35. Madiot, L'Aménagement du Territoire, 227-9.
   36. Pinchemel, La France, 134.
   37. Thompson, I.B., 'Regional planning strategies in France', in Drury, P.J. (ed.), Regional and Rural Development: Essays in Theory and Practice (Alpha Academic Books, Chalfont St. Giles, 1976), 116.
   38. See for example, Hannoun, M. and Templé, P., 'Les facteurs de création et de localisation des nouvelles unités de production', Economie et Statistique, No.68 (1975), 59-70; Ferniot, La Décentralisation Industrielle, 45-51. Hannoun and Templé also stress the importance of the inadequacy of existing premises as a primary motive encouraging firms to look for an alternative location.
   39. A more detailed study of the influence of labour supply is given in Aydalot, P., 'Le rôle du travail dans les nouvelles stratégies de localisation', Revue d'Economie Régionale et Urbaine, No.2 (1979), 174-89.
   40. Certain areas of northern France offered a similar attraction as staple industries shed labour on a large scale.
   41. Bakis, H., 'La sous-traitance dans l'industrie', Annales de Géographie, 84 (1975), 308-11.
   42. Turpin, 'Disparités régionales', 82-3.
   43. Bellon, B., Le Pouvoir Financier et l'Industrie en France (Seuil, Paris, 1980), 48. The two operations may be subsumed within the same firm of course.
   44. Fischer, A., 'Eléments pour une étude des effets spatiaux des concentrations industrielles',

Annales de Géographie, 87 (1978), 302-3. The former situation might be illustrated by the growth strategies of Renault and Michelin, while the latter position is demonstrated by the evolution of the textile operations of Rhône-Poulenc.

45. Aydalot, 'L'aménagement du territoire en France', 249.

46. Hernandez, C. et al., 'La pénétration étrangère dans l'industrie française', Economie et Statistique, No.72 (1975), 3-23.

47. Bachelard, P., 'Décentralisations industrielles et résistance à la crise', Bulletin de l'Association des Géographes Français, No.460 (1979), 151-6.

48. This issue is discussed in Laferrère, M., 'Géographie du pouvoir de décision dans l'industrie lyonnaise', Revue de Géographie de Lyon, 54 (1979), 329; Fischer, 'Eléments pour une étude', 303; Aydalot, 'L'aménagement du territoire en France', 249-52.

49. Valeyre, A., 'Emplois et régions; la polarisation de l'emploi dans l'espace français', in 'Activités et Régions', Travaux et Recherches de Prospective, No.75 (1978), 37.

50. Aydalot, 'L'aménagement du territoire en France', 247-8. See also Estienne, P., La France (Masson, Paris, 1978), vol.1, 94.

Chapter Seven

MAJOR BRANCHES OF FRENCH INDUSTRY

A CONTRASTING PATTERN OF EVOLUTION

Within the industrial sector the contribution of
different branches of activity to total employment,
to the overall value or volume of production and to
the level of exports varies considerably. Equally,
in all these areas individual industries have frequently evolved in a contrasting manner, reflecting
the influence of factors such as a changing pattern
of demand for their products, an increase in competition from other manufacturing countries or the
impact of new technology. Over the post-war period,
these divergent trends have led to a pronounced
modification of the country's industrial structure,
underlined by increasing emphasis upon the manufacture of capital goods to the detriment of consumption and more recently intermediate goods (1). For
the period since 1968 these trends are illustrated
by changes in the level of employment in different
branches of activity indicated in Table 7.1.
        Throughout the 1950s the demands of the recon-
struction programme and the priority accorded to the
industrialisation of the French economy stimulated
the development of industries such as heavy
metallurgy, construction materials and chemicals
(intermediate goods). During the following decade,
the strength of industrial growth contributed to the
greater emphasis upon an extensive range of capital
goods (machines, electronics and vehicles). Conversely, there was little evidence of such vigorous
growth in production or employment in many industries manufacturing consumer products including
textiles, leather articles and clothing. Thus, by
the early 1970s output and employment in the manufacture of intermediate and capital goods was rising
significantly, but there was already a marked trend

Major Branches of French Industry

Table 7.1: Employment in Major Branches of
Industry, 1968-81

	Number of wage-earners ('000)				
	1968	1971	1974	1977	1981
Iron and steel	220	217	223	222	165
Non-ferrous metals	66	64	68	67	79
Construction materials	213	218	216	203	188
Glass	63	66	75	73	67
Chemicals, synthetic fibres	174	185	197	188	177
Foundry and metal working	454	487	536	515	485
Paper, packaging	128	135	144	138	122
Rubber, plastics	168	188	227	226	220
Intermediate goods	1,486	1,563	1,686	1,632	1,503
Mechanical engineering	501	538	592	569	535
Electrical engineering, electronics	428	474	579	578	555
Vehicles	365	417	519	534	503
Aerospace, arms, shipbuilding	212	218	232	236	225
Equipment goods	1,506	1,647	1,922	1,917	1,808
Parachemicals, pharmaceuticals	133	144	160	161	161
Textiles, clothing	730	729	690	612	514
Leather, shoes	143	141	133	121	109
Wood, furniture	312	324	358	340	323
Printing	192	202	219	207	207
Food and drink	491	500	510	505	509
Consumption goods	2,001	1,040	2,070	1,946	1,823

Source: INSEE, Emploi Salarié.

towards a diminished role within the economy for the
group of consumption goods industries.
    Since then, many producers of intermediate
goods have experienced a trend towards a fall not
only in jobs and output but also in investment and
productivity, the latter feature reflecting the considerable extent of spare capacity in many plants
(2). In the manufacture of equipment goods, even in

traditionally expanding branches such as electrical products and electronics, labour requirements have been cut, although production and investment have been less badly hit, partly through an increase in exports; recently, however, this tendency has also moderated as world demand has eased and competition intensified. The continued decline of the sector of consumption goods is largely a reflection of the difficulties of the textile and leather industries. However, the inclusion of parachemical and pharmaceutical industries within this broad category, a particularly dynamic sector of manufacturing, has the effect of moderating these tendencies. It also illustrates the problems of generalisation, for within each of the three groupings used above, there have been divergent trends both between and even within different branches of production (3).

Expanding or contracting industries are generally differentiated by features other than contrasts in the evolution of production and employment (4). Activities in decline are frequently characterised by the absence of adequate investment, reflected in the unsuitable and outdated nature of buildings and machinery, and the non-adaption of output to market demands. It is not uncommon to find these traits linked to a progressively ageing work-force and an inefficient management structure, while they also invariably give rise to low wages. For those industries featuring an underlying trend towards growth, a very different set of features applies. Frequently their development and operation require high capital inputs, more advanced technology is employed, the labour-force has a more youthful age-structure and is generally better qualified, and the level of remuneration is significantly higher. It is not difficult to associate these contrasting sets of structural and operational conditions with various branches of activity, represented in the first instance by part of the textile industry and in the latter case by the electronics, nuclear or aerospace industries. While a reasonable generalisation, this labelling may also be misrepresentative for even within individual industries operating conditions may vary greatly between firms; just as there are modern and highly efficient garment manufacturing plants there are also small, undercapitalised and unproductive engineering works.

MAJOR BRANCHES OF INDUSTRIAL ACTIVITY: A GENERAL
REVIEW

Intermediate Goods

For the greater part, this group comprises a series
of long-established industries which have frequently
strongly marked the urban and industrial landscapes
of the regions in which they are located, not least
due to the generally large and intrusive character
of the associated productive installations. Partly
in view of the considerable age of many of these
plants, added to the erosion or disappearance of the
initial advantage leading to their location in a
particular area, many of these activities have been
linked in recent years with important programmes of
restructuring and, in certain cases, (notably steel),
relocation. This tendency has been reinforced by
the recession and the associated stabilisation or
decline of home demand for many products. Consequently, output has been reduced, but there are also
longer-term factors encouraging this trend as a
number of major producers have sought to increase
their competitiveness by shifting at least part of
their manufacturing activities to areas outside
France where production costs are lower. Employment
within this group (Table 7.1) is concentrated
particularly amongst those activities linked to the
production of metals and chemicals (including the
manufacturing of rubber and plastics).

Metal Industries.

In contrast to the importance of
the iron and steel industries, the production of
non-ferrous metals within France is of much reduced
significance. Aluminium is the only metal produced
in quantity, yet annual output is now less than
400,000 tonnes. Unlike the traditional locations of
the steel industry in northern and north-eastern
France, aluminium production is centred upon south-
eastern and south-western regions, a distribution
related in part, at least originally, to the availability of raw materials and relatively cheap but
abundant supplies of electricity (5). As with the
steel industry, the organisation of the activity is
heavily concentrated, dominated by the group of
Pechiney-Ugine-Kuhlmann, although 60 per cent of the
company's production of aluminium originates from
outside France. In recent years PUK's French operations have become more difficult, in part due to the
fall in world demand but also due to the problem of

the now high cost of energy. This may represent up
to 25 per cent of the total cost of the final
product and consequently one of the company's locational strategies has been to base its activities on
plants in areas where it is able to benefit from
relatively low energy costs (6).

An extensive array of foundry and heavy metallurgical industries depends upon the basic producers
of ferrous and non-ferrous metals, manufacturing an
equally broad range of products including tubes,
wire, girders, boilers and a variety of castings.
Generally, their distribution is also far wider,
although there is not unnaturally still a strong
link with metal manufacturing regions and large
industrial (and thus market) centres (Figure 7.1).
Ownership of the industry is mostly weakly concentrated (7), with the principal exception of the
activities of basic transformation. This branch is
stongly linked to a limited number of large
companies, often subsidiaries of major groups such
as Usinor, Creusot-Loire, Sacilor, and PUK:
Vallourec, for example, a large manufacturer of steel
pipes, is part of Usinor, with production facilities
frequently directly linked to the group's centres of
steel production, as at Dunkerque. Rationalisation
and regrouping of companies, as well as the modernisation of equipment, have also been central to the
recent evolution of these industries. However, one
activity in particular, boiler-making, has been
given a special stimulus through the increasing
emphasis over the last decade upon nuclear energy.

Paper. France produces about 40 per cent of her
requirements in paper, a relatively high proportion
compared with neighbouring countries such an Britain
and West Germany; but, overall, the French paper and
packaging industry remains small and fragmented,
spread throughout a number of regions and between a
variety of manufacturers. The industry's dispersed
character has contributed to its problems of adjustment over recent years. Many of the activity's
difficulties are similar to those affecting the
steel industry. Falling demand and sales in a
highly competitive market have led to a reduction in
output and revenue, leaving considerable excess
capacity. Yet, operating at below optimum conditions only exacerbates the problem of repaying loans
contracted to finance previous investment. The
situation is further complicated by the continuing
need to modernise equipment to raise productivity,

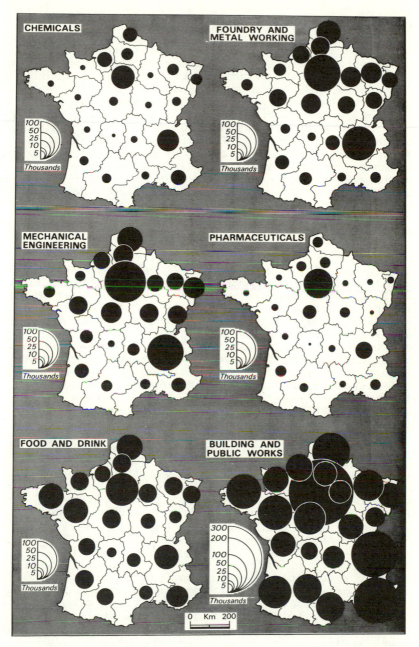

Figure 7.1: Regional Distributions of Employment in Selected Industries, 1981

reduce operating costs and to increase the
industry's competitiveness. Some progress towards
these objectives has been achieved since the launching of a government restructuring plan in the
latter part of 1977, but resulting investment and
rationalisation appear inadequate. This was con-
firmed by the bankruptcy of Chapelle-Darblay, one of
the country's major paper manufacturers, the company
only being able to continue operating through the
injection of government funds. The inevitable
redundancies have aggravated the problem of
unemployment in the region of Rouen (8), not only
one of the major centres of the French paper industry, but also of a number of other heavy industries
experiencing similar difficulties. Continuing
problems of uncompetitiveness led to further proposals for reorganisation in 1982.

Chemicals. The French chemical industry, while
unable to rival the strength of the activity in West
Germany, has grown very substantially over the post-
war period, boosted particularly in the 1960s and
early 1970s by the rapid expansion of petrochemicals. More recently, the downturn in the world
economy, intensified competition and the substantial
rise in the cost of raw materials, have checked the
industry's former dynamism and produced substantial
over-capacity, notably in petrochemicals and synthetic fibres (9).
     While the industry is characterised by the
extensive range of its output, it is also an activity which has become increasingly concentrated
under the control of a restricted number of major
groups (10). The petrochemical sector is dominated
by the subsidiaries of the major oil companies such
as ATO Chimie and Shell Chimie; in the field of
organic chemicals PUK, through its subsidiary
Produits Chimiques Ugine Kuhlmann, Rhône-Poulenc and
CdF Chimie play major roles. In related activities,
Michelin is particularly dominant in the rubber
industry and Rhône-Poulenc in the manufacture of
synthetic textile fibres. Recent nationalisations
have increased considerably the state's control of
the industry, although at the same time the level of
foreign investment in the manufacture of chemicals
has long been relatively high, partly reflecting the
role played by the major oil companies and their
subsidiaries.
     Geographically, the manufacture of basic and
intermediate chemical products is concentrated

predominantly within a limited number of major
production regions, each portraying certain specialisations, but none displaying an entirely comprehensive range of output (Figure 7.1). In Nord-Pas-de-
Calais the early importance of textile manufacturing,
allied to the region's coal resources, were significant influences in the initial development of the
chemical industry. Subsequently, the activity has
been enlarged and diversified, covering the manufacture of both organic and inorganic products. Most
recently the region's production has been further
widened by the launching of a petrochemical industry
based upon the Copénor steam-cracking plant at
Dunkerque which has entailed a shift in location
away from the traditional centres of the Lille
conurbation and the coalfield (e.g. Lens and
Mazingarbe). A certain similarity in production
trends is discernible in Lorraine, with the original
development of a coal-based chemical industry in
centres such as Carling and Marienau, to which was
added more recently a petrochemical component (11).
The region also has a long history of manufacuturing
inorganic chemicals, based on the salt deposits in
southern Lorraine, which have given rise to a series
of production centres, notably at Saaralbe and
Dombasle.
    With the concentration of the greater part of
the country's oil refining capacity in the lower
Seine valley and around the Etang de Berre and Fos,
it is logical that these two areas should have
developed as major production centres of petrochemicals, in both cases supplying industries manufacturing products such as plastics, solvents, detergents
and synthetic rubber. In the Basse-Seine the
industry developed initially in association with the
region's textile manufacturing activities, but has
become increasingly dominated by the production of
fertilisers, reflecting Rouen's rich agricultural
hinterland and its port facilities enabling the
import of raw materials. Finally, Rhône-Alpes also
houses a large and diversified chemical industry,
focused principally upon Lyon (where it was again
originally linked to the textile industry) but also
embracing various other centres, notably Grenoble.
The industry greatly expanded with the production of
petrochemicals following the opening of the Elf oil
refinery at Feyzin in 1964 and, four years later, of
its steam cracking facilities. This is also a
region dominated by the activities of Rhône-Poulenc,
but one that has also suffered from the company's
problems and plant closures related to the

manufacture of artificial fibres.

Equipment Goods

The pronounced expansion of this group of industries
has represented a dominant feature of the post-war
industrialisation of the French economy. Growth
within this sector proved particularly vigorous
throughout the 1960s and early 1970s, demonstrated
by a substantial increase in output and employment
and especially productivity. Such buoyancy corresponded with a period of intense investment and re-
equipment within industry. Since the mid-1970s, the
previously remarkable performance of these industries has been moderated, reflective of a reduction
in demand and indicated by the fall of employment
within all the major branches of this group (Table
7.1). Relatively, however, this remains one of the
most dynamic sectors of French industry, although as
the recession has deepened various structural weaknesses have been highlighted. Certain activities
such as the manufacture of agricultural machinery,
machine tools and domestic applicances are not
strongly developed, or are comparatively uncompeti-
tive by international standards; frequently this
results in a high level of imports. Overall, with
the exception of the sales of transport equipment,
more than half the demand for capital goods is now
met by imports. A number of branches are also
weakly concentrated, and while larger companies are
not necessarily synonymous with greater efficiency,
they at least generally have the resources necessary
to finance research and development. This has
become increasingly significant as the sector's
ability to sustain growth depends to an ever greater
extent upon specialisation in high technology goods,
as industrialising nations become more competitive
in the production of less sophisticated products.
Generalisation, however, masks various contrasts
which exist between the industries within this
group. Certain activities such as electronics and
car manufacturing have in the past expanded
extremely rapidly. Others, despite the recession,
have only recently developed as growth sectors,
illustrated by the microelectronics and aerospace
industries. Conversely, there are a number of
branches, including shipbuilding and machine tools,
from which any dynamism has long been absent.

Aerospace. Aeronautical and aerospace industries

employ over 110,000 workers and have an annual turnover in excess of 35 billion francs (1980), making France the second largest manufacturer in the western world outside the USA (12). Moreover, turnover has nearly quintupled since 1970 and approximately 60 per cent of sales are now made abroad. The greater part of production is controlled by a limited number of companies, notably the Société Nationale Industrielle Aerospatiale (SNIAS), Dassault-Breguet, SNECMA and Matra. Paris remains the major focus for the industry, although decentralisation, initiated originally for strategic reasons in the inter-war years, has led to the substantial expansion of these activities in a number of provincial centres, the most prominent of which are Toulouse and Bordeaux. The former city is now a major focus of production (including manufacture of the Airbus), while the region of Midi-Pyrénées generally now employs over 13,000 workers in these industries. Certain problems have been posed by such long-distance decentralisation (13), but progressively there has been a greater degree of integration with local manufacturers contributing to an increasingly important regional multiplier effect.

The range of production is wide. On the aeronautical side, a variety of civil and military aircraft are manufactured, including major undertakings such as the Airbus and Mirage fighter but also a number of smaller-scale projects, of which the manufacture of helicopters has proved particularly successful (14). In the aerospace industry activity is linked principally to the rapidly growing market for satellites, covering a variety of uses such as telecommunications, the transmission of television programmes, providing additional meteorological information and as a general aid to scientific discovery. While acknowledging the unrivalled American lead in these fields, the French industry has sought to establish itself as an alternative manufacturer of satellites and associated control systems, and of the rockets to launch such materials, the latter being achieved through the Ariane project. These developments also have significant implications for other industries, particularly microelectronics.

Despite considerable success in the above fields, the aeronautical and aerospace industries still portray a certain vulnerability. The huge size of research and development costs is a particular burden, making these industries heavily dependent upon government financial support. So great

has become the necessary level of investment that
international participation in projects is often
essential, illustrated by both the Airbus and Ariane
programmes and by the agreement between SNIAS and
Ford Aerospace to provide a satellite system for a
consortium of Arab states (15). Co-operation,
however, is often difficult to effect, while competition is becoming increasingly more severe.

Shipbuilding. Government aid has been required for
very different reasons in industries such as shipbuilding where French competitiveness has been
progressively eroded, not only by manufacturers in
other industrialised countries (notably Japan), but
also by a growing number of industrialising nations
such as Brazil and South Korea. In an attempt to
arrest the decline in employment and in the new
tonnage being built by French yards a threefold
strategy has been pursued. Production has been concentrated principally at la Ciotat, la Seyne, St.
Nazaire, Nantes and Dunkerque, a reduction has taken
place in the number of major shipbuilders, and
emphasis is being given to specialisation in a
limited range of vessels, particularly those where
the value-added is relatively high, as in the
building of methane or chemical carriers.

Machine Tools and Engineering. Problems of size and
lack of competitiveness also characterise the French
machine tool industry which now employs less than
20,000 workers compared with 27,000 in 1974 (16).
With few exceptions, the industry is composed of a
series of small manufacturers. These are unable to
produce in sufficient quantity to finance essential
research or support an extensive distribution network and after-sales service which would permit them
to challenge with greater effectiveness more efficient foreign companies. Yet, particularly as the
use of complex tools such as robots becomes more
widespread, this sector of production plays a vital
role in maintaining the strength of French industry.
Consequently, in 1981 the government proposed a
number of measures to rationalise the manufacture of
machine tools, giving priority to research and
development and to encouraging greater specialisation, with the expectation of doubling output by
1985 (17).
    The machine tool industry is but a small part
of the much larger branch of mechanical engineering,

which in 1981 employed more than 535,000 workers.
Activities within this group are still relatively
weakly represented outside the country's traditional
industrial regions, indicating in part the strength
and extent of links with other manufacturers (Figure
7.1). Until recently employment and production had
expanded substantially, but, particularly as firms
have reduced investment and replaced machinery less
frequently, demand for the sector's products has
fallen, contributing to a sharp drop in employment
(Table 7.1). Inevitably, regions such as Rhône-
Alpes and Haute-Normandie, with a strong tradition
of this type of manufacture, have suffered the worst
effects.

Consumption Goods
This sector again encompasses a diverse range of
activities which have experienced differing patterns
of evolution. Nonetheless, in general, industries
have been characterised by only a modest growth in
output, the maintenance of a large but declining
labour-force (Table 7.1), allied to a relatively low
ratio of capital to labour, and a worsening external
trading balance, reflecting the intense competition
provided by foreign manufacturers. In addition,
compared with other sections of industry, these
activities remain weakly concentrated both in terms
of the structure of control and the spatial distribution of manufacturing plants. Not all branches,
however, exhibit these features. The production of
pharmaceuticals, for example, has represented a
major source of growth. It is an industry characterised by a high value-added, a skilled and well-
paid work-force, a strong emphasis upon research,
frequent adaptation to new products and production
techniques, and is controlled to a large extent by a
limited number of multinational groups such as
Rhône-Poulenc and Ciba-Geigy. Moreover, unlike the
manufacture of basic and intermediate chemical
products, the industry is strongly represented in
and around the capital, emphasising the more general
tendency for the industrial structure of the Paris
region to become more specialised in the more
advanced and lucrative stages of the productive
process, and in research activities (Figure 7.1).

Textiles. Traditionally, the manufacture of
textiles has represented a major source of production and employment within this sector; despite the

industry's very considerable mutation over an
extended period, it still employs around 500,000
people and is the third most important texile industry (in terms of the volume of materials transformed)
within Western Europe (18). Change has been induced
by various factors. On the demand side, the
consumption of textiles has tended to stabilise and
more recently decline. In part the recession has
reduced sales, but this conceals a longer term trend
towards a lower proportion of households' budgets
devoted to such purchases. On the supply side, the
French industry has been adversely affected, as have
the textile industries of other European countries,
by the heavy and increasing inflow of products from
developing nations notably in south-east Asia and
southern America. As these countries have sought to
build up their industrial sector, the manufacture of
textiles has frequently been amongst the first activities to be encouraged (19). The industry's
technology is relatively straightforward, particularly for the production of standard items at the
lower end of the market; similarly, the necessary
machinery is often obtainable relatively cheaply,
notably second-hand machines from firms in western
countries which have been re-equipped in an attempt
to remain competitive. Furthermore, the activity is
still comparatively labour intensive, requiring a
largely unskilled work-force. Within these
countries the necessary manpower is readily available and, above all, labour costs by European
standards are extremely low; so great is the contrast that even major French firms such as Dollfus-
Mieg have diverted part of their production activities to developing countries. Other advantages
favouring the expansion of this branch include the
small scale of investment necessary to launch
production, a ready overseas market in view of the
price advantage and, in the longer term, the
security of a vast domestic outlet as home consumption of such products begins to increase rapidly.
    The volume of imports from the third world
countries, and the problematic repercussions of such
movements, have grown very substantially since the
early 1970s, leading to frequent calls for a limit
to be placed upon such imported textiles. As a
result of pressure from France and other European
countries to restrict this inflow, a series of
'multifibre' agreements have been concluded with
industrialising countries over recent years, with
the latest covering the period 1982-6 (20). While
this has partially alleviated the difficulties of

the textile industry, guaranteeing the activity's longer term future in France depends just as much upon increasing productivity and rationalising the range of output and location of factories, particularly as strong competition is also provided by manufacturers within the EEC, notably in Western Germany and Italy. Restructuring and modernisation have occurred over a long period, but arguably, in view of the strength of competition and evolution in techniques, investment has been inadequate. Nor have all the policies implemented been successful. Although increased efficiency has been impeded by the presence of a large number of small and often marginal producers, the concentration of control in the hands of a smaller number of large groups has not always proved more successful, forcibly illustrated by the collapse of Boussac-St. Frères and its parent group Agache-Willot, formerly one of France's major textile producers.

Lack of growth in the market for textile goods, intense foreign competition and, above all, programmes of rationalisation and modernisation have caused a sharp decline in the number of firms engaged in the manufacture of textiles and in the industry's labour-force. Since 1970 alone over 200,000 jobs have disappeared, with the rate of loss accelerating over recent years. A major problem of such a reduction in employment has been its concentration in a limited number of regions, where the adverse effect has frequently been exacerbated by the presence of other declining industries (21). Losses have been heaviest in traditional production centres such as Roubaix and Tourcoing in Nord-Pas-de-Calais, various smaller centres in the Vosges as well as in adjacent towns such as Mulhouse and Colmar, and in a number of localities in the Lyon region including St. Etienne and Roanne. Some relief has been provided by special government programmes to generate new employment (for example, the Plan Vosges) (22), but a competitive French textile industry is unlikely to emerge without a further reduction of the labour-force. In a wider context, the government is also faced with combating many of the same structural weaknesses, problems of foreign competition and declining labour requirements in the leather and footwear industries.

Foods and Drinks. Given the size and wide range of output from agriculture, it would be surprising if France did not possess an important branch of industries transforming agricultural produce and manufacturing foods and drinks. Currently these activities employ over 500,000 workers and account for nearly 5 per cent of the country's gross domestic product, with an annual turnover exceeding 330 billion francs (1980). Yet, there are a number of weaknesses which are apparent in the organisation and development of these industries, not least in their relatively poor (although now greatly improving) export performance and the degree to which certain parts of the industry are too fragmented or too small in scale (23). Generalisation, however, needs to be viewed with some caution due to the extreme diversity of this group of manufacturing activities. One example of this is provided by contrasts in the size and manufacturing techniques of different companies. The majority of firms are of extremely small scale, yet through a continuing process of concentration and reorganisation the greater part of production is now controlled by a limited number of large groups, dominated by BSN-Gervais-Danone whose activities include dairy products, mineral waters, beer (Kronenbourg), baby foods and biscuits. Concentration tends to be most fully developed in the major areas of activity and is thus most apparent in the production of milk and dairy products (where a number of co-operative organisations are particularly strong), meats, and drinks.

Despite reorganisation and rationalisation and the depressant effect of the recession over the last decade, employment and output within the industry have increased marginally, with more substantial rises in the value of production and productivity. Such achievements have been aided by the relatively inelastic nature of the demand for food, the constant development of a series of new products and government inspired programmes to encourage investment and reorganisation within the industry. Considerable scope exists to develop further the potential of this branch, hopefully as a means of creating employment in traditionally weakly industrialised but important agricultural areas within regions such as western France; here, in many cases, the industry is already strongly represented (Figure 7.1).

Building and Public Works
The special character of activities within the construction industry sets it apart from other

industrial groups (although particularly strong
links exist with manufacturers of construction
materials) (24). Nevertheless, it is a major sector
of employment within the economy, with a labour-
force of approximately 1.8 million, strongly represented throughout a wide area of the country (Figure
7.1), and is one of the few industrial activities to
be widespread in rural zones. Much of the work-
force is composed, however, of unskilled workers,
many of whom are immigrants. Apart from the nature
of the work and its frequent dependency upon the
vagaries of the weather, this branch is also distinguished by its heavy reliance upon state contracts
or government decisions over investment (25).

Growth within this sector was particularly
marked throughout the 1960s and early 1970s, coin-
ciding with the country's rapid economic and urban
expansion. In the latter instance, the industry had
to respond to a strong demand for housing, intensified by influences such as the previous shortage of
property, the country's post-war demographic boom
and a reduction in the average size of households.
More generally, the vigorous development of the
economy, following an extended period of relative
stagnation, produced a sharp increase in the demand
for factory and office floorspace. This was also a
period during which the country's infrastructure was
greatly expanded, notably in the fields of communications and energy. Moreover, the government also
launched a series of major regional development
projects, many in southern France (in such areas as
Languedoc, Fos and the Rhône valley), giving a
further boost to the civil engineering industry.

Since the onset of the recession and cutbacks
in government expenditure, much of this previous
dynamism has evaporated. New housing starts, for
example, have slipped from a peak of 549,000 in 1974
to an estimated total of around 400,000 in 1982.
Similar reductions are apparent in the construction
of motorways and other extensions of the infrastructure, although certain priority projects such as
nuclear power stations have been less affected. The
latter 1970s also coincided with the completion of
various grandiose construction projects (for example,
Fos) providing a further depressant effect upon the
industry. Employment in this branch still plays a
significant role, however, in the regions of
southern and western France as well as in major
cities.

Inevitably, with a slowing in activity, the
industry has been forced to shed labour with a net

loss of nearly 200,000 jobs between 1974 and 1981.
Many small companies have gone into liquidation,
emphasising the fragmented state of the industry and
the vulnerability of many firms. Some compensation,
however, has been derived through the exploitation
of new markets. In large urban centres such as
Paris the renovation and rehabilitation of property
has attracted far greater significance (as in the
quarter of Les Halles), while civil engineering
firms have sought to extend their activities outside
France, particularly in developing countries and
former French colonies. Similarly, the larger
companies have attempted to diversify activities,
reducing their dependence upon the building and
civil engineering industries (26). In the longer
term, further restructuring and concentration of the
industry appears inevitable in view of its present
sub-divided character and the resulting instability
of companies.

CONFLICTING TRENDS: CASE STUDIES OF THREE KEY
INDUSTRIES

A review of recent trends in the steel, motor
vehicles and electrical and electronics industries
summarises many of the changes and contrasting
evolutionary tendencies which have been features of
the general pattern of industrial development within
France over the last two decades. Following a
period of largely uninterrupted expansion in output
during the 1960s and early 1970s, production and
especially employment have since fallen sharply
within the steel industry, leading to adjustments in
the number and distribution of manufacturing plants,
and in their activities. Throughout much of the
last twenty years the motor vehicle industry has
acted as a major driving force behind the expansion
of French industrial activity, yet by the beginning
of the present decade it too had lost part of its
former vitality, necessitating cutbacks in employment and output. A similar history characterises
the manufacture of electrical goods and electronics
equipment, with the exception that while many traditional fields of production have ceased to grow
rapidly, an important new sector of activity has
become a major source of growth; microelectronics
and the general fields of data processing and transmission have become key areas of expansion and
investment.
It is not only the performance of these three

industries which has been modified, but also their
location. The steel industry has always demonstrated a high degree of spatial concentration, a
trend still apparent despite a move away from traditional production centres. Vehicle manufacturers
have also shifted from their original locations, but
in this case leading to a far wider distribution,
although still to the neglect of a large area of
southern France. The electronics industry is the
most dispersed of these activities, following the
widespread creation of new plants since the early
1960s; as with the vehicle industry, it has played a
significant part in the government's industrial
relocation strategies. More recently, the microelectronics sector, unrestrained by many traditional
locational forces, has been one of the few branches
of activity to expand in some of the country's least
industrialised regions of the south and extreme west
of France.

The Steel Industry

Since the substantial rise in oil prices in 1973
first disrupted the previous tendency towards unimpeded economic expansion, successive French governments and the country's steelmakers (as well as the
policy-makers of the EEC) have attempted to reorga-
nise and revitalise an industry which has suffered a
marked decline in the demand for its product.

The reduction in the market for the output of
the French steel industry is only part, however, of
a more complex set of problems which have afflicted
French (and other European) steel producers for much
of the last decade (27). Given the highly capital
intensive character of steel making and the long
lead times required for investment programmes, if
the balance between supply and demand suddenly
shifts, it is extremely difficult, at least in the
short run, to adjust production capacity. Thus,
when the demand for steel began to ease in 1974 (the
year of peak production - 27 million tonnes) the
French industry had only just completed a series of
projects, such as the enlargement of the Dunkerque
works of Usinor and the launching of a new integrated coastal works at Fos, greatly increasing the
potential for output. Not only were steelmakers
then faced with the expense of idle capacity, but
also with the difficulty of repaying debts engaged
to enable modernisation and expansion. The industry's increasing indebtedness became a major
problem, exacerbated by the aggressive marketing

techniques of competitors faced with similar
difficulties, which led to a fall in prices.
Furthermore, since the mid-1970s a growing number of
manufacturers in the world's industrialising countries, benefiting from modern plant and often lower
production costs, have increasingly challenged the
steel industries of western countries, particularly
in export markets. Consequently, French steelmakers, like many of their European counterparts are
making heavy losses, totalling more than 6 billion
francs for Usinor and Sacilor in 1981. These
problems provoked an initial series of reactions by
the French government and the steel manufacturers,
most of which were implemented between 1977 and
1979. However, the continuation and deepening of
the recession has led to further remedial measures
being required. In particular, the industry's
plight has been aggravated by a reduction in demand
from certain major customers whose sales had
previously held up (for example, the car industry).
    Various responses have been made to this situa-
tion (28). Despite severe financial difficulties,
the steel industry has continued to invest in the
modernisation of its productive apparatus, leading
to improved productivity and greater specialisation
of individual plants; moreover, virtually all steel
is now produced in oxygen-blown or electric arc
furnaces, the former now accounting for over four-
fifths of total output, (compared with less than
three-fifths in 1974) (29). The organisation of the
industry has also been rationalised, so that the
bulk of production is now controlled by Usinor and
Sacilor (30). State involvement in the industry's
restructuring plans has been considerable. Governments have been partly responsible for the program-
med run-down of the work-force, (negotiating two
major agreements in 1977 and 1978 involving the loss
of nearly 40,000 workers, and proposing further major
cuts in 1982) and have been a prime source of
investment finance. In 1978 the state took virtual
control of the industry by acquiring (largely
through the nationalised banks and investment
bodies) a major share of the capital of the above
companies (31); in the latter part of 1981 both
Usinor and Sacilor were fully nationalised.
    The action of the steelmakers and the govern-
ment has also been conditioned by Common Market
policy. In view of the seriousness of the industry's problems, a first major initiative was taken
in 1978 with the publication of the 'Davignon Plan';
it sought, by voluntary agreement, to control the

output of European steel producers, to set minimum
prices and to restrict imports from outside the
Community (32). However, the reluctance of governments and producers to respect these conditions provoked further reaction with the declaration of a
state of manifest crisis in October 1980. By this
mechanism the Commission was able to make legally
binding upon firms, quotas on output for specific
products and limits on prices. Although envisaged
as short-term measures, with the difficulties of the
industry continuing, these restrictions have been
maintained (33). The Commission has also tried to
limit the amount of assistance individual governments are able to accord to their steel industries
(34) and has requested that capacity be reduced to
take account of the much smaller market for their
products. Despite objections to these restrictions,
the EEC's policy has sought to limit the destructive
effects of intense competition and price-cutting
between members of the Community (35). So far, however, the intensity of the crisis in the steel
industry has rendered this extremely difficult.

The complete or partial closure of factories
and a reduction in the industry's labour-force have
been inevitable consequences of rationalisation and
restructuring programmes. At a national level, the
steel industry in 1981 employed 105,000 workers
compared with 158,000 in 1974 (36); between 1979 and
1981 alone, as the problems of the industry
increased, there was a net loss of more than 30,000
jobs. Sacilor, for example, almost halved its
labour-force between 1977 and 1981 to a total of
just over 24,000. Due to the concentrated nature of
the industry, plant closures and employment losses
have been severe in a limited number of localities.
In traditional centres of production in northern and
eastern France it is towns such as Valenciennes,
Denain and Longwy which have been particularly badly
affected (37), emphasising the changing geography of
steel production (Figure 7.2). Most noticeable is
the decline in the position of Lorraine; but even
within the major steel producing areas changes have
occurred, with a shift in Nord-Pas-de-Calais from
the interior to the coast and within Lorraine to the
Moselle valley. Thus output, particularly of basic
steel products, has been focused upon the largest,
most efficient plants benefiting from the greatest
range of locational advantages (38). Principally,
this has favoured the two coastal complexes of
Dunkerque and Fos, a feature emphasised by the
growing and now dominant role played by imported

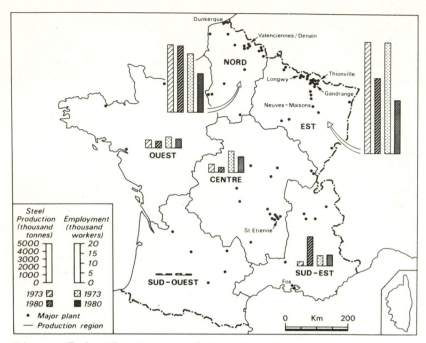

Figure 7.2: The Iron and Steel Industry: Production and Employment

ores and coking coal in steel making, the former now accounting for over 64 per cent of total consumption. Such trends have been to the detriment of smaller, older and generally inland plants which are difficult or expensive to modernise and for which the original <u>raison d'être</u> has long since disappeared. Despite government attempts to bring new industries to these regions, the social and economic consequences of such changes, in terms of unemployment, lost incomes and lost business are substantial.

Although steel output stabilised at around 23 million tonnes between 1978 and 1980 (following a substantial fall), the renewed decline in 1981 indicates the continuing difficulties with which this industry is faced (Table 7.2). In a still highly depressed but extremely competitive market further plant closures and a reduction of employment are unavoidable. Inevitably, these will again be concentrated in the older production centres, already savaged by previous restructuring programmes, where the problem of generating alternative

Major Branches of French Industry

Table 7.2:   Output of Steel, 1972-81

	Output ('000 tonnes)
1972	24,054
1973	25,264
1974	27,023
1975	21,530
1976	23,221
1977	22,094
1978	22,841
1979	23,360
1980	23,176
1981	21,200

Source: La Chambre Syndicale de la Sidérurgie Française.

jobs is critical. The bleak outlook for towns such as Longwy and Denain has been reflected in the violent protests of steelworkers; here communities have long been almost solely dependent upon this one activity.

The Motor Vehicle Industry
The production of motor vehicles, particularly cars, has developed into a major sector and specialisation of French industry (39). Its importance relates to the value and volume of output, the high level of employment and the activity's ability throughout an extended period to create a substantial number of new employment opportunities. France is the second most important vehicle manufacturer in Western Europe (following Western Germany), with a production of over 3.4 million cars and commercial vehicles in 1980. More than half this total is exported, representing nearly a seventh of the over-all value of French exports and considerably exceeding the value of imported vehicles. The industry employs directly over 500,000 people, with at least a similar number employed in ancillary activities (40).
     From the early 1960's until 1973 the expansion of the industry was emphatic, sustained by a particularly buoyant home market as real incomes within France rose substantially. Moreover, growth was

facilitated by the availability of a substantial
labour-force in many areas of the country (through,
for example, the decline of manpower in agriculture),
a strong tradition of inventiveness in car manufacturing techniques, and a low level of penetration of
the French market by foreign competitors. Despite
an initial fall in output and employment in 1974 and
1975, induced by the oil crisis, the industry
recovered significantly in the following year. The
trend was sustained until 1979, reflecting in part
the activity's strong position in export markets
and, at this stage, the comparatively modest impact
of the recession upon consumer demand within the
French economy. Thus, between 1968 and 1979 the
output of cars rose from 1.7 million to 3.2 million
units and employment in the vehicles industry
increased from 365,000 to over 534,000. Since the
latter date, however, growth trends have been
reversed, with both production and jobs decreasing.
Exports have also slipped and foreign car makers now
take nearly thirty per cent of the French market.
In part these tendencies relate to the effects of
the further deepening of the recession, depressing
both domestic and foreign demand, as well as the
increasing competition and aggressive marketing strategies from rival manufacturing nations, not least
Japan. The vitality of the industry has also been
sapped by the problems of restructuring encountered
by the Peugeot group.

Thus, at least in the short-term, the French
car industry's image of dynamism and resilience has
been dented. Both of the major producers (Renault
and Peugeot) made losses in 1981, and the output of
cars slipped substantially to 2.6 million vehicles.
By Britain's standards the trimming of the labour-
force and the introduction of short-time working
have been relatively modest, but given the industry's past record of strong expansion, these
measures have come as a greater shock, contributing
to labour unrest which was a prominent feature of
the latter part of 1981 and the early months of 1982.

Changes in the level of output and employment
have been accompanied by a substantial transformation of the organisation and distribution of the
industry. Renault and Peugeot SA are now the only
two French vehicle manufacturing groups, although
other producers (notably Ford and General Motors)
undertake limited production activities in France.
To compete effectively in international markets, the
increased size of firms has become essential,
enabling the realisation of greater scale-economies,

the development of specialised manufacturing plants
and the use of a large number of standardised parts.
Renault has increased its capacity largely through a
policy of internal expansion, creating a series of
new factories; conversely Peugeot has achieved much
of its growth through the acquisition of rival
companies, first Citroën in 1974 and then in 1978
Talbot, a policy which has tended in the present
economic climate to induce serious problems of
rationalisation. Nonetheless, France now possesses
two major groups capable of effectively challenging,
at least in terms of the scale of their production,
major European competitors such as Volkswagen and
Fiat. Regrouping has also occurred in the manufacture of commercial vehicles, where the current
market is even more depressed and the need for
increased competitiveness far greater. Production
is dominated by Renault-Véhicules-Industriels (RVI),
created through the fusion of the formerly independent manufacturers, Berliet and Saviem. However,
despite the recent acquisition of Dodge (41), the
company has suffered from its small size, making it
difficult to challenge other major European manufacturers such as Volvo, Fiat and Mercedes-Benz.

   One of the most significant changes in the
location of the industry has been its dispersal
away from Paris (Figure 7.3; Table 7.3), a process
particularly evident in the 1960s and early 1970s
(42). The capital formerly dominated overwhelmingly
as the country's major vehicle manufacturing centre,
such concentration linked to the region's importance
as a market and source of labour supply. Now, only
around 30 per cent of employment is concentrated in
Ile-de-France (still making it easily the most
important centre within France - Table 7.3), most of
it linked to the large assembly plants of Renault at
Boulogne-Billancourt and Flins, Citroën at Aulnay-
sous-Bois and Talbot at Poissy. With the increasing
specialisation of plants upon a limited range of
production (43), and the growth of international
sales, close proximity to consumer markets for many
factories has become irrelevant, while labour and
space have become both more expensive and restricted
in supply in the area of the capital. As the industry grew rapidly, the obvious solution became to
expand in provincial locations. Moreover, the
government has long placed special significance on
the decentralisation of the vehicle industry, due to
its past ability to create jobs in substantial
quantities. Over the last decade particular emphasis has been given to the location of manufacturing

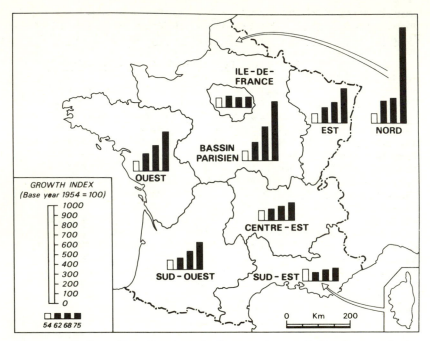

Figure 7.3: The Regional Expansion of Employment in the Motor Vehicle Industry, 1954-75.

plants in depressed regions of Nord-Pas-de-Calais (e.g. Renault at Douai; Peugeot at Valenciennes) and Lorraine (e.g. Renault at Longwy and Thionville; RVI at Batilly); between 1968 and 1981 there was a net gain of over 31,000 jobs in Nord-Pas-de-Calais and more than 10,000 in Lorraine. However, the extent to which this policy will be viable in the future is questionable. Dissemination of plants has also occurred from the two main provincial centres of production, with the expansion of RVI in a series of towns around Lyon, and the extension away from Sochaux of part of Peugeot's production, notably to Susheim (Mulhouse) (44).

In addition to the depressant effects of the recession, which appear likely to continue in the short run, over a longer period there are various other influences which might moderate the growth prospects and modify the structure of the motor industry. With the increasing saturation of the European car market as a growing number of house-holds possess cars, demand is expected to ease; moreover, the battle for a share of this market is

Major Branches of French Industry

Table 7.3: Change in the Regional Distribution of Employment in the Automobile Industry

	Proportion of total employment	
	1968	1981
	(%)	
Ile-de-France	44.8	30.3
Franche-Comté	10.1	10.7
Rhône-Alpes	11.1	8.9
Nord-Pas-de-Calais	1.4	7.1
Haute-Normandie	4.2	5.6
Alsace	2.5	4.8
Picardie	4.0	4.4
Pays de la Loire	3.9	4.2
Centre	2.7	3.6
Basse-Normandie	3.3	3.2
Bretagne	2.7	3.2
Lorraine	0.9	2.7
Others	8.4	11.3
	100.0	100.0

Source: Calculated from INSEE, Emploi Salarié.

likely to be intensified by increased competition, already apparent from Japan, but also from the United States as a new generation of smaller vehicles is developed (45). Export markets seem certain to become more competitive, despite their rapid growth in industrialising countries. Penetration is facilitated by the creation of productive facilities or agreements with manufacturers in foreign countries. There are a limited number of examples of this strategy such as Renault's expansion in South America and more recently Taiwan, and its links with American Motors in the USA (46), but there is potential for a greater extension of this policy. However, with the development of such initiatives, less expansion is likely to occur in France. In the present economic climate this is a sensitive issue, particularly in relation to its implications for employment. But, jobs in the car industry are likely to be less plentiful anyway as increasing automation, and especially the use of robots, reduces substantially the need for manual

labour in many tasks. Finally, as research costs
increase, competition intensifies and large production runs become even more critical for profitability, co-operation between manufacturers not only
within France but also on a European basis is
growing; already this has been pioneered by agreements between Peugeot, Renault and Volvo for the
manfuacture of engines, and Renault and Volkswagen
for the development of gearboxes. Similar under-
standings have also been negotiated between vehicle
manufacturers and component suppliers, illustrated
by the links between Renault and Bendix and Peugeot
and AEG-Telefunken.

Electrical and Electronics Industries

The manufacture of electrical and electronics goods
has long represented a significant growth sector of
industry in France. Its importance has been underlined by a strong French presence in fields of
advanced technology and by the rapid growth of
certain product markets. Despite a recent downward
shift in employment, this group of industries still
employs directly over 550,000 workers, having
enjoyed an exceptional period of expansion between
the mid-1960s and mid-1970s. Not only did employment grow rapidly, but also the scale and volume of
output, the sector's contribution to exports, and
the level of productivity and investment (47).
    The state is heavily involved in the industry's
activities, emphasised most recently by the
nationalisation of CGE, Thomson-Brandt, CII -
Honeywell-Bull and Matra. Over a longer period the
influence of the government has been linked to its
importance as an investor, and to its role as a
major customer in fields such as defence, electricity production and the telecommunications services.
Such involvement relates to factors ranging from
questions of national security to a desire to
promote growth and enhance competitiveness in a
vitally significant area of industrial development.
It is also illustrative of the way in which French
governments have sought to plan jointly with major
branches of industry their expansion and investment
programmes. Government interest has also been
fostered by the relatively high degree of locational
freedom of many manufacturing plants. In the past,
this led the industry to respond positively to
strategies of decentralisation and regional development, favouring certain previously underindustrialised areas. Thus, partly under government pressure,

much of the post-war period has been characterised
by a spread of these activities away from the
capital, where originally the industry was heavily
concentrated, to a series of centres such as Tours,
Angers, Rennes, Dijon and Brest, located principally
in the Paris Basin and parts of western France
(Figure 7.4). The process is reminiscent of that
which has affected the car industry, with access to
a ready supply of labour and the creation of production plants specialising in a limited range of output both features of this pattern of development
(48). Paris still dominates, however, as the
industry's major focus (Table 7.4).

Not unnaturally in view of its large size, this
branch of industry comprises a series of diverse
activities, not all of which have experienced a
similar pattern of development or offer the same
potential for future growth (49). France has long
held a reputation as a manufacturer of electrical
machines and motors and of equipment for the generation of electricity, areas of production in which a

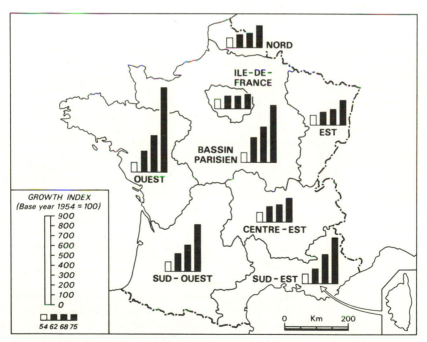

Figure 7.4:   The Regional Expansion of Employment in
Electrical and Electronics Industries, 1954-75

Table 7.4:   Regional Distribution of Employment in
the Electrical and Electronics Industries, 1981

Region	Proportion of total employment (%)
Ile-de-France	34.7
Rhône-Alpes	10.4
Pays de la Loire	5.7
Centre	5.4
Haute-Normandie	4.6
Basse-Normandie	3.4
Bretagne	3.3
Nord-Pas-de-Calais	3.3
Bourgogne	3.1
Alsace	3.0
Provence-Alpes-Côte-d'Azur	3.0
Other	20.1

Source: Calculated from INSEE, Emploi Salarié.

number of large companies such as Merlin-Gerin and
Alsthom-Atlantique have specialised. The French
have also been traditionally strong in the field of
professional electronics which includes the manufacture of products related to aerospace, military,
radar and broadcasting technologies; much of the
success of Thomson-CSF, a subsidiary of Thomson-
Brandt, is due to its expertise in these areas.
This sector's importance is enhanced by the high
value of its exports and a correspondingly strongly
positive external trading balance. Less favourable
is the position of France as a manufacturer of many
domestic appliances and household electrical goods
such as freezers and televisions; the country is a
net importer of these goods although it does have a
number of successful indigenous manufacturers, such
as Thomson-Brandt and Moulinex. Generally, however,
as in other European countries the French industry
has remained too fragmented and the goods too costly
to challenge effectively manufacturers in Japan and,
increasingly, other areas of south-east Asia. For
the future, data-processing and microelectronics
represent two broad areas in which the scope for
expansion is considerable for, despite the American
domination of these activities, France has developed

into one of the leaders within western Europe,
notably in the production of computer peripherals.
Development has been stimulated by the growth of
industries such as aerospace, nuclear energy and
vehicles which are reliant upon technological
advances in these fields, although the high level of
government investment has also been a major factor
aiding their expansion.

From the early 1970s a major boost to electrical and electronics industries was given by the
state's belated commitment to greatly increasing the
capacity and efficiency of the telephone service.
The inadequacy of the network through lack of
investment had become legendary and a strange
anachronism in a country then already engaged in a
series of technologically advanced projects such as
Concorde; yet, previous administrations had regarded
the telephone as a luxury rather than an essential
item of the equipment of homes or businesses. Even
in 1974 only a quarter of French households
possessed a telephone. Recent progress, however,
has been dramatic reflecting a major effort to
improve and extend telecommunication services
initiated during the course of the VIIth plan. By
1980 the proportion of homes equipped with a telephone had risen to 63 per cent, the number of lines
had been increased to 16 million (from 5.7 million
in 1974) (50) and waiting lists for the installation
of a receiver had been greatly reduced. With
approximately 42 telephones per 1,000 inhabitants,
France is still fairly lowly placed on the international league table, but its relative position has
improved substantially. The spin-off for related
industries has been considerable with over 66,000
workers directly related to the production of necessary equipment. Moreover, as the demand for basic
telephone links has been increasingly satisfied,
emphasis has been placed upon the development of
more diverse and advanced telecommunication systems.
These include the Télétel television-based information and data-bank service, a similarly based electronic telephone directory, the Téléfax facsimile
transmission service and the Transpac network for
the transfer of data.

More recently, official encouragement has been
given to developments in office automation, consumer
electronics such as home terminals and, above all,
electronic components vital to the manufacture of an
extended series of products in the general field of
data-processing (51). As early as 1966 the government had attempted to foster an independent

French-based computer industry through the first
Plan Calcul, a policy which culminated in 1975 with
the marriage of the French firm Compagnie
Internationale pour l'Informatique with the American
company Honeywell-Bull, to form CII - Honeywell-Bull.
The link has been criticised due to the apparently
greater benefit it accorded the American partner
(52), although without it, it is doubtful that a
major French interest in the production of computers
could have been maintained. Some success for the
policy might be suggested as CII - Honeywell-Bull
now rivals ICL as the major European-based manufacturer, but the computing industry is still overwhelmingly dominated within France by the activities
of IBM. In 1978 as part of a wider policy to
encourage investment in integrated circuit development and microprocessors the government launched its
'components plan' (Plan Composants) by which it
offered various forms of aid (largely financial) to
companies willing to invest in this field (53).
Again it is an area dominated by American technology.
Reflecting this, and the extremely high research
costs, subsequent developments have frequently taken
the form of agreements with American companies to
undertake common ventures. For example, Saint-
Gobain and National Semiconductors have created
jointly a subsidiary, Eurotechnique, and set up a
new factory at Rousset near Aix-en-Provence; Matra
and Harris are carrying out two similar projects in
the area of Nantes-St. Nazaire (54).
     Given the general buoyancy of the French elec-
tronics industry and the rapid growth in demand for
products both within France and other areas of
western Europe, it is not surprising that foreign
investment, particularly American, is prominent. Of
the American companies, apart from IBM, other firms
such as ITT, Burroughs, Motorola, Hewlett-Packard
and Texas Instruments all have substantial investments within the country. The extent of the
Americanisation of a leading growth sector has led
to some expression of disquiet within France, yet
without access to their resources it seems unlikely
that a viable, wholly nationally-based industry
could survive, especially in view of the intense
international competition in this field.
     A significant geographical by-product of the
general expansion of the electronics and microelectronics industries has been the development of
factories in many centres away from the country's
traditional industrial areas. In this respect,
expansion in the southern and south-eastern regions

of France is particularly apparent. Thus, the urban
areas of Bordeaux, Toulouse, Montpellier, Nice and
Grenoble are amongst those which have benefited from
the electronics revolution, capitalising upon advantages such as their attractive environments for
living and good accessibility to major European and
American cities, as well as in the case of Grenoble,
a long tradition and major research facilities in
this and related fields.

For the future, the present government has
given a strong commitment to supporting French electronics industries, outlining a new five year plan
in 1982. Such interest underlies again the huge
cost of research and development, but also reflects
the sector's potential for growth and, particularly
in the current economic climate, its ability to
create jobs. Success, however, is likely to depend
upon improved performance in certain areas where
French expertise is not yet strongly developed, such
as microcomputers, and greater co-operation and
integration between the major companies.

NOTES

1. Commissariat Général du Plan, Industrie,
(La Documentation Française, Paris, 1980), 205-8.
The French classification of intermediate, capital
and consumption goods industries is based partly
upon the destination of the final product. However,
it is also a reflection of the different structural
and technical characteristics of contrasting sets of
industrial activities. Thus, industries manufacturing basic industrial products (intermediate
goods) tend to be highly capital intensive and concentrated both in terms of ownership and location.
Industries producing capital or equipment goods are
characterised by more elaborate and sophisticated
transformation of the product, and by the more
general use of advanced technology. Conversely, the
consumption goods sector is composed largely of more
traditional manufacturing activites, featuring a
lower level of concentration, less advanced production techniques and a much lower ratio of capital to
labour. Not all branches of industry fit easily
into one of these categories, while, due to their
special characteristics, three areas of activity are
generally excluded from this classification (energy,
food industries and building and public works),
although in the subsequent analysis the second group
has been considered under the heading of consumption

goods industries. More details of the nature and basis of this classificatory system are to be found in:- Desrosières, A., 'Un découpage de l'industrie en trois secteurs', Economie et Statistique, No.40, (1972), 25-39.

2. Dollé, M., 'Les branches industrielles avant et après 1974', Economie et Statistique, No.108 (1979), 3-20.

3. Irrespective of the division of industry into three broad sectors, and of the recent changes, for much of the last twenty years, the car, electrical and electronics, rubber and plastics, and para-chemical and pharmaceutical industries have been a significant force in the growth of French manufacturing. See Dollé, 'Les branches industrielles' and Gachelin, C., 'Crises et défis de l'industrie française', La Documentation Photographique, No.6056 (1981).

4. Estienne, P., La France (Masson, Paris, 1979), vol.1, 87-94.

5. Baleste, M., L'Economie Française (Masson, Paris, 1981), 174-5.

6. Le Monde, 21 Jan. 1982.

7. Brocard, R., 'Les entreprises françaises', Les Collections de l'INSEE, E64 (1979), 138-44.

8. Le Monde, 20 Nov. 1981.

9. See Roux-Vaillard, P., 'L'industrie' in Pagé, J-P. (ed.), Profil Economique de la France (La Documentation Française, Paris, 1981), 203-5; L'Expansion, No.180, Nov. 1981, 50-2; and Marthey, L., 'La chimie de base: données pour une diagnostic', Economie et Statistique, No.91 (1977), 45-67.

10. For a more detailed discussion of such themes see Marthey, L., 'L'industrie chimique en France', Notes et Etudes Documentaires, No.4454 (1978) and Baleste, L'Economie Française, 176-88.

11. Tuppen, J.N., France (Dawson, Folkestone, 1980), 173-4.

12. Le Monde, 4 June 1981.

13. Jalabert, G., Les Industries Aeronautiques et Spatiales en France (Privat, Toulouse, 1974), 374-9.

14. For general details of both aeronautical and aerospace industries see Baleste, L'Economie Française, 203-5.

15. Le Monde, 4 June 1981.

16. Le Monde, 2 Dec. 1981.

17. Le Monde, 3 Dec. 1981; Le Monde, 4 Dec. 1981; Le Monde, 19 Dec. 1981.

18. Approximately half this total is accounted for by the clothing industry.

19.   Stoffaës, C., La Grande Menace
Industrielle (Pluriel, Paris, 1980), 83-6.
20.   Le Monde, 19 Jan. 1982.
21.   More detail of these manufacturing regions
is contained in Baleste, L'Economie Française, 219-
22, and Prévot, V., Géographie des Textiles (Masson,
Paris, 1979).
22.   The Plan Vosges was established in 1978
due to the sharp decline of employment in the
region's textile industries. It has aimed to
improve infrastructure and to offer enhanced incentives (grants and loans) to encourage existing firms
to expand and attract new investors.
23.   Bombal, J. and Chalmin, P., L'Agro-
Alimentaire (Presses Universitaires de France,
Paris, 1980), 70; Klatzmann, L., L'Agriculture
Française (Seuil, Paris, 1978), 57-62.
24.   Estienne, La France, 93.
25.   General details of the industry are also
available in Baleste, L'Economie Française, 189-96
and Tuppen, France, 78-80.
26.   Tuppen, France, 80.
27.   Two detailed studies of the economic and
social consequences of the changed role of the steel
industry in recent years (set against the industry's
longer term evolution) are contained in:-
Freyssenet, M., La Sidérurgie Française 1945-1979
(Savelli, Paris, 1979) and Baumier, J., La Fin des
Maîtres de Forges (Plon, Paris, 1981).
28.   For background to and more detail of these
problems and changes, see Tuppen, France, 64-9 and
Baleste, L'Economie Française, 164-8.
29.   Chambre Syndicale de la Sidérurgie
Française, La Sidérurgie Française en 1980 (Paris,
1981).
30.   Tuppen, France, 67-8.
31.   Malézieux, J., 'Crise et restructuration
de la sidérurgie française', L'Espace Géographique,
9 (1980), 183-96.
32.   Roux-Vaillard, 'L'industrie', 202-3.
33.   Le Monde, 26 June 1981.
34.   More positively, it has agreed to grant
extra aid to help attract new industries to those
areas worst hit by the decline of steel making.
35.   Le Monde, 10 and 11 May 1981.
36.   These figures exclude workers engaged in
the primary transformation of steel.
37.   For an account of the impact see Ardagh,
J., France in the 1980s (Penguin, Harmondsworth,
1982), 57-62.
38.   More detail of the steel producing regions

is given in Baleste, L'Economie Française, 168-73.
For fuller accounts of recent changes in the steel
manufacturing regions of Nord-Pas-de-Calais and
Lorraine consult:- Gachelin, C., 'La Mutation de la
sidérurgie de la région du Nord', Hommes et Terres
du Nord, No.1 (1980), 22-33; Malézieux, 'Crise et
restructuration', 183-96; Thouvenin, M., 'De Wendel-
Sidélor à Sacilor-Sollac: 1968-1980: 13 années de
mutations difficiles en Lorraine', Revue
Géographique de l'Est, 21 (1981), 37-64; Sinou, B.,
'La Lorraine face à la crise sidérurgique', Economie
et Statistique, No.92 (1977), 29-36.

39. Stoffaës, La Grande Menace Industrielle,
135. For a detailed account of the industry, see
Fontaine, P., 'L'industrie automobile en France',
Notes et Etudes Documentaires, Nos.4583-4 (1980).

40. The performance of the motor industry is
obviously strongly linked (and of vital importance)
to a host of component and parts manufacturers.
Unlike the manufacture of completed vehicles the
control of this sector remains relatively fragmented.
There is, however, a high level of foreign investment, reflecting factors such as the size and past
growth record of vehicle manufacturing, France's
good strategic location to serve a European market
and the high level of sub-contracting which is a
feature of the French motor industry.

41. This was the commercial vehicle branch of
Chrysler-Europe, originally acquired by Peugeot.

42. See Nwafor, J.C., 'Facteurs déterminant le
choix des nouvelles sites dans l'industrie
automobile française', Revue Géographique de
Montréal, 30 (1976), 297-307.

43. Numerous illustrations exist. In the
Renault group, for example, its factory at Cléon
specialises in the production of engines and gearboxes, that at Orléans produces precision parts such
as valves, the plant at Dreux manufactures components in plastic (essentially bumpers), while the
plants at Boulogne-Billancourt, Flins, Sandouville
and Douai are orientated towards pressing and
assembly operations.

44. Tuppen, France, 75.

45. In 1981 foreign-made cars took 29 per cent
of the French market, representing a substantial and
(for French manufacturers) worrying increase over
1980 when the proportion was 23 per cent; previously
over a number of years foreign imports accounted for
only approximately 20 per cent of the market.

46. Other examples are given in Ardagh, France
in the 1980s, 68-9.

47.   A detailed account of the industry is provided in Tussau, G., 'Les industries électriques et électroniques', Notes et Etudes Documentaires, Nos.4563-4 (1980).

48.   Two illustrations are provided by the Thomson group. At La Roche-sur-Yon (south of Nantes), a rural area in which agriculture has shed labour, it manufactures dish washers, while at St. Pierre de Varengeville (near Rouen), in an area where the textile industry has declined releasing labour, pumps, motors and thermostats are produced.

49.   Some indication of the diversity is given in Baleste, L'Economie Française, 206-11.

50.   Giscard d'Estaing, C., L'Etat de la France (Fayard, Paris, 1981), 83.

51.   Lloyd, A., 'France's electronic industry: dynamic and wide progress', Datar Newsletter, No.25 (1981), 3.

52.   See, for example, Baleste, L'Economie Française, 208-9, and Le Monde, 21 July 1981.

53.   Baleste, L'Economie Française, 208; Le Monde, 10 April 1981.

54.   Lloyd, 'France's electronic industry', 4-5.

Chapter Eight

INDUSTRIAL REGIONS: THREE CASE STUDIES

Rather than review generally a large number of
industrial areas (1), the present chapter offers a
more detailed portrayal of industry in three contrasting regions, giving some indication of the diversity of manufacturing activity throughout France.
The areas selected are Paris, Nord-Pas-de-Calais and
Brittany. In each case discussion is focused upon
the distinctive features of the contemporary pattern
of industrial development.
    A number of basic differences underlie the
nature, scale and intensity of industrial activity
within each of these areas. There is a strong
contrast between the dense concentration of industrial plant and employment polarised upon the
capital, and the dispersed pattern of industrialisation and comparatively small number of industrial
workers in Brittany. Similarly, the history of
industrial development in this latter region has had
little in common with the expansion of heavy
industry in northern France, although more recently
both areas have benefited from a high level of
investment backed by the government. Furthermore,
in contrast to the relative dynamism of the industrial
sector within Brittany over much of the last
two decades, in Nord-Pas-de-Calais the outstanding
feature has been the extent of employment loss.
    The individuality of each region is emphasised
by other features. In the capital, despite the
strength and array of industrial activities, there
is a growing problem of the loss of jobs in industry
from inner areas of the city, a trend familiar in
Britain but, at least until recently, generally less
evident in France. Nonetheless, there is now
increasing recognition of the extent and adverse
consequences of this decline, not only in Paris but
also in large provincial cities such as Lyon and

Lille (2).

The reduction of manufacturing in the capital's 'inner city' has been part of a wider pattern of locational change contributing to the decline of Paris as an industrial centre. For many years this process produced beneficial repercussions for other regions of the country. Brittany is one such area, although much of the interior remains under-industrialised. The widespread absence of modern manufacturing activity has long been a problematic feature of western France, but the need for new industrial investment is now equally apparent in traditional centres of heavy industry, epitomised by the northern coalfield. Restructuring has become a key element of the industrial strategy pursued within this area.

Viewed together these studies indicate some of the main issues which have been central to the regional pattern of industrial development over the last twenty-five years. In particular, four themes underlie the following assessment - first, the need for a policy of decentralisation and the consequences of both the enforced and spontaneous redistribution of industry; second, the 'take-off' of industry in certain formerly under-industrialised areas; third, the now urgent need to generate new jobs in the older centres of heavy industry; and finally, the emergence of a growing problem of industrial decline in the inner areas of major metropolitan centres.

PARIS: INDUSTRIAL DECLINE IN THE INNER CITY

Paris and its immediate hinterland remain unchallenged as France's major concentration of manufacturing activity, despite the existence over an extended period of government policies designed to reduce the capital's dominance and spread growth to other areas of the country. The Paris region (Ile-de-France) currently accounts for over a quarter of the total value-added in industry within France and houses more than a fifth of the work-force in the secondary sector. However, Paris is no longer expanding as an industrial centre; for more than a decade the volume and value of manufacturing activity carried out in the capital have declined, accompanied by a substantial reduction in the work-force (3). Whereas the level of employment in the secondary sector remained almost stable throughout the greater part of the 1960s, subsequently there

has been an accelerating fall in the number of
people employed in industry. Between 1968 and 1975
industrial jobs dropped by a relatively modest
average of 0.4 per cent per annum, yet between 1976
and 1981 the yearly mean had risen to nearly 2.5 per
cent representing a net annual loss of around 40,000
employment opportunities. In a spatial context this
reduction has been concentrated overwhelmingly in
the central and inner areas of the capital, provoking increasing recognition of the now pronounced
désindustrialisation of the inner city. Until
recently the extent of this process was partially
masked by the continued overall expansion of employment in the Paris region, due to the strong growth
of the tertiary sector in which two-thirds of the
capital's active population is now employed.
However, this trend is now failing to compensate for
the increasing scale of loss of industrial jobs,
leading to a decline in total employment in the
capital and more forceful demands for action to
combat the reduction of manufacturing in inner city
areas.

Industry in the Capital
The rise of Paris as a major industrial centre and
as the primary and undisputed focus of economic
activity within France is a feature of comparatively
recent origin, dating from the latter part of the
nineteenth century and reflected in the strength of
the city's demographic expansion from this period.
Such growth was stimulated by numerous factors, most
of which related to the presence or development of
an increasing range of localisation and urbanisation
economies, linked to the availability of a large and
diverse labour-force and ready access to very
substantial and ever-expanding local and regional
markets. The extent of decision-making power vested
in the capital in both the private and public
sectors of the economy has also long been influential in fixing industrial and commercial development
in the Paris region. So irresistible became the
pull of the capital, that by the 1950s the majority
of new employment created within France was located
in and around Paris; in growth industries such as
cars, electrical goods, pharmaceuticals, aircraft
and armaments, well in excess of half of total
national employment was concentrated in this area.
     Paris still remains the principal focus for
these activities within France, despite the very
considerable expansion of employment in other areas

of the country since the mid-1950s, partly as a result of decentralisation. Not surprisingly, such industries also occupy a dominant position in the composition of manufacturing activities within Ile-de-France. Metal working and engineering, electrical engineering and electronics, motor vehicles and chemicals represent the four principal branches of industry (4); other activities such as printing and publishing, food processing and textiles and clothing, all with a long tradition of establishment in the capital, are also major sectors of employment (Table 8.1) and production. In addition, Paris houses a large work-force engaged in building and public works, reflecting not only the size of the capital (10 million inhabitants) but also the extent to which its urban area is undergoing constant transformation (5).

It is not just the exceptional weight and diversity of industrial activity which distinguishes Paris from other manufacturing regions within France: there are also various qualitative features of the capital's industries which set them apart. These include an emphasis upon activities in which the level of technical innovation is relatively high, upon the more intricate manufacturing processes and upon firms' research and development operations. Such traits are reflected in the extent to which skilled and the more highly qualified labour is concentrated in the capital and also in the strength of white-collar employment subsumed

Table 8.1: Ile-de-France: Employment in Major Branches of Manufacturing Industry, 1981

Branch	Number of employees ('000)
Electrical engineering and electronics	193
Vehicles	153
Mechanical engineering	111
Printing and publishing	94
Chemicals and pharmaceuticals	93
Foundry and metal working	81
Food and drink	65
Textiles and clothing	59
Aircraft and armaments	55

Source: INSEE, Emploi Salarié.

within the secondary sector, although this latter
feature is also a consequence of the overwhelming
concentration of companies' head offices in Paris
(6).
     Within the Paris region considerable spatial
variations exist in the intensity and form of industrial development. The major concentrations of
manufacturing activity have long been located in the
inner suburbs, notably in a broad arc to the north
of the centre stretching from Nanterre through areas
such as Clichy, St. Ouen and St. Denis to
Aubervilliers and Pantin (7). These zones (and
similar districts to the south such as Boulogne-
Billancourt and Vitry), where growth was often
linked to proximity to the Seine valley, still
retain an industrial function, but increasingly the
focus of industry has shifted to the outer suburbs
and urban centres on the periphery of Paris. Here
locations are more dispersed, although in recent
years there has been a growing polarisation upon the
region's new towns, especially Cergy-Pontoise, St.
Quentin-en-Yvelines, Evry, and recently Marne-la-
Vallée (8). The central quarters of the city still
house a diverse range of manufacturers, whose operations are generally small in scale but highly
specialised (9). Such activities are widely spread
throughout this area, although their concentration
tends to be greatest in the northern and eastern
arrondissements; in all these districts, however,
manufacturing has long been declining.

Industrial Decline
This reduction of industrial activity is reflective
of the various constraints (some of them artificially imposed) which have influenced development in
the capital, particularly from the mid-1950s. Since
that period government legislation has sought to
restrict industrial expansion in Ile-de-France and
to channel the growth of firms based in Paris to
less favoured regions of the country; given the
strength and dynamism of the capital's industries at
that time and the underindustrialised character or
weak rate of industrial growth in many provincial
regions, such a policy of decentralisation became an
inevitable and essential instrument of the government's strategy to achieve a more equitable balance
of economic activity and opportunity throughout the
country. With the estimated transfer of over
200,000 jobs away from Ile-de-France, leading to the
creation of a further 300,000 employment

opportunities in provincial areas since 1955, it
seems reasonable to attribute some success to the
attainment of these latter objectives (10).
However, factors other than government restrictions
upon expansion have influenced industrialists to
move from their original sites or to expand production elsewhere, not least the shortage and elevated
cost of land in central and inner areas and the
relatively high labour costs of the Paris region.
Similarly, transfer has not always entailed a move
to an area outside the Paris region. Relocation
within Ile-de-France, largely on the periphery of
the capital, where accessibility is good and prepared industrial sites available, has also represented a major aspect of change, affecting an estimated
movement of around 270,000 workers between 1962 and
1978 (11). As population in the outer suburbs began
to grow rapidly in the 1960s, it seemed logical to
promote a displacement of industry to these
districts. Employment has also been lost in many
inner districts through the closure of firms, a
feature particularly common amongst small, undercapitalised concerns (12), although it may equally
affect larger plants, often following the merger of
firms and the rationalisation of their activities.
In addition, as the recession has led to a fall in
demand for many goods, various existing companies
have reduced output and shed labour. Overall,
survey results suggest that, certainly during the
1970s, employment losses in central and inner areas
were not caused primarily by decentralisation (13);
on the contrary, this accounted for only about ten
per cent of the loss. Instead it was the transfer
of firms towards the outskirts of the city or their
closure which, to an approximately equal degree,
provoked the bulk of the reduction in employment.

The uneven areal spread of job losses is shown
by contrasts in the evolution of industrial employment between the central, inner and outer districts
of the city. These zones may be equated approximately with the grouping of the region's departments
into three concentric zones - Paris, Petite Couronne
(Hauts-de-Seine, Seine-St. Denis, Val-de-Marne) and
Grande Couronne (Essonne, Yvelines, Val-d'Oise,
Seine-et-Marne). Thus, over the period of the late
1960s and early 1970s the number of jobs in industry
fell substantially in the centre, remained roughly
stable in the inner ring and rose markedly on the
outer fringes of the capital (Table 8.2). Since
then, the decline in the centre has persisted, also
becoming a marked feature of the inner suburbs;

Table 8.2:   Industrial Employment Change within
Ile-de-France

	Mean rate of change	
	1968-75	1976-81
	(%)	
Paris	-3.1	-4.6
Petite Couronne	+0.2	-2.1
Grande Couronne	+3.3	-0.7

Source: Calculated from INSEE, _Recensements_ and
Emploi Salarié.

similarly, a net loss of industrial jobs, albeit
modest, is also now a feature of the outer areas of
Paris (Figure 8.1).   It is, however, the pronounced

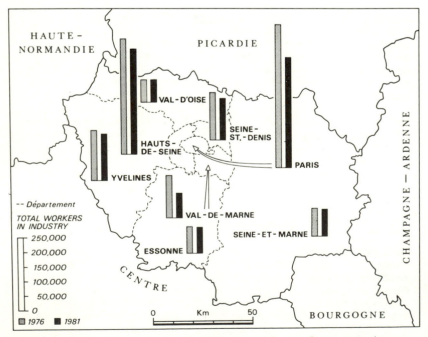

Figure 8.1:   Changes in Industrial Employment in
Ile-de-France

reduction of industrial employment in the
traditional centres of industry of the capital that
is now regarded as excessive in scale and has led to
increasing demands for action to reverse or at least
modify the tendency. There are also many undesirable
side effects of industry's decline, ranging from the
increasing number of abandoned factories and areas
of derelict land (the latter now estimated to cover
at least 350 hectares) to the substantial loss of
local tax revenue. Inevitably, it is many of the
older, heavily industrialised suburbs which have
been worst affected, as in the northern districts of
St. Denis and Gennevilliers, or in southern areas
such as Montrouge, where traditional activities,
particularly engineering, continue to decline (Table
8.3). It is not just small firms which are closing
or shedding labour. Renault, for example, has
reduced employment at its giant Boulogne-Billancourt
works, while Citroën has now long abandoned its
formerly major plant in the XVth arrondissement and
is now proposing the closure of works at Clichy,
Gennevilliers and St. Denis (14).

Action to Counteract Industrial Decline
Official responses to these problems have been
generally limited in terms of the scale and range of
remedial measures proposed. Over recent years
growing representations have been made over the
damaging effect of the agrément and redevance
controls, although opinion over the extent of their

Table 8.3: The Net Loss of Employment in Selected
Industries of the Petite Couronne

Branch	Employment	
	1976	1981
	('000)	
Food and drink	38	26
Foundry and metal working	56	47
Mechanical engineering	70	54
Electrical engineering and		
electronics	109	106
Vehicles	99	88

Source: INSEE, Emploi Salarié.

restrictive character appears divided. Compared
with the early 1960s there are now relatively few
decentralisations each year (an average of between
50 and 60 as opposed to between 200 and 250) involving in total generally fewer than 3,000 workers
(15). This indicates the greatly reduced potential
for shifting employment and adds some support to the
argument that limitations on expansion are no longer
necessary. For large companies the agrément has
been seen frequently as a basis for bargaining
rather than as a measure designed purely to restrict
development in the capital. It is for smaller firms
that controls have probably represented a greater
dissuasive force to growth, yet these are likely to
be the most appropriate candidates to expand in
inner areas. Some acceptance of this viewpoint is
reflected in the partial easing of the agrément
control in 1980, followed in 1981 by the socialist
government's proposal to abolish the redevence
(which had become of only very marginal influence
due to its low ceiling) and to make the granting of
an agrément virtually automatic for small, independent firms. It is hoped that this will remove one
of the obstacles to industrial development in the
inner city, but in seeking to foster growth in this
area, the government and regional authorities have
to reconcile this policy with their much longer
commitment to the expansion of employment in other
priority areas, notably the new towns.

High land costs or rentals, poor accessibility
and an absence of suitable premises represent other
factors capable of suppressing growth, although a
growing number of initiatives are now being taken in
attempts to counterbalance such dissuasive
influences. A number of municipalities have sought
to refurbish large, abandoned factories for use by a
series of smaller enterprises, a policy adopted
notably in the inner suburbs of the north-western
part of the city; here, for example, the former Fiat
factory at Suresnes has been transformed in this
manner (16). In this same area, small firms within
the département of Hauts-de-Seine may now be
eligible for various forms of assistance, including
grants and help with worker retraining (17), testifying to the increased concern of the authorities at
the accelerating loss of industrial jobs.

Various measures aimed at fostering the continued presence of manufacturing activities are also
being pursued within the département of Paris.
Agreement has been reached to develop three sites on
the edge of the central area in the XIIth

arrondissement (at Bercy), the XIIIth arrondissement
(Tolbiac sector) and the XVIIIth arrondissement
(Gazomètres zone). Together these areas are ultimately expected to offer nearly 300,000 square
metres of floorspace for small industrial concerns
(18). Progress in the development of these zones so
far is modest, but their designation is representative of changing official attitudes to the problem
of employment loss. Since 1978, in the revision of
plans for a series of development schemes in this
central area, greater emphasis has been given to the
allocation of land and buildings for use by industrial businesses and craftsmen (19). Areas affected
include the traditional industrial districts of
Belleville and Amandiers in the eastern part of the
city. Inevitably, however, construction costs in
such areas are high and a frequent disincentive to
industrial use. To help overcome this constraint,
therefore, developers will be exempted from payment
of any land tax on premises designed for industry,
in the expectation that lower rents will then be
charged (20). Whether this will occur and act as a
sufficient inducement to counter other possible
limitations to investment has yet to be determined.

Efforts are increasing to at least limit the
scale of employment loss from industry in central
and inner areas of Paris, but as yet there is no
comprehensive policy to deal with this issue. Nor,
apparently, has there been the same appreciation as
in Britain of an inner-city problem, with the loss
of industry linked to a parallel decline in population, social problems and poor housing conditions.
Undoubtedly these conditions co-exist (21), but
their spatial extent and intensity are frequently
restricted. Also, in the past their impact upon
opinion has been limited by various factors; these
have included the continued overall buoyancy of the
employment market due to the expansion of the
tertiary sector, relatively low rates of unemployment (despite an increase in the number unemployed)
and the already large scale of redevelopment in many
inner areas linked to the series of restructuring
poles. However, the situation has now changed,
emphasised by the recent and very sharp rise in
unemployment. With the continuing substantial
reduction of industrial jobs and the inability now
of the service sector to compensate for this loss,
far greater credibility is being attached to the
notion of an inner-city problem.

NORD-PAS-DE-CALAIS: INDUSTRIAL DECLINE AND THE
PROBLEM OF CONVERSION

Although still one of the most heavily
industrialised regions of France, Nord-Pas-de-Calais
is no longer characterised by the dynamism of its
industries and the rapid growth of its population
and towns, features which were central to the area's
development for much of the period from the latter
part of the nineteenth century until the 1950s.
Instead, the region's more recent history has been
increasingly dominated by the economic and social
problems resulting from the continued decline of
formerly staple activities. The need to remodel and
diversify the industrial base has long been apparent,
but as employment losses have become accentuated the
urgency with which remedial measures are required
has grown, as has the scale of such operations;
however, the process of restructuring has been
rendered more difficult by an economic climate which
has become increasingly unfavourable to large-scale
investment. Moreover, the region's living environment, frequently perceived almost exclusively in
terms of a depressed industrial area with a legacy
of poor housing, derelict land and an excessive concentration of heavy, polluting industries, has acted
as a deterrent to potential investors. These
features are not exclusive to Nord-Pas-de-Calais,
also existing in the metallurgical and coal-mining
basins of Lorraine, in the area of St. Etienne and
the Gier valley and in smaller centres such as Le
Creusot and Montceau-les-Mines; but, it is within
this area that the amplitude and spatial extent of
industrial decline are most pronounced.

A number of economic and demographic indicators
attest to the severity of the region's current
problems. Industrial employment has declined over
an extended period. Between 1962 and 1975 the net
annual loss of jobs averaged just under 3,000 but
this concealed an underlying worsening of the position, indicated by the comparative figure for the
period 1975-81 which rose to over 16,000. Thus,
whereas over 710,000 workers were employed in industry at the beginning of the 1960s, twenty years
later this total had fallen to 564,000. Consequently the proportion of the region's work-force
employed in the secondary sector has also declined,
from 53.7 per cent in 1962 to 42.4 per cent in 1981,
as has the relative position of Nord-Pas-de-Calais
as a centre of industrial employment within France.
In the past, the expansion of jobs in tertiary

activities was sufficiently strong to compensate for the drop in industrial employment (as well as the reduction in the agricultural work-force), but as the growth rate of the service sector has eased while the rate of decline of jobs in industry has risen, the level of employment within the region is now falling (Table 8.4).

Table 8.4: The Evolution of Employment in Nord-Pas-de-Calais, 1975-81

	Primary	Secondary	Tertiary	Total
	Employment ('000)			
1975	77.4	661.5	627.6	1,366.5
1976	74.8	640.3	637.0	1,352.1
1977	72.0	640.2	654.6	1,366.8
1978	69.8	618.2	667.8	1,355.8
1979	67.5	597.2	683.5	1,348.2
1980	66.0	585.4	697.5	1,332.9
1981	64.5	564.6	703.8	1,332.9

Source: INSEE, Profils de l'Economie Nord-Pas-de-Calais No.3 (1981).

The total population of Nord-Pas-de-Calais is also declining due essentially to the large and growing net outflow of people. Although there is a long tradition of people moving away from the region (22), previously it had been masked by the high level of natural increase. Recently, however, as the area's economic difficulties have become accentuated, both unemployment and emigration have risen, while simultaneously the birth rate has also eased, reducing the region's former natural demographic vitality. The past dynamism has contributed to the aggravation of current employment problems, as the youthful age structure produces a substantial yearly increase in the active population at a time when the number of jobs is falling (23).

Industries in Decline
Over a long period one of the principal weaknesses of the region's economy has been the restricted nature of the industrial base, dominated

overwhelmingly by a limited group of industries
which progressively have ceased to function as
growth sectors (24); in addition, with the major
exception of textile manufacturing, the jobs related
to these activities have been heavily biased towards
male workers. Such features are still evident in
the pattern of employment (Table 8.5), although the
industrial structure has become more diversified,
related especially to the growth of the vehicle

Table 8.5: Nord-Pas-de-Calais: Employment in Major
Branches of Manufacturing Industry, 1981

Branch	Male workers	Female workers	Total
		('000)	
Textiles and clothing	40.3	57.4	97.7
Food and drink	29.5	12.1	41.6
Mechanical engineering	37.0	3.5	40.5
Foundry and metal working	34.3	3.3	37.6
Vehicles	32.0	3.8	35.8
Iron and steel	33.3	2.0	35.3
Construction materials and glass	25.3	4.3	29.6
Coal	24.8	0.6	25.4
Chemicals/pharmaceuticals	16.6	3.8	20.4
Other	55.4	14.3	69.7

Source: INSEE, Emploi Salarié.

industry. On the negative side, however, industrial
development over the last two decades has been
closely linked to the pronounced decline of the coal,
textile and, belatedly, the iron and steel industries,
although in each case the scale and impact of this
tendency has varied over both time and space. Table
8.6 illustrates the pattern of employment change in
these branches since the early 1960s.

Coal. As in many other mining areas of western
Europe, the importance of the coal industry in Nord-
Pas-de-Calais began to diminish from the late 1950s
through the increasing loss of a series of traditional markets such as domestic and general

Table 8.6: Nord-Pas-de-Calais: Employment Change in Selected Industries

| | Mean annual rate of change | | |
	1962-68	1968-75 (%)	1975-81
Coal	- 4.9	- 6.7	- 7.3
Iron and steel	- 0.8	+ 4.1	- 5.1
Textiles	- 1.7	- 2.9	- 4.4

Source: Calculated from INSEE, Recensements and Emploi Salarié.

industrial users, the power industry and the railways. Coal was unable to withstand the competitive pressure of alternative energy sources, notably oil and natural gas. In addition, the potential of the northern coalfield was further limited by the extent to which the more accessible seams had been exhausted (particularly in the west of the coal basin where extraction had first commenced) and by technical difficulties of mining caused principally by the highly faulted and dislocated nature of the seams (25). Together these factors led to the planned run-down of the coalfield. Thus, over the period 1962-81 output fell from 27.1 to 3.9 million tonnes and the number of miners from just under 100,000 to 16,600 (of which in 1981 only 9,750 worked underground compared with 73,000 in 1962) (26). With the reappraisal of French energy policy giving greater priority to coal, the lifespan of the coalfield has been extended, but it is still anticipated that by the end of the present decade all output will have ceased. Currently mining activity is concentrated in the central zone of the coalfield around Lens and Douai, and to a lesser degree in the east, but these are also the areas in which recent job losses have been greatest.

Textiles. The manufacture of textiles represents one of the oldest industrial activities of the region, yet over the greater part of the post-war period employment has been reduced substantially and, despite an increase during the latter 1960s and early 1970s, output has also fallen. Nonetheless,

225

Nord-Pas-de-Calais remains the major centre of the
textile industry within France, featuring a diverse
range of production (27). To remain competitive the
region's industries have had to adapt to new techniques and to the increasing use of synthetic
fibres; equally, improvements in productivity have
been essential, gained largely through investment in
new machinery and the rationalisation of companies'
operations, all tendencies leading to a decline in
manpower. A reduction in the number of manufacturers and increased concentration of ownership
within the industry have also occurred. Maintaining
competitiveness has been rendered particularly
difficult, however, by the changing world pattern of
textile manufacturing, and the loss of trade due to
increased imports has further aggravated the
industry's difficulties, particularly since the
early 1970s. Between 1968 and 1975 the net annual
rate of loss of jobs within the industry averaged
2.9 per cent, yet over the period 1975-81 this rose
to 4.4 per cent. Geographically, textile manufacturing is dispersed widely throughout the region,
although the greater part of employment and production is concentrated within and around the Lille
conurbation, based upon the three centres of
Roubaix-Tourcoing, Lille and Armentières, each with
its own specialisations (28). Naturally, therefore,
job losses have been highest in this area, totalling
over 16,000 between 1975 and 1980.

Iron and Steel. There is also a long tradition of
iron working and subsequently steel manufacturing in
Nord-Pas-de-Calais, activities which during the
nineteenth century became centred increasingly upon
the coal basin and particularly the area around
Denain and Valenciennes. In the period immediately
following the second world war the region's iron and
steel industry was still of relatively modest size,
but during the 1960s and early 1970s it expanded
substantially, leading to an increase in employment,
output and productivity. Thus, between 1962 and
1974 production of steel more than doubled to over
9.0 million tonnes and the labour-force increased
from 38,000 to 46,000 workers, contrasting strongly
with the coal and textile industries. This pattern
of overall growth concealed, however, a progressive
shift of activity away from the traditional centres
of the industry on the coalfield and in the Sambre
valley in favour of the coast (29). Already, in the
early part of the present century, two small works

had been established at Boulogne and to the north of
Dunkerque, but the changes that began to occur in
the 1960s related to the decision by Usinor to con-
struct a large, integrated works on a coastal site
at Dunkerque (30). Not only would the new plant be
able to benefit fully from the changing pattern of
supply of the industry's raw materials, but such a
location would also facilitate the export of production and offer an ample reserve of land for subsequent extension. Moreover, the progressive development of this site over more than a decade enabled
the introduction of a series of technological
advances in steel making, greatly increasing the
plant's efficiency. Since the mid-1970s, however,
the fall in the demand for steel has had serious
repercussions upon the industry, particularly, for
the older factories of the interior, despite in
certain cases their relatively recent modernisation
(31). Production and employment have been concentrated to an even greater extent upon Dunkerque,
with the consequent loss of jobs and closure or
partial shut-down of works in the interior. Thus,
Usinor has ceased to produce iron and steel at its
plants at Denain and Valenciennes, retaining only a
series of rolling and finishing operations. The
social consequences in terms of lost jobs have been
substantial and caused frequently violent protest.
By 1980, for example, Usinor's Denain plant employed
only 1,500 workers compared with over 8,500 at the
beginning of the 1970s (32); overall, the region of
Valenciennes-Denain suffered a net loss of around
7,000 jobs in the steel industry between 1975 and
1980. Moreover, despite concentration upon
Dunkerque, so severe are the industry's problems
that production is well below capacity and Usinor is
now shedding rather than recruiting labour. Between
1975 and 1980 jobs in Dunkerque's steel industry
remained approximately stable at around 12,500
workers, contrasting markedly with a mean annual
increase of 18 per cent between 1968 and 1975.

A number of common features underlie the
decline of these three formerly dominant activities.
First, the loss of jobs has been related essentially
to male employment, thus exacerbating dispropor-
tionately the problem of unemployment amongst male
workers. Second, the spatial distribution of job
losses has been unequal, affecting over the last
decade principally the eastern and central areas of
the coal basin, and the Lille conurbation. Finally,
the consequences of closure are not limited solely to
employment losses, but have frequently been

associated with the legacy of a disfigured urban
environment characterised by derelict land, spoil
heaps, abandoned factories and decaying housing, all
tending to thwart the process of conversion.

Restructuring the Nord's Industrial Economy
By concentrating upon only three activities in
decline, this tends to under-state the problem of
employment loss, for in recent years a reduction of
jobs has become a growing feature of a series of
industries including metal working and shipbuilding,
chemicals, glass and construction materials. This
is not intended to imply, however, that efforts have
not been undertaken to restrict or compensate for
the decline. On the contrary, numerous initiatives
have been launched over an extended period with the
aim of revitalising the industrial economy and,
above all, generating new employment. These have
originated from the government as well as a range of
regional based authorities including local Chambers
of Commerce and notably, the Association pour
l'Expansion Industrielle de la Région Nord-Pas-de-
Calais (APEX), a branch of DATAR whose very presence
attests to the gravity of the region's economic
difficulties. In addition one of the earliest
bodies to intervene was the regional coal authority
(HBNPC) through its specialist services SOFIREM and
SAII, promoting the reindustrialisation of the coal
basin and the retraining of displaced miners (33).
          Various strategies have been employed (34). In
an attempt to provide a setting conducive to economic growth, considerable investment has been devoted
to the improvement of infrastructure, exemplified by
the expansion of the region's motorways; most
recently the route between Lille and Valenciennes
has been completed (1981), while that between Calais
and Cambrai (A26), ultimately linking with Reims, is
being gradually extended. Not only has this greatly
improved accessibility but many sections of motorway
in Nord-Pas-de-Calais also have the advantage of
being free of tolls. The many potential advantages
offered for heavy industry by a coastal site
adjacent to deep-water port facilities, allied to
the decline of the coalfield, led to the idea of
developing a major heavy industrial and port complex
between Calais and Dunkerque (35), with the expectation that this 'growth pole' would stimulate expansion in the flagging industrial zones of the
interior. Since the early 1960s and particularly
over much of the last decade, Dunkerque certainly

did expand greatly as a heavy industrial centre, linked to the growth of the iron and steel, oil refining, petrochemical and nuclear industries; the port has also been extended, notably through development of the new 'western port' (36). However, while Dunkerque itself may have become the regional focus of such industries, to the detriment of the coal basin, the extent to which it has fostered growth in the region's interior is questionable (37).

Greatest emphasis upon the replacement of jobs has been placed upon the area of the coalfield, the Lille conurbation and the Sambre valley, all affected by the substantial decline of at least one group of industries. A number of incentives have been used to encourage industrial investment. Over a long period former mining areas have been rehabilitated and a series of new and large industrial estates have been established as at Béthune, Douvrin and Douai. Equally, selected zones of the three areas outlined above have long qualified for maximum assistance under the government's regional policy, while the coalfield has also benefited from aid provided by the European Coal and Steel Community. Not unnaturally there has also been the advantage of a plentiful, if not always highly trained, labour-force. Less easy to measure, but undoubtedly influential, particularly for larger investment projects has been the effect of government 'persuasive' tactics.

Many new industrial plants have now been established within the region, exhibiting considerable diversity in size and the nature of manufacturing activities. The most substantial contribution to the generation of new employment has been made, however, by the car and car components industry (38). In 1962 this branch employed fewer than 6,000 workers, but by 1981 the total had risen to over 35,000, reflecting a series of investments by both major French manufacturers. Renault's factory at Douai now employs over 7,000 workers, while in terms of recent investment Peugeot is developing a new plant near Valenciennes and Renault a new works near Bruay.

Some success in the remodelling of the region's industrial structure due to these factors and to the influence of the various bodies promoting development is evident. Since the SAII started to intervene in 1967 it alone has been involved in the creation of over 16,500 jobs, while from a similar date APEX has contributed to the generation of over

60,200 jobs, nearly 60 per cent of which have been
located throughout the coalfield. Yet, with the
principal exception of the area around Dunkerque,
industrial employment within the region continues to
decline, frequently heavily, as in the eastern part
of the coal basin (Figure 8.2). For example, in the
sub-region of Lens there was a net loss of 11,000
jobs between 1975 and 1980, while in the area of
Douai, despite an increase of over 5,000 workers in
car production, overall industrial employment fell
by 4,000. These trends are mirrored in the continued outflow of population, emphasising the amplitude of problems within the region and the limitations of measures which have been taken to improve
the position (39).

Given the continued dominance within the
region's industrial employment structure of activities with an underlying tendency towards decline,
present trends seem likely to continue; moreover, it
is questionable for how long the car industry will
continue to expand. However, restructuring is not

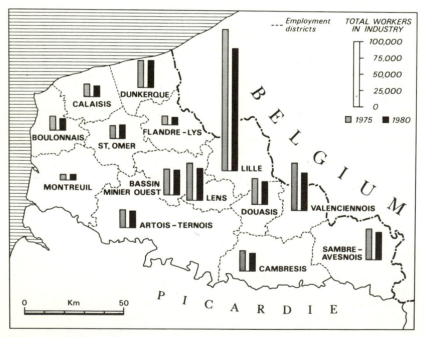

Figure 8.2: Changes in Industrial Employment in
Nord-Pas-de-Calais

only confined to generating new industrial jobs.
The tertiary sector is still relatively weakly
represented within the region, offering scope for
development; it has long been argued that one of the
constraints on the region's development, encouraging
people to leave the area, is the lack of diversity
of employment opportunities created by this situation (40). Expansion of the service sector would
also help solve the problem of a continuing inadequate number of jobs for women, although the most
propitious location for such growth, Lille, is
unfortunately not the area of greatest imbalance in
the employment structure.

THE UNDERINDUSTRIALISED WEST: THE CASE OF BRITTANY

Brittany, unlike Nord-Pas-de-Calais, has never been
marked by a strong industrial tradition. This is
despite a long history of predominantly small,
rural-based manufacturing activities related to
products such as textiles, leather goods and
articles made out of wood, or to the limited processing of the region's agricultural output (41).
Moreover, with few exceptions heavy industry and
large-scale manufacturing plants have never been
features of a region long characterised by the weakness of its industrial sector. From the early 1960s,
however, the number of jobs in industry began to
increase substantially, accompanied by a diversification of the industrial structure through the
choice of Brittany as the location for factories in
a series of growth activities such as electronics
and vehicle manufacturing. This has represented an
important component of the region's more general
transformation, as agriculture has been modernised
and infrastructure improved, notably through the
upgrading of the road network. In addition, the new
dynamism of the industrial sector has induced its own
consequences, helping to arrest the previous decline
of Brittany's population and encouraging a redistribution of the region's inhabitants in favour of its
urban centres. Government intervention and the
attraction of branch plants of firms based in Paris
have been vital factors in the revival of industrial
activity.
    Nonetheless, despite the creation of a large
number of new industrial jobs, Brittany remains
weakly industrialised compared with many regions of
the country, with extensive areas of the interior
still largely devoid of industry. Only 28 per cent

of the region's labour-force is employed in the
secondary sector. In addition, those industries
within Brittany which, in comparison with the
national average, are over-represented tend also to
be those which experienced at best a modest rate of
expansion prior to the more recent period of widespread contraction of industrial employment; shipbuilding, food and drink, construction materials and
leather goods are representative of these activities
(42). Furthermore, a significant number of jobs in
the secondary sector are concentrated in building
and public works (43), a group of industries characterised by a strongly fluctuating level of employment and an unstable structure, reflective of the
large number of small enterprises whose lifespan is
often shortlived. In contrast, the automobile
industry and electrical and electronics industries,
which have expanded strongly at a national level,
now represent a significant feature of the region's
industrial structure (Table 8.7).

Table 8.7: Brittany: Employment in Major Branches
of Manufacturing Industry, 1981

Activity	Employment ('000)
Food and drink	40.6
Aeronautical industries, shipbuilding	19.4
Electrical engineering and electronics	18.3
Vehicles	16.0
Construction materials and glass	10.1
Wood and furniture	9.6
Heavy metallurgy	9.3
Mechanical engineering	8.6
Textiles and clothing	8.3
Other	29.3

Source: INSEE, Emploi Salarié.

The Take-Off of Industry
The previous absence of industrial development has
been linked to a variety of factors, not least the
region's relative isolation and inaccessibility
within France (44). Not only was the region inadequately connected to other areas of the country,

including Paris, but internal routes, particularly
between the northern and southern parts of Brittany,
were poorly developed. Thus, the region has been
handicapped by its remoteness from the country's
major markets and centres of innovation. Also,
during the nineteenth century, lacking the necessary
raw materials or easy access to them, it remained
largely untouched by the industrial revolution and
major advances in production techniques. Such
progress was further inhibited by the absence of a
strong regional banking network capable of generating the necessary capital for industrial investment.
Generally, therefore, in a predominantly rural
region, highly dependent upon agriculture and dominated by small and medium sized towns, over a long
period few attractions existed for the industrialist
(45).
      Yet, throughout much of the last two decades
there had been substantial investment in industry
and a correspondingly large number of new jobs
created within this sector, suggesting a re-
evaluation of the region's potential assets as an
industrial centre or the intervention of a series of
new locational factors. Both processes appear to
have been active. In a period of strong economic
growth (from the mid-1950s until the mid-1970s), and
a general shortage of labour, the release of manpower from agriculture and declining rural-based
industries, combined with the widespread existence
of underemployment amongst the labour-force in
traditional activities, represented valuable assets
in attracting industrial investment. Moreover, not
only was labour abundant, particularly in relation
to the relatively unskilled worker, but also comparatively cheap, certainly in the early growth years
before trade union membership became more widespread.
Improvements have been made to communications (for
example, the Plan Routier Breton) and to the provision of energy. Initiatives have also come from
enterprising local authorities through a variety of
means ranging from the sponsorship of new industrial
estates to the 'marketing' of their respective
localities. Throughout the region government grants
(payable at the maximum rate in certain western
areas), have also long been available to encourage
new firms, although their precise influence is
difficult to evaluate. Of equal if not greater
significance has been the extent to which regional
action groups and promotional organisations and
political personalities have been able to persuade
the government to exert its influence in stimulating

industrial and related development within the
region. One example is the expansion of the electrical and electronics industries (many of which are
highly dependent upon state contracts in fields such
as telecommunications), a process linked in part to
factors such as the location of the Centre National
d'Etudes des Télécommunications at Lannion, a region
in which over three-quarters of industrial employment is now in these activities (46). Industries
linked to telecommunications have played a significant role in the industrial revival of Brittany, but
if this sector is to maintain this function there is
a need in certain cases to re-orientate production
away from the manufacture of basic telephone equipment (for which the market is increasingly
saturated) to new growth areas.

Certain changes in other economic activities
within the region have helped promote industrialisation. Thus, the increased specialisation within
agriculture upon the intensive rearing of pigs and
poultry has led to the growth of firms manufacturing
animal feeds (47), while more generally the
previously underdeveloped and fragmented agricultural processing industry has been expanded and
reorganised. Despite certain structural weaknesses,
the overall importance of agriculturally based
industries is considerable. Nearly a quarter of
employment in manufacturing industry is concentrated
within these activities and they also make a
substantial contribution to regional turnover and
value-added in industry, and have attracted a high
level of investment (48). Moreover, not only does
this branch constitute a major area of industrial
specialisation within Brittany, but it also represents one of the principal concentrations of food
processing industries within France. Activity is
centred upon dairying and meat and cereal based
products, although marked intra-regional variations
exist (49). All these features attest to the
continuing important role of agriculture in Brittany,
but they also conceal the extremely heterogeneous
character of this branch of industry, still dominated by numerous small often out-dated production
units.

Given the previous pattern of stagnation of the
region's industrial activities, the creation of new
jobs since the mid-1950s has been impressive,
although against these increases has to be offset
the loss of employment opportunities in many traditional industries. Various statistics illustrate
the strength of change. Since the early 1960s

development grants have been accorded on the
understanding that nearly 70,000 new jobs would be
created (50). In the early years a number of major
companies such as Citroën and Thomson established
large factories in Brittany (51). Subsequently,
many have continued to expand, contributing to a
process of self-sustained rather than induced
growth. By the early 1970s between 6,000 and 8,000
new jobs were being created in industry each year
(52), and in total over the period 1962-75 there was
a net increase of over 82,000 in the industrial
labour-force. Since the latter date expansion has
slowed dramatically, even amongst those activities
such as the automobile, electronics and food
processing industries which have underlain the
modern industrial revolution in Brittany. By the
early 1980s much of the dynamism formerly associated
with this movement had disappeared, at least
temporarily, as the total number of jobs in the
secondary sector started to fall (53).

Brittany as an Industrial Region
Important as these changes have been, Brittany still
possesses a relatively weak industrial base, characterised by a number of continuing structural
deficiencies and considerable spatial contrasts in
the distribution and intensity of manufacturing. A
third of all employment in manufacturing is concentrated in the region's five towns above 50,000
population, while only four urban centres have more
than 10,000 industrial workers (Rennes, Brest,
Lorient and St. Brieuc) (54). The principal concentrations of industry (with the major exception of
Rennes) are located around the periphery of Brittany,
reinforcing a long-standing contrast between the
more developed coastal belt and the more impoveri-
shed rural interior (Figure 8.3). In such rural
areas there is a pronounced absence of industrial
activity and in the small centres of industry which
do exist there is often an excessive specialisation
upon a very restricted range of industries. For
some areas, however, particularly those in relative
proximity to larger urban centres with more diversified labour markets, such limitations are partially
offset by commuting to industries in these towns.
This tendency is most pronounced in the region of
Rennes, principally reflecting the wide area from
which employees of Citroën travel to work (55).
Moreover, for many small-holders in rural areas, the
growth of industry in adjacent urban centres has had

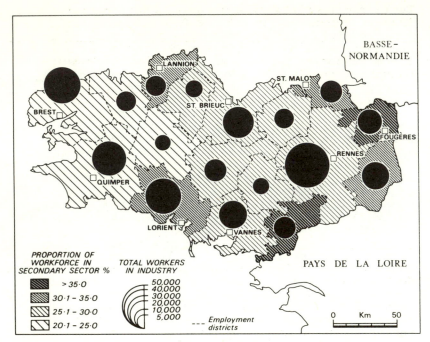

Figure 8.3:   Industrial Employment in Brittany in
1980

the advantage of enabling them to maintain their
interest in farming while combining this with an
industrial job.
　　Despite a limited number of large establishments (56), overall the region's industries are
still dominated by small productive units (Table
8.8), although decentralised plants have tended to
be of a larger size than indigenous factories. Decentralisation, however, although beneficial to the
region in terms of the volume of new employment
generated, has resulted in little improvement in the
qualitative aspects of such provision, with many of
the additional jobs relating to largely unskilled
work on production lines or in assembly operations
(57). The process has also contributed to the high
level to which industrial firms in Brittany are
dependent upon decision-making centres external to
the region. Thus, it is estimated that over half of
all industrial employment and investment is controlled by companies with headquarters in another
region of France, principally Paris (58).
　　Some support for the success of

Table 8.8: Brittany: Industrial Plant Structure,
1980

Size of plant (no. of employees)	Number of plants
0	6,871
1-5	4,986
6-9	840
10-19	696
20-49	721
50-99	313
100-199	182
200-499	105
500-999	22
1,000+	15

Source: Chambre Régionale de Commerce et d'Industrie de Bretagne.

industrialisation policies is provided by the altered demographic performance of the region, as the previous tendency towards an overall loss of population has been reversed, largely due to a now positive migrational balance. While it seems logical to suggest that an enlarged and streng-thened industrial base has assisted in this trans-formation, economic growth within the region is now related increasingly to the expansion of jobs in the tertiary sector, implying that other influences are also involved. Moreover, the overall increase in population conceals a continuing outward migration of young people, largely compensated by the inflow of retired persons, and a still strong reduction in the inhabitants of rural areas. Other indices, relating to incomes and living standards, suggest that Brittany is still disadvantaged compared with many French regions (59). Industrialisation has represented an important strand of policies designed to ameliorate this position, but despite an impres-sive record of new jobs created, Brittany's indus-trial base remains characterised by a certain fragility and duality.

NOTES

1. This is undertaken elsewhere; see, for example, Tuppen, J.N., *France* (Dawson, Folkestone, 1980), 111-21.

2. See, for example, Bonneville, M., 'La désindustrialisation urbaine: le cas de Villeurbanne', *Revue de Géographie de Lyon*, 50 (1975), 97-105; Dumolard, P., 'Croissance et réorganisation de l'ensemble urban lyonnais', *Revue de Géographie de Lyon*, 56 (1981), 5-27.

3. In the early 1960s nearly a third of the total value-added in French industry derived from the Paris region and approximately 28 per cent of the labour-force in the secondary sector was located here. See Lefèvre, G., 'Les zones d'activité de l'est de l'agglomération parisienne', *Analyse de l'Espace*, No.2 (1979), 1-26.

4. Tuppen, *France*, 113-16. This takes into account both the level of employment and the value of production.

5. For a more detailed appraisal of the labour-force see, for example, Beaujeu-Garnier, J., *Atlas de Géographie de Paris et de la Région d'Ile-de-France* (Flammarion, Paris, 1977), vol.2, 16-22, or Estienne, P., *La France* (Masson, Paris, 1980), vol.2, 115-16.

6. Pinchemel, P., *La Région Parisienne* (Presses Universitaires de France, Paris, 1979), 13-14.

7. Beaujeu-Garnier, *Atlas et Géographie de Paris*, vol.1, 107-19.

8. Tuppen, J.N., 'The development of French new towns: an assessment of progress', *Urban Studies*, 20 (1983), forthcoming.

9. For more details see Beaujeu-Garnier, *Atlas et Géographie de Paris*, vol.2, 21-2.

10. 'Un Bilan de décentralisation industrielle', *Problèmes Economiques*, No.1747 (1981), 3.

11. 'L'évolution industrielle de l'Ile-de-France', *Informations d'Ile-de-France*, No.53 (1981), 5.

12. Demangeat, D., 'Réflexions sur la désindustrialisation de la région parisienne', *Analyse de l'Espace*, No.2 (1979), 36.

13. Derot, F. and Du Pasquier, G., *Réflexions sur la politique industrielle de l'Ile-de-France* (Institut d'Aménagement et d'Urbanisme de la Région d'Ile-de-France, Paris, 1977); Demangeat, 'Réflexions sur la désindustrialisation'; *Le Monde*,

14 Feb. 1978; Le Monde, 22 March 1980.
14. Le Monde, 31 July 1981.
15. 'L'évolution industrielle de l'Ile-de-France', 5.
16. Le Monde, 6 March 1982.
17. Such aid is provided and financed by the département's Conseil Général.
18. Le Monde, 11 Aug. 1981 and 14 Oct. 1981.
19. 'Politique nouvelle de la rénovation urbaine', Paris Projet, No.21-2 (1982), 16-17. Wherever possible it is also intended to facilitate the continued operation of existing small businesses.
20. 'Politique nouvelle de la rénovation', 16-17.
21. See, for example, Bentham, G. and Moseley, M., 'Socio-economic change and disparities within the Paris agglomeration: does Paris have an "inner-city problem"?' Regional Studies, 14 (1980), 55-70; Madge, C. and Willmott, P., Inner City Poverty in Paris and London (Routledge and Kegan Paul, London, 1981).
22. Thumerelle, P.J., 'La population du Nord-Pas-de-Calais au seuil des années 80: héritages et mutations', Hommes et Terres du Nord, No.1 (1980), 2.
23. Thumerelle, P.J., 'Crise économique et décroissance démographique - l'exemple de la région Nord-Pas-de-Calais', Annales de Géographie, 89 (1980), 148-50.
24. Tuppen, France, 146-53.
25. For more details of the development of this industry see Flatrès, P., Atlas et Géographie du Nord et de la Picardie (Flammarion, Paris, 1980), 165-77.
26. The majority of underground workers are foreigners (principally Moroccans) reflecting the increasing rejection of this type of work by Frenchmen.
27. See Flatrès, Atlas et Géographie du Nord, 187-98.
28. Flatrès, Atlas et Géographie du Nord, 187-90.
29. See Flatrès, Atlas et Géographie du Nord, 178-87.
30. Tuppen, J.N., 'The role of Dunkerque in the industrial economy of Nord-Pas-de-Calais', in Hoyle, B.S. and Pinder, D.A. (eds.), Cityport Industrialisation and Regional Development (Pergamon, Oxford, 1981), 270-1.
31. Fuller details of the recent development and problems of the industry are contained in,

Malézieux, J., 'Crise et restructuration de la sidérurgie française', L'Espace Géographique, 9 (1980), 183-96, and Gachelin, C., 'La mutation de la sidérurgie de la région du Nord', Hommes et Terres du Nord, No.1 (1980), 21-33.

32.   Gachelin, 'La mutation de la sidérurgie', 25.

33.   HBNPC - Houillères du Bassin du Nord et du Pas-de-Calais. SOFIREM (Société Financière pour Favoriser l'Industrialisation des Régions Minières) is a subsidiary of Charbonnages de France and was created in 1967. It is basically a finance company which, for example, through becoming a minority share-holder for a limited period, assists new firms to establish in the coal basin. Assistance is intended primarily for small firms. In Nord-Pas-de-Calais SOFIREM has assisted 66 companies involving over 6,600 jobs (by 1982). SAII (Service d'Acceuil Implantations Industrielles) is a promotional organisation operated to encourage industrial development in current and former mining regions.

34.   Battiau, M., 'Un essai d'analyse des difficultés du Nord-Pas-de-Calais', L'Information Géographique, 45 (1981), 99-100; Flatrès, Atlas et Géographie du Nord, 217.

35.   Flatrès, Atlas et Géographie du Nord, 217.

36.   Ducret, B., 'Port de Dunkerque', L'Information Géographique, 45 (1981), 122-6.

37.   Perret, J.M., Usinor-Dunkerque ou l'Espoir Déçu des Flamands (Westhoek-Editions, Dunkerque, 1978). Tuppen, 'The role of Dunkerque', 276-9.

38.   Flatrès, Atlas et Géographie du Nord, 219-21.

39.   Battiau, M., 'Le rôle des données structurelles dans l'évolution du nombre des emplois industriels dans le Nord-Pas-de-Calais des années 1950 à nos jours', Hommes et Terres du Nord, No.1 (1980), 15.

40.   Battiau, 'Un essai d'analyse', 97.

41.   Le Lannou, M., La Bretagne et les Bretons (Presses Universitaires de France, Paris, 1978), 102-3.

42.   Larivière, J-P., 'Données sur la répartition du secteur secondaire dans l'espace breton', Norois, 28 (1981), 395.

43.   79,000 workers representing 32 per cent of employment in the secondary sector in 1981.

44.   Estienne, La France, vol.2, 159-61.

45.   A general account of the region's economic and demographic situation in the nineteenth and early twentieth centuries is contained in

Meynier, A., <u>Atlas et Géographie de la Bretagne</u> (Flammarion, Paris, 1976), 35-40.

46.   Larivière, 'Données sur la répartition du secteur secondaire', 396.

47.   Diry, J-P., 'L'industrie française de l'alimentation du bétail', <u>Annales de Géographie</u>, 88 (1979), 694-702.

48.   James, J-P., 'Dynamisme des industries agricoles et alimentaires en Bretagne', <u>Octan</u>, No.5 (1981), 5.

49.   James, 'Dynamisme des industries agricoles', 9.

50.   <u>Rapport d'Activité</u> (DATAR, Paris), various years.

51.   Two Citroën factories on the outskirts of Rennes now employ around 12,000 workers. However, most of the new factories created within Brittany are much smaller, rarely exceeding 500 workers.

52.   <u>Le Monde</u>, 8 Feb. 1977.

53.   Part of this reversal has been caused by the reduction of labour in the construction industry. Between 1975 and 1981 there was a net decline of nearly 10,000 jobs.

54.   Larivière, 'Données sur la répartition du secteur secondaire', 395-6.

55.   Larivière, J-P., 'La zone de recrutement de main-d'oeuvre de l'usine Citroën en Chartres-de-Bretagne', <u>Norois</u>, 28 (1981), 389-94.

56.   Meynier, A., 'L'annuaire industriel de Bretagne', <u>Norois</u>, 28 (1981), 405.

57.   Estienne, <u>La France</u>, vol.2. 162.

58.   James, J-P., 'L'industrie bretonne et ses faiblesses', <u>Octant</u>, No.1 (1980), 8.

59.   Estienne, <u>La France</u>, vol.2. 162.

Chapter Nine

THE TERTIARY SECTOR: AN OVERVIEW

THE ROLE OF THE TERTIARY SECTOR

Although the remarkable post-war revival of the
French economy is frequently attributed to the very
substantial rise in the volume of industrial output
and the increased efficiency of the country's
industries, important changes have also taken place
in the service sector. Since the early 1960s the
rapid growth of employment in this latter field
underlies one of the major transformations of French
society over the post-war period [1]. Tertiary
activities now employ approximately 58 per cent of
the French labour-force and contribute around 50 per
cent of the country's gross domestic product.
However, by the early 1980s, with the downturn in
the economy leading to a lower rate of growth in the
service sector, and an accentuated decline of industrial jobs, the expansion of employment in tertiary
activities was failing to compensate for losses in
agriculture and industry.
    The extent to which the tertiary sector has
expanded is indicated by the substantial growth of
employment, but the strength of this change is
frequently made more obvious by the associated
transformation of rural and urban landscapes.
Accommodating the increase in retailing and office
activities has led to the radical alteration of the
physical structure of the central areas of many
cities; growth has also resulted in the largely
unstructured proliferation of commercial outlets on
the outskirts of urban areas. The expansion of
tourism has produced equally profound alterations to
the environment, both in areas which are highly
urbanised (such as the Côte d'Azur), and in regions
predominantly devoid of large settlements (for
example, the Pyrenees and Alps). So great has been

the scale of change, that a reappraisal of the
desirability of certain forms of development has
occurred, accompanied by increasing measures of
control.

Given the high rate at which jobs have been
created in tertiary activities, measures to
influence the distribution of such employment have
taken on an increasingly important role in regional
policy. The government first intervened in the
early 1960s, seeking to divert offices away from the
capital, partly through the now abandoned policy of
métropoles d'équilibre. Subsequently, its interest
was extended to research laboratories and now
greatest priority is accorded to those activities
likely to act as catalysts for growth in their new
locations.

The significance of the tertiary sector to
regional development is not confined, however, to
offices and research institutes. In many rural
areas, for example, if the continued outward migration of population is to be arrested and communities
are to remain viable, the maintenance or increase of
services upon which residents depend is vital.
Similarly, in such areas the encouragement of
tourism represents one means by which to help
reverse the tendency towards depopulation, and
generate new employment and income. More generally,
throughout much of the country (particularly in the
south) tourism with its many offshoots has become a
major factor in economic development. This does not
mean, however, that such growth has always been seen
as beneficial. On the contrary, it has often been
highly controversial, indicative of the many less
attractive features of the 'tourist explosion'
ranging from overcrowding to the despoilment of
areas of outstanding natural beauty; the current
controversy over the extension of skiing facilities
on the slopes of Mont Blanc is an apt illustration.
Thus, the forces for new employment growth are often
opposed to those for conservation.

THE DIVERSE NATURE OF TERTIARY ACTIVITIES

The sub-division of the tertiary sector into a broad
series of activities offers some indication not only
of the diversity of pursuits subsumed within it, but
also of the relative contribution of each branch to
total employment. These characteristics are
summarised in Table 9.1 (2). It is apparent that
employment is not equally spread amongst these

Table 9.1:   Employment in Tertiary Activities, 1981

| | Number of wage-earners | | |
	Male	Female ('000)	Total
Wholesaling	543	231	814
Retailing	468	646	1,114
Car retailing and repair	275	54	329
Hotels, cafes, restaurants	191	205	396
Transport	689	137	836
Telecommunications, postal services	265	194	459
Market services (firms)	448	387	835
Market services (households)	427	1,108	1,535
Property leasing	30	27	57
Insurance	59	76	135
Banking and finance	211	205	416
Non-market services	1,621	1,964	3,585
Total	5,227	5,274	10,501

Source: INSEE, Emploi Salarié.

categories. Thus, major employers are represented
by the varied group of retailing and wholesaling
businesses and above all non-market services, relating to employment in, for example, central and
local government and education: in 1981 this latter
branch accounted for 3.6 million employees.
Services provided to firms and households also
represent a large category of employment, together
offering in excess of 2.3 million jobs. These activities relate to fields such as consultancy,
research, sporting activities and, notably, jobs in
the health services. With around 826,000 employees,
transport industries are also important employers,
whereas (at least in terms of total employment) the
branches of banking, finance and insurance, and
telecommunications are of much reduced significance.
    Tertiary activities are also distinguished by
the relatively large number and high proportion of
female jobs offered (Table 9.1). Whereas in 1981
only a third of the 6.9 million industrial wage-
earners were women, in the tertiary sector the
number of female employees stood at around 5.3
million, representing 50 per cent of the total

labour-force. Nonetheless, even between service
activities there are considerable variations in the
role of female employment, ranging from its comparatively strong position in the provision of domestic,
health, administrative and educational services to
its much weaker influence in the transport and
wholesaling branches.

Various other structural contrasts exist within
the tertiary sector and between service activities.
Just as in industry there is considerable variation
in the size of businesses, although small and medium
sized enterprises predominate overwhelmingly; moreover, the high level of control exercised by relatively few companies over a branch of industry, a
comparatively common feature of the secondary sector, is far less apparent in relation to tertiary
activities (3). In the same way that various forms
of industry have existed and evolved over a long
period, so too have many service functions, not
least those linked to commerce and administration.
However, as the economy has become greatly enlarged,
more complex to manage and experienced substantial
modifications and specialisation, birth has been
given to an extended series of new services in
fields such as advertising and promotion, data-
processing, technical advice and financial consultancy. Equally, many established services have not
only grown substantially in size, but have also
taken on new forms; in the health sector the range
of specialist services provided has been greatly
enlarged, many new recreational and leisure activities have become increasingly popular, while a
variety of specialist organisations servicing firms
(such as office cleaning companies) have flourished.
The growth and enlargement of the economy since the
early 1960s, therefore, has been characterised by
the development of a series of 'modern' services,
many of which are directly related to industrial
expansion, population increase or changing consumption patterns of that population.

As well as assessing the size and structure of
the tertiary sector by branches of activity, it is
also possible to analyse its role by the use of
occupational data (Table 9.2). Thus, in 1980 there
were over 9.7 million people working in tertiary
occupations of which the largest group of around 4
million workers was represented by office staff and
a much smaller number of sales assistants (around 20
per cent of this total). There were also a substantial number of employees classified as junior
executives and administrators, but this is a

Table 9.2:   Evolution of Tertiary Employment by
Socio-Economic Grouping, 1954-80

Socio-economic group	Total workers				
	1954	1962	1968 ('000)	1975	1980
Retailers and wholesalers	1,434	1,307	1,236	1,100	1,104
The professions, senior executives and administrators	554	766	995	1,459	1,763
Junior executives and administrators	1,113	1,501	2,006	2,765	3,181
Office and shop workers	2,068	2,396	2,996	3,841	3,682

	Mean annual rate of change			
	1954-62	1962-68 (%)	1968-75	1975-80
Retailers and wholesalers	- 1.1	- 0.9	- 1.6	+ 0.1
The professions, senior executives and administrators	+ 4.8	+ 5.0	+ 6.7	+ 4.2
Junior executives and administrators	+ 4.4	+ 5.6	+ 5.4	+ 3.0
Office and shop workers	+ 2.0	+ 4.2	+ 4.0	- 0.9

Source: Calculated from INSEE, Tableaux de
l'Economie Française, 1981 and Enquête sur l'Emploi
d'Octobre 1980 (1981).

relatively heterogeneous category of employment
which includes nearly 830,000 technicians and around
740,000 teaching staff. Other major occupational
groups are of lesser significance, although the
professions and upper management account for nearly
1.8 million people including 800,000 senior executives. Many of these occupations, however, are not
confined to activities classified within the
tertiary sector. Industrial firms frequently depend
upon a substantial number of management, administrative, marketing, research and clerical staff, all
tertiary occupations, yet when categorised by
activity, these are included within the secondary

sector. Moreover, various industrial firms, apart from selling their manufactured goods, also market their engineering or research expertise, adding to their complement of tertiary workers. Overall, however, the largest group of white-collar workers within manufacturing firms is generally represented by those engaged in management and administrative tasks (4). Similarly, various jobs classified (by activity) within the service sector are essentially industrial (manual) occupations, as for example in the branch of transport. It is estimated that nearly 24 per cent of employment in the tertiary sector is accounted for by industrial jobs, whereas over 18 per cent of employment in industry is represented by tertiary occupations (5).

THE POST-WAR EXPANSION OF TERTIARY ACTIVITIES

Throughout the greater part of the post-war period the expansion of the tertiary sector has been emphatic. Between 1954 and 1981 employment in service activites rose from under 7 million employees to over 12 millions. For much of this period mean growth rates exceeded 2 per cent per annum (Table 9.3), considerably above those achieved in the industrial sector. Even during the years of exceptional strong economic growth of the late 1960s and early 1970s, the expansion of employment in tertiary activities easily outdistanced that in industry, and between 1962 and 1975 the expansion of employment in the service sector accounted for three-quarters of the net increase in jobs within France (6). Moreover, between 1968 and 1975 service

Table 9.3: The Growth of Employment in the Tertiary Sector

	Mean annual growth rate (%)
1954-62	2.4
1962-68	1.8
1968-75	2.7
1975-81	2.0

Source: Calculated from INSEE, Recensements and Rapport sur les Comptes de la Nation de l'Année 1981.

activities accounted for a net annual increase of
215,000 jobs compared with only 64,000 in the
industrial sector (7). Since then the contrast in
performance has been accentuated. Whereas employment in the tertiary sector showed a net increase of
1.2 million jobs between 1975 and 1981, that in
industry experienced a net decrease of over 0.6
million. Despite the relative buoyancy of service
activities, recent trends also indicate a now
generally much lower rate of growth in employment
(8). This has occurred as the depressant effects of
the recession deepen and widen, as real incomes have
started to fall and as certain structural adjustments (leading to lower labour requirements) have
also taken place within the tertiary sector.

Within this general increase of employment in
service activities, the growth of female jobs has
been particularly strong, reflecting not only the
nature of the work, but also a progressive increase
in the number of women actively seeking employment.
Thus, of the 1.5 million jobs created in the
tertiary sector between 1968 and 1975, 62 per cent
were taken by women (9). Similarly, over the period
1975-81, 64 per cent of the net increase in employment was accounted for by female jobs; moreover,
whereas the number of employees in the tertiary
sector overall expanded by 13.7 per cent, the rate
for female workers was 18.1 per cent, leading inevitably to an increase in the proportional significance of women employed in service activities. In
addition, most women are employed full-time, despite
a general growth of part-time work (10).

Although the expansion of employment has been a
general feature of the development of the tertiary
sector for an extended period, not all branches of
activity have evolved in a comparable manner or at a
similar rate. Table 9.4 illustrates the contrasting
pattern of evolution of the major branches of
service activities between 1975 and 1981. While
certain traditional areas of growth remained relatively buoyant (banking and insurance) (11) the
branches where growth has been most pronounced
relate to the provision of a variety of services to
firms and particularly households (12). Furthermore,
since the early 1970s there has been a very substantial rise in the number of temporary employees (13),
such as secretaries, currently totalling around
200,000; this reflects a change in both the nature
of employment being sought, notably as more women
have joined the labour-force, and a more flexible
attitude towards the organisation of work by

The Tertiary Sector

Table 9.4: Growth of Tertiary Employment by
Activity, 1975-81

| | Number of wage-earners | | Rate of growth |
| | 1975 | 1981 | |
	('000)		(%)
Wholesaling	757	814	7.5
Retailing	1,003	1,114	11.1
Car retailing and repair	286	329	15.0
Hotels, cafes, restaurants	340	396	16.5
Transport	812	826	1.8
Telecommunications, postal services	400	459	14.7
Market services (firms)	650	835	28.5
Market services (households)	1,154	1,535	33.0
Property leasing	51	57	11.8
Insurance	122	135	10.6
Banking and finance	374	416	11.2
Non-market services	3,286	3,585	9.1

Source: INSEE, Emploi Salarié.

employers (14). Just as variations in the pattern
of development exist between major branches of
activity, there are also frequently contrasts within
individual categories, particularly where a diverse
range of jobs is grouped together. The overall
stability of employment in transportation conceals,
for example, a rise of the number of workers in the
road haulage industry compared with a fall in those
working for the railways (15).
    A further indicator of differential growth
within the service sector, shown over a much longer
period, is provided by the contrasting pattern of
development of the various tertiary occupations
(Table 9.2) (16). For most groups there has been a
pattern of an increasing rate of growth throughout
the 1950s and 1960s, which was largely sustained
during the early 1970s; then, over the period 1975-
80 rates moderated, with the previous tendency
towards expansion even reversed in the case of office
workers. Within these broad categories the rate and

pattern of growth over time have often varied
considerably; for example, amongst junior administrative personnel, the number of health service
staff has expanded very rapidly throughout most of
the post-war period whereas teaching occupations
have tended to grow at a much slower rate over
recent years following a rapid phase of expansion in
the 1960s and early 1970s. The main exception to
these patterns is represented by the group of wholesalers and retailers, whose number has declined
virtually continuously since the mid-1950s, strongly
linked to the disappearance of many small shopkeepers.
  The consequences of the expansion of the
tertiary sector within the economy are not only confined to the growth of employment. Progressively an
increasing proportion of gross domestic product has
been generated by service activities, which now also
make a significant contribution to the French
balance of payments. Services represent a valuable
export 'commodity', particularly in areas such as
the provision of technical advice and expertise to
developing countries, notably to assist in major
construction projects (17). In 1981 a net surplus
of 32.7 billion francs was realised on external
exchanges in the service sector, although this is a
relatively recent feature, comparing with only 2.7
billion francs in 1974 (18). Somewhat paradoxically,
however, in view of the apparent strength of growth
within the tertiary sector given by the various
indicators above, productivity has increased less
rapidly than in other areas of the economy (although
rising nonetheless by over 3 per cent per annum for
much of the period from the mid-1950s to mid-1970s)
(19). This reflects the extent to which it has
proved relatively difficult to effect technical
progess within certain tertiary activities (compared,
for example, with many industrial processes) (20),
although increasingly, computerisation and general
advances in data-handling and office equipment are
enabling higher productivity to be achieved, notably
in fields such as banking.

Growth Processes and the Tertiary Sector
The rapid growth of the tertiary sector and its now
very sizeable contribution to national employment
and income generation might be viewed as natural
outcomes of the development of the French economy
since the end of the second world war. As economic
activity has increased in scale, intensity and

complexity, greater emphasis has been placed upon
such functions as control, administration, research
and decision-making, while transactional operations
generally have expanded greatly (21). At the same
time, the demand for services has risen in response
to the general increase in both population and
affluence. It has also been stimulated by the substantial rise in the proportion of households'
income devoted to expenditure on services, which
rose from approximately 28 per cent in 1959 to
nearly 40 per cent in 1980. This trend has been
related not only to greater wealth but to other
factors, such as improved living standards and
changing spending preferences, the latter often
linked to longer holidays and more leisure.

Change within industry has had various repercussions for activities within the service sector
and for tertiary occupations. For example, in the
past there has been a strong relationship between
the increase in the manufacture of vehicles and the
expansion of employment in firms specialising in
related sales and servicing. Similarly, the growth
of the construction industry in the 1960s and early
1970s, and the associated property boom, led to a
strong demand for architects and planners as well as
a general upsurge in the number of people employed
in related development agencies.

The increasingly complex nature of the productive process has spawned a growing number of
ancillary and advisory services. These have
frequently developed as functionally specialised
departments of the firm or more recently and more
widely as independent organisations, illustrated by
the rapid growth of companies offering expertise and
servicing connected with computer systems. This
latter and now rapidly developing trend has not led
to a pronounced overall growth of employment in the
economy, but it has resulted in a strengthening of
the tertiary sector as many operations formerly
subsumed within manufacturing firms, and therefore
classified within the secondary sector, have now
become divorced from such ties. The important technological revolution which has underlain the modernisation of industry has led to a modification not
only in the amount of labour required in production
activities, but also in the type of manpower
demanded. There has been an increase, therefore, in
the number of workers performing various control
functions, raising the need for white-collar as
opposed to blue-collar employees.

Just as pressure for the growth of service

activities has come from industry, it has also
originated from within the tertiary sector. Here a
significant influence has been the extension of both
central and local government activities, leading to
a corresponding increase in civil servants, administrative personnel and other support staff. In 1980
there were over 4 million government employees in
various tertiary occupations, of which 1.2 million
were represented by clerical staff (22). The
increase in population and the vast extension of
state services, notably in the fields of health,
education, housing and social welfare have contributed to the substantial rise in the number of jobs
in the public sector. Growth has been equally
apparent in the services offered by private firms,
often in many of the above areas such as health and
education. More particularly, it has been linked to
the extension of retailing (despite the decrease in
small shopkeepers) and the rapid expansion of a
broad range of leisure industries.

The development of certain forms of tertiary
activity may also result in an important multiplier
effect, implying a valuable role in regional
development policy. In the same way that the needs
of many industries, and particularly large manufacturing plants, spawn jobs in dependent suppliers and
servicing agents, the presence of selected services
within an area often acts as an inducement for
economic expansion. This process relates primarily,
however, to certain quaternary activities with an
important command function, related to decision-
making and research (23). Thus, the presence of the
headquarters of industrial companies and banks, or
of the main offices of leading consultants, makes
demands on a series of other services, stimulating
expansion.

Despite the underlying tendency towards the
growth of employment and businesses within the
tertiary sector, matched against this is the absolute or relative decline of certain activities and
occupations. Limits on public spending under the
essentially monetarist policies pursued by the
governments of Raymond Barre (1976-81) were one
factor which helped depress the growth rate of white-
collar jobs in the state sector, (just as the
opposed economic philosophy of the socialist party
is likely to result in a rise in such employment).
In certain cases this coincided with a longer-term
downturn in the requirements for certain occupations.
For example, the need for primary school teachers
has eased as the school population of this age has

declined, reflecting the fall in birth rates in the late 1960s and 1970s. Just as technological change has frequently reduced labour requirements in industry, it has also had this effect amongst tertiary activities, not least through the compu-terisation of many routine tasks related to data handling and the development of more sophisticated office equipment. Rationalisation and the concen-tration of ownership are, again, characteristics of restructuring within the tertiary sector. Many small retail outlets, for exmaple, have closed or been incorporated within larger companies, unable to withstand the competition from larger retailing units and organisations; nonetheless, the slowing in the rate of decline of the number of small retailers suggests the process may be easing, particularly in view of the resurgence of popularity of certain small specialised shops.

SPATIAL ASPECTS OF TERTIARY ACTIVITIES

Inter-Regional Contrasts
Within the majority of French regions, by 1980 over half of total employment was concentrated in the tertiary sector (Table 9.5). This contrasts with the situation in 1954 when in only three regions did the proportion of the work-force employed in service activities exceed 40 per cent, and in only eight was it above 35 per cent. Nonetheless, at both dates the outstanding features were the intensity of employment in tertiary activities in Ile-de-France and Provence-Alpes-Côte d'Azur, and the extent to which this situation contrasted with that in other areas of the country. In these two regions over two-thirds of all workers were employed in the service sector by 1980.
        Since the mid-1950s all regions have experienced a strong growth of employment in the tertiary sector, although not all to the same extent. It is above all those regions of Mediterranean and south-eastern France in which the highest growth rates have occurred (24). Tourism, and the many activities linked to it ranging from property development to the hotel and catering trade, is one obvious factor which accounts for the sector's particular vitality in the seaboard and alpine regions of this part of France; but others have been influential. Government encouragement of both private and state firms to decentralise part of

Table 9.5: Proportion of Total Employment working
in the Tertiary Sector by Region, 1980

	%
Ile-de-France	66.9
Champagne-Ardenne	52.1
Picardie	45.8
Haute-Normandie	51.6
Centre	49.5
Basse-Normandie	43.3
Bourgogne	49.0
Nord-Pas-de-Calais	53.9
Lorraine	55.4
Alsace	50.2
Franche-Comté	39.4
Pays de la Loire	46.5
Bretagne	53.8
Poitou-Charentes	52.9
Aquitaine	53.5
Midi-Pyrénées	51.5
Limousin	51.6
Rhône-Alpes	51.1
Auvergne	47.9
Languedoc-Roussillon	56.4
Provence-Alpes-Côte d'Azur (including Corse)	68.6

Source: INSEE, Enquête sur l'Emploi d'Octobre 1980
(1981).

their administrative or research activities has also
played a significant role, demonstrated by the
expansion of banking and financial organisations at
Lyon and research laboratories at Grenoble. More
generally, for activities and firms with few locational constraints to their operation (a growing
trend as improvements in telecommunications have
greatly facilitated the transfer of information),
their movement to areas of high environmental quality
has increased, particularly as it is relatively easy
to attract management and skilled technical staff to
such regions. Unquestionably this factor has had a
favourable influence upon south-eastern France.
Finally, the strong growth of the tertiary sector in
this broad area corresponds with a marked increase
in population and an intense movement of urbanisation.

The Case of the Paris Region

Despite differential regional growth rates, there has been relatively little change in the overall distribution of tertiary employment during the post-war period (25). Ile-de-France remains the primary focus of such activity within France, housing nearly 28 per cent of employment in the service sector; this compares with under 9 per cent in Rhône-Alpes (Table 9.6), the second largest regional concentration, and emphasises the extent to which Paris dominates outstandingly as the country's principal centre of tertiary activities. This is reflected in

Table 9.6: Relationship between Total Population and Employment in the Tertiary Sector, 1980

	Proportion of total population within France (%)	Proportion of total employment in tertiary activities within France
Ile-de-France	18.8	27.8
Champagne-Ardenne	2.5	2.3
Picardie	3.2	2.3
Haute-Normandie	3.1	2.9
Centre	4.2	3.8
Basse-Normandie	2.4	2.1
Bourgogne	3.0	2.7
Nord-Pas-de-Calais	7.3	5.8
Lorraine	4.3	3.8
Alsace	2.9	2.8
Franche-Comté	2.0	1.6
Pays de la Loire	5.3	4.5
Bretagne	4.9	4.3
Poitou-Charentes	2.9	2.4
Aquitaine	4.8	4.5
Midi-Pyrénées	4.2	3.6
Limousin	1.4	1.2
Rhône-Alpes	9.2	8.6
Auvergne	2.5	2.0
Languedoc-Roussillon	3.4	3.0
Provence-Alpes-Côte d'Azur (including Corse)	7.7	7.7

Source: Calculated from INSEE, Population au 1er Janvier 1980 and Enquête sur l'Emploi d'Octobre 1980 (1981).

the much higher density of tertiary employment
(compared with the resident population) in the
capital than in other regions of France, and in the
exaggerated extent to which employment within Ile-
de-France is concentrated in the service sector (26).
Further confirmation of the capital's predominance
is given by comparing regional shares of total population (Table 9.6). The imbalance between Ile-de-
France and other regions of the country is evident
in both quantitative and qualitative terms. Thus,
Paris houses a disproportionate share of employment
in the more skilled, more qualified and more highly-
paid tertiary occupations (27). The capital has
become the prime focus of companies' control,
administrative and research functions, a feature
illustrated by the far greater representation of
senior management and highly qualified technical
staff within the labour-force (28); whereas this
category accounts for 11 per cent of firms' total
employment in Ile-de-France, for the majority of
other regions it is below 6 per cent (29). Above
all, Paris stands out due to its monopoly of
highest-level decision-making functions.

    Whereas Ile-de-France is distinguished by the
strength of the service sector, a number of other
regions of the country are equally prominent due to
relative weaknesses in the size or structure of
tertiary employment (30). Two broad types of region
may be identified. The first relates to the
country's old industrial centres and is epitomised
by the region of Nord-Pas-de-Calais; here the number
and particularly the range of service sector jobs is
comparatively restricted with an underprovision of
more qualified, responsible jobs, partly reflecting
the region's long and excessive dependency upon a
limited series of heavy industries. Similar
features, although with a contrasting origin, are
apparent in a second group of regions characterised
by their recent industrialisation and illustrated by
many areas in the Paris Basin and western France.
Again there is a predominance of low level white-
collar employment, in this case partly resulting
from the character of industrial development which
has been strongly linked to the expansion of branch
plants with a high proportion of semi-skilled
industrial jobs and very little provision of qualified tertiary sector employment. A somewhat
contrasting pattern is evident, however, in selected
southern regions which have also been characterised
by underindustrialisation. Here, alongside the
traditional range of tertiary activities such as

commerce, in which growth rates have generally been modest, has been grafted a series of modern service functions linked to tourism, health care and industrial and scientific research; in these latter cases the level of qualification is frequently much higher.

The Concentration of Tertiary Activities

For a number of reasons, not least that of market accessibility, the locations and expansion patterns of many tertiary activities are strongly linked with the distribution of urban centres and the process of urbanisation. Thus, it might be more appropriate to view certain aspects of their development at a sub-regional level. Just as there are broad inter-regional contrasts in the intensity and rate of growth of employment in the tertiary sector, there are also significant intra-regional variations. Figure 9.1, for example, indicates that those areas in which tertiary employment is strongly represented are relatively limited. Generally, they correspond with larger urban centres, although this is less true in south-eastern France where tourism is an important component of the service sector, and jobs induced by it are by no means restricted to the major towns. Similar spatial contrasts are also evident in the pattern of employment growth, illustrated by expansion over the period 1962-75 (Figure 9.1). Growth rates were generally highest in and adjacent to the capital, throughout much of south-eastern France, particularly in the area to the east of the Rhône, and in a number of the regional centres of the Paris Basin such as Orléans, Tours, Le Mans, Caen and Reims; these towns have experienced a very rapid growth of their population and the extension of their urban area since the early 1960s.

One of the principal features of the French urban hierarchy is the imbalance between Paris and other large urban centres (31). There are no effective provincial counter-weights to the capital, with an unusually large size differential (of approximately 8 to 1) between Paris and the second largest city of Lyon; moreover, with the major exceptions of Lyon, Marseille and Lille, most of the remaining regional centres have populations of less than 500,000 inhabitants. Not only is there an unusual rank-size distribution of the larger urban centres within France, there is also an irregular pattern of spatial distribution, reflecting in part the

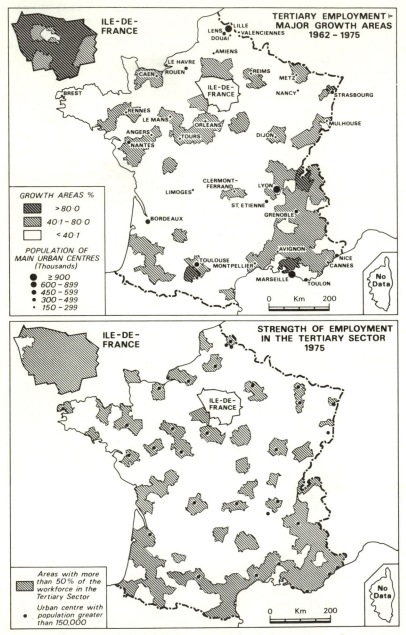

Figure 9.1: The Expansion and Intensity of Employment in Tertiary Activities

excessive dominance of the capital over its regional hinterland. Thus, the larger provincial cities within France are characterised by their essentially peripheral location.

Inevitably, outside of Paris, these urban centres represent the principal concentrations of tertiary activities and employment within France. The country's ten largest provincial centres house approximately 15 per cent of all employment in the tertiary sector which when combined with the proportion for the Paris agglomeration amounts to 39 per cent of the total for the country (32). There are, however, significant contrasts between these provincial centres, not only in terms of the degree to which employment is biased towards the service sector, but also in the nature and relative strength of the tertiary functions themselves. In the cities of Marseille and Strasbourg, for example, over two-thirds of total employment is provided by the tertiary sector, whereas the proportion is much lower (although still well over half) in certain cases, notably in the more industrial cities of Lyon and Lille. Similarly, in terms of specialisation, Lyon, Lille and Strasbourg are all more significant banking and financial centres than Marseille (33); conversely, in the latter city, a much higher proportion of workers in the tertiary sector is employment in transport industries, indicating the influence of Marseille's port function. Other contrasts are apparent; for example, Lyon and Lille house a greater number of the headquarters of major companies than Marseille (34), although the role of all three cities in this capacity is insignificant compared with the capital. Together, these indicators reflect the differences in the mix of activities within these centres, implying contrasts in their present function and economic health, and in the influences which have underlain their growth. On a wider scale, a number of studies have emphasised the spatial variability in the extent to which urban centres depend upon the tertiary sector (35). There is, for example, a general opposition between many of the towns of northern and eastern France where the bias is generally towards industrial activities and those of southern and western France where the proportion of tertiary employment is far greater.

All the major cities referred to above have been linked with a substantial increase of employment in the tertiary sector (although actual growth rates have often been higher in smaller centres),

but their distinctiveness derives much more from the
presence and expansion of quaternary activities. It
is only within agglomerations of this size that contact patterns and external economies, upon which
such functions depend, are likely to be generated.
Equally, in view of their specialist character,
these tend to be activities found at relatively few
locations, the latter being selected on the basis of
most effective accessibility to the widest possible
market. Relatively few of the large provincial
agglomerations have functioned effectively in this
manner, however, with the exception of Lyon. Most
lack the necessary regional environment of intense
industrial and commercial activity, allied to a high
density of population. Thus, for a variety of
reasons such as an inadequate range of labour skills
they are unable to attract quaternary functions and
dependent services in substantial quantity. Inevitably, therefore, these activities have tended to
concentrate in those regions where conditions are
more conducive to development; all too frequently
this has meant not Lyon or Lille, but Paris.

FUTURE DIRECTIONS

For more than two decades the expansion of the
tertiary sector has been of fundamental importance
to the creation of new employment within France.
Even with the more recent slowing of the rate at
which jobs are being generated within this group of
activities, it is only amongst tertiary occupations
that a net increase in employment is occurring. In
the present context of high rates of unemployment,
the extent to which jobs will continue to be created
within service activities is crucial. However,
while there is little doubt that the underlying
sectoral shift within the economy in favour of the
tertiary sector will be maintained, leading to new
employment growth, various forces might limit the
strength of this process.
   Underlying factors such as the currently
depressed state of the economy and continued slowing
of the rate of demographic growth are likely to have
a restraining influence upon the rate at which new
jobs are generated. A major but more specific
impact is also likely to be made by the rapid introduction and extension of computerised processes,
although there is some ambiguity about the effects
upon employment (36). While this will undoubtedly
result in the further loss of many jobs involving

the routine handling of data, the use of automated
techniques ought at the same time to widen the
possibilities for production, offering the potential
for the creation of new jobs. Equally, the greater
use of computers and their adoption for a much
larger number of applications is increasing the need
for advisory and servicing agencies, leading again
to further employment growth. However, the impact
of computerised technology and the scope for the
automation of data handling and related office
operations, vary considerably between branches of
activity. Thus, while substantial advances have
occurred in certain areas such as banking, progress
and the potential for change in for example retailing and transportation are much more limited.

Just as the structure and organisation of many
tertiary activities are being remodelled, modifications are also taking place in locational patterns.
These are varied in character, ranging from the
intra-urban displacement of services (notably
retailing) towards the outer-suburbs, to the inter-
urban transfer of activities, particularly associated with decentralisation. Once again computerised technology and advances in telecommunication
systems ought to facilitate both these processes,
although previous tendencies suggest some hesitancy
by firms to respond to such a lessening of the
constraints on distance, noticeably in terms of
movement away from the capital. In this respect
there has been the interesting paradox that despite
the enhanced locational freedom offered by developments in the above fields, the heavy concentration
of computing hardware and expertise within the Paris
region has previously restricted decentralisation
(37).

In the same way that French industry is undergoing structural and locational change, similar
processes of transformation characterise the
tertiary sector and individual activities within it.
Arguably, however, in view of the continued generation of an important net surplus of jobs within this
sector its significance to the general problem of
combating unemployment and particularly of counteracting imbalances in the regional distribution of
employment is at least as crucial as that of industry. But the dilemma which still faces the government is that in the past certain tertiary activities
capable of generating strong employment growth,
particularly related to decision-making functions,
have demonstrated a far greater reluctance to for-
sake traditional location centres than many

industrial firms. Nonetheless, there are more optimistic trends. Tourism and leisure industries, embracing sporting and recreational facilities and dependent businesses, are likely to continue to grow in significance as the average working week becomes shorter, paid holidays become longer and living standards rise further (albeit currently at a slow rate); significantly, these are generally activities with different sets of locational requirements.

NOTES

1.   Braibant, M., 'L'économie des services marchands de 1960 à 1980', Archives et Documents, No.37 (1981), 6.
2.   The figures refer only to salaried employees in the tertiary sector and, therefore, undervalue the size of the total labour-force.   This is particularly apparent in the retailing branch where it is estimated (1981) that there are a further 500,000 self-employed workers represented essentially by the large number of small shopkeepers.
3.   Pinchemel, P., La France (Armand Colin, Paris, 1981), vol.2, 153.
4.   Commissariat Général du Plan, Emplois dans les Services (La Documentation Française, Paris, 1980), 261-70.
5.   Lipietz, A., 'La dimension régionale du développement du tertiaire', in 'Activités et Régions', Travaux et Recherches de Prospective, No.75 (1978), 70.
6.   'La place du secteur tertiaire dans l'économie française', Problèmes Economiques, No. 1569 (1978), 14.
7.   Huet, M., 'Emploi et activité entre 1968 et 1975', Economie et Statistique, No.94 (1977), 63.
8.   For the year 1980 this had dipped to below 1.0 per cent per annum.
9.   Huet, 'Emploi et activité', 67.
10.   Sigogne, P., 'Conditions d'emploi et coût de la main-d'oeuvre dans les économies européennes', Economie et Statistique, No.140 (1982), 68.
11.   Huet, 'Emploi et activité', 67.
12.   It is not just over the period since 1975 that these services have expanded rapidly: it has been a dominant trend since the latter 1950s. Between 1959 and 1980 employment doubled to around 3.8 million workers.   See Braibant, 'L'économie des services marchands', 9.
13.   Such employment is classified under the

heading services to households and enterprises.
14. Commissariat Général du Plan, Emplois,
147-8.
15. Huet, 'Emplois et activité', 67.
16. For a more detailed analysis of the
pattern of evolution between 1954 and 1975 see
Thevenot, L., 'Les catégories sociales en 1975:
l'extension du salariat', Economie et Statistique,
No.91 (1977), 3-31.
17. Detailed reference to the sector's significance as an export commodity is made in 'La place
du secteur tertiaire, 10-12.
18. Parodi, M., L'Economie et la Société
Française depuis 1945 (Armand Colin, Paris, 1981),
138; 'Rapport sur les comptes de la Nation de
l'année 1981', Les Collections de l'INSEE, C101-2
(1982).
19. Parodi, L'Economie et la Société, 137.
20. Pinchemel, La France, 153.
21. For a detailed discussion, see Lipietz,
A., 'Polarisation interrégionale et tertiarisation
de la société', L'Espace Géographique, 9 (1980), 36.
22. 'Enquête sur l'emploi d'octobre 1980',
Collections de l'INSEE, D81 (1981), 49.
23. Pinchemel, La France, 154. The ability of
decentralised research bodies to stimulate employment locally outside of their own organisation is,
in many cases, questionable. Functional linkages
are often almost exclusively orientated towards the
capital. See Brocard, M., 'Aménagement du
territoire et développement régional: le cas de la
recherche scientifique', L'Espace Géographique, 10
(1981), 61-73.
24. Mary, S. and Turpin, E., 'Panorama
économique des régions françaises', Collections de
l'INSEE, R42-3 (1981), 159-60.
25. Mary and Turpin, 'Panorama économique',
139-40.
26. Lipietz, 'Polarisation interrégionale',
38.
27. For example, around 40 per cent of all
senior executives and administrators are employed
here. Additional examples are given in Pinchemel,
P., La Région Parisienne (Presses Universitaires de
France, Paris, 1979), 13-14.
28. This is illustrated generally in Lipietz,
'La dimension régionale du développement du
tertiaire', 110-11.
29. Calculated from details given in
'Structure des emplois en 1979', Collections de
l'INSEE, D84 (1981).

30. The basis for the following remarks is taken from Lipietz, 'Polarisation interrégionale', 39-41.

31. See, for example, Noin, D., L'Espace Français (Armand Colin, Paris, 1976), 25-36.

32. Corresponding figures for proportions of total population are 12 per cent and 28 per cent respectively. These calculations are based upon the results of the 1975 census.

33. This is measured by the proportion of tertiary employees working in this branch.

34. Valeyre, A., 'Emplois et régions', in 'Activités et Régions', Travaux et Recherches de Prospective, No.75 (1978), 59.

35. See, for example, Pumain, D., 'La composition socio-professionnelle des villes françaises', L'Espace Géographique, 5 (1976), 227-38; Thibault, A., 'La structure économique des espaces locaux en France', L'Espace Géographique, 5 (1976), 239-49; Noin, D., 'Essai d'établissement d'une carte économique de la France sur les bases comtables', L'Espace Géographique, 2 (1973), 257-65. In addition, a review of various studies undertaken with the aim of classifying French towns is provided in Pumain, D. and Saint-Julien, Th., 'Fonctions et hiérarchies des villes françaises', Annales de Géographie, 85 (1976), 385-440.

36. Commissariat Général du Plan, Emplois, 62-8.

37. Huet, P., Télématique et Aménagement du Territoire (La Documentation Française, Paris, 1981), 55-8.

Chapter Ten

THE GROWTH OF OFFICES AND OFFICE EMPLOYMENT

As in various other advanced western capitalist
societies, one of the central features of post-war
economic change in France has been the pronounced
growth of office activities and related employment.
This has been a major factor accounting for the
increasingly dominant position of the service sector
and of the substantial rise of jobs in tertiary
occupations. It is, above all, the comparatively
recent but now marked expansion of quaternary functions that has given a particular impetus to the
development of the office sector (1).
     Many of the processes encouraging the growth of
office activities have been influential over a long
period, but, over the last two decades especially,
they have operated with a heightened intensity,
reflecting in part the extent of economic change.
Not only has the economy grown substantially, but it
has also become far more complex in operation and,
thus, difficult to manage. Similar features characterise the evolution of individual firms and in both
cases have increased the need for administrative,
managerial and secretarial staff. Moreover, continuing technical advances have given additional
significance to control and supervisory jobs;
equally, the greater sophistication of many products
and more intense competition between companies have
increased greatly the need for research and development. In general, therefore, the increasing
division of labour associated with economic progress
has underlain the expansion of the tertiary sector
and notably office activities.
     In this respect, such processes have had a
number of consequences. Many traditional services
linked to trading and industrial development (for
example banking) have expanded very significantly.
The administrative and research operations of the

larger industrial firms have also grown rapidly,
associated in many cases with the physical separa-
tion of companies' control and manufacturing functions, a process which has often been strengthened
by mergers, amalgamations and takeovers. As firms
have come to rely increasingly heavily upon a range
of specialised business services, many have grown
independently of the enterprises utilising their
expertise, leading to a very substantial rise in the
size and number of an extended series of consultancy,
financial and promotional agencies. At the same
time, the activities of both central and local
government have also grown in volume, complexity and
diversity. All the above trends have been linked to
a rise in employment, but equally have been trans-
lated into the need for a substantial increase in
office floorspace. By the late 1960s the strong
demand for additional space, coupled with a totally
inadequate supply, prompted a wave of office
building. It has involved the construction of a
wide range of purpose-built accommodation, as well
as the growth throughout France of an important
market for speculative developments, a feature
previously almost entirely lacking outside Paris.
These changes have affected most of the larger urban
centres of France, leading to a pronounced modification of their townscapes.
     Traditionally, due to its qualities of accessi-
bility, the central area of the city grew as the
primary focus of office activities, but in many
cases the strength of demand for new floorspace has
exceeded the absorptive capacity of such zones.
This problem, coupled with the increased asphyxia-
tion of the centre due to severe congestion caused
by the very rapid expansion of business and
commercial activity in an area ill-adapted to such
growth, led to the decision in a number of cities to
create new, specialised business quarters adjacent
to the existing central business district. Such
developments are epitomised by La Défense at Paris,
but are now also a feature of many of the large
provincial cities; La Part-Dieu at Lyon, the Bourse
and Mériadeck quarters at Marseille and Bordeaux and
the Saint-Sever and Place des Halles operations at
Rouen and Strasbourg are all illustrative of this
concept. These centres were conceived not only to
enlarge substantially the availability of office
floorspace, but also to respond to the previous
inadequacy in the number and range of retail outlets
by the provision of new shopping centres. Other
trends in the more recent location of office

activities are observable, not least an increased but often apparently random drift towards suburban and peripheral areas, representing nonetheless logical responses to lower land costs, the availability of space or improved accessibility. While all these changes testify to a marked growth of business activity, they also need to be viewed in the context of the pronounced urbanisation of French society which occurred in the post-war period.

THE PATTERN OF GROWTH OF OFFICE ACTIVITIES AND EMPLOYMENT

Providing an accurate assessment of the role of office activities within the economy is rendered difficult by certain conceptual and practical difficulties (2). As a result, the indications given here are intended as a general guide rather than a precise measurement of the size, significance and evolutionary tendencies of this field of employment. The increase in office floorspace over the period 1965-80 offers a general indication of the extent to which such activities have expanded in France. In 1965 floorspace totalled approximately 43.4 million square metres: by 1980 this had risen to over 70.7 million square metres, with a marked acceleration in the rate of growth during the early 1970s (Table 10.1). Occupational data provide a further and more detailed measure of the expansion of office activities. In 1980 the number of people employed in those socio-economic groups dominated by office jobs stood at 5.2 millions (Table 10.2). This compares with a total of only 2.5 millions in 1954 and indicates the large scale of the increase

Table 10.1:   Office Floorspace in France

Year	Total (million square metres)	Period	Mean annual rate of growth (%)
1965	43.5	1965-70	2.2
1970	48.3	1970-75	5.0
1975	60.4	1975-80	3.4
1980	70.7		

Source: Association Bureaux-Provinces.

Table 10.2:   The Expansion of Office Occupations

Occupational Category	1954	1962	1968 ('000)	1975	1980
Engineers	76	138	186	256	308
Upper management	277	378	455	654	801
Middle management	534	626	740	970	1,208
Office employees	1,628	1,886	2,371	3,104	2,903
Total	2,515	3,028	3,752	4,984	5,220

Source: INSEE, Recensements and Enquête sur l'Emploi d'Octobre 1980 (1981).

in jobs over the intervening period. Following a relatively modest rate of expansion during the latter 1950s and early 1960s, the period until the mid-1970s was characterised by an exceptionally strong increase, although since that time the pace of growth has eased noticeably. Nonetheless, by 1980 nearly a quarter of the total work-force was employed in an office job compared with only 13 per cent in 1954. Moreover, this masks the very substantial growth in the employment of women in office occupations; by 1980, they represented 52 per cent of those employed in such jobs.

Just as growth rates have varied over time, they have also differed between various types of office employment (3). In terms of recent trends, the most noticeable feature has been the reduction in clerical, secretarial and typing staff, partly reflecting the general contraction of the employment market over this period, but also indicating the lower requirements for such personnel as many routine tasks have become automated and compu-terised. This tendency seems likely to reduce the ability of the office sector to continue to provide a large number of new female employment outlets, for it is this group of office jobs which has the highest proportion of female employees (67 per cent of the total in 1980 which, for example, compared with only 19 per cent for the occupational category of upper management).

A broadly similar pattern of employment growth emerges through an analysis of the expansion of office activities grouped within the tertiary sector (Table 10.3). Thus, between 1968 and 1981 jobs in

Table 10.3: The Evolution of Employment in Office
Activities in the Tertiary Sector

Office activities	Wage-earners		
	1968	1975 ('000)	1981
Market services (firms)	485	650	835
Property dealing	20	51	57
Insurance	89	122	135
Banking	230	374	416
Non-market services (e.g. public administration and education)	2,814	3,286	3,585
	3,638	4,483	5,028

Source: INSEE, Emploi Salarié.

this field rose by over 38 per cent, although since
the mid-1970s the rate of increase has dipped substantially, falling from a yearly mean of 3.3 per
cent between 1968 and 1975 to only 2.0 per cent
between 1975 and 1981. Considerable variations
exist again between activities. For example, despite the importance of employment in non-market
services (3.6 million wage earners in 1981) (4),
this branch grew by only 27 per cent between 1968
and 1981 compared with a rate of expansion of over
80 per cent and over 72 per cent respectively for
the much smaller but more dynamic groups of banking
and business services. Even in these fields,
however, the rate of growth has eased in recent
years, notably in the former case. Throughout the
greater part of the period 1960-75 banking activities (and associated employment) grew rapidly in
France, linked to factors such as a propitious
economic and demographic climate, an extension of
banks' services, a far greater number of people
being paid monthly by cheque and a generally underdeveloped banking network in relation to the potential demand (5). Since the mid-1970s, however,
growth has slowed significantly, partly reflecting
the success of past efforts to enlarge the system
and partly indicating a downturn in economic
activity. However, in relation to the slowdown in
the expansion of employment a more fundamental cause

relates to the impact of modern computerised data
handling techniques which have not only greatly
increased banks' information handling capacities,
but also reduced the need for personnel and considerably improved productivity.

Certain similarities in the pattern of development are evident in the growth of those activities
grouped under the heading 'market services'. This
diverse category includes specialists in industrial
engineering, a variety of financial transactions,
technical and legal affairs, publicity and property
development. With the rapid expansion of the French
economy until 1974, there was a corresponding rise
in demand for such services; but, the slower rate of
growth of business activity since the mid-1970s has
reduced the overall rate of expansion of this group
of activities, although selected services have
continued to expand rapidly, such as those offering
technical or financial advice (6).

The Spatial Pattern of Office Activities

In view of its already large share of tertiary
employment within France, it is of little surprise
that Paris should also dominate overwhelmingly as
the country's primary centre for office employment.
For example, the capital houses approximately 31 per
cent of all those employed in office occupations,
compared with only 3 per cent located in France's
second largest city, Lyon. For certain categories
of employment the degree of concentration in Paris
is even greater. Thus, 37 per cent of all senior
management personnel are employed in this region,
indicating that in addition to the capital housing a
disproportionate share of the nation's office jobs,
this trend is particularly accentuated in relation
to more highly qualified and better remunerated
employment opportunities. The same tendency is
reinforced by the extent to which the capital acts
as the predominant research centre within France,
employing around 60 per cent of all such personnel
(7). Moreover, not only is Paris a major centre for
office employment within France, but such jobs also
represent a substantial proportion of total employment within the capital, accounting for 36 per cent
of the work-force.

The excessive weight of Paris is further
demonstrated when employment is measured by categories of activity occupational groups. Thus, in
1981 30 per cent of all jobs in tertiary activities
were located in the region of Ile-de-France. When

broken down into more restricted groups of services,
some show a much stronger concentration upon Paris;
the proportion exceeds 40 per cent in the case of
banking, insurance and business services. One final
and significant indicator of the dominance of the
capital is provided by the location pattern of head
offices of companies, particularly of large corporations. Half of all companies in France have their
headquarters situated in Ile-de-France, while for
the largest firms (by turnover), over three-quarters
are based in the capital (8). Amongst the 20 most
important groups within France, Michelin is the only
company to retain its administrative and control
centre outside of Paris. Moreover, not only are the
majority of head offices of large companies found in
the capital, but this tendency has been reinforced
over the post-war period. After Ile-de-France, the
regions of Nord-Pas-de-Calais and Rhône-Alpes rank
second and third for the number of company head
offices which are located within them, but compared
with Paris their role is insignificant; they contain
only 4 and 3 per cent respectively of the headquarters of the 500 most important companies.
Although the predominance of the capital is not in
question, it is possible to overestimate its significance. While numerous firms maintain a headquarters at Paris, this does not mean that all
management and control functions are located here;
in many cases at least part of these operations is
conducted elsewhere. Arguably, as companies have
increased in size and scope, this has provided
greater opportunities for the decentralisation of
certain decision-making and administrative activities, particularly where the operational divisions
within a group are based on products rather than
functions (9). The Renault group, for example, has
its head office in the capital, yet control of its
commercial vehicle subsidiary, RVI, is centred at
Lyon, although this also reflects its origin as the
Lyon-based firm of Berliet.

Within provincial France a limited number of
the larger urban centres stand out as the main
centres of office employment, particularly Lyon,
Marseille and Lille (Table 10.4), although none
challenges Paris. Together, however, Paris and the
ten largest provincial centres of office employment
house 46 per cent of those people working in such
occupations, indicating a general spatial imbalance
in the distribution of such jobs. The same areal
disequilibrium is demonstrated by the regional
distribution of office floorspace; nearly half of

Table 10.4: Major Centres of Office Employment in France

Agglomeration	Number of office employees 1975	Proportion of total office workers in France (%)
Paris	1,538,660	30.9
Lyon	150,820	3.0
Marseille	119,420	2.4
Lille	104,300	2.1
Bordeaux	76,405	1.5
Toulouse	64,310	1.3
Nantes	55,230	1.1
Strasbourg	46,880	0.9
Rouen	46,090	0.9
Grenoble	44,720	0.9
Nice	44,135	0.9

Source: INSEE, Recensement (1975).

the total is concentrated in Ile-de-France (35 per cent), Rhône-Alpes (8 per cent) and Provence-Alpes-Côte-d'Azur (6 per cent) (10). A further indicator of this situation is provided by Figure 10.1 which depicts the main centres of speculative office development in towns and cities outside Paris. The dominant position of the three largest provincial metropolises is again emphasised, although a number of relatively small cities have also developed as important centres of office floorspace, notably Strasbourg and Grenoble, where major redevelopment schemes have been partly responsible for the substantial increase in supply.

There is now some evidence that the importance of the Paris region as a focus for offices is being marginally but progressively reduced. This is suggested by the rate at which employment in office activities grew between 1975 and 1981 (Table 10.5). In Ile-de-France the increase totalled 10.0 per cent, while in provincial regions it attained 13.1 per cent over the same period. A similar trend is indicated by comparing the amount of new floorspace under construction in these two areas over the same period (Table 10.6).

It is not only the imbalance between Paris and

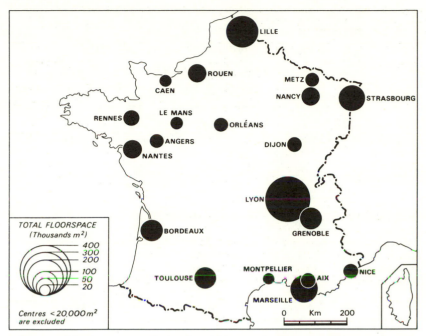

Figure 10.1: Completed Office Floorspace in Major Provincial Cities, 1981

Table 10.5: Growth of Employment in Office Activities, 1975-81

	Total employment		Rate of growth
	1975	1981	1975-81
	('000)		(%)
Paris	1,359	1,495	10.0
Provincial regions	3,124	3,533	13.1
France	4,483	5,028	12.2

Source: INSEE, Emploi Salarié.

the rest of the country, however, which is slowly being reversed; within provincial France the launching of a series of speculative developments in many small and medium-sized towns has begun to act

Table 10.6:   Increase in Office Floorspace, 1975-80

	1975	1976	1977	1978	1979	1980
			Floorspace completed			
			('000 square metres)			
Ile-de-France	730	342	209	236	125	202
Provincial regions	197	297	173	154	185	103
Ile-de-France (% share)	79	54	55	61	40	66

Source: Association Bureaux-Provinces.

as a counterweight to the larger office centres.
Whereas in 1973 the ten largest towns accounted for
73 per cent of the total stock of offices, by 1980
this proportion had shrunk to 63 per cent (Table
10.7). However, the availability of office floorspace does not guarantee its commercialisation, and
the existence of vacant offices is often a particular problem of the smaller centre. Here many developments were launched in the property boom of the
early 1970s; since then not only has demand eased,
but the supply has greatly increased and in many

Table 10.7:   Stock of Office Floorspace in Major
Provincial Cities (speculative developments only)

	1973	1980
	(square metres)	
Lyon	49,400	325,600
Lille	39,900	159,100
Marseille	42,200	118,100
Strasbourg	10.200	100,500
Grenoble	16,300	72,100
Toulouse	300	69,500
Bordeaux	10,000	67,900
Nancy	10,000	49,800
Nantes	8,100	48,800
Rouen	5,000	48,200

Source: Association Bureaux-Provinces.

towns the range of external economies available is inadequate to tempt certain potential clients.

The uneven spatial distribution of offices, particularly those related to quaternary functions, and the dominant position of the capital as a centre for related employment, are not features which are unique to France. Similar traits are observable for example in Britain, and the general importance of centralising forces in the location of offices is well documented (11). While the exceptional growth of Paris may be linked to these latter processes, it is also related to specific changes in the control and organisation of business activity. Increasingly a greater share of economic activity is becoming controlled by large national and multinational groups which tend to select major metropolitan centres for the location of their headquarters; moreover, mergers and takeovers, an integral part of the process of the formation of large corporations, have tended to reinforce the centralisation of control. Not only do the administrative centres of such enterprises frequently themselves employ a large personnel, but their presence exerts an impor- tant multiplier effect upon dependent services.

Major groups appear to be attracted to large urban centres for a variety of reasons. Three sets of factors have been distinguished as being of para- mount importance (12). First, location in such areas facilitates face-to-face contacts between firms and other decision-making organisations and between companies and their clients. Second, firms have access to a vast range of essential external services which are complementary or supplementary to their operations. Third, companies are also able to benefit from a high degree of inter-metropolitan accessibility, a factor of vital significance as firms have grown in size and degree of spatial dispersion and their trading activities have exten- ded to cover a much wider area.

Many of these factors would appear to have been influential in the growth of offices in Paris. The French capital is a major centre of control and decision-making in both the public and private sectors of the economy, reflecting the still high centralised character of the nation's organisation. Numerous business services have mushroomed in Paris, their disproportionate concentration in Ile-de- France having been indicated already. Equally, Paris has long benefited from its position as the major focus of communication systems within France, although increased congestion is but one of a number

of diseconomies which have progressively influenced
certain firms and organisations to shift at least
part of their operations away from the capital.
However, it is still characteristic of many state
and private firms and organisations that the ultimate power of decision remains vested in the
capital, a situation which limits the effectiveness
of decentralisation strategies and efforts to
achieve a more equitable distribution of economic
activity within France.

THE DECENTRALISATION OF OFFICES

Just as industrial employment was heavily concentrated in the Paris region in the 1950s, particularly in a number of 'growth' sectors, a similar
pattern of distribution characterised the location
of certain office activities, especially those
linked to control and research functions and notably
in such fields as banking and insurance. With the
subsequent rapid expansion of the French economy and
the associated strong growth of these activities, it
became inevitable that a degree of spontaneous dispersion should occur, reflecting factors such as the
increasingly fierce competition for land in the
capital and the development of larger provincial
market centres. However, the extent of such movement was limited with the result that many areas
outside Paris remained noticeably poorly endowed
with the decision-making centres of firms, restricting their growth potential and weakening the
diversity of their labour markets.
By the early 1960s it was also apparent that
the tertiary sector had become the major generator
of new employment within the economy. Taken
together, therefore, these factors suggested to the
government the desirability of trying to regulate
further expansion in the capital and of encouraging
it in various provincial localities. Such a
strategy responded to the increasing emphasis being
given to the need to redress the imbalances of job
opportunity and living standards between Paris and
many other areas of the country. Without manipulating artificially the location of offices it seemed
unlikely that a substantial and widespread
spontaneous redistribution would take place. Moreover, it had become recognised that the build up
within a region of selected higher order services
could exert a significant attractive force upon
industrial development, thus helping to promote a

further strand of regional planning strategy. Since
the late 1950s, therefore, successive governments
have introduced measures to encourage the decentralisation of office activities.

The Control of Office Development

Various policies have been pursued, largely through
government initiatives, which have aimed to promote
the expansion of offices in provincial locations in
preference to the capital. As with industrial
development, controls have been introduced to limit
growth in the Paris region and financial inducements
have been offered to attract firms to certain other
areas of the country. The government has also
sought to persuade sections of its own ministries
and services to relocate at least part of their
activities in provincial centres. Similarly, the
policy of métropoles d'équilibre was directed
particularly towards the creation of a limited
number of major regional service centres concentrating state administrative services and offering an
important supply of office floorspace for business
activities. Although elements of this policy have
lapsed since its introduction in 1964, from the
early 1970s increasing emphasis was placed upon
ameliorating the range and quality of financial
institutions in a number of these 'poles' with the
aim of enhancing their appeal as business centres.
The achievement of this objective has been facilitated by the readiness of a number of banks to
decentralise various commercial functions and to
widen the range of services offered in provincial
locations. In a wider context, the regional reforms
of 1964 and 1972 gave a general impetus to the
decentralisation or employment through the considerable enlargement of regional administrative
services; the further reforms of 1982 seem likely to
produce a similar impact.
     A package of building controls and monetary
incentives has played a fundamental role in governments' attempts to promote the expansion of tertiary
activities away from Paris. Restrictions on the
construction of offices in the capital were first
formally introduced in 1958 with the extension of
the agrément procedure, already applicable to industrial land uses, to such development. Then in 1960
the redevance, a tax on new building, was introduced. It was not until 1967, however, that grants
were made available to further encourage location
outside the Paris region; initially they were

provided in only a limited number of the country's larger urban centres (13). Since then some modifications have occurred. The areas eligible for government grants (and certain tax concessions (14)) have been increased in extent to include a number of other major towns (1972) and to cover virtually all of France with the exception of the central part of the Paris Basin (1976). Also, in 1977 grants became available for research activities located in a limited number of urban centres.

Further modifications in 1982 have aimed to provide a simplified but more generous system of aid, while maintaining the priorities outlined above. Thus, for the greater part of the country there is now a single rate of grant covering non-industrial and research operations (Figure 10.2). In various urban centres for one or other, or both, of these activities higher grants are payable. Certain conditions of eligibility apply, but the main prerequisite is the creation of at least 10 jobs in an existing or new undertaking. Grants are

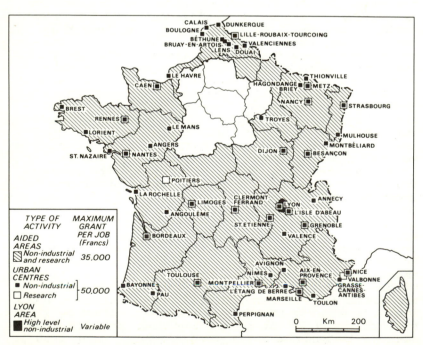

Figure 10.2: Government Grants and Assisted Areas for Non-Industrial and Research Operations, 1982

accorded on the basis of the number of employment
opportunities generated and range up to maxima of
35,000 or 50,000 francs depending upon location (15).
For the Lyon area, special conditions apply; small
projects are unlikely to qualify for assistance
given the area's inherent attraction as an office
and research centre, but in view of the desire to
enhance the city's appeal as an international business centre, large undertakings with an important
command function would be eligible for aid.
Progressively, therefore, governments have given
greater emphasis to the decentralisation of non-
industrial activities (16).

Restrictions on development in and around the
capital remain and in some cases have been reinforced. The redevance is levied over a limited zone
of the central area of Ile-de-France, and in 1982 it
was proposed to raise its maximum rate to 1,300
francs per square metre of floorspace (17). It is
the system of agrément, however, which represents
the government's major dissuasive force, and applies
to the whole of Ile-de-France and the five southern
cantons of the département of Oise. Such approval
is granted by the Comité de Décentralisation (Decentralisation Committee), a body of up to thirty
members representing various government ministries
as well as a number of interested parties (for
example, the DATAR and Préfet of Ile-de-France).
Currently, an agrément has to be obtained for any
new building project in excess of 1,000 square
metres of floorspace or for the extension of existing premises above this limit. In cases where the
developer and user(s) of an office block are not the
same, these requirements apply, nonetheless, to both
parties (18).

The problem of persuading firms to locate away
from the capital is not only a consideration of the
Decentralisation Committee. One of the principal
functions of DATAR is to direct economic growth
towards the less favoured regions of France. Its
actions in the field of office activities led to the
creation in 1974 of the Association Bureaux-
Provinces whose services are available to encourage
and assist firms to establish in localities outside
of Ile-de-France: the organisation closely resembles
the former Location of Offices Bureau in Britain,
for it is also charged with trying to persuade
foreign companies to establish their European headquarters in France, including Paris.

The Results of Decentralisation

The decentralisation (19) of tertiary activities appears to have involved far fewer operations and a smaller number of jobs than the corresponding movement of industry. Evidence suggests that after the relatively slow growth of decentralisation during the early and mid-1960s, the number of moves rose substantially over the late 1960s until the mid-1970s (20). Since then there has been a decrease, although it is estimated that since the late 1970s approximately 5,000 jobs in the tertiary sector (of which the majority are in offices) have been shifted away from the capital each year (21). Most of these moves relate, however, to the partial rather than complete transfer of a firm's activities. Decentralisation has concerned a varied range of businesses and organisations. There is some evidence to suggest, however, that it has been a characteristic particularly of the growth strategies of financial institutions and insurance companies and of firms specialising in business services, and that it has been a significant feature in the location of research activities (22). Many of these moves relate to firms in the private sector but, in addition, government departments and agencies have been responsible for the decentralisation of administrative and technical services; since measures were first introduced to curb expansion in the capital this has involved around 37,000 jobs (23).

For each firm or organisation the specific determinants influencing the decision to decentralise are likely to vary. Nonetheless, certain general factors appear to underlie the majority of moves. A number of diseconomies of continued concentration at Paris have emerged for various firms, relating to problems of poor access, lack of space for expansion or high rentals. Frequently, these are related to the difficulty or elevated cost of renewing leases, and to the constraints of government legislation. The high cost of operation in the Paris region represents an unnecessary burden for the maintenance in the area of a number of administrative and data handling tasks and for certain research activities which do not require close spatial linkage with major metropolitan centres (24). Various major banks and insurance companies have moved at least part of their routine administrative services away from the capital, although given their need for a relatively large (but generally modestly qualified) labour-force they have often been relocated in or adjacent to large urban areas. The computing centre of Crédit Lyonnais and BNP's administrative centre, both on the outskirts of Lyon, illustrate this trend.

Changing marketing strategies or the internal restructuring of companies may also have locational implications, favouring decentralisation. The desire to enlarge the market area of a business represents one of the many factors drawing firms to provincial locations; such commercial reasons have acted as a strong influence upon the shift of banking and business services away from Paris (25), reflecting the strength of economic growth in areas outside the capital over the last two decades. Other attractions include the availability of suitable office accommodation, frequently at a considerably lower cost. For example, even in a city the size of Lyon, the average cost of renting office floorspace in the city centre may be up to half that in areas such as La Défense or the inner western suburbs of Paris (26). Unlike the past pattern of industrial decentralisation, however, it appears that the need to gain access to a large labour-force, while in certain cases important, has not exerted the same overriding influence in encouraging the transfer of office activities from the capital. Equally, there is some evidence to suggest that the availability of government grants has not acted as a major influence upon firms' decisions to decentralise (27).

The Spatial Pattern of Decentralisation
Compared with the pattern of industrial decentralisation, two major contrasting traits characterise the redistribution of tertiary activities; first, for many firms, the much greater distance over which the move has taken place and, second, the important role played by the larger provincial urban centres in localising decentralised employment. Some support for these generalisations is provided by the location of jobs resulting from the award of government grants, although these have been taken up by firms other than those which have moved from Paris. Between 1976 and 1980, for example, most jobs were created in a limited number of regions dominated by one or a restricted number of major urban centres; Rhône-Alpes and Provence-Alpes-Côte d'Azur offer two examples (Figure 10.3). Until the recent changes in legislation, grants were payable at a higher rate throughout much of 'western' France; but there is little evidence that they have led to preferential

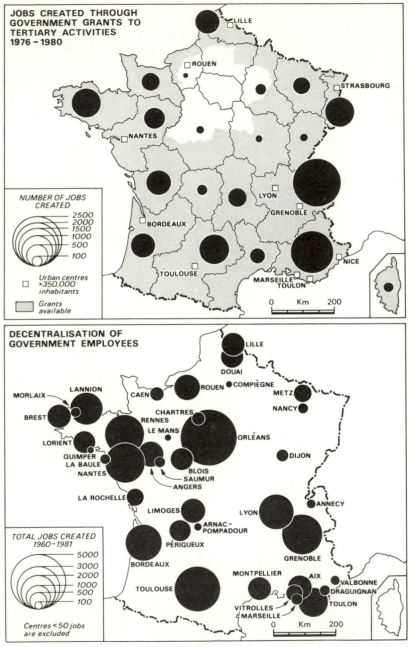

Figure 10.3: The Decentralisation of Tertiary Employment

investment in this area and thus responded to the
government's commitment to widening the range of
employment in this generally less prosperous part of
the country. The general effectiveness of grants is
also questionable. Relatively few jobs have
resulted (around 2,300 each year between 1976 and
1980), suggestive of the inherent difficulty of
decentralising certain office-based activities and
indicative of the modest value of payments (28).
Overall, the government's financial outlay has been
insignificant compared with its support for industry; between 1976 and 1980 grants for tertiary
activities totalled 181.3 million francs as opposed
to 2,535.3 million francs allocated to industry
through regional development grants (29).

A more refined spatial classification of decentralised employment has been outlined linking location with different forms of activity (30). Three
forms of decentralisation are distinguished. The
first relates to the major provincial cities,
particularly Lyon, Bordeaux and Strasbourg, to which
a large number and broad range of activities have
moved, attracted by the expansion and growth potential of the local market; banking and consultancy
services are typical of this process. Secondly, a
wide area of western France and the region of Centre
is defined, to which generally larger units have
been transferred, frequently in the public sector
and in fields such as administration and data-
processing. Here growth has often been induced
rather than spontaneous. Finally, much of southern
France (and to some degree Brittany) have become
areas to which research laboratories have been
attracted, partly under government pressure but in
certain cases reflecting the influence of an attractive natural environment or the presence of an
existing research base. Some support for this
assessment is given by the distribution of decentralised employment in the public sector (Figure 10.3).
Priority appears to have been accorded to parts of
'western' France, benefiting, for example, towns in
Brittany and the two cities of Bordeaux and
Toulouse, largely through the movement of scientific
and educational establishments linked to electronics
and aerospace. However, the largest concentration
of jobs (approximately 5,000) has resulted at
Orléans, many linked to the transfer of sections of
research organisations such as the CNRS, INRA and
BRGM (31). The town has also been selected by
various firms in the private sector such as IBM. In
both cases this choice of location appears to have

been influenced by the desire to maintain easy
access with services in Paris, underlining a common
difficulty in promoting decentralisation (32). The
state's influence has not been directed, however,
solely to the western part of the country; employment has also been generated in south-eastern
regions, notably at Lyon and Grenoble, the latter
city having become a major focus for research into
nuclear energy.

This latter aspect reflects a further aim of
government strategy: to promote a policy of concentrated decentralisation, partly to facilitate the
generation of various external economies and partly
to establish a series of specialised and integrated
research centres. Just as these aims have also been
pursued within the public sector, private firms have
also been encouraged to follow a similar policy.
Certain concentrations have developed: Toulouse has
grown as the centre for activities linked to aerospace, Rennes and to a lesser degree Brittany in
general, for telecommunications, and Grenoble for
electronics and nuclear science.

The same principle applies to the development
of a number of 'tertiary and science parks', illustrated by the growth of administrative and research
activities at Valbonne between Nice and Cannes (33).
This project was launched in the early 1970s and has
since become the focus of an extensive area and
range of tertiary activities including research
(e.g. electronics, pharmaceuticals), higher education (e.g. Ecole des Mines de Paris; Ecole
Supérieure des Communications), administration (e.g.
Dow Chemicals; Texas Instruments). It perpetuates
an already established tendency for the location of
such activities in this region of southern France, a
trend pioneered in 1962 by IBM's decision to transfer its research headquarters from Paris to La Gaude
(to the west of Nice). Then, as now, the potential
for this form of economic growth reflected the
appeal of the area due to factors of climate and
landscape, good accessibility, particularly the
close proximity of Nice airport, and an already
established base for research at the University of
Nice. Nonetheless, despite such attractions the
rate of expansion has been slower than anticipated,
although this is partly a reflection of the excessively optimistic character of the original employment predictions (up to 35,000 jobs by 1990).
Currently nearly 2,000 jobs have been generated
directly at Valbonne and in the surrounding area,
most of them for skilled and highly qualified

personnel. Few operational linkages exist, however, between the various activities.

Decentralisation: an Assessment

Some disappointment has been expressed over the relatively modest scale of decentralisation and the extent to which many control and decision-making functions have remained in Paris, often resulting in decentralised units remaining dependent upon the capital (34). Whatever the shortcomings of official policy, this suggests, at least in part, that for many office activities, the forces of agglomeration remain strong; even large cities such as Lyon are still perceived as unable to offer the range of contacts, access to an extensive clientele or quality of personnel required by many firms. It is, perhaps, of little surprise that the majority of companies' head offices remain firmly rooted in the capital, for it is at this level of policy formulation and negotiation that ease of access to external contacts is vital. In contrast, decentralisation has been associated with the establishment of a number of regional organisational centres, notably in the fields of banking and insurance, and with the movement of an increasing number of routine operations. However, the lead which the state wished to demonstrate, by the transfer of its own administrative services and research institutes, has been unimpressive despite the relatively large number of jobs decentralised. Delays have been frequent and opposition by employees reluctant to leave the capital considerable, both traits illustrated by the protracted polemic over the transfer of part of the SNCF's administrative services to Lyon and Lille (35).

It is possible, however, to distinguish a number of more encouraging trends. Government controls have considerably slowed the expansion of office floorspace in Paris, while a number of official initiatives have helped create the necessary environment for decentralisation. Communications between the capital and major provincial centres have been improved, the range of state services and higher educational establishments in these cities widened and strengthened, and major banks have accorded far greater discretionary and decision-making powers to their principal regional offices.

Rapid developments and improvements in data-processing equipment and the telecommunications system are also providing the means to increase the

decentralisation of certain tasks (36). Previously,
with data handled principally by large computers
based in Paris, the opportunities for the dispersion
of even routine tasks was limited. This handicap is
now being removed by the introduction of more and
smaller machines and greatly increased capacity for
the transmission of information, as through the
Transpac network (37). Above all, firms in provincial locations now have much easier direct access to
data banks based in Paris. However, the process of
decentralisation is still partly slowed by the
continued overwhelming concentration of computer
operators and advisors in Paris. But, whatever the
desirability and potential for decentralisation, in
the current period of more restrained economic
growth, the scale of new investment and, therefore,
movement, is likely to be restricted.

OFFICE DEVELOPMENT AT A LOCAL LEVEL: TWO CASE
STUDIES

So far office activities have been viewed largely in
a national or regional context with little emphasis
upon their structural or spatial characteristics at
a local level. To offer some insight into specific
centres of office employment, a more detailed
appraisal will be undertaken of the situation in the
cities of Paris and Lyon. The former represents the
principal focus of offices within France, while the
latter serves as the major office centre outside of
the capital.

Paris
Spontaneous outward movement from the capital and
decentralisation encouraged by government policy
have done little to diminish the dominance of Paris
as a location for office activities. Within the
département of Paris alone there are over 14 million
square metres of office floorspace where more than
1 million workers are employed, representing over 50
per cent of the area's wo𝗄-force (38). As stressed
elsewhere, it is not only the volume of office
activity which distinguishes the capital, but also
the qualitative features of associated employment,
particularly the diversity of functions and high
proportion of qualified workers: in the major growth
area of computing and data-processing, over 60 per
cent of the highly trained technical and engineering
personnel are located in the capital (39).

The Growth of Offices

Despite the wide range of office activities, three key functions testify further to the capital's distinctiveness. First, Paris acts as a major administrative centre, not only in a local and regional context, but more significantly, in a national and international setting; second, it dominates as a leading banking and financial centre, and third, it houses a large number of company head offices, particularly those of major national and multinational groups (40). Traditionally, the business, administrative and government quarter of the city was located in the 'west end' of the centre in a broad area around the Champs-Elysées. However, government restrictions on development, linked with natural limitations on space for expansion have led to a dispersion of activities away from this nucleus, notably towards the inner western suburbs.

This lessening of the dominance of the central area of the city, to the advantage of other areas of the capital became an increasingly significant feature of office location strategy pursued in the Paris region during the 1970s, particularly as the office boom of the late 1960s and early 1970s generated a strong pressure for further development. Other priorities also emerged. First, it appeared desirable to try to encourage a higher level of growth in the eastern parts of the city, an area traditionally shunned by office activities which had thus led to an imbalance in the employment structure and to journey-to-work problems. Second, many of the outer suburban districts of the capital had long suffered from the lack of a large number or broad range of job opportunities in offices; with the launching of the new towns in the early 1970s and the desire to provide them with a balanced employment structure, it became even more essential to attract office activities to these outer areas.

Thus, over the last decade, policy towards the location of offices within the Paris region has aimed at a redistribution of activity away from the centre towards a series of suburban and peripheral sites. Such priorities need to be viewed in the wider context, however, of the objective at a national level of directing expansion away from the capital, leading in certain cases to a conflict of interest between, for example, the priorities of the new towns and the desirability of decentralisation. Control of development within the region has been effected in part by the dissuasive influence of the redevance which is levied at a variable rate in the central and inner areas of the capital (highest in the west), and is not applicable in the new towns; far more stringent control has been applied by the agrément procedure. These restrictions have been applied, however, against the background of a substantial change in the conditions of supply and demand.

In the early 1970s the demand for office floorspace in the capital was high, yet the availability, particularly of new offices, was limited, provoking a marked surge of speculative investment. Despite restrictions, approval was given for extensive office development, exceeding 1.7 million square metres of floorspace in 1971 (Table 10.8). The desire for stricter control of the market led in 1975 to the government's decision to limit the annual total of floorspace approved within the region to 700,000 square metres, of which in principle a third was to be directed towards the new towns and no more than 40,000 square metres approved in the centre. However, since the mid-1970s economic conditions have changed and the previous boom in the property market has been superceded by a marked slump. Together, these influences resulted in a substantial decline in the amount of new floorspace approved (Table 10.8), followed by a considerable fall in the amount of office property released onto the market and acquired. In the short term this

Table 10.8: Approval of New Office Floorspace

	Agréments granted	
	Ile-de-France	Paris (département)
	('000 square metres)	
1970	1,450	401
1971	1,736	294
1972	1,188	272
1973	1,199	115
1974	897	112
1975	563	30
1976	334	77
1977	375	80
1978	261	27
1979	625	37
1980	700	20

Source: Atelier Parisien d'Urbanisme.

slow take-up produced a vast surplus of supply, with the excess of new office floorspace alone exceeding 1 million square metres; since then, due to a more restrained building programme, this has been reduced to around 400,000 square metres (41).

<u>Internal Contrasts</u>. Over recent years restrictions on the construction of new offices in central areas of the capital have been strictly enforced, illustrated by the substantial reduction in the amount of floorspace approved each year (Table 10.8). Most of the current movement in the market is related to the re-use of existing premises or the sale or lease of renovated office buildings. The era of major redevelopment schemes such as Maine-Montparnasse and Front-de-Seine, which augmented considerably the centre's stock of offices, has now largely ceased; even where renewal is occurring, office floorspace is often limited, as at Les Halles (42), again reflecting the restrictive character of official policy. Exceptions exist in only a limited number of areas such as the Gare de Lyon. In this latter case it is anticipated that, with good suburban rail links to the east and south-east of the city, the further provision of office jobs in this area will help redress the previous under-provision of such employment in this part of the capital.
    Within the inner suburbs the improved accessibility theoretically offered by the <u>boulevard périphérique</u> has attracted a number of office schemes, but the greater part of new development has been concentrated in the series of restructuring poles spread throughout this area. Of these, La Défense has been the most ambitious, successful and controversial (Figure 10.4). It was conceived in the late 1950s with one of its principal aims to create a prestige office centre capable of relieving the traditional congested business quarter of the capital. By 1982 over 860,000 square metres of floorspace had been completed, virtually all of it had been taken up and a further 200,000 square metres was under construction. In addition, a host of major national and multinational companies, including Société Générale, Union des Assurances de Paris, IBM, Crédit Lyonnais, Esso and Rhône-Poulenc, had established their French headquarters or Paris offices at La Défense, creating over 45,000 new jobs. A number of companies have transferred to this area due to their inability to gain approval for expansion in the centre. Despite such apparent success,

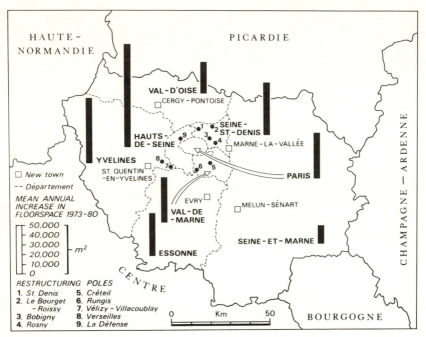

Figure 10.4: The Increase of Office Floorspace in Ile-de-France (refers to private sector only)

La Défense has not been without its difficulties, notably in the mid-1970s when, following a period of rapid take-up of floorspace, demand fell substantially. The complex was adversely affected by the first repercussions of the recession and a surplus of floorspace in the Paris region as a number of speculative projects launched in the early 1970s were released onto the market. As a result, the Decentralisation Committee discriminated in favour of La Défense in its allocations of agréments, although this represented a contradiction of the policy of trying to promote location in the city's inner eastern suburbs. Here office schemes such as Les Mercuriales at Bagnolet, despite its location adjacent to the périphérique and much lower cost, have long remained largely unoccupied, reflecting their relative isolation from the city's main business quarter.

In the outer suburbs the main focus for office development has increasingly become the new towns (Figure 10.4). For much of the period between 1975 and 1980, for example, the average amount of

floorspace approved within the towns exceeded the
minimum requirement laid down by the government
(Table 10.9). Nonetheless, in terms of the amount

Table 10.9: New Office Floorspace approved in the
New Towns of Ile-de-France

	Amount of floorspace (square metres)	Proportion of regional total (%)
1975	135,381	29
1976	112,758	35
1977	140,291	38
1978	73,919	28
1979	188,236	30
1980	280,658	38

Source: Association Bureaux-Provinces.

of new floorspace taken up each year, the new towns
still play a relatively modest role in the property
market of Ile-de-France, averaging only 6 per cent
of the total between 1975 and 1980. The problem of
an excessive supply of vacant floorspace which
characterised the new towns in their earlier years
(43) has now been greatly reduced, particularly at
Cergy-Pontoise, St. Quentin-en-Yvelines and Evry.
All now offer an increasingly large and diverse
labour market, and the cost of renting or buying
offices is relatively modest compared with many
sites closer to the centre although accessibility to
the central area is good. The same processes which
have encouraged growth in many provincial centres
appear to have operated also in favour of the new
towns, particularly in relation to the attraction of
activities in the financial and data-processing
fields (44). Marne-la-Vallée has so far experienced
a lower level of office development and the problem
of vacant floorspace remains significant, partially
reflecting its more recent development. It belies,
however, its potential as an office centre due to
excellent accessibility with the centre, notably
through the RER (45), but it does imply again that
the eastern part of the capital is still relatively
disadvantaged as an office centre.
      Thus, whilst certain adjustments have been made
to the spatial distribution of office employment

within the region, notably provoking the relative decline of the centre (46), certain imbalances persist. At a regional level there is some indication of an increasing reduction of available floorspace with relatively few new major projects under construction, reflecting investors' reluctance to commit resources during the previously depressed state of the market. Pressures for further office development are increasing, therefore, not least to offer an alternative to La Défense as this operation nears completion.

Lyon
Since the late 1960s France's second city has expanded rapidly as a centre for office activities and now ranks by a substantial margin as the principal focus for offices outside of Paris. It is estimated that since 1965, over 1.1 million square metres of office floorspace have become available at Lyon, almost more than twice the total for any of the other large provincial agglomerations (47). Over this period, however, the pattern of growth has varied considerably, with a marked decline in the amount of floorspace completed since 1977. This is illustrated by reference to the provision of space in speculative developments (Table 10.10) (48).
    In the capital one of the major features of the expansion of offices has been the emphasis upon development in suburban locations in preference to

Table 10.10: Annual Increase in Floorspace of Speculative Office Development in Lyon

	Floorspace (square metres)
1973	27,350
1974	95,550
1975	31,650
1976	31,650
1977	66,100
1978	24,100
1979	19,950
1980	8,950

Source: Association pour le Développement Economique de la Région Lyonnaise.

the centre. At Lyon, although a spontaneous drift of certain office activities towards the periphery is observable, the outstanding feature of growth over the last decade has been the creation and commercialisation of a new central business district, La Part-Dieu, which has played a crucial role in the city's rise as an office centre (Figure 10.5). Prior to this development, there was no recognisable office quarter within Lyon, and a virtual absence of speculative building, leading to considerable pressure for additional floorspace.

Other forces have underlain the increase in office building at Lyon. A number are of local origin. For example, as a major urban and industrial centre, situated amidst a region which for much of the post-war period has experienced rapid demographic and economic growth, the city possesses a number of obvious attractions for business activity. In addition, Lyon is easily reached (particularly by road) from much of its regional hinterland; and with continuing improvements to communications such as the opening of Satolas international airport in 1975 and the launching of the TGV in 1981 (49) it has also become increasingly accessible to Paris and other major business capitals. External influences have also been significant, notably in the context of regional policy. As part of the government's strategy of creating a number of provincial counterweights to Paris, Lyon has benefited from a substantial increase in the capacity and functions of the city's banking facilities (50). Also, certain tendencies which have operated nationally have promoted growth, such as the general increase and diversification of business services and the increasing spatial disassociation of firms' control, administrative and manufacturing activities.

The expansion of the office sector has been fostered by various types of organisations and firms. In part it has been induced by the indigenous growth of local companies and by the growth of state, regional and municipal services already located in the city. In addition, various public and private concerns, based elsewhere, have extended their operations through expansion at Lyon. Growth in this latter area has been particularly apparent in relation to banking and insurance, with companies such as Société Générale and UAP setting up their regional headquarters at Lyon. Associated with these different forms of expansion are contrasting patterns of location. It has been suggested that office activities linked to industrial firms have

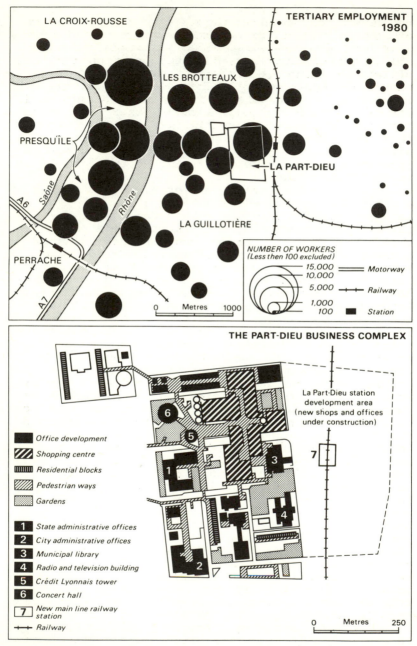

Figure 10.5:   Central Lyon: Tertiary Employment and the Central Business Complex of La Part–Dieu

tended to expand either adjacent to the main zones
of industry (particularly in the outer eastern
suburbs), or in selected inner areas of the city
(51). Conversely, companies seeking ready-built
office accommodation in a prestige location have
shown a strong preference for La Part-Dieu, the area
in which the major part of the public administrative
sector has also become concentrated. A more random
distribution characterises those firms building
their own office complexes, ranging from inner city
sites such as the Le Tonkin redevelopment area, to
more attractive peripheral locations such as Ecully
in the western suburbs.

La Part-Dieu. Amidst these various developments,
La Part-Dieu represents a symbol of the city's
growth and importance as an office centre (52).
Located adjacent to the traditional retailing and
business quarters, it offers (in addition to a major
retailing complex and a number of public amenities)
380,000 square metres of office floorspace, divided
between public administrative services (160,000m^2)
and commercial activities (220,000m^2) predominantly
in the private sector (Figure 10.5). The first
office block was completed in 1971; by 1982 the
greater part of the available floorspace had been
taken up and around 12,000 jobs created. These
should not necessarily be regarded as 'new' employment, however, for many firms have regrouped at La
Part-Dieu jobs previously dispersed or poorly accom-
modated elsewhere in the local area; the same principle applies to a part of the employment in
administrative services. Moreover, despite the
virtual completion of the project, the commercialisation of office floorspace in the private sector
has not been without its problems, notably in the
latter 1970s following the release of 30,000 square
metres, spread over 40 floors, in the Crédit
Lyonnais tower. Designed as the principal prestige
building of the complex, initially takers for the
floorspace proved difficult to attract. In part
this reflected a depressed market but it also
resulted from the relatively high cost of space, a
consequence of the building's design features (e.g.
full air conditioning) and height (leading to strict
security regulations and, inevitably, higher charges).
       Part of the strategy behind the launching of La
Part-Dieu was to attract control and decision-making
elements of major national and multinational groups
to Lyon, given their ability to generate employment

in a wide range of ancillary activities. To some
extent this policy has succeeded. Within the Crédit
Lyonnais building alone, apart from the bank's
administrative offices, RVI, Rhône-Poulenc-Textile
and Technip (a major engineering consultancy firm)
all have a substantial grouping of office activities. The city, however, has as yet to attract a
major divisional headquarters of one of the
country's leading industrial groups from which the
spin-off in terms of jobs and investment ought to be
far greater. If this objective is to be pursued,
with the completion of La Part-Dieu, the problem now
is where to provide the necessary floorspace (53).

La Part-Dieu has had a major influence upon the
growth and concentration of office activity within
Lyon. However, it has a wider significance as a
model of the way in which various large provincial
urban centres responded to the substantial demand
for office floorspace which existed in the early
1970s. Now, in a period of more restrained economic
growth and revised thinking on the design and location of office accommodation, it is questionable
whether the experience will be repeated in response
to future requirements.

NOTES

1. A general discussion of this area is given
in Tauveron, A., 'Le tertiaire supérieur: moteur du
développement régional?' L'Espace Géographique, 3
(1974), 169-78.
2. The notion of an office job is open to
different interpretations. In addition, problems
exist in the use of employment data for groups of
activities within the tertiary sector which are
composed essentially of office jobs. Not only are
certain occupations inevitably included which do not
relate to office employment, but this neglects the
important component of office jobs subsumed within
the secondary sector. Occupational data offers a
more attractive alternative and a reasonable, albeit
slightly narrow, approximation of the number of
office jobs is provided by use of the definition
employed by the Paris Urban Planning Authority (see
Foucher, J., Les Bureaux dans les Agglomérations de
50,000 à 250,000 Habitants (La Documentation
Française, Paris, 1974), 24). This definition of
office employment is used here. An alternative and
complementary measure of the importance of offices
is provided by floorspace statistics. Few are

available on a comprehensive basis, however. One reliable source is provided by data collected and published by the Association Bureaux-Provinces. In most cases, however, this information relates only to offices built by developers on a largely speculative basis. While this acts as a useful indicator of the market, floorspace in these developments is but a minor element of the total stock of offices; it is estimated that in provincial France, floorspace provided on this basis represents less than 5 per cent of the overall total.

3. These features are discussed in some detail in Thevenot, L., 'Les catégories sociales en 1975: l'extension du salariat', Economie et Statistique, No.91 (1977), 3-31.

4. Given the variety of activities subsumed within this category, this figure undoubtedly represents an over-estimate of the number of office jobs.

5. Commissariat Général du Plan, Emplois dans les Services (La Documentation Française, Paris, 1980), 171-87.

6. For a more detailed study, see Braibant, M., 'L'économie des services marchands de 1960 à 1980', Archives et Documents, No.37 (1981).

7. Pinchemel, P., La Région Parisienne (Presses Universitaires de France, Paris, 1979), 14. This is also forcibly demonstrated in Brocard, M., 'Aménagement du territoire et développement régional: le cas de la recherche scientifique', L'Espace Géographique, 10 (1981), 61-9.

8. Pinchemel, La Région Parisienne, 14. Valeyre, A., 'Emplois et régions: la polarisation de l'emploi dans l'espace français' in 'Activités et Régions', Travaux et Recherches de Prospective, No. 75 (1978), 39-41 and 59.

9. Fischer, A., 'Eléments pour une étude des effets spatiaux des concentrations industrielles', Annales de Géographie, 87 (1978), 306-7.

10. Bureaux en Province (La Documentation Française, Paris, 1977).

11. Daniels, P., Office Locations: An Urban and Regional Study (Bell, London, 1875).

12. Pred, A., City Systems in Advanced Economies (Hutchinson, London, 1977), 116-20.

13. For fuller details, see Ferniot, B., 'La réglementation relative à la localisation des activités tertiaires en France (1958-70)', Analyse de l'Espace, No.4 (1978), 50-4.

14. Yuill, D. et al., Regional Policy in the European Community (Croom Helm, London, 1980), 71-7.

15. Originally 100 jobs had to be created for

a firm to become eligible for a grant, and until
1982 the maximum grant per job was 20,000 francs.

16.   Apart from the Regional Development Grant,
other forms of aid are available. It is also now
possible for non-industrial projects to qualify for
a small business grant (prime à l'emploi) authorised
by individual Regional Councils. Various other
forms of aid exist to encourage decentralisation,
notably to facilitate the movement of staff affected
by a decentralisation operation. Grants are payable
to help offset the costs of movement for key personnel and since 1980 a system of location contracts
(contrats de localisation) has been introduced,
sponsored by the government and negotiated between
the firm and the local authority in the area to
which the move takes place. Under this scheme
advice and financial aid are provided to assist with
rehousing and with the problem of the loss of
employment by the spouse of the person whose job has
been decentralised.

17.   Originally the maximum was 100 francs per
square metre; in 1971 it was raised to 400 francs
and remained unchanged until the present proposal.

18.   Just as with industrial projects, the
agrément has often been used as a means of negotiation between the government and a firm or organisation. Thus, if agreement is reached on the transfer
of certain services and jobs to provincial areas,
limited expansion in the Paris region may also be
authorised.

19.   The term decentralisation is used loosely
to cover principally three types of operation: the
complete move of a firm from Paris to provincial
France, the partial transfer of part of a firm's
activities, and the creation of new employment in
areas outside Paris by a firm based in the capital,
independently of any transfer of activity.

20.   Bonnet, J., 'La décentralisation des
activités tertiaires en France', Revue Géographique
de Lyon, 54 (1979), 358.

21.   The information is provided by the
Association Bureaux-Provinces.

22.   Bonnet, 'La décentralisation des activités
tertiaires', 358.

23.   Association Bureaux-Provinces, Bulletin
No.15 (1981), 7-8. The major areas of activity
involved related to the Ministries of Postal and
Telecommunication Services, Industry, Defence and
the Environment.

24.   Bonnet, 'La décentralisation des activités
tertiaires', 359.

25. Bonnet, 'La décentralisation des activités tertiaires', 359.

26. Le Marché Immobilier en France 1982. Report published by the consultants Bourdais, Paris, 1982.

27. Ferniot, B., 'Bilan de 48 enquêtes sur la décentralisation tertiaire effectuées d'avril à juin 1977', Analyse de l'Espace, No.4 (1978), 78.

28. These ranged between maxima of 10,000 and 20,000 francs per job.

29. Calculated from details provided in the annual Rapports d'Activité of DATAR.

30. Bonnet, J., 'La décentralisation des activités tertiaires: analyse géographique', Analyse de l'Espace, No.4 (1978), 19-20.

31. CNRS - Centre National de la Recherche Scientifique; INRA - Institut National de la Recherche Agronomique; BRGM - Bureau de Recherches Géologiques et Minières.

32. Bonnet, 'La décentralisation des activités tertiaires: analyse géographique', 18.

33. Background to this development is contained in Hall, R., 'Sophia Antipolis: ville nouvelle', Town and Country Planning, 43 (1975), 119-22.

34. See, Madiot, Y., L'Aménagement du Territoire (Masson, Paris, 1979), 216-21; Perrin, N., 'L'aménagement du territoire et le développement régional' in Pagé, J-P. (ed.), Profil Economique de la France (La Documentation Française, Paris, 1981), 430; Pinchemel, P., La France (Armand Colin, Paris, 1981), vol.2, 169-70; Brocard, 'Aménagement du territoire et développement régional', 61-73.

35. Pinchemel, La France, 170-1; Le Monde, 6-7 Sept. 1981 and 11 Nov. 1981.

36. Huet, P., Télématique et Aménagement du Territoire (La Documentation Française, Paris, 1981).

37. Huet, Télématique, 11.

38. Les Bureaux à Paris 1970-80 (Atelier Parisien d'Urbanisme, Paris, 1981).

39. Huet, Télématique, 90.

40. Beaujeu-Garnier, J., Atlas et Géographie de la Région d'Ile-de-France (Flammarion, Paris, 1977), vol.2, 62-77.

41. Le Marché des Bureaux en France en 1980 (Association Bureaux-Provinces, Paris, 1981), 22.

42. Tuppen, J.N., 'Les Halles: a major central area redevelopment', Town and Country Planning, 50 (1981), 137-9.

43. Tuppen, J.N., 'New towns in the Paris

region: an appraisal', Town Planning Review, 50
(1979), 58-62.
    44.   Evry, for example, houses the regional
administrative centres of banks such as the BNP,
Crédit Lyonnais and Société Générale, as well as
general administrative or data-processing activities
for companies such as Hewlett-Packard, Digital
Equipment, Sofinco-la-Hénin, Harvester International
and Lyonnaise des Eaux.
    45.   Réseau Express Régional - the limited
stop, high-speed métro system. See Tuppen, J.N.,
'Public transport in France: the development and
extension of the métro', Geography, 65 (1980), 127-
30.
    46.   In terms of floorspace, the proportion of
the regional total concentrated in the centre has
declined from approximately 75 per cent in 1962 to
around 60 per cent in 1980.
    47.   Bonneville, M., 'La construction des
bureaux dans l'agglomération Lyonnaise', Revue de
Géographie de Lyon, 54 (1979), 350.
    48.   Peaks shown in 1974 and 1977 represent the
completion of major phases of the Part-Dieu operation. The depressed property market has influenced
the recent decline in new floorspace.
    49.   TGV - Train à Grande Vitesse. See Tuppen,
J.N., 'Le train à grande vitesse: its development
and implications', Geography, 67 (1982), 343-4.
    50.   More detail of these objectives is
contained in Lyon: Place Bancaire (La Documentation
Française, Paris, 1974).
    51.   Bonneville, 'La construction des bureaux',
350-1.
    52.   Described in greater detail in Tuppen,
J.N., 'Redevelopment of the city centre: the case of
Lyon-La Part-Dieu', Scottish Geographical Magazine,
93 (1977), 151-8; Bonnet, J., 'L'essor du tertiaire
supérieur à Lyon: le centre régional de la Part-
Dieu', Revue de la Géographie de Lyon, 51 (1976),
5-33.
    53.   As an illustration of the problem, the new
Part-Dieu railway station complex contains provision
for up to 50,000 square metres of floorspace, but in
predominantly small units of 5-10,000 square metres,
too small for this purpose.

Chapter Eleven

CHANGING PATTERNS OF RETAILING

Over the last two decades retailing in France has
altered radically, although the activity has long
been characterised by innovation and change (1).
However, since the early 1960s the scale, pace and
extent of transformation have all increased greatly,
sweeping aside the traditional image of a nation
dominated by small and often inefficiently run
retail businesses.
      Small shops still predominate but their signi-
ficance has been substantially eroded by the
development of new forms of retailing. Above all,
change has been linked to the very rapid growth of
mass merchandising and the self-service selling
technique. Unlike Britain, France has been much
more prepared to imitate forms of retail organisation pioneered in the USA.
      The transformation of retailing has involved
much more than a modification of the form of the
outlet and the manner by which the product is sold.
Equally profound changes have occurred in the
organisation of the activity, associated with the
rationalisation of distribution networks and a concentration of ownership. Thus, the control of an
increasing volume of retail sales is now assured by
a limited number of large frequently vertically
integrated groups. Even small retailers have associated in various ways, principally to strengthen
their bargaining position as purchasers. These
mutations have also been linked to new location
patterns. Many traditional central shopping areas
have been remodelled and revitalised, but the overriding feature of this form of change has been the
suburbanisation of retailing, with the widespread
growth of large free-standing stores and shopping
complexes on the outskirts of urban areas.
      Such developments have occurred against a

backcloth of substantial social and economic change in post-war France. Thus, factors such as improved living standards, the redistribution of population, increased personal mobility and altered consumer preferences have all contributed to the growth of new forms of retailing.

THE ROLE OF RETAILING IN THE ECONOMY

Various indicators attest to the importance of retailing within the French economy and to its dynamism. In 1980 the activity employed over 1.6 million people, spread between more than 600,000 retail outlets, and generated a turnover of just under 700 billion francs (2). Moreover, since 1962 jobs have increased by nearly 300,000 (3). Such generalisation masks, however, a more complex pattern of development, with growth trends varying over time and between different retail activities. A more detailed appraisal of the increase in wage-earners within this branch between 1968 and 1981 illustrates these points (Table 11.1). Although such employment has increased yearly by more than 2.1 per cent over this period, growth has been lower than in the tertiary sector as a whole; moreover, variations have occurred between the food and non-food retailing sectors. In the former case a relatively high rate of growth has been sustained since the latter 1960s, whereas amongst non-food retailing activities (which account for a far larger share of employment) expansion has been at a lower rate, with a tendency to decline over recent years. By 1980, however, the previous vitality of the combined retailing sector was less apparent; employment growth has eased to an annual rate of 0.6 per cent, concealing a modest net decrease of jobs in the non-food retailing branch.

This altered performance appears related to the depressive effects of the recession upon consumer demand and upon new investment. However, over a longer period the creation of new jobs has been counterbalanced by the continuing decline of the small shopowner, from a total of over 1.2 millions in 1954 to around 875,000 in 1980. Part of the explanation for this tendency lies in the severe competition posed for many small retail outlets, particularly in the grocery trade, by the proliferation of supermarkets and hypermarkets and the spread of self-service shopping; small traders have often been reluctant or unable to adapt to new selling

Changing Patterns of Retailing

Table 11.1: Employment in Retailing: Changes 1968-81

a. The Increase of Employment in Retailing

	Total wage-earners		
	1968	1975 ('000)	1981
Food retailing	294.7	352.3	414.0
Non-food retailing	575.0	650.9	700.4
Total	869.7	1,003.2	1,114.4

b. The Rate of Employment Increase

	Mean annual rate	
	1968-75 (%)	1975-81
Food retailing	2.8	2.9
Non-food retailing	1.9	1.3
Total	2.2	1.9

Source: INSEE, Emploi Salarié.

techniques. However, a slowing in the rate of their decline since 1975 suggests that in this particular case the recession, rather than hastening closure may have encouraged certain owners to retain their businesses due to the difficulty of finding alternative employment (4); it may also indicate the renewed fashionability of certain forms of small retail outlet, and their undoubted convenience value.

In common with many other tertiary activities retailing also represents an important source of female employment. In 1981 over 646,000 women wage-earners were employed in this branch, representing 58 per cent of the total salaried labour-force. Since 1975 alone their number has increased by over 82,000. Similarly, employment growth in retailing has been characterised by a substantial rise in

part-time working, particularly amongst women, with
such employees now accounting for at least a sixth
of the total labour-force (5).
   Variations are also evident over time in the
pattern of openings and closures of retail outlets.
Throughout much of the period from the mid-1950s
until the mid-1970s, there was a tendency for the
number of outlets to decline; however, since 1975
there has been a progressive rise (6). For example,
whereas the total fell by a yearly average of 2,000
between 1971 and 1975 (7), over the period 1975 to
1981 the annual net increase averaged 9,260, the
figure increasing each year to exceed 14,100 in 1980
(8). Despite the recent overall picture of expansion, there are noticeable contrasts in the performance of different branches of retailing. The
opening of new outlets has been more pronounced in
the non-food sector, particularly in relation to
goods such as furniture, clothes and shoes, electrical products and chemists (9). Conversely, closures
have been heavy in food retailing, representing a
net loss of 8,000 outlets each year between 1975 and
1979 (10); in particular, they have occurred in
shops specialising in meat, groceries and dairy
produce (11). Together these trends indicate a very
substantial degree of change and renewal of
retailing outlets over recent years.

THE DETERMINANTS OF CHANGE

Many factors account for the post-war growth and
transformation of retailing, making it difficult to
evaluate the precise effect of specific influences
(12). Nonetheless, the unprecedented expansion of
the French population for much of this period,
greatly enlarging the potential market, has played a
fundamental role in the increase of this activity.
Moreover, this overall rise in population has been
accompanied by a pronounced shift of people away
from rural areas to urban centres, helping to
provoke in many towns and cities the rapid increase
of retail turnover, emphasising the essentially
urban characteristic of this latter feature.
Temporary migration has also stimulated the expansion of certain forms of retailing in selected
areas; activities related to tourism in regions such
as France's southern coastal seaboard offer one
example. The impact of these demographic changes
has been heightened by the comparative lack of
growth or movement prior to the second world war;

further, due to an inevitable lag in the expansion
of retailing facilities in response to population
growth, in the more recent past there has frequently
been a problem of the under provision of shops,
strengthening the need for the extension and modification of the retail system. This has been a particular feature and problem of many outer suburban
areas.

It is not only the increase in population that
is of significance, but also the enhanced purchasing
power of consumers that has underpinned retail
expansion. The strong growth of the French economy
throughout much of the post-war period has been
accompanied by a substantial rise in incomes,
improved living standards and higher levels of
personal consumption. Moreover, the inclination to
spend has also been promoted by new buying techniques, notably in recent years by the very rapid
increase in credit card sales; it has also been
encouraged by an upsurge in advertising. However,
consumption patterns have altered, offering some
explanation for the contrasting evolution of
different forms of retail outlet. Thus, whereas in
1959, 34 per cent of household expenditure was taken
by the purchase of food and drink, by 1980 this had
fallen to 21 per cent; similarly, expenditure on
textile and leather goods fell from 12 to 8 per
cent (13). Conversely, the proportion spent on
major durable goods rose from 7 to 9 per cent (14).
Several minority markets have also expanded rapidly,
reflecting not only increased affluence, but other
factors such as shorter working hours and changing
fashions; growth has been strong, for example, in
the field of sports and leisure goods and home
improvements. Demographic and social changes have
also led to the development of new forms of clientele, demanding particular types of goods. The
considerable increase in the number of young adults
(consequent upon post-war population trends) is one
illustration of the expansion of an important group
of purchasers; similarly, with the progressive rise
in the number of women in the labour-force and the
associated increase in their purchasing power, this
has helped generate a growing market for feminine
products. More generally, the ever-expanding range
of consumer goods has led to the creation of retail
outlets to promote their sale; the 'fast food' revolution, belatedly hitting France, is a similar case.

Other influences have led not only to an
increase in the number and range of new retail outlets, but also to a modification of pre-existing

shops. The rapid spread of the 'self-service'
selling technique, particularly in food retailing,
led to the opening of new stores or the modernisation of existing shops; so too did the trend towards
much larger retailing units as owners sought to
enlarge their product range, adapt to the demand for
self-service or realise scale economies. Consumers
themselves have helped induce change in retailing
provision through altered shopping habits and preferences. Greater emphasis is placed on relatively
infrequent, bulk-buying trips under the influence of
increased car ownership, higher levels of female
employment and improved storage facilities, notably
through the rise in the proportion of households
possessing freezers (28 per cent in 1980 compared
with 10 per cent in 1973). This has been combined
with the apparent desire for more convenience in
purchasing and a more attractive shopping
environment.

Change has been conditioned by factors other
than market forces. Government policy, the initiative and drive of certain businessmen and the action
of various pressure groups have also played their
part. Official attitudes have varied, but more
recently have tended to favour the small retailer
(15), whose cause has also been stoutly defended by
lobbies within the profession. In the latter case,
therefore, the pressures have been for the immuta-
bility of the system rather than its transformation.
Conversely, much of the original momentum for change
was generated by enlightened pioneers of mass
merchandising such as Leclerc and Fournier (16), the
latter founding the now giant hypermarket chain of
Carrefour. Despite their success, and the widespread adoption of their principles, opposition to
their selling techniques has been considerable.

There is now some evidence to suggest a slowing
in the previously rapid pace of transformation and
modernisation. After an extended period of continuous expansion, an increasing equilibrium between
the supply of certain forms of retail outlet and the
potential demand for their services has developed;
this is partly the case in relation to the slow-down
in the opening of new hypermarkets, although this
also reflects the influence of artificial constraints in an attempt to maintain a balance between
this and more traditional forms of retailing. The
recession has also exerted a depressive influence,
particularly in deterring potential investors in
major development projects, not least due to the
high cost of borrowing (17). Nonetheless, despite

temporal and spatial fluctuations, the general underlying trend within France is the continuous metamorphosis and expansion of retailing activity, even if for certain outlets, due to changes in fashion, their existence is essentially ephemeral.

There are, however, areas in which the tendency is towards a reduction of the amount of retail trade and the closure of shops. This is apparent in the inner areas of certain large cities (18) in which there has been a sizeable reduction in population or problems of urban decay, often associated with planning blight; it is also a feature of certain depressed industrial towns in traditional areas of heavy industry in northern and north-eastern France (19). In particular, however, it is a characteristic of many small rural communities where depopulation has often been intense and occurred over a long period. Not only has the local clientele for many shops been diminished, but due to the increased mobility of many of those remaining, trade has been lost to adjacent towns with a wider range of often cheaper goods. In recognition of the extent to which this has taken place, some attempt to maintain a minimum level of services in rural areas has been made by the government through financial incentives offered to shopkeepers (20).

CHANGES IN THE STRUCTURE OF RETAILING

Retail Organisation - The Growth of Concentration
As the volume of retailing activity has grown, the organisation of the industry has altered radically, taking account of such influences as the need to supply an increasing number of consumers with a more diverse range of products and, in doing this, to maximise efficiency in a highly competitive market. Retailing is still dominated by a large number of small and medium-sized businesses, frequently family concerns; but, in response to the above demands, an ever-growing proportion of retail sales is being controlled by a relatively restricted group of large, multiple-branch companies. The trend is particularly marked in food retailing, where such firms now control nearly 50 per cent of all sales, compared with only a tenth in the early 1950s (21).

Various forms of large company exist. One of the oldest is represented by the major department/variety store chains; the three most important, in terms of turnover, are the groups of Nouvelles

Galeries, Printemps-Prisunic and Layfayette-
Monoprix. Despite the relatively large floorspace
and high turnover of many of the shops within these
companies, the number of such outlets is comparatively limited. Many other chain-store groups now
exist, although their activities tend to be more
specialised and the retail outlets smaller in size.
This form of organisation is typical amongst food
retailers, illustrated by the numerous Félix-Potin
and Viniprix stores which form part of the Socadip
group. It is not uncommon to find firms controlling
both wholesaling and retailing operations. Many
such companies grew up on a regional basis, but
progressively they have become part of much larger
national organisations; one of the most powerful is
now the Paridoc group. Associations of the type
outlined above have existed since the mid-nineteenth
century, but a more recent form of major retailing
company is represented by various large independent
operators, linked particularly with the growth of
hypermarkets and other sizeable free-standing
stores. The Carrefour group is representative of
this form of evolution.

Despite their different origins, a number of
common traits characterise the commercial strategies
of these groups. Their present form results from an
intense and continuing process of concentration
involving takeovers, mergers and various looser
forms of association. As this has occurred, various
companies have also sought to control a greater
range of the operations linked to retailing such as
wholesaling and distribution, with the aims of
raising efficiency, guaranteeing supply and
achieving further economies of scale. The extent of
this process is illustrated by the Casino-Epargne
group which, apart from incorporating the above
operations, also manufacturers a number of its own
products (22). A further example of concentration
is provided by the growth of large purchasing
organisations, frequently acting on behalf of a
number of groups and which, in certain instances,
also possess their own retail outlets (23).

Concentration of control and ownership has also
been accompanied by a diversification of activities,
notably where companies have been absent from growth
sectors of the market. Moreover, for some of the
hypermarket chains whose expansion has been
curtailed by government legislation, this process
represents an important means by which to expand
their business. Diversification has occurred in
several ways. For example, many of the

long-established department store groups and other
chain store retailing organisations have invested
in hypermarkets; the group Printemps-Prisunic has a
major holding in the Euromarché hypermarket network,
while the large food retailing chains of Casino-
Epargne and Cofradel now also operate hypermarkets
trading respectively under the names Géant Casino
and Mammouth. Many companies which originated with
this form of trading have also sought to vary their
activities, expanding into fields such as sports
and leisure goods, restaurants and cafeterias and
home improvements; in this latter area, for example,
Carrefour has acquired the chain of Castorama shops.
    Although many of these large groups have
expanded rapidly, leading in certain market areas to
an increasingly ologopolistic tendency (24), small
businesses still account for a large volume of
retail sales, albeit a continually declining share
of their total value. In their attempt to remain
competitive, many of these concerns have adopted
practices similar to those employed by the major
retailing chains, with the formation of voluntary
chains and centralised purchasing organisations.
Small retailers are, however, an extremely heterogeneous group; not all are prone to decline. In
particular, it is independent family businesses in
both the food and non-food retailing sectors which
are losing ground (25).

Retail Techniques - the Boom in Self-Service
Since the early 1960s selling techniques have been
revolutionised, accompanied by the spread of new
types of retail outlet. Within Western Europe these
changes are not unique to France, but the rapid pace
and extent of transformation make the French experience highly distinctive. One of the principal
forms of change is the growth of self-service,
especially for the retailing of food. Its spectacular increase has led to the opening of numerous
supermarkets and hypermarkets, the conversion of
many pre-existing shops and the closure of a large
number of small retail outlets unable to compete
with the price-cutting policies which are generally
an integral part of the self-service marketing
philosophy. It is estimated that self-service
stores (of which there are now more than 27,500
employing over 260,000 people) account for more than
60 per cent of total food sales, illustrating the
strength of this movement (26); the first super-
market opened in France in 1957.

Hypermarkets epitomise this revolution of retailing methods and of consumer habits, although their development has often been controversial (27). The rise in the number of these stores has been meteoric. The first hypermarket opened in 1963: by 1982 this total had risen to 466 following a particularly rapid phase of expansion in the late 1960s and early 1970s (28). Such growth is reflected in their increasing impact upon sales. In 1970 less than 3 per cent of total retail turnover was generated by hypermarkets, but by 1981 this had risen to nearly 12 per cent; for food products the proportion was 16 per cent, with sales in this sector alone amounting to 60 billion francs (29). With the expansion of these stores, an increasing number of companies have sought to exploit their potential, although the majority of outlets and floorspace are still controlled by a limited number of chains; the ten major groups, for example, possess 83 per cent of the total floorspace (Table 11.2). Carrefour, the innovator of this form or retailing in France, no longer has the greatest number of outlets, but its sales' area is still considerably greater than its competitors.

Hypermarkets are now a feature of most areas of France, with a number of obvious exceptions such as parts of the interior regions of the Alps and Massif Central (Figure 11.1.). Nor is it surprising to observe a concentration of outlets and a relatively high ratio of floorspace to population in the

Table 11.2: Principal Hypermarket Chains, 1982

Chain	Floorspace (square metres)	Number of outlets
Carrefour	447,638	49
Mammouth	337,438	67
Euromarché	278,791	45
Auchan	243,944	30
Rond-Point	173,600	39
Leclerc	165,281	49
Cora	156,600	24
Continent	147,455	22
Géant Casino	123,657	18
Rallye	101,831	16

Source: Libre Service Actualités, No.825/6 (1981).

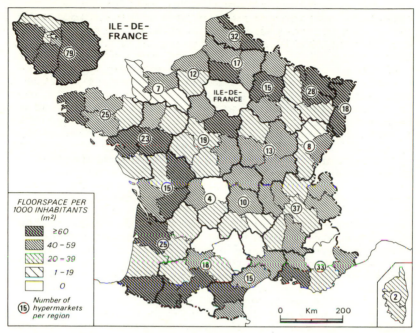

Figure 11.1:   The Distribution of Hypermarkets, 1981

country's more densely populated and urbanised
regions; for example, the Paris region, northern and
north-eastern France and around some of the larger
southern cities such as Marseille, Bordeaux and
Toulouse.   Certain areas of Brittany also have a
comparatively high incidence of such stores, partly
reflective of an above average density of population, but also of the greatly increased number of
potential purchasers resulting from the influx of
tourists.   Moreover, western France was an area of
innovation in the growth of hypermarkets (30).   Not
all regions, however, conform to these generalisations.   The level of development is comparatively
weak, for example, around Lyon, despite the size and
high density of urban population.   This is one
indication that there are factors which have limited
the spread of super-stores, ranging from the lack of
availability of land suitable for expansion, to
opposition from existing local traders.   The
strength of this latter protest was one factor
leading to greater control of such developments.
This was effected principally by legislation passed
in 1973 (Loi Royer) which, amongst other provisions

311

to assist shopkeepers generally, required new
retailing developments above a specified floorspace
(1,500 square metres for communes of more than
40,000 inhabitants) to seek prior approval from
newly created Departmental Urban Commercial Planning
Committees (Commissions Départementales d'Urbanisme
Commercial) (31). While there is some evidence of a
slowing in the number and rate of new openings since
that date (Table 11.2), this appears attributable to
factors other than just restrictive legislation,
such as a downturn in property investment and the
saturation of certain urban markets (32, 33).
    Since its introduction, the concept of the
hypermarket has evolved considerably. Initially,
the trend was towards ever larger stores, culmina-
ting in the early 1970s with the opening of a
limited number of giant outlets, notably by
Carrefour; on the outskirts of Toulouse and
Marseille, for example, their hypermarkets exceed
20,000 square metres of retailing floorspace. Since
then there has been a tendency towards more modestly
sized units, prompted by various factors. These
include the relative scarcity of sites able to
accommodate such large developments, difficulties of
access and parking, increased competition, an outcry
against such huge complexes on environmental grounds
and problems of management. The functions of the
hypermarket have also tended to become more diversified, frequently through the addition of a series of

Table 11.3: The Increase in Hypermarkets

	Number of additions
1968-74*	41
1975	19
1976	34
1977	30
1978	18
1979	26
1980	24
1981	34

*yearly average

Source: Ministère du Commerce et de l'Artisanat, La
France des Commerces 1981, and Libre Service
Actualités, No.825/6 (1981).

smaller, specialised shops and services housed
within the same building, perpetuating an earlier
trend towards the inclusion of self-service restaurants. The idea of adding an additional range of
retail outlets meets various objectives; it tends to
widen the appeal of the hypermarket, attracting a
broader clientele, and, by enabling smaller
retailers to benefit from the drawing power of the
major store, (rather than be squeezed out by it), it
helps moderate their opposition to les grandes
surfaces.

It is not only the structure of the hypermarket
which has evolved, but also its location. Typically
a retailing form located on the periphery of urban
areas, it has now become a feature of development
within the central and inner areas of towns, particularly where part of the infrastructure costs are
borne by another developer. Thus, in the shopping
centre of the new town of Evry and in the huge
commercial complex at La Défense (Quatre Temps) one
of the main anchor stores is in each case a hypermarket (Euromarché and Auchan respectively). In the
latter case, Auchan replaced an earlier project of a
major department store chain, and the company's
decision to locate here is indicative of an aggressive and dynamic development strategy adopted by
many of the hypermarket groups, in turn reflecting
the sophisticated character of their operations
(34).

Discussion of changes in retailing techniques
has been focused upon hypermarkets and their trading
methods, but revised selling practices are not
unique to this field. Large discount stores
employing self-service techniques have been established in other more specialised areas of retailing,
illustrated by the FNAC chain (records, books, hi-fi
and photographic equipment) (35). Similar
principles apply to other types of retailing such as
home furnishings and improvements, where the number
of large out-of-town stores has increased substantially; the 'Atlas' furniture chain is one example.
Moreover, it is not uncommon for these shops to be
attracted to sites of hypermarkets, to their mutual
benefit. Even the traditional department stores
have sought to shed their staid image and to cater
for markets they tended to neglect previously (teen-
age and young people's fashions, leisure goods), not
least in response to the strength of competition
from new forms of outlet. These examples offer a
further demonstration, therefore, of the profound
mutation of the French retailing system.

INTRA-URBAN RETAILING: SPATIAL CHANGES

Just as the organisation and techniques of retailing
have altered radically over the last two decades,
intra-urban location patterns have also been substantially modified, frequently involving the
replacement of a formerly ordered, hierarchical
arrangement of services by a more complex, less
structured distribution of retail outlets. Rather
than review all the many changes which have
occurred, two key themes have been selected for more
detailed appraisal; first, the remarkable growth of
retailing in suburban and above all peripheral zones
of the urban area, and, second, the transformation
of the central business district, a process provoked
at least in part by the challenge represented by the
expansion of retailing in the outer suburbs.

The Shift towards the Periphery
As the majority of French urban centres have
expanded rapidly over the post-war period, not only
in population but also in areal extent, it is not
unnatural that a corresponding spatial adjustment of
retail provision should take place. The extent to
which this has occurred is more surprising, but is
reflective of the varied influences which have
prompted the movement. Demographic growth has been
strongly concentrated in the suburbs, particularly
through the joint migrational forces of an influx of
population from regions external to the urban area
and internal redistribution. This differential
pattern of expansion between central and outer areas
has been most marked in the capital, although the
trend has been repeated consistently in the larger
provincial cities. In relation to retailing activity it is the shift in purchasing power represented
by this contrast which is most significant.
     In the early post-war period there was a marked
lag between the growth of suburban housing estates,
often on a huge scale, and an increase in retail
provision. In part this was due to imperfections in
the planning system, but it also reflected the
reluctance of retailers at this time to invest in
these projects, failing to appreciate the amplitude
of the suburbanisation movement. By the 1960s there
were many instances of a chronic under-equipment in
retail outlets in the suburbs, most pronounced in
the Paris region, where the inadequate pattern of
post-war provision aggravated a marked imbalance
which had developed in the inter-war period. So

serious did the situation become, that the
government sought actively to encourage the expansion of retail facilities in these areas (contrasting with its later, more restrictive policy) (36).
     By the latter 1960s conditions had become
particularly propitious for the growth of suburban
and out-of-town retailing centres. Apart from the
factors outlined above, this period coincided with
the introduction of major innovations in retailing
techniques. As developers sought locations for
their new super-stores, peripheral sites where land
was available at relatively cheap cost, (highly significant in terms of the design of buildings and
their car parking requirements), became particularly
attractive. Moreover, as communications were
improved, the accessibility of these areas was
greatly enhanced, while at this time development was
not impeded by strict land use controls. Equally,
the ever-increasing degree of mobility of households
through rapidly rising levels of car ownership,
offered these new shopping centres the potential of
an extensive catchment area. Thus, a wave of
creations has resulted, on a scale previously
unseen.
     Various types of peripheral shopping centre
have become established. The simplest structure is
represented by a single, large, free-standing store,
most commonly a hypermarket. To this has often been
added a limited series of other retail outlets,
located either adjacent to the hypermarket or housed
within it. More complex forms have evolved from
these simple models, relating to the growth of new
peripheral shopping centres incorporating a much
wider range of retail outlets (37). These are exemplified in their ultimate stage of development by
the series of regional shopping complexes which now
encircle the capital, the majority of which were
opened in the early 1970s (Figure 11.2). Although
in nearly all cases these are extremely large
centres, they differ in form and conception (38).
Typically, the emphasis is away from food retailing
(contrasting with the hypermarket) and orientated
much more towards an extensive range of specialist
shops, with a strong emphasis upon clothes and
durable goods. These varied retail facilities are
housed collectively in a single covered and air-
conditioned building; in addition, the whole centre
is animated by at least one large 'anchor' store
(generally major department stores) and may contain
a number of complementary services such as banks,
cinemas and restaurants. The centres of Parly 2,

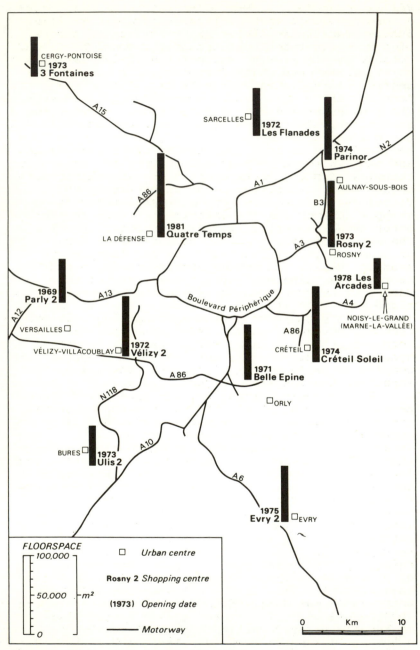

Figure 11.2: Regional Shopping Centres around Paris

Vélizy 2 and Rosny 2 are illustrative of this model.
A more developed form is represented by Evry 2 and
Quatre Temps where the shopping centre is just part
of a much wider and more integrated complex, linked
notably to the presence of offices (39); furthermore, at Evry and Cergy-Pontoise and to a lesser
degree, Noisy-le-Grand, the centres' principal
function is to serve their respective new towns.
The centres at Aulnay and Bures have a simpler
structure, comprising a series of shops based around
a hypermarket.

Not surprisingly, in view of their large size
and number, the impact of all these forms of
retailing centre has been considerable. It is estimated that the huge Carrefour hypermarket at
Vitrolles (to the north of Marseille) attracts
shoppers from up to 50 kilometres, and on an average
Saturday serves approximately 18,000 people (40).
The effect of hypermarkets has generally been
greatest in relation to food sales. At Lyon, for
example, a city relatively underequipped in such
stores, the value of food retailing in the two
Carrefour hypermarkets at Vénissieux and Ecully
alone exceeds that of the whole of the central area;
overall, hypermarkets accounted in 1980 for 22 per
cent of food sales in the Lyon urban region (41).
Moreover, the total turnover of the Vénissieux
hypermarket exceeded that of the whole shopping
complex of La Part-Dieu, further demonstrating the
impact of these stores (Figure 11.3).

In the Paris region the retailing structure and
people's shopping habits have been transformed by
the proliferation of hypermarkets and notably by the
regional shopping centres indicated above.
Generally, this has resulted in a substantial reduction in the previous spatial imbalance between the
location of population and retail outlets, although
for certain services there is still inadequate provision and heavy reliance upon the city centre (42).
However, for most durable consumer goods there is no
longer an obligation to travel to the centre,
although, paradoxically for many food items dis-
tances travelled for their purchase have increased,
reflecting the polarised nature of these new forms
of provision (43). Inevitably, as these centres
have increased their turnover, this has produced a
corresponding negative effect in older, traditional
shopping areas. In part the major department stores
in the centre have been adversely affected (44),
although they have responded by opening in the new
regional shopping complexes. Above all, however, it

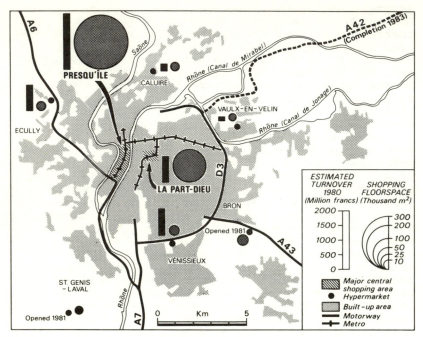

Figure 11.3: Retailing Activity at Lyon: Centre versus Periphery

appears to be the inner suburbs and the small retail outlets within them which have suffered most, a trend reflected elsewhere as at Lyon and Bordeaux (45). Finally, in certain cases difficulties have also been posed for retailers in neighbouring rural communes, particularly in areas in which there is already an established trend towards the decline of population.

Despite the attractions of hypermarkets (e.g. lower prices, convenience of shopping), there appears to be some disaffection with this form of retailing (46). Moreover, given the extent of past expansion, there is now often competition between hypermarkets, suggesting a point of saturation is being reached, a condition also applying to the regional shopping centres (47). Thus, not only in the Paris region, but elsewhere in France there is some suggestion that the out-of-town movement may have reached its apogee.

Changing Patterns of Retailing

Redevelopment at the Centre
Change on the periphery has been most marked by the
creation of a range and volume of retailing facilities previously unencountered in these areas. In
central districts new development has often been no
less apparent, although in this case supplementing
an inadequate or outdated existing retailing
nucleus. Not unnaturally, the extent of transformation has been greatest in the country's larger urban
centres (48).

Here the pressure for change has emanated from
a variety of sources. Inevitably, as these cities
entered a phase of rapid demographic and economic
growth from the middle or latter part of the 1950s,
and in the general absence at that time of redevelopment projects, the congestion of central quarters
became an increasing problem. The situation was
often exacerbated by an already dense pattern of
land use and a heritage of narrow streets, ill-
adapted to the substantial rise in vehicular
traffic; moreover, conflict between the differing
needs of cars and pedestrians arose. As the population of these cities grew, the demand for an increase
in the provision of central retail outlets was
expressed in various ways. Not only was there a
need to augment the number and range of shops but
also to enlarge the floorspace of existing stores,
responding not just to an increase in their trade,
but also to the modification of selling techniques.
More recently, as various forms of peripheral shopping centre have been developed, often representing
formidable competition for the traditional retailing
core, this has offered an additional incentive for
revitalising the quality of both the shops and
shopping environment of the central area.

Major additions to the retailing capacity of
the central area are an essentially recent phenomenon, occurring over the last decade. Frequently
they have formed part of a wider process of transformation of this quarter, linked to large-scale
redevelopment schemes which have also included
offices and cultural and recreational facilities;
moreover, such change has commonly been associated
with the improvement of public transport. These
features have been most apparent in the majority of
the larger provincial cities of France. Purpose-
built shopping centres, reminiscent of certain of
those constructed in the Paris region such as Parly
2 (49), have been added as an integral part of much
more extensive new business and commercial centres.
As such they have not only greatly increased the

provision of shops, but also introduced a very
different concept of retailing. Numerous examples
of this type of development exist, including the
Part-Dieu (Lyon), Bourse (Marseille) and Mériadeck
(Bordeaux) centres, and the Saint Sever, Place des
Halles and Centre Jaude complexes in the smaller
cities of Rouen, Strasbourg and Clermont-Ferrand.
Change has also been apparent in the capital,
notably with the opening of the Forum shopping
centre, a major element of the more extensive
renewal and renovation programme in the Les Halles
district (50).

These complexes represent major additions to
the retailing capacity of their related central
areas. At La Part-Dieu (51), for example, 110,000
square metres of retail floorspace have been added,
including two leading department stores, a limited
series of other large stores (for example, Marks and
Spencer and C&A) and over 220 smaller retail
outlets; in addition, there is a series of restaurants and cinemas spread over three main levels.
The shopping centre in the Place des Halles development at Strasbourg is on a smaller scale, but still
contains 47,000 square metres of retail floorspace
including 6 major stores and 120 supporting shops.
In most cases these new business centres have not
replaced part of the pre-existing commercial area,
but have been located adjacent or even some distance
away from it. Various factors have governed such a
choice, ranging from the desire to conserve
buildings of historic interest, to the availability
of land. In many instances at least part of the
area redeveloped was already disused or readily
available for re-use; at Lyon, for example, the
greater part of La Part-Dieu is located on a
formerly obsolete army barracks, this new centre
lying approximately 1,500 metres east of the traditional CBD (Presqu'île).

The comparatively recent opening of many of
these centres makes a realistic assessment of their
impact difficult. Given their large-scale, however,
it is reasonable to suppose that their influence is
considerable, a trait which is clearly evident in
the case of La Part-Dieu (Figure 11.3). Since its
opening in 1975, turnover has risen progressively,
amounting to approximately 870 million francs in
1980. The bulk of sales is accounted for by non-
food items, for which annual turnover now totals
more than half that of the Presqu'île (52); the
relative importance of the traditional centre for
shopping has declined, reflective of competition not

only from La Part-Dieu, but also new suburban
retailing complexes. However, had it not been for
the substantial growth of La Part-Dieu, the significance of the retailing function of the central area
as a whole would have been reduced to a much greater
extent. Even the Part-Dieu complex, however, has
certain shortcomings, not least relatively poor
accessibility by road, a feature typical of other
such centres; conversely, it does benefit from a
location astride the city's métro system (53).

Faced with such competition, an increasing
specialisation of services available within city
centre has often occurred, linked with attempts to
rejuvenate this area, notably through pedestrianisation. At Lyon two of the principal shopping streets
in the Presqu'île were modified in this manner,
while the area also benefits from the arrival of the
métro (54). Elsewhere, pedestrianisation schemes
have multiplied rapidly, to cover an increasing area
of the central parts of cities such as Bordeaux,
Strasbourg and Rouen: moreover, this is not a
feature confined only to larger urban centres, being
equally characteristic of smaller towns such as
Annecy and Colmar. Certainly in Lyon, the results
of such measures appear to have been an upsurge in
commercial activity, slowing the centre's relative
decline.

Now that most of France's larger urban centres
have been equipped with new retailing centres, the
vogue for this form of redevelopment, reflective of
the general 'gigantism' philosophy which reigned
supreme throughout much of the 1970s, seems to have
passed. This has been encouraged naturally by
moderated growth rates and altered views on urban
renewal and design. There appears now to be a trend
towards more modest adjustments, incorporating
existing buildings where possible and giving greater
prominence to the traditional shopping street.

NOTES

1.   Cazes, G., and Reynaud, A., Les Mutations
Récentes de l'Economie Française (Doin, Paris,
1973), 156-7.
2.   Le Monde, 6 May 1981; La France des
Commerces (Ministère du Commerce et de l'Artisanat,
Paris, 1982).
3.   La France des Commerces.
4.   Commissariat Général du Plan, Emplois dans
les Services (La Documentation Française, Paris,

1981), 19.
    5. Commissariat Général du Plan, Emplois, 19.
    6. Dobler, H., 'Le commerce et les services commerciaux', in Pagé, J-P. (ed.), Profil Economique de la France (La Documentation Française, Paris, 1981), 262-3.
    7. Commissariat Général du Plan, Emplois, 116.
    8. La France des Commerces.
    9. Dobler, 'Le commerce et les services commerciaux', 263.
    10. Commissariat Général du Plan, Emplois, 116.
    11. It may appear strange that the number of wage-earners in food retailing has increased yet the number of outlets has declined substantially. This reflects that the former statistic does not include small shop owners (many of whom have gone out of business) and the fact that the closure of many small premises has been compensated by the opening of a limited number of large outlets (notably super-markets and hypermarkets) which have generated a large number of new jobs.
    12. For further discussion of some of these general points see, for example, Beaujeu-Garnier, J. and Delobez, A., Geography of Marketing (Longman, London, 1979), 44-7; Dawson, J., 'Retail trends in the EEC', in Davies, R.L. (ed.), Retail Planning in the European Community (Saxon House, Farnborough, 1979), 21-30; Smith, B.A., 'Retail planning in France', Town Planning Review, 44 (1973), 279-306.
    13. La France en Mai 1981 - Les Activités Productives (La Documentation Française, Paris, 1982), 318.
    14. La France en Mai 1981, 318.
    15. Beaujeu-Garnier, J. and Bouveret-Gauer, M., 'Retail planning in France' in Davies, Retail Planning in the European Community, 99-112; Dawson, J., 'Shops and shopping: France restructures', Geographical Magazine, 49 (1976), 200.
    16. Ardagh, J., France in the 1980s (Penguin, Harmondsworth, 1982), 396-409.
    17. These general points are briefly discussed in, Commissariat Général du Plan, Emplois, 19.
    18. Research undertaken by the Agence d'Urbanisme shows this to be the case, for example, at Lyon.
    19. Cazes and Reynaud, Les Mutations Récentes, 160.
    20. Beaujeu-Garnier and Bouveret-Gauer, 'Retail planning in France', 110.

21. Dobler, 'Le commerce', 272.
22. Estienne, P., La France (Masson, Paris, 1979), vol.1, 116.
23. Baleste, M., L'Economie Française (Masson, Paris, 1980), 266-7.
24. Beaujeu-Garnier and Delobez, Geography of Marketing, 51.
25. Dobler, 'Le commerce', 272.
26. Libre Service Actualités, No.766 (1980), 67-70.
27. Various details of the development of hypermarkets in France are given in Dawson, J.A., 'Hypermarkets in France', Geography, 61 (1976), 259-62. The definition of a hypermarket is based partly on size (more than 2,500 square metres of retail floorspace), but the concept of shopping which the term embodies is equally important. Essential features include a broad range of keenly-priced items of food and drink (accounting for at least a third of the floorspace, although the greater part of turnover), a general series of non-food goods (especially clothing and household products), self-service and payment through a large number of check-outs; these facilities are housed in a single-storey building, surrounded by extensive car parking space.
28. Libre Service Actualités, No.825/6 (1981), 162.
29. Libre Service Actualités, No.825/6 (1981), 169.
30. Dawson, J.A., 'Shopping centres in France', Geography, 66 (1981), 143; Ardagh, France in the 1980s, 396-402.
31. Dobler, 'Le commerce', 277; Beaujeu-Garnier and Bouveret-Gauer, 'Retail planning in France', 104-7.
32. Beaujeu-Garnier and Bouveret-Gauer, 'Retail planning in France', 108-10.
33. In recognition of the continuing debate over the desirability of the continued proliferation of hypermarkets and large retailing complexes (principally in peripheral locations) the new socialist government called a temporary moratorium on the granting of further planning permission for such development to enable a more accurate assessment of the level of existing provision - Le Monde, 12 Jan. 1982.
34. Libre Service Actualités, No.840 (1982), 19.
35. Ardagh, France in the 1980s, 405-6.
36. Beaujeu-Garnier and Bouveret-Gauer, 'Retail planning in France'.

37. A fuller discussion of this subject is given in Dawson, 'Shopping centres in France', 143-6.

38. Metton, A., 'Centres périphériques: regards sur l'expérience parisienne', Revue Géographique des Pyrénées et du Sud-Ouest', 50 (1979), 107-11.

39. A more detailed example is given in Cazes and Reynaud, Les Mutations Récentes de l'Economie Française, 195, and in Beaujeu-Garnier and Delobez, Geography of Marketing, 224.

40. Vaudour, N., 'Les grandes surfaces périphériques de vente dans les Bouches-du-Rhône', Annales de Géographie, 87 (1978), 49-52.

41. Enquête sur le Comportement d'Achats des Ménages de la Région Lyonnaise (Agence d'Urbanisme, Lyon, 1982).

42. Metton, 'Centres périphériques', 111-12.

43. Delobez, A., 'L'évolution de l'activité commerciale depuis l'implantation des grandes surfaces', Analyse de l'Espace, No.4 (1973), 46.

44. Delobez, 'L'évolution de l'activité commerciale', 45.

45. Cassou-Mounat, M., 'L'évolution récente des structures commerciales dans l'agglomération de Bordeaux', Revue Géographique des Pyrénées et du Sud-Ouest, 49 (1979), 93.

46. Delobez, 'L'évolution de l'activité commerciale', 51.

47. Barrère, P. and Cassou-Mounat, M., Les Villes Françaises (Masson, Paris, 1980), 197.

48. For a general discussion of this theme see Beaujeu-Garnier and Delobez, Geography of Marketing, 193-6.

49. This is not surprising in certain cases as the same developer has been responsible for the schemes: for example, the Société des Centres Commerciaux has undertaken developments which include Parly 2, Rosny 2, Vélizy 2 and Là Part-Dieu.

50. Tuppen, J.N., 'Les Halles: a major central area redevelopment', Town and Country Planning, 50 (1981), 137-9.

51. Tuppen, J.N., 'Redevelopment of the city centre: the case of Lyon-La Part-Dieu', Scottish Geographical Magazine, 93 (1977), 151-8. In describing and assessing change in the central area particular.reference is made to the very substantial transformation which has occurred at Lyon.

52. Retailing floorspace within La Part-Dieu, however, amounts to only approximately a third of that located in the Presqu'île. Turnover figures

are taken from <u>Enquête sur le Comportement d'Achats des Ménages de la Région Lyonnaise</u>, 17.

53. The same applies at Marseille; see, Tuppen, J.N., 'Public transport in France: the development and extension of the métro', <u>Geography</u>, 65 (1980), 127-30.

54. Tuppen, J.N., 'The métro comes to Lyon', <u>Town and Country Planning</u>, 44 (1976), 311-14.

Chapter Twelve

TOURISM - A KEY SECTOR OF GROWTH

GENERAL FEATURES

From an activity which in the middle of the
nineteenth century concerned a highly restricted,
largely affluent clientele and affected only a
limited range of localities, tourism over the last
thirty years has expanded on a vast scale, embracing
a much wider spectrum of the population and exerting
an impact over a far greater extent of the country.
Its growth highlights the greatly enhanced role
within society of leisure and recreational activities. With the development of mass tourism over the
post-war period the nature of the activity itself
has also altered very considerably. New forms of
tourist provision have evolved, both as a response
to a changing pattern of demand and as a means to
widen the potential market, particularly in favour
of the lower income groups. The mode of development
has also altered. Initially, growth was largely a
spontaneous and uncontrolled process, illustrated by
the expansion of resorts along the Côte d'Azur which
began in the last century. Since the early 1960s,
however, many tourist complexes have become increasingly planned and 'imposed', often resulting from
government decisions and forming part of wider
regional development plans.
        Tourism plays a significant role in the French
economy, generating a turnover estimated at 220
billion francs in 1980. This represented more than
8 per cent of the country's gross domestic product
which exceeded, for example, the contribution made
by the whole of the primary sector; moreover, since
the early 1970s the .activity has made a sizeable
positive contribution to the French balance of payments, representing a net gain of over 9 billion
francs in 1980 (1). In the same year employment

directly created by tourism in fields such as catering, accommodation and travel agencies was evaluated at around 310,000 persons. However, when jobs resulting indirectly are taken into account, estimates suggest that around 1.5 million people are dependent in some way upon this activity, making precise definition of the 'tourist industry' difficult (2). Numerous linkages exist with other activities (3). These range from connections with various transport operators to links with manufacturers of products such as boats, skis and tents, and with the building industry, their diversity emphasising the importance of the multiplier effect. Tourism also involves significant movements of resources between different regions of the country (4), represented not least by the transfer of spending power. Often this has been to the considerable benefit of many local and regional economies, particularly in selected mountainous and coastal areas which lack other forms of productive enterprise as in parts of the Alps, Massif Central, Brittany and southern France.

The significance of tourism to the French economy also relates to the degree to which the activity has expanded, generating employment, investment and income. One measure of the emphatic character of growth is given by the rise in the number of French people taking a holiday each year. Estimates vary, but in the late 1930s it is generally accepted that those people going on holiday at least once a year totalled less than 2 millions; by the late 1950s this had increased to nearly 10 millions (5). A decade later the total had more than doubled to over 21 millions in 1969, and by 1980 the number exceeded 29 millions, representing over 56 per cent of the population (6). Other indicators attest to the strength of this expansion. For example, over the 1970s the number of classified hotels and campsites increased by averages of nearly 3 per cent and over 5 per cent respectively each year; comparable trends were observable in the provision of other forms of holiday accommodation and in the creation of tourist amenities such as moorings for pleasure craft. Growth has also been reflected in the increase of employment in activities linked to tourism, a feature which has persisted despite the more recent depressive effects of the recession (Table 12.1) (7).

Expansion is attributable to a variety of social and economic influences, although it also

Table 12.1: Employment Growth in Activities related
to Tourism, 1976-81

Activity	Mean annual rate (%)
Travel agents	10.8
Tourist offices	5.9
Restaurants	6.1
Hotels	2.1
Cafes	2.2

Source: Ministère de la Jeunesse, des Sports et
Loisirs.

needs to be viewed against the backcloth of a
country possessing a number of undoubted natural
advantages for tourist activity relating to favourable climatic influences and the diversity and richness of natural landscapes. A major factor underlying growth has been the marked improvement in the
material well-being of the majority of French
families over the post-war period. Incomes have
risen substantially in real terms, enabling people
to afford holidays more easily and more frequently,
while for lower wage-earners various measures have
been introduced by successive governments to help
reduce the financial burden. These range from the
idea of low-cost accommodation in holiday complexes
(villages de vacances) to that of the holiday-cheque
launched in 1982 (8). Equally fundamental to the
growth of tourism has been the institution and
extension of paid holidays. Since legislation in
1936 first established this principle, the minimum
allowance of 15 days has been raised, first to three
weeks in 1956, then to four weeks in 1969, with more
recently a fifth week added in 1982 (9). It might
be argued also that certain forms of tourist activity have been stimulated by the shortening of the
working week, which by 1982 stood officially at 39
hours.
     Greater personal mobility and improved acces-
sibility have acted as further major stimuli to
development, linked primarily to the growth in car
ownership (10). However, travel generally has
become easier and relatively cheaper, not only due
to the influence of the car. French Railways, for
example, has long operated a policy of reduced fares

for families travelling to their holiday destination
by train, while more recently a similar strategy has
been adopted on certain airline routes. Various
social pressures also encourage tourism, ranging
from the increasing urbanisation of society and the
associated desire to seek out a more relaxed
environment, to the influence of publicity campaigns
and fashion; the 'selling' of holidays has developed
into a major activity, facilitated by media such as
the television, while the skiing holiday, for
example, now stands alongside the car and various
items of household equipment as an important symbol
of social status.

Just as many factors have increased the demand
for holiday facilities, tourism has also been
encouraged by a substantial development in the
supply of accommodation and amenities. Again, this
has occurred in many ways ranging from major,
government-sponsored development schemes exemplified
by the transformation of the Languedoc coast, to
more modest initiatives of Local Authorities or
private developers (such as Ribourel and Merlin).
To encourage investment, particularly in new or
improved accommodation, the government has made
available various grants and low-interest loans
(11), while during the course of the VIIth Plan
special financial provisions were made to promote
the increased provision of hotels, gîtes and camping
sites in rural areas (12).

THE STRUCTURE AND PATTERN OF TOURISM

The term tourism embraces a diverse range of
activities including day trips effected from home
and visits of longer duration spent away from a
person's permanent place of residence. In the
present review emphasis is focused upon this latter
category. By far the greatest number of French
people are on holiday in the two summer months of
July and August, rising in the latter case to around
15 millions. Secondary but far less accentuated
peaks of between 3 and 4 million holidaymakers
correspond with the Easter and Christmas breaks; in
addition, a growing number of people are now depar-
ting in the period of the school holidays in
February.

Not all of the population, however, benefits
from holidays to the same extent. Thus, whereas
over 85 per cent of senior executives and professional people of similar status take at least one

holiday a year, the equivalent proportion of farmers and farm workers is less than 17 per cent (Table 12.2); not only is the propensity to take a holiday greater amongst the higher socio-economic groups, but also the mean length of stay is considerably longer. These tendencies may be related in part to

Table 12.2: Proportion of People taking Holidays by Socio-Economic Category, 1980

Socio-economic group	(%)
Upper management and the professions	85
Middle and lower management	81
Other white collar workers	69
Blue collar workers	53
Farmers and farm workers	17

Source: Ministère de la Jeunesse, des Sports et Loisirs.

differences in income but they also reflect factors such as the difficulty for many workers in the farming community to absent themselves for more than a short period due to the nature of their work. Variations in departure rates are also evident between urban and rural areas, being much higher in the former case and increasing markedly with the size of urban centre. Again this reflects the interplay of various factors such as the spatial distribution of different socio-economic classes, the proximity of rural dwellers to the countryside and the stress induced by living and working in major towns and cities (13). There is far greater uniformity, however, in the mode of transport used by the majority of holiday-makers; the car counts for over four-fifths of all visits effected in France (Table 12.3).

The destinations chosen by tourists naturally vary greatly, although a number of broad tendencies are discernible (Table 12.4). The coast represents the most popular location, followed by rural areas and mountainous districts, although the relative importance of these three regions varies between the winter and summer seasons. Certain of these charac-teristics are illustrated further in Figure 12.1. The distribution of the number of days spent on holiday reflects the strong attraction of the coast

Tourism - A Key Sector of Growth

(above all the Atlantic and Mediterranean seaboards) and a more restricted number of inland locations, principally in the Alps. In this latter case the area's relative importance as a tourist centre is

Table 12.3: The Form of Transport used to Travel to Holiday Destinations, 1980

Transport mode	(%)
Car	81
Train	13
Coach	3
Aeroplane	2
Others	1

Source: Ministère de la Jeunesse, des Sports et Loisirs.

most apparent in winter, although it is visited by a greater number of people in summer. Places available on campsites attest to the pull of coastal regions, particularly in the south of France and Brittany. In many instances, however, the actual extent of the areas affected by this form of tourism is limited to a narrow maritime facade with little penetration inland. The distribution of hotel rooms presents a somewhat contrasting pattern, with Paris as the principal centre, reflecting in part that

Table 12.4: Pattern of Holiday-making, 1980

Type/location of holiday	Winter	Summer	Overall
	(% total holidays)		
Touring	4	5	4
Seaside resort	15	45	47
Mountain region	33	17	17
Rural area	30	27	28
Urban area	18	6	4
	100	100	100

Source: Ministère de la Jeunesse, des Sports et Loisirs.

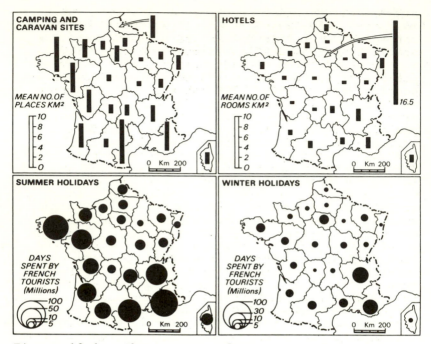

Figure 12.1:   The Pattern of Tourism and Tourist Accommodation, 1980

hotel accommodation caters not only for the tourist but also the businessman.   France's capital is, nonetheless, an important centre for tourism, particularly for foreign visitors; the Pompidou Centre and the Eiffel Tower dominate as the two most-visited places amongst the classified sites and monuments in France.   All the maps indicate, however, the importance of the broad area of south-eastern France for tourism, testifying to the exceptional quality of the region's scenery, the attractiveness of its climate and its greatly improved accessibility.

Aspects of Change
Tourism is a highly dynamic activity.   Over the post-war period the number of people taking a holiday has greatly increased, seaside resorts and mountainous regions have reinforced their popularity and new forms of tourism have developed.   The scale of activity has been greatly enlarged, a reflection not just of the much higher number of tourists, but

also of the growing international character of
movement. In 1980 over 30 million visits by
foreigners were recorded in France, with nearly half
originating from Western Germany and Belgium (14).

One indicator of change is represented by the
pattern of holiday accommodation utilised by French
people (Table 12.5). Although a large proportion
still uses the homes of friends or relatives, two
areas of growth are apparent: second homes and the
use of caravans or tents (15). Both trends are
evidence of the diverse character of tourism,
although each is a response to different forces: the
former is often a sign of affluence, while the
latter has been an important factor in the democra-
tisation and vastly increased scale of tourist
activities. The number of second homes has grown
substantially, from around 960,000 in 1962 to an
estimated 2 million in 1980. As a result approximately 10 per cent of all households now possess
such a property, although ownership rates are
inevitably much higher amongst the upper income
groups (16). It is not uncommon for a second home
to be inherited, although with the outflow of population from many rural areas the acquisition of
property used to be relatively easy. However, as
this source has become increasingly exhausted, a
growing number of specialist complexes have been
built, essentially in the more popular coastal and
mountainous areas. Second homes are widely scat-
tered, although there is a greater concentration in

Table 12.5: Proportional Significance of Different
Forms of Holiday Accommodation

| | 1964 | 1980 |
	(% total)	
Hotel	8	7
Rented property	16	15
Second home	11	14
Home of parent or friends	45	38
Caravan or tent	11	18
Other	9	8
Total	100	100

Source: Ministère de la Jeunesse, des Sports et
Loisirs.

traditional tourist areas and in the hinterlands of
major cities, notably Paris (17). As well as
offering holiday accommodation, frequently they have
an additional function as weekend residences, especially in those areas easily accessible from major
urban centres (18); also, in the longer term, they
may serve as a place for retirement (19).

Camping and caravanning holidays have grown in
appeal, partly due to the greater flexibility which
they offer; equally, however, they represent cheaper
alternatives than staying in hotels and thus have
enabled a greater number of people to go away. In
this respect they represent but one of an increasing
range of relatively inexpensive alternatives for
holiday accommodation, often run on a non-profit
making basis: a common formula is represented by the
village de vacances (20). A number of specialist
organisations such as <u>Tourisme et Travail</u> and
<u>Villages-Vacances-Familles</u> now promote this type of
holiday (21). Similar communal forms of holiday
centre have also grown, organised on a commercial
basis, but again with the emphasis upon relatively
low-cost accommodation and the provision of a range
of facilities to cater for the diverse needs of
families; this concept is epitomised by the Club
Méditerranée, which pioneered the idea in the 1950s.

Efforts to encourage or enable more people to
take a holiday have been a central feature underlying change. This is illustrated by many of the
above examples. It is also demonstrated by various
other tendencies such as the growth of package tours
or the attempt to add a 'tourist' component to other
activities. Hence, the increasing interest in
catering for participants in major conferences and
the revival of certain spa-towns such as Vichy and
Le Mont-Dore.

THE IMPACT OF TOURISM: AN ALTERNATIVE VIEW

Although the growth of tourism has generally been
viewed favourably, it does not follow that all
aspects of its development have been uncontrover-
sial. On the contrary, there are various unattractive and problematic features which have accompanied
expansion. Protests have been registered at the
increasing scale of construction and the destruction
of the natural beauty of many attractive sites
through the building of tourist complexes. Moreover, despite the generation of employment and
income, not all communities have welcomed the summer

flood of tourists and the associated problems of
congestion and loss of tranquility. Even where jobs
are created, many are only of a seasonal nature and
not necessarily well-paid.

One of the major problems, however, is coping
with the increasing volume of movements associated
with tourism. Not only are more people holidaying
in France, but the flows of tourists are concentrated over relatively short periods and are
directed towards a limited number of major regions.
Various difficulties arise, therefore, from the
temporal and spatial concentration of tourist activity. In addition, the situation is aggravated by
the contrast in location of the bulk of the population in the northern part of the country (dominated
by the Paris region), and the principal holiday
areas in the south (particularly the south-east),
inducing an intense movement between the two areas
and placing considerable pressure on the communication network. French Railways, for example, is
faced with various organisational problems in
catering with peak flows to winter sports resorts
(22); while on the major weekends for the departure
and return of holiday-makers in the summer, the
Autoroute du Soleil is notorious for its congestion.
Moreover, movement to and from the south is made
more difficult by the additional flow of tourists
traversing France to reach other regions of Europe.

In an attempt to ease the problems, initiatives
such as the staggering of school holidays by
different regions have been tried but their impact
is hard to evaluate. A further related and more
intractable problem arises from the saturation of
many resort areas, most evident along the Riviera.
The longer term solution to this type of over-use
probably lies in trying to divert tourists to other
less-crowded areas (this was one consideration in
the development of the Languedoc coast) rather than
attempting to increase existing capacity, but
breaking people's habits is not an easy task.

SUMMER TOURISM

The huge scale and profound impact of tourism are
most clearly demonstrated during the summer months
(principally July and August), a period of intense
activity. In 1980 over 53 per cent of the French
population went on holiday at this time of the year
(compared with only 41 per cent in 1964), with
nearly a half spending their time in a seaside

locality (23). For the remainder, the majority
stayed in predominantly rural areas inland, with
over recent years an increasing preference for
mountainous regions.

The Attraction of the Coast

An ever-growing number of French and foreign
tourists now invade France's coastal resorts each
summer. Not all areas of the coast, however, appear
equally attractive and spatial variations are evident in the extent to which the number of visitors
has grown (Figure 12.2). The Riviera and Brittany
are easily the most frequented areas but, despite
the rise in the number of tourists, increasing
difficulties are being encountered in accommodating
the inflow. Conversely, the north-western coastline
appears comparatively unpopular, with a stable
rather than expanding clientele. Growth has been
most apparent in parts of western France and in the
region of Languedoc-Roussillon, in the latter case
reflecting the very substantial increase in

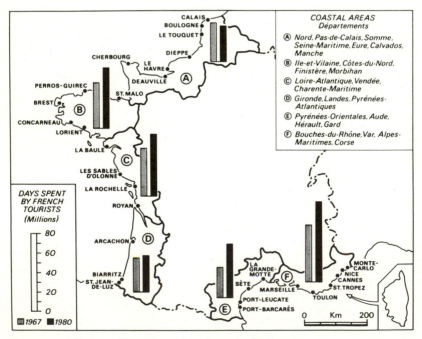

Figure 12.2: Tourism in Coastal Areas

accommodation and amenities. As the number of
tourists has risen, changes have occurred in the
pattern of holidaymaking, principally in relation to
the growing popularity of camping and caravanning,
necessitating a corresponding adaptation in the
provision of facilities. This is but one aspect,
however, of a more comprehensive pattern of transformation which has been a feature of many coastal
areas. New tourist complexes have been developed
and in many existing resorts there has been an
increase in capacity and in the range of amenities,
in the latter case aimed at widening the centres'
appeal. Inevitably, this has led to an extension of
urbanisation along the coastal fringe, provoking in
certain areas a hostile reaction and demands for
conservation rather than transformation.

Change in Traditional Areas: the French Riviera.
Between Marseille and the Italian border stretches
France's premiere resort area, universally renowned
for its natural charm and beauty. Now, however, it
has become characterised increasingly by some of the
less attractive features of mass tourism, linked to
the area's inability to absorb satisfactorily the
vast influx of summer visitors and to the many and
often conflicting pressures upon scarce land
resources. The early growth of tourism during the
nineteenth century was associated with an affluent
and largely foreign clientele, attracted mainly to
the area west of Cannes (Côte d'Azur), principally
during the mild winter period (24). It was not
until the inter-war years that the pattern was
reversed in favour of the summer, which is now overwhelmingly the most important season; the growth of
Nice (over 400,000 inhabitants), the region's
principal resort, exemplifies this evolution (25).
The present scale of tourist activity is demonstrated by the number of annual visitors to the
département of Alpes-Maritimes, evaluated at over 6
millions of which more than 80 per cent come during
the summer (26); it is also estimated that between
60 and 80 per cent of the takings of hoteliers and
shopkeepers result from trading during the main part
of the summer season, indicating the importance of
tourism on the local economy (27).
     Throughout this area tourist activity has
resulted in an increasingly dense pattern of urban
growth, largely restricted, however, to a narrow
coastal belt with expansion inland severely restricted by the mountainous character of the terrain,

particularly along the Côte d'Azur. One partial
solution to the lack of space has been to expand
seawards, as with the marina developments at Port
Grimaud and the Baie des Anges at Cannes: such
operations, however, represent extremely expensive
undertakings.

Congestion symbolises the problems provoked by
the region's attractiveness and is manifest in
several ways. Despite improvements, elements of the
infrastructure are inadequate for the peak elements
of summer, notably in relation to water supply and
the road network. The shortage of land has had many
consequences, not least a substantial rise in price,
an increase in speculation, a growing temptation not
to respect planning controls, a decline of agricultural activity and a tendency towards high-rise
buildings, highlighted at Monte-Carlo. Beaches have
become excessively overcrowded and certain forms of
accommodation, notably campsites, woefully inadequate, creating severe problems of uncontrolled
camping or the unacceptable saturation of existing
sites (28). Supply has failed to keep pace with
demand, but in an area of scarce land resources
camping grounds are not always strong competitors in
the land market, particularly as their use is
restricted to a relatively limited period of the
year. These difficulties, allied to other problems
such as an increase in pollution and fire hazard,
have led to a certain disaffection amongst some
tourists for this area; they also indicate that,
despite the undoubted economic benefits of tourism
in the region, there are also a number of social
costs which result from the intensity of development
and usage. This implies the need for improved
management, but with so many interests at stake such
an objective is difficult to realise.

Major Development Schemes. In a limited number of
cases attempts to improve the organisation of
tourist activities have been allied to much broader
regional development strategies conceived on the
basis of harnessing an area's potential for tourism.
This policy is exemplified by the proposals which
were drawn up for developing the Languedoc coast,
and is also illustrated by similar plans which have
sought to expand tourism along the coastal areas of
Aquitaine and Corsica (29). Although local and
regional initiatives have generally contributed to
the elaboration of development programmes, much of
the inspiration and impetus for expansion have

originated from the government and particularly the DATAR; thus, these specific projects need to be viewed in the wider context of regional planning strategies.

A number of aims are common to the development proposals for all the above areas. Given the growing saturation and often narrow range of facilities in many traditional resort areas (notably the Côte d'Azur), an early priority became the desire to spread tourist activity more evenly around French coastal regions, combined with a diversification of accommodation, particularly to take account of the growing demand for cheaper options (campsites, holiday camps) and second homes (30). Secondly, these projects were seen as a vital means towards reviving flagging regional economies, particularly in the case of Languedoc and Corsica (31). In proposing major development schemes there was also the desire, however, to avoid creating the less attractive features of already congested areas by preventing an uninterrupted pattern of urbanisation along the coastal fringe and by designing an adequate road network. These have been central features of the Languedoc and Aquitaine projects, with development concentrated in a series of nodes separated by broad areas of 'protected' natural environment (32). More recent thinking, illustrated in the case of the Aquitaine coast, has placed emphasis upon the idea of seeking to integrate the development of the coast with its hinterland, so widening the appeal of a tourist complex and extending the benefits accruing from tourism to the often neglected rural interior.

Progress has varied greatly between these different schemes, with the most substantial changes having taken place along the Languedoc coast. Since this project was launched in 1963, development has been spread over a coastal area extending approximately 180 kilometres in length which previously was largely devoid of settlement and economic activity (33). Five tourist complexes incorporating a number of entirely new resorts such as la Grande-Motte, le Cap d'Agde and Gruissan have been built, together offering over 60,000 dwellings, 180,000 sites on camping grounds, 1,800 hotel rooms and 1,200 rooms in holiday villages, involving a total investment of over 6 billion francs (34). Development, however, has involved many other changes, including the provision of new infrastructure, the eradication of malaria from the area, the reclamation of a series of coastal lagoons, the construction of nine harbours for pleasure craft and the reafforestation of 3,000 hectares of land.

The programme outlined for the Aquitaine coast is considerably less advanced, in part an inevitable consequence of its launching a decade after the Languedoc operation: (the master plan was finally approved in 1972). Initially an ambitious scheme was proposed, involving the creation of nine resort centres strung out over 230 kilometres of coast between the Gironde and Bayonne, and separated by a series of protected forest zones. This coastal belt also features an area of inland lagoons where originally it was also aimed to promote tourism. Although modelled on the Languedoc project, the scale and pace of change have been much more modest and the consequences far less dramatic. By 1980 less than 7,000 holiday dwellings were completed (although a further 33,000 were being built) (35), and few of the centres had progressed very far (36). A similarly limited pattern of expansion has charac- terised the official government programme in Corsica, with organisational difficulties and inad- quate financial resources inhibiting development (37). This should not imply that the tourist industry has not greatly expanded for undoubtedly it has, reflecting the island's natural vocation for tourism and a long history of such activity. However, much of the recent impetus has come from private rather than state initiatives, associated with a marked shift away from the provision of hotel accommodation towards more varied and less expensive alternatives (38).

Evaluation of the development projects of Languedoc and Aquitaine suggests certain contradic- tions. In the former case, there are various out- ward signs of success; over 30,000 jobs have resulted and since the scheme was initiated the number of visitors to the area has quadrupled to around 2 millions (39). But certain difficulties also prevail, many of which relate to an initially unrealistic assessment of the scheme's potential. Despite the increase in employment, jobs have not been created to the extent that was anticipated, and many of the more recently launched resorts such as Gruissan have expanded relatively slowly reflecting high construction costs and greater uncertainty over future demand. In addition, exacerbating the latter problem, the hopes of an extended summer season have not been fulfilled, possible reflecting an inadequate range of inherent attractions other than the beach and the sun (40).

Tourism - A Key Sector of Growth

    Along the Aquitaine coast the original
ambitious objectives have been modified and reduced
considerably in scale, accompanied by the abandonment of a number of projects, notably in the
interior; despite the attraction of the idea of
developing this latter area, it has proved hard to
implement, not least due to the reluctance of developers to invest in areas which appear commercially
far less attractive. More general problems have
included difficulties over the acquisition of land,
hostility from local interests due to the 'imposed'
nature of the scheme, opposition from ecologists and
a coastal environment more difficult to manage than
in Languedoc, not least due to the destructive power
of the sea (41). Together these factors have combined to slow development, with the result that the
construction of new accommodation has often been
greater in pre-existing resorts, notably around the
Bassin d'Arcachon. The project has also been the
victim of the recession and just as the transformation of the Languedoc coast symbolises the era of
grandiose development schemes in the late 1960s and
early 1970s, the remodelling of the Aquitaine
coastal area is reflective of a more restrained
philosophy of development and a more subdued period
of economic growth.

Other Priorities
Despite the popularity of the coasts, many inland
areas receive a large number of summer visitors,
notably in the Alps where picturesque towns such as
Annecy are important tourist centres. Given the
growth potential of tourism and, in contrast, the
problems of declining population and a loss of
economic activity which characterise many rural
areas, it is understandable that the government
should support this activity. In such environments,
however, its policy has not been to promote large-
scale development but to encourage the limited
expansion of campsites, holiday villages and rented
dwellings such as gîtes. However, an increase of
accommodation alone is unlikely to prove successful;
additional amenities are necessary such as swimming
pools, tennis courts, boating facilities, sign-
posted walks, pony-treking and, not least, a minimum
level of service provision. This implies, however,
the need for local enterprise and co-operation, qua-
lities not always apparent in rural communities; it
also considerably increases the size of necessary
investment, generating its own problems. Still, the

development of this type of tourist venture has become an integral part of government and regional policy in the improvement programmes for rural areas in parts of the Massif Central and south-west France.

The consequences of an increase in the number of tourists and the facilities to cater for them are frequently expressed in problems of overcrowding, pollution and destruction of the natural environment. These are features of both inland and coastal sites and have led to increasing demands for limits to growth and environmental protection. Responses to such pressure have been reflected in a number of government policies which might be illustrated by reference to two examples. First, over the last two decades a series of national and regional parks has been created. In the former instance the idea was launched in 1963 with the opening of the Parc National de la Vanoise (Alps); since then a further four parks have been established (42). In these zones the main objective is to preserve the natural environment, especially where there are rare animal or plant species (43). Regional parks are more varied in character. Although protection of the environment is still important, various forms of development are permitted and the areas are managed with the aim of catering for certain recreational needs; since 1968 twenty-one have been established (44).

A second example is offered by various protective measures implemented in coastal areas (45). These reflect the extent to which many coastlines are now built-up (over 90 per cent of the coastal fringe in the département of Alpes-Maritimes (46)) and the desire to limit this tendency. They also represent a response to the problems of over-use and the degree to which such areas have come under private ownership. Since 1975 a Coastal Conservatory (Conservatoire de l'Espace Littoral et des Rivages Lacustres) has been established with the aims of safeguarding coastal areas and maintaining access to them; but, despite the acquisition of 10,000 hectares and the desirability of these objectives, financial constraints have limited the effectiveness of this body. Similarly, building within 100 metres of the coast has been prohibited since 1979. For this and other measures to be effective, however, it is also essential that attitudes change. Despite mounting pressures for conservation and improved environmental management, in the past there appears to have been considerable apathy associated with the implementation of the necessary controls (47).

WINTER HOLIDAYS

Just as the number of French people taking a summer holiday has risen substantially over the last fifteen years, so too has the total of those going away in winter. By 1980 it was estimated that more than 12 million people went on holiday at least once during the winter months, representing nearly 23 per cent of the population (48). The choice of location and purpose of these holidays varied widely, but nearly a third of the total number of days spent by people holiday-making was accounted for by stays in mountainous regions, associated with winter sports. In view of the very rapid growth of this latter activity and its many and often controversial consequences, the remainder of this chapter is devoted to a discussion of these issues.

The spectacular increase in the popularity of winter sports, particularly over the last decade, is illustrated by the rise in related holidays. Compared with 630,000 French people taking a skiing holiday over the winter period 1958-9, by 1974-5 this had grown to 1,950,000; by the winter of 1979-80 this latter total had more than doubled to 4.2 millions, representing almost 8 per cent of the population (49). Despite the sizeable growth in numbers, however, the clientele of ski resorts remains relatively restricted, concentrated amongst the higher status socio-eocnomic groups; blue collar workers, for example, account for only around a sixth of all French visitors to winter sports centres (50). The resorts also play host to a growing number of foreign tourists, estimated to account for approximately 10 per cent of the total number of days spent there by holidaymakers. In addition, for certain centres easily accessible from adjacent, large urban centres (such as Lyon and Grenoble), there is also an important weekend clientele.

The French Alps dominate as the main centre of winter sports. Around three-quarters of all skiing holidays spent by French people are located within this area, with an estimated 60 per cent of stays of foreign tourists and weekend visitors also concentrated in the region (51). Even here, however, the distribution is unequal, with the départements of Savoie and Haute-Savoie dominating as the principal

destinations. These two areas contain a varied
selection of resorts, both in terms of size and conception, including the majority of the larger and
more popular centres such as Courcheval, La Plagne
and Val d'Isère (Figure 12.3). The Paris region
represents the single most important source of
visitors, accounting for a third of the total. In
other mountainous areas outside of the alpine region
winter sports are carried out on a much reduced
scale. Resorts are generally smaller and often
serve very different catchment areas: for example,
the main skiing centres of the Massif Central such
as Le Mont-Dore and Super-Besse draw a large number
of visitors from western France (52).

Many factors, such as increased affluence and
leisure time, already cited in explaining the
general growth of tourism in France are also very
relevant to the upsurge in winter sports holidays.
To these may be added a number of more specific
influences (53). Over the post-war period skiing
has become an increasingly popular activity, boosted
by the Winter Olympics at Grenoble in 1968 and by
intense publicity; furthermore, the increasing popularity of cross-country skiing as opposed to classi-
cal alpine skiing has helped to widen considerably
the potential clientele. In responding to this
demand, the Alps in particular possess many advantages, not least the extent, high quality and
variability of skiing areas, allied to the frequently
favourable weather during the main season (54). As
a result, many new resorts have been built, and
existing winter sports complexes increased substantially in size. These trends have been encouraged
by the greatly improved accessibility of this
region, most evident in relation to the growing
alpine motorway network, but equally reflected in
the improvement of air services to this general
area.

Government action has also been influential,
inspired by the joint aims of ensuring that French
mountainous regions participated in a rapidly
growing and lucrative market, and of bringing a new
source of economic development to declining rural
areas. Thus, over the period of the mid-1960s to
mid-1970s the government launched a number of
initiatives in the context of a Plan-Neige aimed at
encouraging the construction of new resorts; also
established were the Service d'Etudes pour
l'Aménagement Touristique de la Montagne (SEATM) and
the Commission Interministérielle pour l'Aménagement
Touristique de la Montagne (CIAM) which have both

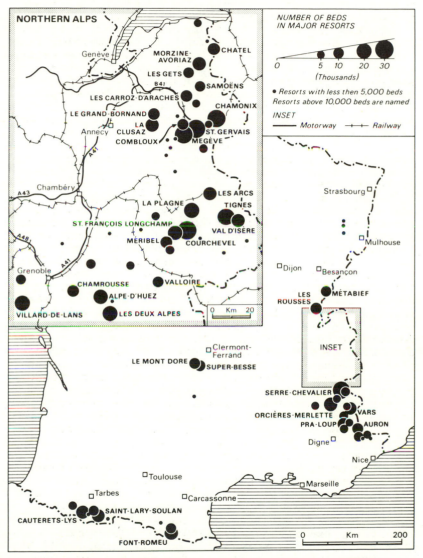

Figure 12.3:   Major Winter Sports Resorts, 1981

played key roles in stimulating and co-ordinating development (55).

Skiing Resorts - General Characteristics
A number of general trends are discernible relating to the greatly increased demand for skiing facilities (56). The area accessible to skiers has been extended very considerably, aided by the installation of an ever-growing number and variety of cable-cars and ski-lifts, with more than 3,000 such services now in operation. At the same time, the amount of accommodation has increased substantially, as well as its form, with a varied range of purchasing and renting options now available. These changes have been accompanied by a sharp rise in the number of skiing resorts and centres; from a total of 50 in 1960, there are now more than 220.

With the increase in resorts, there have also been marked changes in their conception and location; it is possible to distinguish four broad stages of evolution. During the inter-war period, as skiing slowly became more popular, the majority of centres catering for this activity grew spontaneously from existing settlements which generally already functioned as summer tourist centres. By present standards, the accommodation and often the ski slopes were located at a relatively low altitude. Numerous resorts illustrate this pattern of growth including, amongst the more important, Chamonix, Morzine and La Clusaz (57). There was also a limited expansion of a number of settlements orientated more exclusively towards skiing, often at a high altitude, such as Megève and l'Alpe-d'Huez. In the period immediately following the second world war a second phase of development was initiated based on specifically planned, higher altitude resorts, generally of a much larger scale; most of the stimulus for such expansion came from departmental authorities, anxious to diversify the local economic base and increase their revenue. The resort of Courcheval exemplifies this form of development, along with other centres such as Chamrousse and Orcières-Merlette (58) (Figure 12.3).

Then, from the early 1960s, a third more dramatic and controversial stage commenced with the launching of the idea of the 'integrated' resort (59). The essence and originality of this type of development lay in the desire to create highly efficient winter sports resorts with the amount of accommodation and number of ski lifts carefully calculated in relation to the capacity of the skiing area. Development was not based on an existing village nucleus but on a greenfield site (facilitating the planning of the complex) at a high altitude, usually around 1,700-1,800 metres. This latter characteristic was determined not only by the far greater extent of the area available for skiing, but also by the better quality and longer duration of the snow cover; moreover, with much of the necessary land communally owned at this level, its acquisition ought to be easier. The majority of the accommodation is in the form of apartments, with relatively few conventional hotels; disposal of this property has been crucial to the operation, offsetting the high development costs. In most cases all activities relating to the construction and running of the resorts have been undertaken or co-ordinated by a single developer, further underlining the integrated character of these complexes. Many examples of this generation of resort exist including La Plagne, Les Arcs, Avoriaz and Tignes (60). Their development has also corresponded with the government's wish to expand French skiing facilities, particularly to encourage foreign tourists; the policy appears to have proved successful (61).

More recently, with a number of changes in the design and development of resorts, a fourth phase of evolution has emerged. Partly as a response to some of the less attractive features of the 'integrated' centres, subsequent creations have tended to be smaller in scale, contain a greater diversity of accommodation and possess a wider range of facilities; also, a stricter control has been exerted by Local Authorities over the development. This revised and more modest approach is illustrated by the resorts of Val Cenis and Valmorel. When looking at these new forms of development it should be remembered, however, that many of the older resorts have continued to expand, often on a considerable scale.

The Unacceptable Face of Skiing

Although the proliferation of skiing facilitites has responded to an increase in demand, this has not been without problems and criticisms, many of which accompanied the very rapid phase of expansion between the mid-1960s and mid-1970s. Growing opposition was expressed over the destructive impact upon areas of considerable natural beauty caused by the increasing 'urbanisation' of the mountainside.

Consequently, since 1977 the government has
introduced stricter controls over expansion (62).
The highly functional nature of many of the integrated resorts, sometimes referred to as usines à neige
has also provoked adverse comment, as did the highly
unattractive character of much of the accommodation
in some of the early centres, resembling the appart-
ment complexes of the grands ensembles and meriting
the description of Sarcelles des neiges (63). This
has been one factor leading to the more recent preference for development of more modest dimensions,
based upon groups of chalets. Even in the older
resorts criticism has been levelled at the unattractive character of certain elements of the accommodation and the general lack of control over expansion;
the first land use plan for Chamonix dates only from
1971 (64). Given the difficult environment in which
skiing resorts are developed and the high cost of
many of the necessary installations, notably ski-
lifts, it is not unnatural that winter sports are
expensive. Nonetheless, there is a comparative
absence of low cost accommodation and therefore
opportunities for the less affluent to participate
in such activities (65). Again, therefore, some of
the more recent creations such as Val Cenis have
placed emphasis on catering for this market (66).
    Supply has not always been finely adjusted to
demand and in certain areas one outcome of the wave
of speculative development over the last two decades
has been strong competition between resorts, helping
to produce financial difficulties (67). Under the
pressure for expansion, resorts have also spread to
more marginal areas such as the southern Alps,
encouraged by both developers and communal authorities anxious to benefit from the boom in winter
sports. But the risks here are higher due to
greater uncertainty cver the level of snowfall;
inadequate falls and a resulting loss of tourists
were particular problems of the winter 1980-1 (68).
    It is not only the winter season which is
important to a resort's commercial success; often
the ability to attract visitors in summer is of
vital importance. Thus, although many high altitude
winter sports centres benefit from excellent skiing
conditions, due to the absence of other facilities
and the less attractive character of the natural
landscape, they have little appeal for summer
tourism; hence, the more recent trend to lower altitude resorts, although certain of the centres
located at around 2,000 metres such as Super-Tignes
have benefited from summer skiing on glaciers.

Tourism – A Key Sector of Growth

Often the best compromise has been reached by the
older resorts benefiting from a double season; such
is the situation at Morzine and Chamonix, where in
the latter case there are more visitors in the
summer than winter (69).

An Assessment: Employment and Demographic Changes

Whatever the shortcomings associated with the
exploitation of the potential offered by l'or blanc,
the result has been the marked transformation of
rural society in many mountainous areas. The creation or expansion of resorts has frequently produced
various advantages for the wider community, particularly in the field of infrastructure where changes
have included the provision of new or improved
roads, far more effective snow clearance and the
installation of telephone lines; together these
measures have all contributed to a lessening of the
previous isolation of many settlements (70).
      The pattern of economic activity has also
experienced substantial modification. In areas
previously characterised by the decline of employment, winter sports complexes have generated a
series (and often a considerable number) of new
jobs. These range from activities directly related
to skiing, such as instructors and chair-lift
operators, to employees in allied fields such as
restaurants, hotels and accommodation services,
shops, craft industries and the building trade.
Despite an influx of outsiders attracted by such
employment opportunities, in many cases local inhabitants have taken on these jobs (71). The impact
upon the traditional agricultural economy, however,
has often been ambiguous; while the growth of a new
source of employment and income has generally
encouraged the abandonment of farming, it has also
enabled certain farmers to maintain their holding by
combining its running with some other activity.
Overall, the influx of tourists has had a beneficial
multiplier effect upon communities, especially
through the increase in income which has resulted.
But, not all expectations have been fulfilled.
Fewer jobs than anticipated have resulted and many
are part-time or seasonal in character and relatively poorly paid.
      Employment growth has been accompanied by an
increase in population, frequently entailing a
marked reversal of previous trends (72), whereas in
those communes unaffected by winter sports the loss
of inhabitants has in many cases continued (73).

Tourism - A Key Sector of Growth

An illustration of the combined rise in employment and population, much of which has been stimulated by the growth of winter sports, is provided by the commune of Bourg-St. Maurice; the resort of Les Arcs is located here (Table 12.6).

Table 12.6: The Evolution of Population and Employment in the Commune of Bourg-St. Maurice

	1954	1962	1968	1975
Population	3,910	3,498	4,436	4,900*
Employment	1,874	1,462	1,636	2,235
(of which farmers and farm workers)	745	475	318	170

*total in 1982 - 5,700

Source: INSEE, Recensements.

Many settlements in mountainous regions have been drastically modified by the explosive growth of winter sports. Moreover, in areas such as the northern Alps, this trend has contributed greatly to a wider movement of economic and demographic regeneration. Not all mountainous regions share this dynamism, however, nor has the growth of resorts been a feature of all such areas. For example, this feature is far less apparent in the southern Alps and Massif Central, both regions in which the rural population continues to decline. Any policy to revive the upland areas of France, therefore, should not be based on winter sports alone, despite their ability to induce growth.

NOTES

1. Le Tourisme en France en 1980 (Ministère de la Jeunesse, des Sports et Loisirs, Paris, 1981), 7-11.
2. Le Tourisme en France, 8.
3. Cazes, G. and Reynaud, A., Les Mutations Récentes de l'Economie Française (Doin, Paris, 1973), 162-3.
4. Estienne, P., France (Masson, Paris, 1979), vol.1, 118.
5. See Cazes and Reynaud, Les Mutations Récentes, 161 and Wolkowitsch, M., 'Le tourisme en France', Profils Economiques, No.2 (1980), 104.

6. 'Les vacances des français en 1980', _Regards sur l'Economie du Tourisme_, No.28 (1980).

7. In certain cases (for example, hotels, cafes and restaurants) trade obviously does not result only from tourism.

8. The idea is that the savings of a lowly-paid worker towards his holiday are supplemented by a contribution from his employer, the total distributed in the form of special cheques. See _Le Monde_, 25 March 1982 and 26 March 1982.

9. This additional week, however, cannot be added to the pre-existing month's holiday to make a continuous period of five weeks holiday.

10. Rognant, L., 'La France et la civilisation des loisirs', _Profils Economiques_, No.6 (1981), 47.

11. Madiot, Y., _L'Aménagement du Territoire_ (Masson, Paris, 1979), 208-10.

12. _VIIe Plan de Développement Economique et Social_ (Union Générale d'Editions, Paris, 1976), 285-6.

13. Beauchamp, C., 'Activités et aménagements touristiques en France', _Profils Economiques_, No.6 (1981), 30.

14. _Le Tourisme en France_, 21.

15. The table excludes accommodation used by foreign visitors. This is one factor which explains the relatively weak role of hotels - over 50 per cent of foreigners stay in hotels. Similarly, the growth of caravanning and camping holidays is under-valued as the figures ignore foreign tourists, of which a sixth use this type of accommodation.

16. Wolkowitsch, 'Le tourisme en France', 108. For a broader discussion of second homes see Boyer, M., _Le Tourisme_ (Seuil, Paris, 1972), 123-30.

17. Estienne, _France_, 122. For more detailed studies of this phenomenon in specific localities see, for example, Clout, H.D., 'Second homes in Auvergne', _Geographical Review_, 61 (1971), 530-53 and Boyer, J-C., 'Résidences secondaires et 'rurbanisation' en région parisienne', _Tijdschrift voor Economische en Sociale Geografie_, 71 (1980), 78-87.

18. A more detailed discussion of the distribution of second homes and of differences between holiday and weekend residences is given in Barbier, B., Les résidences secondaires et l'espace rural français', _Norois_, No.95ter (1977), 11-19.

19. Clout, H.D., 'Résidences secondaires en France', in Coppock, J.T. (ed.), _Second Homes: Curse or Blessing_? (Pergamon, Oxford, 1977), 47-62.

20. Various forms of 'village' exist, but in

general the aim is to provide comparatively simple
but pleasant surroundings for a family holiday.
Apart from the accommodation and essential amenities,
a number of central services are provided (restau-
rant, crèche) as well as certain recreational
facilities; families are encouraged to participate
in the activities of the complex. See Lanquar, R.
and Reynouard, Y., Le Tourisme Social (Presses
Universitaires de France, Paris, 1978), 46-57.
>   21.   Lanquar and Raynouard, Le Tourisme Social,
37-9.
>   22.   Le Monde, 3 Feb. 1981.
>   23.   Le Tourisme en France, 14-18.
>   24.   A wider discussion of the development of
tourism over this period is given in Boyer, Le
Tourisme, 109-23.
>   25.   See Livet, R., Atlas et Géographie de
Provence, Côte d'Azur et Corse (Flammarion, Paris,
1978), 166-8.
>   26.   Wolkowitsch, 'Le tourisme en France', 112.
>   27.   Livet, Atlas et Géographie de Provence,
164.
>   28.   Le Monde, 21 July 1979.
>   29.   A number of more generalised, less ambi-
tious regional development plans have been formula-
ted for other coastal regions such as Brittany and
Basse-Normandie where there is already a well-
established tourist industry. Here the aims have
been not only to encourage further expansion but to
control more effectively the nature and location of
facilities. The most recent programme was launched
in 1980 in the region of Vendée.
>   30.   For a more detailed account of the objec-
tives underlying the development of the Languedoc
coast see Ferras, A. et al., Atlas et Géographie du
Languedoc et du Roussillon (Flammarion, Paris,
1979), 204-6.
>   31.   The problems are outlined in, for example,
Thompson, I.B., Modern France (Butterworths, London,
1970), 422-51.
>   32.   For details of the proposals to develop
the Aquitaine coast see Barrère, P. and Cassou-
Mounat, M., 'Le schéma d'aménagement de la Côte
Aquitaine', Revue Géographique des Pyrénées et du
Sud-Ouest, 44 (1973), 303-20.
>   33.   Thompson, I.B., The Lower Rhône and
Marseille (Oxford University Press, London, 1975),
30-2. A fuller account of the scheme's outline is
given in this source.
>   34.   Aménagement du Territoire - Rapport
d'Activité 1980 (DATAR, Paris, 1981), 72.

35. Le Monde, 21 June 1980.

36. A more detailed assessment is given in Cassou-Mounat, M., 'Actions d'aménagement et croissance spontanée sur la Côte Aquitaine', Revue Géographique des Pyrénées et du Sud-Ouest, 52 (1981), 41-60.

37. Bonnet-Pineau, E., 'L'aménagement des littoraux français', Profils Economiques, No.6 (1981), 95. The government first sought to promote tourism through the creation of SETCO (Société pour l'Equipement Touristique de la Corse) in 1957. This organisation was then replaced by a special inter-ministerial body for tourist development, which itself was superseded in 1977.

38. Renucci, J., La Corse (Presses Universitaires de France, Paris, 1982), 76-82.

39. Aménagement du Territoire, 72; Beauchamp, 'Activités et aménagements touristiques', 39.

40. Fuller assessments of the project are given in, for example, Ferras, et al., Atlas et Géographie du Languedoc, 214-18, and Pearce, D., Tourist Development (Longman, London, 1981), 99-102.

41. Cassou-Mounat, M., 'Tourisme et espace littoral: l'aménagement de la Côte Aquitaine', L'Espace Géographique (1976), 132-44.

42. Neboit, R., 'Les français et leur environnement', Profils Economiques, No.2 (1980), 126-8.

43. More general details are given in Clout, H.D., The Geography of Post-War France (Pergamon, Oxford, 1977), 53-5, and Monod, J. and de Castelbajac, Ph., L'Aménagement du Territoire (Presses Universitaires de France, Paris, 1978), 66-9.

44. A detailed assessment of the character of one regional park is given in Guillemette, J-P., 'Le parc régional d'Armorique 10 ans après...', Octant (Cahiers Statistiques de la Bretagne) No.5 (1981), 27-34.

46. Cazes, G. et al., L'Aménagement Touristique (Presses Universitaires de France, Paris, 1980), 72.

47. Le Monde, 4 Aug. 1980.

48. Les Vacances des Français en 1980, 23.

49. Figures published by the Observatoire Economique Rhône-Alpes at Lyon.

50. Bertherat, J., 'Les stations de ski: une affaire en plein essor', Points d'Appui Pour l'Economie Rhône-Alpes, No.8 (1980), 35.

51. Bertherat, 'Les stations de ski', 35-6.

52. For a fuller discussion see Jamot, Ch.,

'Les sports d'hiver en Auvergne', La Revue
d'Auvergne, 92 (1978), 39-84.
53. Cazes, et al., L'Aménagement Touristique,
85.
54. Veyret, P., Atlas et Géographie des Alpes
Françaises (Flammarion, Paris, 1979), 175-9.
55. Cazes, et al., L'Aménagement Touristique,
85.
56. Cazes, et al., L'Aménagement Touristique,
77.
57. A more detailed study of a similar but
smaller resort (Peisey-Nancroix) is contained in
Thompson, Modern France, 186-7.
58. Veyret, P., 'La grande mutation du ski
dans les Alpes françaises', L'Information
Géographique, 40 (1976), 160.
59. Further details are given in Cazes, et
al., L'Aménagement Touristique, 83-9; Veyret, 'La
grande mutation du ski', 160-1; Pearce, Tourist
Development, 16-21. The most detailed and specialised study is contained in Knafou, R., Les Stations
Intégrées de Sports d'Hiver des Alpes Françaises
(Masson, Paris, 1978).
60. For the detailed history of one of these
resorts (Les Arcs) see Godino, R., Construire
l'Imaginaire (Presses de la Cité, Paris, 1980).
61. Veyret, 'La grande mutation du ski', 161.
62. Le Monde, 21 Aug. 1979.
63. Le Monde, 19 Jan. 1980.
64. Cazes, et al., L'Aménagement Touristique,
91.
65. Lanquar and Raynouard, Le Tourisme Social,
88-91.
66. Le Monde, 27 March 1982.
67. Le Monde, 12 Jan. 1980.
68. An example is provided by the problems
experienced by Isola 2000. See Le Monde, 12 Jan.
1981.
69. Veyret, Atlas et Géographie des Alpes
Françaises, 161.
70. Cazes, et al., L'Aménagement Touristique,
89-90.
71. See, for example, Marnexy, A., 'Les
stations de ski de la Haute-Maurienne: un exemple
original d'aménagement touristique', Revue de
Géographie Alpine, 67 (1979), 294; Cazes, et al.,
L'Aménagement Touristique, 90.
72. A number of illustrations are provided in
Veyret, Atlas et Géographie des Alpes Françaises,
260-1.
73. Veyret, 'La grande mutation de ski', 164.

Chapter Thirteen

THE FRENCH ECONOMY IN THE 1980s

A CHANGED ENVIRONMENT

The current image of the French economy is very
different from the one apparent a decade ago. At
that time, following a period of exceptional growth,
the country's transformed and revitalised economic
base symbolised the 'new' France which had been
created following the second world war. Since then
the economy has faltered under the pressure of a set
of problems largely unencountered during the preceding post-war period. Although the adverse effects
triggered by the first oil crisis were countered
relatively successfully, the repercussions of the
deuxième choc pétrolier have had a much more profound depressant impact.

The country has been faced with a sharp rise in
the rate of inflation and a dramatic increase in the
level of unemployment, accompanied by a marked
slowing in the pace of economic growth. These are
not, however, problems which are unique to France.
On the contrary, such conditions have all been
features of the recent history of the majority of
the world's advanced industrial nations. Moreover,
the duration and intensity of the recession, reflected in the continuing fall in the levels of profits
and investment, suggest that the events of the last
decade represent a major break-down in the capitalistic system rather than a cyclical down-turn in
activity.

Faced with this modified environment, French
society has entered a further phase of adaptation.
Transformation of the economy, however, is not only
the result of the pressures indicated above. New
directions to change also reflect an altered political background and modified attitudes within society
to the nature of development. The election of a

socialist President and government has created an
alternative (albeit contested) framework for the
management of the economy, involving greater state
intervention and control, the devolution of certain
decision-making powers and commitment to greater
social equality in the distribution of the benefits
of growth. Progressively, there has also been a
growing disenchantment with the philosophy of
gigantisme and the overriding concern with technical
efficiency which underpinned development during the
1960s and early 1970s. The less attractive features
of such an approach have led to demands for greater
concern to be given to the social consequences of
economic expansion and to its impact upon the
environment. It is not just the recession, therefore, that has influenced and moderated the scale
and form of change.

Problems of the employment market highlight the
country's altered economic performance. Jobs continue to be lost in agricultural activities, despite a
slowing in the rate of decline; the level of employment in industry has failed to increase since the
early 1970s and is now falling rapidly, while the
rate of growth in tertiary activities has eased
considerably. Not surprisingly, therefore, a major
strand of the socialist government's revised and
Keynsian inspired economic strategy has become the
control of unemployment. Some success is apparent
but only at the expense of a deterioration of the
balance of payments deficit, a weakened franc and a
continuing high rate of inflation.

It is these adverse consequences which have
helped make the management of the economy such a
controversial issue, with the more monetarist orientated policies of the opposition contrasting
strongly with the present government's strategy.
But, the adoption of the former approach under the
Barre administration in the latter 1970s, while
strengthening France's foreign trading position and
limiting the rise of the rate of inflation, did
little to stem the increase in unemployment. A
greater measure of concensus is apparent over the
need in the longer term to render French producers
more competitive and to restructure the economy with
the aim of greater penetration of new growth
sectors. However, just as the country's economic
difficulties are common to many other nations, and
partly attributable to external influences, effective solutions are unlikely to result unless remedial action is undertaken con-jointly; this emphasises the high degree of interdependence of the

world's major capitalist economies.

SPATIAL DIMENSIONS TO CHANGE

The past remodelling of the economy has been
characterised by substantial variations in both the
extent and consequences of the process. Generalisation about individual sectors often conceals important areal contrasts. Thus, although radical
changes have affected agriculture, linked to greater
efficiency, higher incomes and improved living
standards, not all regions have benefited to the
same extent. Conditions of poverty are still widespread amongst the farming population in areas such
as the Massif Central, while the problems generated
by excessive specialisation in highly speculative
forms of production remain an underlying feature of
agriculture in Mediterranean regions.
      Change within the secondary sector has long
been associated with the reduction of the importance
of Paris as an industrial centre. Throughout the
1960s a strong movement of decentralisation (which
has now virtually ceased) underpinned a significant
redistribtuion of industry, although the extent to
which this was effective in achieving a more equitable spread of economic activity throughout the
country is questionable. Certainly, many towns
close to the capital gained considerable benefit, as
did various other urban centres in the wider areas
of the Paris Basin and western France. Conversely,
little change occurred in many regions more distant
from Paris, such as the south-west. Nor did government regional policy generally have any marked
impact upon slowing the decline of population in the
more remote and frequently upland regions of the
country.
      Other shortcomings have been apparent in the
spatial pattern of economic growth. Attempts to
shift office-based and research activities from the
capital have encountered only limited success,
contributing to a more fundamental problem of the
existence of marked regional imbalances in the
quality of employment provision. Even in those
regions benefiting from decentralisation, in either
the secondary or tertiary sectors, resulting jobs
have often been heavily biased towards occupations
requiring a low level of skill or qualification,
resulting in an inadequate diversity of the local
employment market. The redistribution of activities
has been accompanied by a polarisation of command

functions upon Paris, a process reinforced through
the concentration of ownership and made more
apparent as basic manufacturing operations and
routine administrative tasks have become the prime
candidates for transfer to or expansion in provincial locations.

The more recent phase of restructuring has had
equally important spatial ramifications, although
associated more with the decline rather than the
expansion of employment. Thus, the severe problems
encountered by many of the country's staple industries such as heavy metallurgy, shipbuilding, coal
and textiles have had a highly selective areal
impact. Certain traditional manufacturing districts
have also been adversely hit due to changing locational preferences, illustrated by the increasing
exurbanisation of industry to the detriment of many
inner suburban areas. Yet there are other regions
of the country where the need for new employment is
equally great and where living standards remain
depressed. Parts of the southern Alps, Pyrenees,
Massif Central and even rural zones in regions such
as Lorraine, Bourgogne and Aquitaine continue to
exhibit such features. In a number of these areas
the expansion of tourism has acted as one means to
attenuate the decline of jobs in traditional activities, but it is often only a palliative and by no
means a universal panacea.

FUTURE DIRECTIONS

These difficulties are indicative of some of the
factors which present a dilemma for the government
in designing economic and regional policies and in
ordering its priorities. Inducing the spatial redistribution of jobs and the creation of new employment opportunities in those areas where the need is
greatest is rendered particularly problematic in a
period of slow economic expansion. Similarly, the
extent to which it is realistic or feasible to
promote development in some of the more isolated and
inhospitable rural areas has to be balanced against
the needs of many urban centres where the incidence
of unemployment and the scale of contracting industries are far greater.

There is also a problem of choice for the
government in deciding in which branches of activity
to concentrate investment and encourage development.
Particular emphasis has been placed upon industries
such as electronics and data-processing, reinforcing

the strategy of restructuring and giving support to
sectors with a strong potential for growth. The
state is also committed, however, to maintaining
many of its older, less efficient manufacturing
activities, notably steel. Here, development
programmes are designed in part to improve productivity, but there are often strategic and social
factors involved, in the latter case reflecting the
concentration of jobs in limited areas where communities are still heavily dependent upon a narrow
range of activities. A more generous system of
regional aids has also been instituted to assist in
counteracting such problems and in eradicating the
inequalities of living standards and opportunities
which persist within the country.

There is no doubting the necessity for these
initiatives, but again their implementation is made
more difficult, and their likely effectiveness more
uncertain, by a sluggish economy and other substantial demands upon public finance (such as the health
and social services). It is highly questionable,
therefore, whether the French economy has the
capacity to meet satisfactorily all these various
demands. At the same time, a more intricate problem
of regional imbalance in economic activity has
developed compared with the simpler 'Paris versus
the provinces' model pertaining in the 1950s; but,
the economic environment in which adjustments need
to be made has also altered. Stimulating the
expansion of the economy and manipulating the
regional distribution of jobs, therefore, represent
far more onerous and challenging tasks in the 1980s.

SELECT BIBLIOGRAPHY

Allard, P. et al., Dictionnaire des Groupes
    Industriels et Financiers en France (Seuil,
    Paris, 1978).
Ardagh, J., France in the 1980s (Penguin,
    Harmondsworth, 1982).
Attali, J., La Nouvelle Economie Française
    (Flammarion, Paris, 1978).
Aydalot, P., 'L'aménagement du territoire en France:
    une tentative de bilan', L'Espace Géographique,
    7 (1978), 245-53.
Aydalot, P., 'Le rôle du travail dans les nouvelles
    stratégies de localisation', Revue d'Economie
    Régionale et Urbaine, No.2 (1979), 174-89.
Badouin, R., Economie et Aménagement de l'Espace
    Rural (Presses Universitaires de France, 1979).
Bakis, H., 'La sous-traitance dans l'industrie',
    Annales de Géographie, 84 (1975), 297-317.
Baleste, M., L'Economie Française (Masson, Paris,
    1981).
Barrère, P. and Cassou-Mounat, M., Les Villes
    Françaises (Masson, Paris, 1980).
Bastié, J. and Dézert, B., L'Espace Urbain (Masson,
    Paris, 1980).
Battiau, M., 'Quelques remarques sur l'évolution de
    la répartition géographique des emplois
    industriels en France entre 1954 et 1975',
    L'Information Géographique, 45 (1978), 170-88.
Battiau, M., 'Un essai d'analyse des difficultés du
    Nord-Pas-de-Calais', L'Information
    Géographique, 45 (1981), 98-102.
Baumier, J., La Fin des Maîtres de Forges (Plon,
    Paris, 1981).
Beauchamp, C., 'Activités et aménagements
    touristiques en France', Profils Economiques,
    No.6 (1981), 24-43.
Beaujeu-Garnier, J., 'Toward a new equilibrium in

France', <u>Annals of the Association of American Geographers</u>, 64 (1974), 113-25.

Beaujeu-Garnier, J., <u>Atlas et Géographie de Paris et de la Région d'Ile-de-France</u> (Flammarion, Paris, 1977), 2 vols.

Beaujeu-Garnier, J. and Bouveret-Gauer, M., 'Retail planning in France', in Davies, R.L. (ed.), <u>Retail Planning in the European Community</u> (Saxon House, Farnborough, 1979).

Beaujeu-Garnier, J. and Delobez, A., <u>Geography of Marketing</u> (Longman, London, 1979).

Bellon, B., <u>Le Pouvoir Financier et l'Industrie en France</u> (Seuil, Paris, 1980).

Bentham, G. and Moseley, M.J., 'Socio-economic change and disparities within the Paris agglomeration: does Paris have an "inner city problem"?', <u>Regional Studies</u>, 14 (1980), 55-70.

Béteille, R., 'L'industrie en milieu rural en France', <u>L'Information Géographique</u>, 42 (1978), 28-43.

Bombal, J. and Chalmin, P., <u>L'Agro-Alimentaire</u> (Presses Universitaires de France, Paris, 1980).

Bonnet, J., 'La décentralisation des activités tertiaires: analyse géographique', <u>Analyse de l'Espace</u>, No.4 (1978), 5-30.

Bonnet, J., 'La décentralisation des activités tertiaires en France', <u>Revue Géographique de Lyon</u>, 54 (1979), 357-68.

Bonneville, M., 'La désindustrialisation urbaine: le cas de Villeurbanne', <u>Revue Géographique de Lyon</u>, 50 (1975), 97-105.

Bonneville, M., 'La construction des bureaux dans l'agglomération Lyonnaise', <u>Revue Géographique de Lyon</u>, 54 (1979), 349-56.

Boyer, J-C., 'Résidences secondaires et 'rurbanisation' en région parisienne', <u>Tijdschrift voor Economische en Sociale Geografie</u>, 71 (1980), 78-87.

Boyer, M., <u>Le Tourisme</u> (Seuil, Paris, 1972).

Boyle, M. and Robinson, M.E., 'A further note on French nuclear energy', <u>Geography</u>, 67 (1982), 148-9.

Braibant, M., 'L'économie des services marchands de 1960 à 1980', <u>Archives et Documents</u>, No.37 (1981).

Brémond, J., <u>Les Nationalisations</u> (Hatier, Paris, 1981).

Brocard, M., 'L'aménagement du territoire et développement régional: le cas de la recherche scientifique', <u>L'Espace Géographique</u>, 10

(1981), 61-73.
Brocard, R., 'Les entreprises françaises',
    Collections de l'INSEE, E64 (1979).
Calmès, R. et al., L'Espace Rural Français (Masson,
    Paris, 1978).
Carré, J.J. et al., Abrégé de la Croissance
    Française (Seuil, Paris, 1973).
Carrère, P. et al., 'Evolution de la situation
    économique des régions françaises de 1972 à
    1977', Economie et Statistique, No.100 (1978),
    39-50.
Cassou-Mounat, M., 'Tourisme et espace littoral;
    l'aménagement de la côte Aquitaine', L'Espace
    Géographique, 5 (1976), 132-44.
Cassou-Mounat, M., 'Actions d'aménagement et
    croissance spontanée sur la côte Aquitaine',
    Revue Géographique des Pyrénées et du Sud-
    Ouest, 52 (1981), 41-60.
Cazenave, G. and Monteil, J., Les Revenus des
    Agriculteurs (Presses Universitaires de France,
    Paris, 1980).
Cazes, G. and Reynaud, A., Les Mutations Récentes de
    l'Economie Française (Doin, Paris, 1973).
Cazes, G. et al., L'Aménagement Touristique (Presses
    Universitaires de France, Paris, 1980).
Chardonnet, J., L'Economie Française (Dalloz, Paris,
    1976), vol.3.
Chevalier, J-M., L'Echiquier Industriel (Hachette,
    Paris, 1981).
Chombert de Lauwe, J., L'Aventure Agricole de la
    France de 1945 à nos Jours (Presses
    Universitaires de France, Paris, 1979).
Clout, H.D., The Massif Central (Oxford University
    Press, London, 1973).
Clout, H.D. (ed.), Themes in the Historical
    Geography of France (Academic Press, London,
    1977).
Clout, H.D., The Geography of Post-War France
    (Pergamon, Oxford, 1972).
Clout, H.D., 'France', in Clout, H.D. (ed.),
    Regional Development in Western Europe (Wiley,
    Chichester, 1981), 151-77.
Clout, H.D., 'A new France?', Geography, 67 (1982),
    244-50.
Commissariat Général du Plan, Agriculture,
    Industries Agricoles et Alimentaires (La
    Documentation Française, Paris, 1980).
Commissariat Général du Plan, Emplois dans les
    Services (La Documentation Française, Paris,
    1980).
Commissariat Général du Plan, Industrie (La

Documentation Française, Paris, 1980).

Dalmasso, E., Les Activités Tertiaires (SEDES, Paris, 1976).

Dawson, J.A., 'Hypermarkets in France', Geography, 61 (1976), 259-62.

Dawson, J.A., 'Shopping centres in France', Geography, 66 (1981), 143-6.

Delors, J. 'L'économie française: une modernisation entravée, une dynamique à retrouver', in Dahrendorf, R. (ed.), La Crise en Europe (Fayard, Paris, 1982), 79-102.

Demangeat, D., 'Réflexions sur la désindustrialisation de la région parisienne', Analyse de l'Espace, No.2 (1979).

Diry, J-P., 'L'industrie française de l'alimentation du bétail', Annales de Géographie, 88 (1979), 671-704.

Dollé, M., 'Les branches industrielles avant et après 1974', Economie et Statistique, No.108 (1979), 3-20.

Dubois, P., 'La rupture en 1974', Economie et Statistique, No.124 (1980), 3-20.

Dumont, R. and de Ravignan, F., Nouveaux Voyages dans les Campagnes Françaises (Seuil, Paris, 1977).

Durand, P., Industrie et Régions (La Documentation Française, Paris, 1974).

Essig, F., DATAR: des Régions et des Hommes (Stanké, Paris, 1979).

Estienne, P., La France (Masson, Paris, 1978-9), 4 vols.

Ferrandon, M-C. and Waquet, I., La France depuis 1945 (Hatier, Paris, 1979).

Ferras, A. et al., Atlas et Géographie du Languedoc et du Roussillon (Flammarion, Paris, 1979).

Fischer, A., 'Eléments pour une étude des effets spatiaux des concentrations industrielles', Annales de Géographie, 87 (1978), 294-313.

Flatrès, P., Atlas et Géographie du Nord et de la Picardie (Flammarion, Paris, 1980).

Fontaine, P., 'L'industrie automobile en France', Notes et Etudes Documentaires, Nos.4583-4 (1980).

Fourastié, J., Les Trente Glorieuses ou la Révolution Invisible de 1946 à 1975 (Fayard, Paris, 1979).

France: Annual Economic Survey (Organisation for Economic Co-operation and Cultural Development).

Freyssenet, M., La Sidérurgie Française 1945-79 (Savelli, Paris, 1979).

Froment, R. and Lerat, S., La France au Début des Années 80 (Bréal, Montreuil, 1981), 2 vols.

Fruit, J-P., 'L'évolution récente de la population active rurale en France (1968-75)', L'Information Géographique, 42 (1978), 159-67.

Gachelin, C., 'Crises et défis de l'industrie française', La Documentation Photographique, No.6056 (1981).

George, P., France (Martin Robertson, Oxford, 1973).

Gervais, M. et al., Une France sans Paysans (Seuil, Paris, 1965).

Gervais, M. et al., Histoire de la France Rurale - Tome 4: La Fin de la France Paysanne - 1914 à nos Jours (Seuil, Paris, 1976).

Gilly, J.P. and Morin, F., 'Les groupes industriels en France', Notes et Etudes Documentaires, Nos.4605-6 (1981).

Girard, J-P. et al., 'Les agriculteurs - Tome 1', Collections de l'INSEE, E46-7 (1977).

Giscard d'Estaing, V., L'Etat de la France (Fayard, Paris, 1981).

Godino, R., Construire l'Imaginaire (Presses de la Cité, Paris, 1980).

Gombert, M., 'De moins en moins d'agriculteurs', Economie et Statistique, No.100 (1978), 26-34.

Guibert, B. et al., 'La mutation industrielle de la France', Collections de l'INSEE, E31-2 (1975).

Hannoun, M., 'L'industrie française face au second choc pétrolier', Economie et Statistique, No.135 (1981), 59-63.

Hannoun, M. and Templé, P., 'Les facteurs de création et de localisation des nouvelles unités de production', Economie et Statistique, No.68 (1975), 59-70.

House, J., France: An Applied Geography (Methuen, London, 1978).

Huet, M., 'Emploi et activité entre 1968 et 1975', Economie et Statistique, No.94 (1977), 59-76.

Huet, M., Télématique et Aménagement du Territoire (La Documentation Française, Paris, 1981).

Jalabert, G., Les Industries Aeronautiques et Spatiales en France (Privat, Toulouse, 1974).

Juillard, E., Atlas et Géographie de l'Alsace et de la Lorraine (Flammarion, Paris, 1978).

Kayser, B., 'Le changement social dans les campagnes françaises', Economie Rurale, No.135 (1979), 5-11.

Klatzmann, J., L'Agriculture Française (Seuil, Paris, 1978).

Klatzmann, J., Géographie Agricole de la France (Presses Universitaires de France, Paris, 1979).

Knafou, R., _Les Stations Intégrées de Sports d'Hiver des Alpes Françaises_ (Masson, Paris, 1978).

Labasse, J. _L'Espace Financier_ (Armand Colin, Paris, 1974).

La France en Mai 1981: Les Activités Productives (La Documentation Française, Paris, 1982).

Lanquar, R. and Raynouard, Y., _Le Tourisme Social_ (Presses Universitaires de France, Paris, 1978).

Larivière, J-P., 'Données sur la répartition du secteur secondaire dans l'espace breton', _Norois_, 28 (1981), 395-404.

Le Lannou, M., _La Bretagne et les Bretons_ (Presses Universitaires de France, Paris, 1978).

'Le monde paysan', _Les Cahiers Français_, No.187 (1978).

Lerat, S., 'Collecte et commercialisation des céréales en France', _L'Information Géographique_, 42 (1978), 15-27.

Le Roy, P., _L'Avenir de l'Agriculture Française_ Presses Universitaires de France, Paris, 1975).

Le Roy, P., _Le Problème Agricole Français_ (Economica, Paris, 1982).

Les Chiffres Clés de l'Industrie Française (Ministère de l'Industrie, Paris, 1982).

'Les multinationales', _Les Cahiers Français_, No.190 (1979).

Limouzin, P., 'Les facteurs de dynamisme des communes rurales françaises', _Annales de Géographie_, 89 (1980), 549-87.

Lipietz, A., 'La dimension régionale du développement du tertiaire' in 'Activités et Régions', _Travaux et Recherches de Prospective_, No.75 (1978), 65-121.

Lipietz, A., 'Polarisation interrégionale et tertiairisation de la société', _L'Espace Géographique_, 9 (1980), 33-42.

Livet, R., _Atlas et Géographie de Provence, Côte d'Azur et Corse_ (Flammarion, Paris, 1978).

Livet, R., _Les Nouveaux Visages de l'Agriculture Française_ (Les Editions Ouvrières, Paris, 1980).

Madiot, Y., _L'Aménagement du Territoire_ (Masson, Paris, 1979).

Malezieux, J., 'Crise et restructuration de la sidérurgie française', _L'Espace Géographique_, 9 (1980), 183-96.

Marchand, O. and Revoil, J-P., 'Emploi et chômage: bilan fin 1980', _Economie et Statistique_, No.130 (1981), 23-44.

Marthey, L., 'L'industrie chimique en France', _Notes_

et Etudes Documentaires, No.4454 (1978).

Mary, S. and Turpin, E., 'Panorama économique des régions françaises', Collections de l'INSEE, R42-3 (1981).

Merlin, P., 'Aménagement du territoire et localisation des activités en France', Tijdschrift voor Economische en Sociale Geografie, 65 (1974), 368-80.

Metton, A., 'Centres périphériques: regards sur l'expérience parisienne', Revue de Géographie des Pyrénées et du Sud-Ouest, 50 (1979), 107-13.

Meynier, A., Atlas et Géographie de la Bretagne (Flammarion, Paris, 1976).

Moliner, J., 'L'évolution de la population agricole du XVIII siècle à nos jours', Economie et Statistique, No.91 (1977).

Monod, J. and de Castelbajac, Ph., L'Aménagement du Territoire (Presses Universitaires de France, Paris, 1978).

Mormiche, P., 'Chômage et qualification dans les régions', Economie et Statistique, No.119 (1980), 23-34.

Morvan, Y., La Concentration de l'Industrie en France (Armand Colin, Paris, 1972).

Noin, D., L'Espace Français (Armand Colin, Paris, 1976).

Noin, D., 'Essai d'établissement d'une carte économique de la France sur les bases comptables', L'Espace Géographique, 2 (1973), 257-65.

Pagé, J-P. (ed.), Profil Economique de la France (La Documentation Française, Paris, 1981).

Parodi, M., L'Economie et la Société Française depuis 1945 (Armand Colin, Paris, 1981).

Perret, J-M., Usinor-Dunkerque ou l'Espoir Deçu des Flamands (Westhoek-Editions, Dunkerque, 1978).

Pinchemel, P., La Région Parisienne (Presses Universitaires de France, Paris, 1979).

Pinchemel, P., La France (Armand Colin, Paris, 1981), 2 vols.

Pitié, J., L'Exode Rural (Presses Universitaires de France, Paris, 1979).

Prévot, V., Géographie des Textiles (Masson, Paris, 1979).

Pumain, D., 'La composition socio-professionnelle des villes françaises', L'Espace Géographique, 5 (1976), 227-38.

'Redéploiement ou protectionnisme?', Les Cahiers Français, No.192 (1979).

Renucci, J., La Corse (Presses Universitaires de

France, Paris, 1982).

Royer, J-F., 'L'exode agricole: des départs sans relève', Economie et Statistique, No.79 (1976), 59-63.

Scarth, A., 'New nationalisations in France', Geography, 67 (1982), 155-6.

Servan-Schreiber, J-J., Le Défi Mondial (Fayard, Paris, 1980).

Smith, B.A., 'Retail planning in France', Town Planning Review, 44 (1973), 279-306.

Spindler, F., 'L'élevage en France', Notes et Etudes Documentaires, Nos.4341-2 (1976).

Sorlin, P., La Société Française, 1914-68 (Arthaud, Paris, 1971).

Stoffaës, C., La Grande Menace Industrielle (Pluriel, Paris, 1980).

Stoffaës, C., 'Les talents industriels des Français' in Reynaud, J-D. and Grafmeyer, Y. (eds.), 'Français, qui êtes-vous?', Notes et Etudes Documentaires, Nos. 4627-8 (1981), 157-74.

Tauveron, A., 'Le tertiaire supérieur: moteur du développement régional?', L'Espace Géographique, 3 (1974), 169-78.

Thevenot, L., 'Les catégories sociales en 1975: l'extension du salariat', Economie et Statistique, No.91 (1977), 3-31.

Thibault, A., 'La structure économique des espaces locaux en France', L'Espace Géographique, 5 (1976), 239-49.

Thompson, I.B., Modern France (Butterworths, London, 1970).

Thompson, I.B., The Lower Rhône and Marseille (Oxford University Press, London, 1975).

Thompson, I.B., The Paris Basin (Oxford University Press, London, 1981).

Thumerelle, P.J., 'Crise économique et décroissance démographique - l'exemple de la région Nord-Pas-de-Calais', Annales de Géographie, 89 (1980), 144-56.

Tuppen, J.N., 'Fos - Europort of the south?', Geography, 60 (1975), 213-7.

Tuppen, J.N., 'Redevelopment of the city centre: the case of Lyon-La Part Dieu', Scottish Geographical Magazine, 93 (1977), 151-8.

Tuppen, J.N., France (Dawson, Folkestone, 1980).

Tuppen, J.N., 'The role of Dunkerque in the industrial economy of Nord-Pas-de-Calais', in Hoyle, B.S. and Pinder, D.A. (eds.), Cityport Industrialisation and Regional Development (Pergamon, Oxford, 1981), 265-79.

Tuppen, J.N., 'Les Halles: a major central area

redevelopment', Town and Country Planning, 50 (1981), 137-9.

Tuppen, J.N., 'Le train à grande vitesse: its development and implications', Geography, 67 (1982), 343-4.

Tuppen, J.N., 'The development of French new towns: an assessment of progress', Urban Studies, 20 (1983), forthcoming.

Turpin, E., 'Disparités régionales, croissance et crise', Economie et Statistique, No.133 (1981), 77-99.

Tussau, G., 'Les industries électriques et électroniques', Notes et Etudes Documentaires, Nos.4563-4 (1980).

Vadour, N., 'Les grandes surfaces périphériques de vente dans les Bouches-du-Rhône', Annales de Géographie, 87 (1978), 40-58.

Valeyre, A., 'Emplois et régions: la polarisation de l'emploi dans l'espace français', in 'Activités et Régions', Travaux et Recherches de Prospective, No.75 (1978), 5-64.

Veyret, P., 'La grande mutation du ski dans les Alpes françaises', L'Information Géographique, 40 (1976), 159-65.

Veyret, P., Atlas et Géographie des Alpes Françaises (Flammarion, Paris, 1979).

'Vie et transformation de l'industrie en Ile-de-France: 1954-78', Cahiers de l'Institut d'Aménagement et d'Urbanisme de la Région d'Ile-de-France, 63 (1981).

Wolkowitsch, M., 'Le tourisme en France', Profils Economiques, No.2 (1980), 102-16.

A number of annual publications of INSEE (Institut National de la Statistique et des Etudes Economiques) also contain useful information. These include:-

Annuaire Statistique de la France
Les Comptes de l'Industrie
Les Comptes de l'Agriculture Française
Le Commerce en France
Rapport sur les Comptes de la Nation
Statistiques et Indicateurs des Régions Françaises
Tableaux de l'Economie Française

arable farming 30-4
    see also cereals
Arcachon 336, 341
Ardennes 37
Ariane 185, 186
armaments industry 120,
    177, 214, 215
Armentières 226
Association Bureaux
    Provinces 279
Association pour
    l'Expansion
    Industrielle de la
    Région Nord-Pas-de-
    Calais (APEX) 228,
    229-30
Atlantic coast 331,
    338-41
ATO Chimie 182
Aube 55, 57
Aubervilliers 216
Auchan 310, 313
Aulnay-sous-Bois 199,
    316, 317
automobile industry
    see motor vehicle
    industry
Auvergne 8, 33, 95, 104,
    106, 111, 149, 164,
    254, 255
Avignon 70, 258, 278
Avoriaz 345, 347

Bagnolet 290
balance of payments 3-4,
    326
banking and insurance
    244, 248-9, 259, 265,
    269-70, 271, 276, 277,
    280-1, 283, 287
barley see cereals
Barre, Raymond 83, 252,
    256
Bas-Rhin 55, 57
Basse-Normandie 7, 8, 30,
    149, 154, 171, 201,
    204, 254, 255
Basse-Seine see Seine
    valley
Batilly 200
Bayonne 278, 340

Beauce 30, 101
Belgium 10, 333
Belleville 221
Bendix 202
Benelux 138
Berliet 199, 271
    see also Renault
    Véhicules Indus-
    trielles
Berre 17
Besançon 278
Béthune 229, 278
Biarritz 336
Blois 282
BNP 281
Bobigny 290
Bordeaux 40, 42, 70,
    147, 157, 159, 168,
    185, 207, 258, 266,
    272, 273, 274, 278,
    282, 283, 311, 318,
    321
Bouches-du-Rhône 76, 90
Boulogne 45, 227, 278,
    336
Boulogne-Billancourt
    199, 216, 219
Bourgogne 8, 149, 163,
    171, 204, 254, 255,
    358
Bourg-St. Maurice 350
Bourse, commercial
    centre 266, 321
Brazil 122, 139, 186
Bresse 71
Brest 203, 235, 236,
    258, 278, 282, 336
Bretagne 7, 8, 12, 90,
    148, 149, 154, 201,
    204, 254, 255
    see also Brittany
Briey 278
Brittany 30, 33, 38, 42,
    45, 61, 71, 88, 92,
    95, 103, 104, 112,
    150, 157, 159, 168,
    212, 213, 231-7, 283,
    284, 311, 327, 336
Bruay-en-Artois 229, 278
BSN-Gervais-Danone 93,
    190

370

crisis 3, 15, 21,
131-2, 355
consumption 15, 16-19
imports 122
refining 17, 19, 130,
138, 183, 229
oil seed 29
Oise 279
Orcières-Merlette 345,
346
organic chemicals 183
Orléans 150, 257, 258,
273, 282, 283
Orly 316

Pactes Nationaux pour
l'Emploi 14-15
Pantin 216
paper industry 127, 177,
180-2
parachemicals 130, 182,
183, 229
Paribas 22
Paris 105, 147, 158, 162,
166, 167, 170, 185,
192, 199, 203, 212,
213-21, 233, 236, 257,
259, 260, 265, 270-7
passim, 280, 281, 284,
285, 286-92, 293, 331,
334, 357
see also Ile-de-France
Paris Basin 7, 23, 30,
33, 34, 36, 42, 53,
61, 67, 95, 103, 106,
148, 150, 152, 153,
154, 160, 167, 168,
171, 256, 257, 278,
357
Paris region see
Ile-de-France
Parly 2 315, 316, 319
Pas-de-Calais 42
Pau 278
Pays de la Loire 8, 12,
37, 90, 101, 148, 149,
154, 171, 201, 204,
254, 255
Pechiney-Ugine-Kuhlmann
127, 138, 141, 179-80,
182

Périgueux 282
Perpignan 278
Perros-Guirec 336
petrochemicals 130, 182,
183, 229
Peugeot 138, 139, 141,
165, 198, 199, 200,
202, 229
see also Citroën,
Talbot
pharmaceutical industry
138, 177, 178, 181,
187, 214, 215, 224,
284
Picardie 8, 101, 148,
149, 152, 163, 201,
254, 255
pig farming see live-
stock rearing
Place des Halles,
commercial centre
266, 320
Plan Avenir Jeunes 15
Plan Calcul 206
Plan Composants 206
Plan Neige 344
plastics industry 108,
179
Plogoff 20
Poissy 199
Poitiers 148, 278
Poitou-Charentes 8, 31,
148, 149, 150, 254,
255
polyculture 30, 49, 67,
93, 101
Pompidou, Georges 137
Port-Barcarès 336
Port-Leucate 336
poultry see livestock
rearing
Prime d'Installation
Artisanale 113
Printemps-Prisunic 308,
309
printing industry 177,
215
property leasing 244,
249, 269
Provence 40, 42

379

Provence-Alpes-Côte
d'Azur 7, 8, 9,
31, 34, 149, 204,
253, 254, 255, 272,
281
Pyrenees 72, 242, 358

quaternary activities
252, 259-60, 265,
275
Quatre Temps 313, 316
Quimper 236, 282

rape 36
recession 3, 123, 131-2,
355
redevance
industry 158, 219,
220
offices 277
regional councils 23,
159
regional parks 341
regional planning
development grants
159, 160, 278-9
general policy 23
industry 157-66
offices 277-86
Reims 228, 257, 258
remembrement see farm
consolidation
Renault 22, 93, 134, 139,
141, 161, 162, 165,
168, 198, 199, 201,
202, 219, 229, 271
see also Renault
Véhicules Industriels
Renault Véhicules
Industriels (RVI)
199, 200, 271, 296
Rennes 148, 203, 235,
236, 258, 273, 278,
282
research activities
79-80, 170, 215, 254,
256, 278, 283, 284
Réseau Express Régional
(RER) 291
retailing 242, 244, 249,
253, 261, 301-25

central area
redevelopment 319-21
food 302, 303, 304,
307, 309, 317
growth 302-4
hypermarkets 71, 302,
306, 308, 309-13,
315, 317
non-food 302, 303,
304, 309
organisation 308-9
regional shopping
centres 315-17
self-service 301,
302, 309-13
small shopkeepers
253, 301, 302-3, 306,
309
see also Loi Royer
Rhône, valley 19, 34,
40, 42, 67, 90, 92,
191
Rhône-Alpes 8, 9, 108,
111, 147, 149, 152,
155, 183, 187, 201,
204, 254, 255, 271,
272, 281
Rhône-Poulenc 93, 127,
139, 141, 161, 182,
183, 187, 289, 296
rice see cereals
Riviera 335, 336, 337-8
Roanne 189
robots 121, 186
root crops 31
Rosny 290
Rosny 2 316, 317
Roubaix 189, 226, 278
Rouen 70, 182, 183, 258,
266, 272, 273, 274,
282, 320, 321
Roussillon 42
Royan 336
rubber industry 179, 183
Rungis 69-70, 290
rural areas 28, 95,
103-14, 115, 143-4,
243, 307, 341-2
aid and management
policies 106-14
industry 104, 108-9,

Troyes 278

unemployment 3-4, 9-15
  remedial measures
  13-15
  spatial distribution
  10-12
  women unemployed 12
  youth unemployment
  12-13, 15
Union des Assurances de
  Paris (UAP) 289, 293
United Kingdom see
  Great Britain
urban population 28
USA 120, 138, 139, 140,
  185, 201, 301
Usinor 127, 133, 141,
  170, 180, 193, 194,
  227

Valbonne 278, 282, 284-5
Val Cenis 347, 348
Val-de-Marne 218, 290
Val d'Isère 344
Val-d'Oise 218, 290
Valence 40, 278
Valenciennes 17, 165,
  170, 195, 196, 200,
  226, 227, 228, 229,
  258, 278
Vallourec 180
Vannes 236
Var 76
vegetable production 31,
  33, 34, 41-3, 65, 69,
  74, 75, 90, 92, 101
Vélizy 2 316, 317
Vélizy-Villacoublay 290,
  316
Vénissieux 317, 318
Vern-sur-Seiche 17
Verseilles 290, 316
Vichy 334
Vienne 40
village de vacances 328,
  334
vines see viticulture
viticulture 31, 33, 34,
  39-42, 74, 75, 76, 103
  see also wine

production
Vitry 216
Volkswagen 199, 202
Volvo 199, 202
Vosges 30, 37, 72, 189

Western Germany 10, 120,
  138, 182, 189, 197,
  333
wheat see cereals
white-collar workers 6,
  215-6, 245-7, 249-50,
  256, 268-70
wholesaling 244, 245,
  249
wine production 29, 35,
  39, 40, 69, 70, 101
winter sports see
  tourism
wood industry 108, 177,
  231, 232

Yvelines 218, 290

Zones de Rénovation
  Rurale et de Montagne
  73, 112